They Do What?

They Do What?

A Cultural Encyclopedia of Extraordinary and Exotic Customs from around the World

JAVIER A. GALVÁN, EDITOR

 ABC-CLIO

Santa Barbara, California • Denver, Colorado • Oxford, England

Library of Congress Cataloging-in-Publication Data

Galván, Javier A., 1965–
    They do what? : a cultural encyclopedia of extraordinary and exotic customs from around the world / Javier A. Galván, editor.
        pages cm
    Includes index.
    ISBN 978-1-61069-341-7 (hardback) — ISBN 978-1-61069-342-4 (ebook)
1. Manners and customs—Encyclopedias.   2. Rites and ceremonies—Encyclopedias.   I. Title.
    GT76.G35   2014
    390—dc23   2013050254

ISBN: 978-1-61069-341-7
EISBN: 978-1-61069-342-4

18 17 16 15 14   1 2 3 4 5

This book is also available on the World Wide Web as an eBook.
Visit www.abc-clio.com for details.

ABC-CLIO, LLC
130 Cremona Drive, P.O. Box 1911
Santa Barbara, California 93116-1911

This book is printed on acid-free paper ∞

Manufactured in the United States of America

The publisher has done its best to make sure the instructions and/or recipes in this book are correct. However, users should apply judgment and experience when preparing recipes, especially parents and teachers working with young people. The publisher accepts no responsibility for the outcome of any recipe included in this volume and assumes no liability for, and is released by readers from, any injury or damage resulting from the strict adherence to, or deviation from, the directions and/or recipes herein. The publisher is not responsible for any reader's specific health or allergy needs that may require medical supervision, nor for any adverse reactions to the recipes contained in this book. All yields are approximations.

Contents

List of Entries

Geographic Guide to Entries

Asia (North)

Boryeong Mud Festival

Konaki Sumo, Crying-Baby Sumo Competition

Log-Riding Onbashira Festival

Mizuko Kuyō, Miscarried and Aborted Fetus Ceremony

Qingming Festival, Tomb-Sweeping Day

Sannakji, Eating Live Octopus

Sapporo Snow Festival, *Yuki Matsuri*

Scorpions on a Skewer

Setsubun, Bean-Throwing Children's Festival

Umbilical Cord as Family Treasure

Visiting-Girls Courting Tradition

Australia and the Pacific

Cannibalism

Corpse High-Platform Exposure

Land-Diving Ceremony

Lotus Births

Moko: Māori Male Facial Tattoos

NAIDOC Aboriginal Week in Australia

Penile Subincision Ceremony

Tuna-Throwing Competition

Yams, Sex, and Marriage in Trobriand Traditions

British Isles

Abbots Bromley Horn Dance

Black Pudding Throwing Championship

Blackening the Bride

Bog Snorkeling

Carrying Flaming Tar Barrels

Cheese Rolling Competition

Goose Day

Gurning

Haxey Hood Game

Man versus Horse Marathon

Puck Fair

Sprinkling Cake on a Child's Head

Up Helly-Aa, Fire Festival

Whuppity Scoorie Children's Celebration

Caribbean and Central America

Animal Sacrifice in Santería Rituals

Fiesta de Santiago y Vejigantes

Junkanoo Bahamas Festival

Little Devils Festival, *Los Diablitos*

Nyabingi Rastafarian Sessions

Parranda de Remedios Christmas Festival

Quema del Diablo, Burning the Devil

Santería Cleansing Rituals

Turks and Caicos Conch Festival

Europe

Baba Marta: A Bulgarian Spring Celebration

Bochnia Salt Mine Underground Relay Race

Bone Houses and Ossuaries

Burning of Witches Event

Chess Boxing Championships

Infiorata Festival, Flower-Petal Tapestries

Brushing Teeth with Cow's Dung
  Ashes
Burying the Placenta
Cow Jumping Initiation
Dipo Womanhood Ceremony
Fantasy Coffins
Fattening Rooms
Female Genital Cutting and Mutilation
Forehead-Cutting Initiation
Kung Musical Healing Ceremony
Lobola: Bridal and Financial Contract
Maasai Circumcision Ceremony
Menstrual Isolation Ritual

Reed Dance Chastity Ceremony
Scarification of Children's Faces
Sharo: Public Flogging and Bravery
Spitting as Greeting Tradition
Washing Hands with Cow's Urine
Wodaabe Courtship Dance and Festival

International (Multiple Locations)

Eating Human Placenta
Rogaining International Competitions
World Beard and Moustache
  Championships

Thematic Guide to Entries

Beauty and Health

Brushing Teeth with Cow's Dung
    Ashes
Moko: Māori Male Facial Tattoos
Neck Stretching in Thailand
Washing Hands with Cow's Urine

Birth Customs

Baby-Naming Ceremonies in Ghana
Baby's Feet Off the Ground
Burying the Placenta
Lotus Births
Mizuko Kuyō, Miscarried and Aborted
    Fetus Ceremony
Umbilical Cord as Family Treasure

Coming of Age/Rites of Passage

Breast Ironing
Bullet Ant Initiation
Cow Jumping Initiation
Dipo Womanhood Ceremony
Fattening Rooms
Female Genital Cutting and
    Mutilation
Forehead-Cutting Initiation
Land-Diving Ceremony
Maasai Circumcision Ceremony
Matis Hunting Trials
Menstrual Isolation Ritual
Penile Subincision Ceremony
Reed Dance Chastity Ceremony
Rumspringa Amish Run
Russefeiring
Scarification of Children's Faces
Tooth-Filing Ceremony

Competitions and Sports

Black Pudding Throwing
    Championship
Bochnia Salt Mine Underground Relay
    Race
Bog Snorkeling
Buzkashi, Afghani Sport on Horseback
Camel Racing
Camel Wrestling
Cheese Rolling Competition
Chess Boxing Championships
Gurning
Haxey Hood Game
Man versus Horse Marathon
Redneck Games
Rogaining International Competitions
Running of the Bulls
Tuna-Throwing Competition
Varzesh-e Bastani Iranian Wrestling
Wife-Carrying Competition
World Beard and Moustache
    Championships

Festivals and Celebrations

Abbots Bromley Horn Dance
Baba Marta: A Bulgarian Spring
    Celebration
Barong Dance Ceremony
Boryeong Mud Festival
Burning of Witches Event
Carnaval Do Rio de Janeiro
Carrying Flaming Tar Barrels
Feria de las Flores, Festival of Flowers
    in Medellín
Fiesta de Santiago y Vejigantes
Fiestas de Quito

Religious Ceremonies

Animal Sacrifice in Santería Rituals
Burying Llama Fetuses
Candomblé Religion and Animal
  Sacrifice
Diablada Dance, Dance of the Devils
Firewalking
Inti Raymi, Festival of the Sun
Kapparot Ritual
Krampus and Christmas
Kumbh Mela Spiritual Pilgrimage
Kung Musical Healing Ceremony
Ngaben Cremation Ceremony

Nyabingi Rastafarian Sessions
Parranda de Remedios Christmas
  Festival
Qingming Festival, Tomb-Sweeping Day
Quema del Diablo, Burning the Devil
Ramadan: Fasting, Prayer, and Charity
Santería Cleansing Rituals
Sharo: Public Flogging and Bravery
Snake Handlers in Christian
  Appalachia
Thaipusam, Extreme Flesh
  Modification
Virgen del Carmen, Fiestas de Cusco

Acknowledgments

This encyclopedia was a collective effort from its inception. First of all, this project would not have been possible without contributions of dozens of authors who shared their cultural traditions and experiences with me. I owe them a mountain of gratitude. From the publishing perspective, the editorial staff at ABC-CLIO offered suggestions (and corrections) that turned this project into a much more polished final manuscript. However, I must specifically thank my acquisitions editor, Kaitlin Ciarmiello. She provided valuable advice, and she always kept this project on the right track. In addition, I will be eternally indebted to two people who have provided me with unconditional support. They are the two consistent pillars of my life. My wife Maya has supported all my academic ventures, including this book. We met twenty-five years ago, and she continues to surprise me with her internal strength. Overall, she has made me a better man. My son Marco is now seven years old. During his short lifespan, he has already been exposed to a plethora of cultural experiences throughout six continents. He has become my faithful traveling buddy. Finally, this encyclopedia is dedicated to my mother, Evelia Cervantes de Galván, who passed away while I was writing this book. May she rest in peace.

Introduction

This one-volume encyclopedia is focused on traditions and customs that might seem unusual, unique, or exotic to typical American students. At the initial stages of gathering a list of possible topics for this project, I enlisted the help of multiple experts who included anthropologists, artists, historians, geographers, travel writers, dancers, musicians, religious leaders, medical doctors, teachers, and stay-at-home mothers. Many of them subsequently also agreed to write a few entries. As a result, the authors of this book are dedicated writers who currently live, study, work, or come from all corners of the world, including Africa, Europe, Asia, the Caribbean, North America, the Middle East, Latin America, the British Isles, India, and Australia. They provide a truly international dimension to this book, and they all offer their unique view of the world. After much careful consideration and collaboration with multiple contributors, I have included entries organized into coherent categories, such as peculiar marriage and dating practices, distinct birth customs, exotic funeral traditions, rites of passage rituals, unique competitions, uncommon food, wacky sports, as well as both religious and secular celebrations. Each entry consists of an overview of the origins of the custom and where it takes place, as well as an explanation of how and why the tradition is practiced.

Every culture has unique characteristics that make it stand out in comparison to other groups of people. Social elements such as history, religion, culinary traditions, and family life have influenced the development of modern cultural practices for centuries. Cultural identity often includes multiple elements such as art, music, spirituality, and celebrations, especially when they mark important milestones in a person's life, as in the case of pregnancy, birth, adolescence, adulthood, weddings, and death. Over time, they become established customs that transcend individual generations, and they evolve into cultural markers of a specific group of people. In this book, I avoided the use of the adjective "weird" to describe any cultural traditions because it would be offensive to practitioners of multiple customs. While many cultural practices have a long history dating back to hundreds of years (e.g., the Matis hunting trials in Brazil, the Kumbh Mela spiritual pilgrimage in India, and the Day of the Dead in Mexico), others have been recently established (including the tuna-throwing competition in Australia and the bog snorkeling event in Wales). In addition, there are a few customs that are still being practiced, but they are now limited to agricultural and rural communities; such traditions are often diluted in urban settings or succumb to disuse and eventual extinction (e.g., the practice of washing hands with cow's urine by the Nuer groups in South Sudan).

One of the most attractive and intriguing manners to experience another culture is through food and festivals, and they often go well together. When it comes to food, there seems to be a spectrum of personal preferences ranging from dishes viewed as "interesting," to acceptable, to unusual, to unwilling to try, to only-for-dare-devils, and then right out disgusting. There are several culinary traditions that might seem a bit odd, but lots of people are willing to try, such as rooster-comb soup in Spain or eating live octopus (Sannakji) in South Korea. Yet, only people with adventurous palates are willing to taste foods such as fried tarantulas in Cambodia; duck eggs with embryos (Balut) in the Philippines; and a wide variety of insects available in Mexico, Colombia, and Thailand. Other food items are mostly rejected by Westerners, such as eating scorpions on skewers in China or consuming the human flesh of a deceased relative (endocannibalism) by the Wari tribes of Brazil. These topics are covered in detail because they offer an important insight into multiple regional cultures.

Exploring cultural traditions can certainly be fun and intriguing. Some of my fondest memories of traveling and living abroad are related to experiences with local festivals. Large exotic celebrations bring families and communities together, and they break the monotony of the daily routine. Special events such as the *Up Helly-Aa* Fire Festival in northern Scotland, the Holi Indian festival of colors, the vibrant Carnaval in Rio de Janeiro, the Nyabingi Rastafarian Jamming sessions in Jamaica, and the biggest food fight in the world (La Tomatina in Spain) remind us that people like to have fun. This book covers them in detail. However, it also explores the history behind such celebrations to explain how they were established and why they have had such a long enduring power. These festivities offer a captivating window into another culture. Such customs might appear to highlight cultural differences, but they also allow us to discover how much we all have in common. Globalization and transportation have brought people closer together, and traditions have expanded beyond their original borders. As a result, most urban centers in the United States now offer an exposure to multiple cultural festivals and food.

There are, however, multiple traditions that are more solemn and spiritual in nature. Such customs include the special manner in which cultures deal with mourning the loss of a loved one, including finger amputation in Papua Guinea, and how the Yanomami people of Brazil and Venezuela eat the ashes of a cremated family member. In addition, the cyclical nature of death has produced ancient traditions of funerary practices, including the extravagant funerals of the Ashanti people in Ghana, the use of bone houses in Austria and Portugal, and the ceremonial sky burials in Tibet. This books covers them all in detail (and many others) highlighting the traditions that for centuries have blended religion, local celebrations, personal spirituality, and sometimes a little bit of superstition.

While certain traditions covered in this book might seem unusual to average young Americans (e.g., breast ironing, fire walking, or penile subincision), they are absolutely commonplace in other parts of the globe. In contrast, events such as participating in the Redneck Games in Georgia, following the Rumspringa Amish Run tradition in Pennsylvania, observing Christian snake handlers in Appalachia, or eating honey (bee's vomit) seem rather "strange" to people outside the United States. A few traditions covered in this encyclopedia appear to be exotic, but they are widely accepted (e.g., the intricate Māori male facial tattoos in New Zealand, the wife-carrying competition in Finland, and blackening the bride in Scotland). However, there are other customs that are often viewed with a strong disapproval from a Western perspective, such as the case of female genital mutilation, brushing teeth by using cow's dung ashes, and eating human placenta. All the cultural entries included in this book are covered with respect regardless of how unusual they might seem to American readers.

I do not pretend to suggest that this book includes a complete set of topics related to unique and peculiar customs from around the world. That would be arrogant. I actually had to limit the number of entries due to space and time restrictions; this was a regrettable necessity. My hope is that this book actually sparks further discussion so that readers would be interested in finding out more information. Consequently, every entry offers a section titled "Further Readings" to serve as a guide for additional enquiry.

Since this book has an encyclopedia format following an alphabetical order, it is foremost a reference book. As a result, it can be used as a general resource for specific research papers by exploring the list of entries provided at the front. It can also be read from cover to cover to offer a wide approach to cultural traditions in a global setting. Readers can also find the index at the end of the book as a useful tool to quickly identify specific topics they want, which are then linked with other cross-referenced materials. In addition, the geographical list of topics offers the option to find customs in a specific country or region. Overall, the book offers information to readers who might not necessarily have an academic background on comparative cultures or interdisciplinary studies. Each individual entry can stand alone, but they are also part of a larger theme, such as funeral customs, unusual food, or marriage traditions. This practice allows readers to make connections among different entries. My ultimate hope is that readers enjoy the journey of cultural discovery.

ABBOTS BROMLEY HORN DANCE

The Abbots Bromley Horn Dance is one of the oldest and most celebrated of English folk calendar customs, and it takes place only once a year. The dance is performed annually in the village of Abbots Bromley, Staffordshire, on the first Monday after September 4, usually between September 5 and September 12. This date coincides with a village celebration dedicated to the patron saint of the local church. There is much speculation as to the origins of the Abbots Bromley Horn Dance. The first recorded mention of the rite can be found in Robert Plot's *Natural History of Staffordshire*, written in 1686, in which Plot describes a famous Staffordshire dance occurring variously at Christmas, New Year, and Twelfth Night, and it always involves a hobby horse and multiple deer heads. An earlier reference (written in 1532) refers to a hobby horse dance, but it does not mention any horns at all. It has been noted that the dance was known to have been performed at the Barthelmy Fair in 1226, and some folklorists theorize that the dance may be a surviving Druidic custom.

The dance is performed by a team of twelve men who live in the village of Abbotts Bromley, England. These men are allotted roles, which range from being one of the six dancers known as the Deer-men (each of whom carries a set of reindeer antlers) to being a Jester or Fool, a character called Maid Marian, a Bowman, a Hobby Horse (a dancer wearing a wooden head–shaped like that of a horse and a caparison) or that of one of two musicians (one of whom carries a triangle on which he beats time and the other one carries a melodeon accordion or a fiddle). Since the early 1800s, the Fowell Family of Abbots Bromley has had the honor of providing the lead Deer-man and of selecting the other eleven dancers.

On the day of the dance, the antlers carried by the Deer-men are taken to the local parish church of Saint Nicholas where they are blessed and subsequently handed out to the dancers. These antlers, after which the Abbots Bromley Horn Dance is named, were carbon-dated by the Department of Geological Sciences at Birmingham University in 1976, and they were found to date back to 1065 (plus or minus eighty years). The age of the horns, together with the fact that the antlers came from reindeer, suggests that the horns were brought to England during the time of the Vikings for reindeer have been extinct in Britain since before the time of the Norman conquest of England in 1066. The weight of the horns ranges from 16 to 25 pounds (7 to 11 kilograms). Three of the horns are painted white with brown tips, and another three horns are decorated brown with gold tips. Each set of antlers is attached to a carved deer head mounted on a short wooden handle for ease of transportation and to lessen the physical strain of carrying the horns

Costumes used for the Abbots Bromley Horn Dance. (Christopher Elwell/Dreamstime.com)

for many hours. The dancers receive the horns at about eight in the morning, and they return them around twelve hours later after having danced at various sites around the village. At the conclusion of the festivities, the horns remain in the church until the dance is performed again the following year.

During the ritual, as the dancers approach a performance site, they form a serpentine line that weaves in and out of itself in the shape of the number eight, always continuing to advance until the dancers bearing the horns form a circle. This circle revolves clockwise and anticlockwise and then flattens to form two lines so that the men carrying the white horns face those carrying the brown horns. At one end, the Maid Marian faces the Jester or Fool and the Hobby Horse faces the Bowman, who pretends to shoot the Hobby Horse with a toy bow and arrow. Each line of dancers then advances three steps, retreats, and advances again. Then, the Deer-men lower their horns to suggest they are stags about to fight. As the Deer-men pretend to ready themselves for action, the Hobby Horse snaps his jaws in time with the music, which is traditional English folk music, including tunes such as "The Farmers Boy" and "Uncle Mick." The steps are repeated many times until a single line of dancers forms once more and dancers head off to another part of the village where the dance continues. Local people considered it unlucky if the group of dancers does not stop at their home, or at least in their part of the village. By the end of the day, the dancers (fuelled by refreshments proffered by the villagers) will have covered over 10 miles. The refreshments donated to the performers hark back to the cakes and ale traditionally doled out to the dancers.

In 1887, the daughters of the local vicar decided that the dancers should wear pseudo-medieval costumes possibly inspired by illustrations found in a compendium of plays by Shakespeare, thereby breaking with the tradition which saw the dancers wear everyday clothing decorated with ribbon and scraps of cloth. The new costumes consisted of green tunics and blue trousers patterned with brown spots. The costumes have altered little over the years with the design of the current costumes dating back to 1948 and consisting of a cap, knitted stockings, knee breeches, and a jerkin.

The fame of the Abbots Bromley Horn Dance now draws tourists from as far away as Canada and Indonesia to witness the celebratory spectacle and elaborate dances, which continue to bring a great many visitors to the village each year.

Victoria Williams

Further Readings

"Abbots Bromley Horn Dance." *BBC.co.uk*. November 2009. http://www.bbc.co.uk/stoke/content/articles/2008/07/09/horn_dance_feature.shtml (Accessed on October 9, 2012).

Alexander, Marc. *The Sutton Companion to British Folklore, Myths and Legends*. Stroud, UK: Sutton Publishing, 2005.

Burne, C. S. "Staffordshire Folk and Their Lore," *Folk-Lore* 7, no. 4 (December 1896). http://en.wikisource.org/wiki/Folk-Lore/Volume_7/Staffordshire_Folk_and_their_Lore (Accessed on October 9, 2012).

Official Website of the Horn Dance of Abbots Bromley. http://www.thehorndanceofabbotsbromley.co.uk/index.htm (Accessed on October 9, 2012).

Ravenscroft, John. "The Abbots Bromley Horn Dance." *TimeTravel-Britain.com*. 2005. http://www.timetravel-britain.com/articles/history/horndance.shtml (Accessed on October 9, 2012).

Simpson, Jacqueline, and Steve Roud. *Oxford Dictionary of English Folklore*. Oxford: Oxford University Press, 2000.

ANIMAL SACRIFICE IN SANTERÍA RITUALS

Santería is an Afro-Caribbean religion that is widely practiced in Cuba, Puerto Rico, Colombia, Dominican Republic, Venezuela, Panama, and parts of the United States. It blends aspects of African beliefs from the Yoruba groups in Nigeria with those of European Catholicism and Native American traditions from the Caribbean. The result is a religion that includes traditions such as sacred drumming sessions, attempts to communicate with their ancestors, and a direct relationship with multiple male and female gods. However, one of the most controversial aspects of santería is the practice of animal sacrifice during religious ceremonies, especially chickens and goats. While images of blood and decapitated animals have mobilized animal rights groups in the United States to declare the practice as animal cruelty, santería followers have argued that sacrificial blood is a crucial component of their offerings to their gods. In the United States, such differences of

A *santero* (priest) holding roosters for sacrifice. (AP Photo/Javier Galeano)

opinion have resulted in confrontations with local police departments attempting to enforce regional ordinances and also legal battles in U.S. federal courts debating basic constitutional concepts such as freedom of religion.

Santería has multiple names (including *Regla de Ocha*, *La Regla de Lucumí*, and simply *Lukumí*); each name reflects a specific historical struggle to survive. The slave trade from Africa forced the migration of Yoruba slaves from southern Nigeria to the Caribbean sugar plantations, especially to Cuba, Puerto Rico, and Haiti. They brought with them their religion, language, and customs, which were based on the worship and respect of nature. However, the European colonial period (roughly 1500 to 1800s) immediately criminalized their religion and forced them to convert to Roman Catholicism. All of the sudden, slaves were supposed to worship one single God they knew nothing about, while being simultaneously surrounded by a wide array of saint statues. Since their main purpose was to survive their harsh living conditions, they went along with the European religious requirements, but they slowly started to assign one of their own gods (*Orishas*) to individual saints. For example, the Catholic saint of Santa Barbara was aligned with Changó, one of the most powerful gods in Yoruba religion. On the surface, the slaves were seen as praying to European saints, but they were actually worshipping their own African-origin deities. This phenomenon known as syncretism was the genesis for multiple Afro-Caribbean blended religions such as Brazilian Candomblé, Haitian Voodoo, and Cuban and Puerto Rican santería. In fact, the current name of *santería* is a misnomer that was used by catholic religious leaders as a pejorative term for the practice of slaves who showed more devotion to saint statues than to Jesus Christ himself. As an extension, the term *santeros* or *santeras* (depending on their gender) later applied to male and female santería priest and priestesses. When the Spanish colonial period was over in the Caribbean by the end of the 1800s, santería was a well-established religion that continued to flourish throughout the 1900s. After a few decades, a large number of santería practitioners arrived in the United States mainly through migration of Cubans and Puerto Ricans. When the U.S. Congress granted U.S. citizenship to Puerto Ricans in 1917, they migrated in large numbers mainly to Florida and New York. Later, two waves of Cuban immigrants settled mostly in Florida during the 1960 and the 1980s. The first santería church in the United States was officially established in 1974 in the city of Hialeah, Florida; it was named the Church of the Lukumí Babalu-Aye.

In order to understand animal sacrifice as a crucial component of santería rituals, it is necessary to understand its broader context and the structure of the religion. Overall, there is a general sense of secrecy regarding its beliefs and traditions. For example, there is no central religious book to guide its believers, and there

PUBLIC DISPLAY OF SANTERÍA IN CUBA VERSUS PUERTO RICO

Cuba and Puerto Rico display different social attitudes toward santería in public settings. In general, it is noticeable that Cubans are much more open and accepting of santería as part of the larger society than their Puerto Rican counterparts. In Cuba, the santería tradition of small informal gatherings (rather than practicing in large religious venues) actually facilitated its survival during the 1960s and 1970s under Communist rule—a political system in which religions did not officially exist on the island. During the late 1980s and 1990s, religious practice became much more acceptable in Cuba, and it is now commonplace to see *santero* and *santera* priests in training wearing their white clothing openly throughout the island. On the other hand, Puerto Ricans are much more reserved about openly expressing their affiliation to santería. Actually, this syncretic religion is more popular in specific towns in Puerto Rico with a strong Yoruba African heritage such as Loíza, Bayamón, and Carolina. To complicate matters a bit more, most santería followers and *santero* priests are also baptized Catholic, even though the practice is no longer necessary for their survival as it once was during the European colonial period (1500s–1800s). A good example of how these two religions are intertwined into daily life is revealed when a Puerto Rican family moves into a new house. They usually invite a Catholic priest to offer a blessing of the house. However, they also invite a *santero* to practice a cleansing of the property, just in case.

Javier A. Galván

is no central leader to follow. Instead, knowledge is passed on mostly orally and by actually participating in rituals and celebrations. Another unique feature of santería is that its practitioners aim to achieve spiritual balance during their life-time rather than seeking a reward in the afterlife. In addition, santería gatherings do not take place in massive cathedrals or ornate churches. Instead, modern-day ceremonies still reveal their humble origins and a cautious distrust of outsiders. Most ceremonies take place in an *ilé*, or *Casa de Santos* (Saints' Home), which are mostly located inside a priest's home. These *ilés* usually have a small shrine des-ignated to several gods. The modest altars are traditionally decorated with satin fabric in vibrant red, white, and dark colors. These houses of worship include a group of practitioners, an ordained priest or priestess, and a group of individuals who are being initiated into priesthood. The trainees go through a series of initia-tion rituals, including a cleaning session, earning a necklace bathed in herbs and sacrificial blood, and a rebirth celebration. Afterward, the future priests spend one year as part of a purification period during which they must wear only white clothing, avoid physical contact with anyone who is not initiated into santería, and eat only naturally grown food. After twelve months, the initiation ceremony takes place when the priests and priestesses are finally ordained; this celebration always requires an animal sacrifice. Once ordained, priests and priestesses are viewed as direct representatives of the *Orishas*, and they can serve as messengers between santería practitioners and the gods.

Animal sacrifice is absolutely essential to santería traditions. Sacrifices are per-formed in rituals marking milestones of birth, marriage, and death, as well as heal-ing sessions, and the initiation of priests. Chickens are the most common animals used for sacrifices, but others also include goats, pigeons, sheep, ducks, and tur-tles. The animals are killed in a quick manner by cutting the carotid arteries in a single stroke with a sacrificial knife. However, the only part of the animal offered to the *Orishas* is its blood; the meat and other food is usually prepared and eaten by the worshippers who participate in the ceremony. Nothing is wasted. The only time that the meat is not consumed is when the animals were used for a healing ceremony or a death ritual since practitioners believe that the illnesses were passed onto the animals. As part of the offerings, the priest might also offer candles, flow-ers, fruit, and prayers.

The practice of killing animals for sacrifice has been challenged in U.S. courts alleging animal cruelty and health hazards. During the 1990s, the city of Hialeah, Florida, passed several ordinances with the goal of prohibiting the killing of ani-mals for sacrifice and not intended for food consumption. These laws reflected the uneasiness that the general U.S. population has regarding the idea of animal sacrifice. As the ordinances were being approved, it became clear that they were targeting the practices of the local santería church of Lukumi Babau-Aye, and the religious leaders appealed the rulings alleging that their constitutional rights of freedom of religion granted by the first amendment of the U.S. constitution were being violated. The local ordinances were originally upheld in the local courts, but the case made it all the way to the U.S. Supreme Court, which overturned the city of Hialeah's animal cruelty laws for being unconstitutional. The U.S. Supreme

Court declared on June 12, 1993, that santería is an established religion, and its practitioners have the constitutional right to practice animal sacrifice as part of their ceremonies and rituals. The 1993 ruling has not since been challenged.

Javier A. Galván

Further Readings

Clark, Mary Ann. *Santería: Correcting the Myths and Uncovering the Realities of a Growing Religion.* Westport, CT: Praeger, 2007.

Galván, Javier A. *Culture and Customs of Puerto Rico.* Westport, CT: Greenwood Press, 2009.

Grenhouse, Linda. "Court, Citing Religious Freedom, Voids a Ban on Animal Sacrifice." *The New York Times*, June 12, 1993, p. 9.

Mason, Michael Atwood. *Living Santería: Rituals and Experiences in an Afro-Cuban Religion.* Washington, DC: Smithsonian Institution Press, 2002.

Pérez y Mena, Andrés I. "Cuban Santería, Haitian Vodun, Puerto Rican Spiritualism: A Multicultural Inquiry into Syncretism." *Journal of Scientific Study of Religion* 37, no. 1 (1997): 15–27.

"Text of 1993 U.S. Supreme Court Decision in the Hialeah Case: Church of the Lukumi Babalu Aye, Inc. et al. versus the City of Hialeah, FL." *Journal of Church and State* 35, no. 3 (Summer 1993): 668.

ASH EATING

The custom of ash eating is a fundamental part of the religious life of the semi-nomadic Yanomami Indians who live in Brazil and Venezuela. As a consequence of the fear of losing one's soul in the case that the body is not burned and the ash is not eaten by relatives, the practice of ash eating is extremely important for the afterlife of this Indian group.

The Yanomami Indians—who are also known as Yanam, Yanoama, Yanomanö, or Sanema—are the largest indigenous tribe in South America with approximately 10,000 people living in the southern part of Venezuela and roughly 9,000 of them living in the northwest region of Brazil. Their settlements are as are bordered by the rivers Orinoco, Rio Negro, Casiquiare, and the Rio Branco. The Yanomami people follow a semi-nomadic lifestyle because they have to keep moving to different hunting grounds. The Yanomami Indians are the most famous tribe of South America, and there has been a great deal of public attention regarding their situation in the past three decades. During the Brazilian gold rush in the 1980s, they became victims of gold miners, who encroached into the settlement areas of the Indians and killed many of them in order to obtain their land for gold panning. Multiple aid organizations intervened on their behalf to fight for their rights, and today the Yanomami seem to be able to live without interference again.

The life of the Yanomami people is highly segregated and isolated. One of the main reasons is that the Yanomami language is not part of another familiar family of languages in South America, and the different dialects are not understood by different tribal communities. In addition, the Yanomami people live in smaller communities, between which wars are fought sometimes. Due to this potentially volatile condition, they set up strategic alliances to ensure victory over their rival groups located nearby. Since they live in an antagonistic condition of constant peril, there is rarely any interaction between the individual communities. Usually the Yanomami live in an open *Shabono*, which is a single pitch roof with a height of 6 meters (19 feet). Inside, all families are housed together without any walls, a fact that ensures a close community feeling. The Yanomami Indians are usually small in stature. Men are rarely taller than 1.60 meters (5 feet 2 inches) and women average 1.45 meters (4 feet 9 inches). They all live together and usually interact completely naked. Only the men use a hip string to cover their penis, which is protected from parasites in this position. Struggles are solved by a fight between the participating men, who alternately beat each other with a wooden club on the back of the head, where the Yanomami men traditionally have a tonsure. For hunting, a very long bow and curare poison are used. In addition to meat, they eat plantains, manioc or corn, which they cultivate themselves on small fields they create by using slash and burn methods. Once they leave their settlement position, this field will become jungle again, so their semi-agrarian lifestyle has no negative consequences on the nature of the Amazon as rain forest.

The soul is the most important factor in the religious beliefs of Yanomami people—who will not tell their real name to strangers and non-Indians—because of the fear of losing their soul by doing so. Their worldview is animistic, which means that they believe that each part of the cosmos might contain a soul. A soul could be inside an animal as well. To protect their own souls from evil forces, the Yanomami execute strict rituals to protect themselves, especially after the death of a group member. When a person dies, the major task of the remaining relatives is to protect the soul of the dead person. To highlight this purpose, a special communal ceremony is held. During this ceremony, the relatives of the dead person use *genipapo* or grime to blacken their face and bodies, and they sing traditional elegies and poems. An important part of the ceremony is to burn the body as well as all the personal belongings of the deceased member of their *Shabono*. When the body is burnt, the relatives take the bones and crumble them. The bone powder will subsequently be kept (sometimes for months) in the community until a festive occasion in the future. When the celebratory time arrives, the ash is mixed with banana mush and eaten by the remaining relatives. This ritual symbolizes a society which absorbs a lost member again. The whole process is viewed as crucial for the salvation of the soul of the deceased. Only the burning of the body will release the death soul which is able to rise to heaven. If deceased members of the Yanomami community are not burned and their ash eaten, their soul will become an evil spirit, which in turn will harm and bring diseases to the other members of the community. During times of tribal wars, it is considered fatal if a body is lost. Enemies threaten their adversaries by promising not to eat their ash after their death. The loss of the body is like a loss of the soul. The whole ceremony of burning and eating the ash with the remaining relatives can release the soul for redemption. The Yanomami people believe that a part of the soul—the so-called shadow soul—can be reborn in animals, which is why they are forbidden to hunt some animals. For example, they are not allowed to hunt the harpy eagle, because it could eventually contain the soul of a dead Yanomami. To contact the dead, the shaman of each community will connect this world with the afterworld. It is believed that the shamans can contact the souls to ensure the success of the ash-eating ritual.

Frank Jacob

Further Readings

Chagnon, Napoleon A. *Yanomamo—The Fierce People.* New York: Holt, Rinehart and Winston, 1968.

Diaz, Maria Eugenia, and William Neumann. "Venezuela to Investigate Report That Brazilian Miners Massacred Indian Village." *The New York Times.* August 30, 2012. http://www.nytimes.com/2012/08/31/world/americas/venezuela-to-investigate-report-that-miners-massacred-indians.html?_r=0 (Accessed on March 21, 2013).

Ferguson, Brian. *Yanomami Warfare. A Political History.* Santa Fe, NM: School of American Research Press, 1995.

New Pictures of Brazil's Isolated Amazon Yanomami Tribe. *The Telegraph.* November 23, 2011. http://www.telegraph.co.uk/news/worldnews/southamerica/brazil/8909937/New-pictures-of-Brazils-isolated-Amazon-Yanomami-tribe.html (Accessed on March 21, 2013).

Salamone, Frank A. *The Yanomami and Their Interpreters. Fierce People or Fierce Interpreters?* Lanham, MD: University Press of America, 1997.

ASHANTI EXTRAVAGANT FUNERALS

Funeral ceremonies play an important role in many of the cultures of sub-Saharan Africa. The Ashanti (or Asante), an ethnic group numbering over 2 million people whose homeland is in central Ghana, are known for funerals that are public, elaborate, and expensive—to the point where some observers characterize them as extravagant.

An Ashanti funeral is often held several weeks after a death. During this period, while the body is preserved in a mortuary, the family of the deceased works to prepare for the event. Funerals are traditionally the responsibility of a person's *abusua* (matriclan); these are relatives who are linked through common maternal ancestors. They notify distant relatives, refurbish the deceased person's house, and memorialize the departed family member on posters, T-shirts, and in other images that will be distributed to mourners. When all is ready, the body is brought back to the house and prepared for the funeral, draped in kente cloth and adorned with gold jewelry. The ceremonies can last several days. They begin with a lying-in-state at the family home, which culminates in the presentation of burial gifts for use by the deceased in his or her journey to *asamando*, the land of the dead. Then come the burial, the interment, and finally the great funeral, a public event honoring the deceased person with music, dancing, food, and drinks. During this ceremony, as a way of demonstrating their connection to the deceased and the family, relatives and community members publicly make donations of money and traditional, prestigious goods, including textiles, golden funeral objects, and displays of imported liquors and soft drinks.

These public funerals (with processions, music, and ceremonies organized for maximum impact) have become a tourist attraction that guidebooks and websites advise visitors to Ghana not to miss. At the same time, however, they are criticized within Ghana and even among the Ashanti themselves for wasting money and demonstrating misplaced priorities. Critics charge that families who neglect their elders in life will provide extravagant funerals when they die. The funerals are also criticized for absorbing money that could otherwise be used for priorities like education or health care. Ghana is considered by the World Bank to be a lower-middle income country, with a 2011 gross national income of only $1,410 per person. Concerns that funerals squander valuable resources reflect these circumstances. Nevertheless, despite a long history of attempts by the state and traditional Ashanti authorities to limit funeral expenditures, the ceremonies continue to become more elaborate.

Ashanti funerals express the way in which the religious traditions of Akan peoples, the larger cultural group to which the Ashanti belong, understand the relationship between the living and the dead. Traditionally, they believe that their ancestors continue to influence the lives of living descendants. The funeral serves as a way of demonstrating respect and establishing a good relationship with a newly departed ancestor. They also believe that people occupy the same social position in *asamando* (land of the dead) that they did in life, so a funeral that demonstrates wealth, connections, and respect makes sure the new ancestor is as well-off as possible in the land of the dead. Even among Ashanti Christians, who no longer share this understanding of the role of ancestors and the afterlife, the tradition of remembering and honoring the departed is considered very important.

By building and demonstrating solidarity within an *abusua* (matriarchal clan), funerals also reinforce the importance of the extended family in a world that increasingly emphasizes the individual. For the *mmusua* (plural of *abusua*) who organize and host these events, funerals are expressions of their social position or the position to which they aspire. In order for the funeral to achieve its goals, families must demonstrate that the deceased lived a successful life by presenting a well-maintained house, a richly dressed body, and public displays of gifts and donations. Although large numbers of attendees at the ceremonies add to the expense by expecting to be entertained with music, dance, and drink, their presence shows that the deceased had many connections and relationships in his or her community. Likewise, many people attend funerals to build their own connections, understanding that when they die others will do the same for them. Even if the deceased failed to achieve economic or social success in life, a successful funeral can rewrite history by suggesting that the opposite was true.

Technological innovations have shaped the evolution of the Ashanti funeral into its modern, spectacular form. The introduction of the modern mortuary has made it possible to preserve bodies and include them in the funeral rites rather than interring them immediately after death. Increased access to print media has allowed the dead to be memorialized in obituary notices, on posters, and even on signs and billboards. Funerals are now documented on video and sometimes shown on television. Social change has made it possible for more families to participate, since a funeral industry now offers services like mortuary care, "body decorating" or preparation of a corpse, and even rental outlets providing the furniture, regalia, and jewelry necessary for a high-status funeral.

In order to present these displays of wealth and prestige, families often go into debt, even though the donations presented by attendees at the great funeral defray some of the costs. This is one reason that the funerals are characterized as extravagant. Yet, Ashanti funerals are also democratic in character. Prior to the early twentieth century, only members of the ruling elite were able to present elaborate memorial services for the dead. During the 1930s and 1940s, income from Ghana's expanding cocoa industry allowed a wider range of Ashanti people to adopt this custom. Although Ghana's economy has cycled through periods of growth and contraction since the country achieved its independence in 1957, funerals continued to be acknowledged as a central part of Ashanti culture and communal life. Today, even though local governments in the Ashanti region of Ghana might attempt to regulate or limit funeral expenses, many *mmusua* continue to honor their ancestors by presenting the most elaborate funeral services they can afford.

Sara C. Jorgensen

Further Readings

De Witte, Marleen. *Long Live the Dead! Changing Funeral Celebrations in Asante, Ghana.* Amsterdam: Aksant Academic Publishers, 2001.

Gott, Suzanne. "'Onetouch' Quality and 'Marriage Silver Cup': Performative Display, Cosmopolitanism, and Marital *poatwa* in Kumasi Funerals." *Africa Today.* December 22, 2007. http://www.accessmylibrary.com/article-1G1-172946887/onetouch-quality-and-marriage.html (Accessed on November 30, 2012).

Mensah, Kwabena. "Funeral Celebration—Costly to the Economy." *Ghana Web.* January 18, 2007. http://www.ghanaweb.com/GhanaHomePage/features/artikel.php?ID=117472 (Accessed on November 30, 2012).

World Bank. "Ghana: Data." 2012. http://data.worldbank.org/country/ghana (Accessed on November 30, 2012).

BABA MARTA: A BULGARIAN SPRING CELEBRATION

Baba Marta is an ancient spring celebration that is rooted in pagan traditions and national legend. This tale may be traced before the founding of Bulgaria in 681 ACE; the historical lore associated with the festival is tied to Bulgaria's founder, Khan Asparuh. The connotations of *Baba Marta* have remained virtually unchanged despite Christian appropriation of certain symbols beginning in the seventh century. This celebration begins each year on March 1 and lasts throughout mid-April. *Baba Marta* is the mythical figure that symbolizes the end of winter and the beginning of life-affirming spring. Her name literally translates to "Grandmother March," and she is depicted as an irascible old woman whose moods are as erratic as the March weather. Sunny and warm spring days signify that "Grandmother" is happy, while cold spells mean that she is sad or angry. *Marta* is further called so because in pagan tradition, March is the "female" month that gives birth to light and life after the dark cold. This tradition also originates from the tragic legend of an elderly mountain woman who died as a result of the fickle March days. Lured into believing that spring had finally settled in Bulgaria after a succession of beautifully warm weather, the old woman hiked into the Balkan Mountains to let her goats graze when a sudden cold enveloped the countryside and killed the woman. Early observers attributed *Baba Marta* to the spirit of the woman who suffered from March's unpredictability.

Today, however, Bulgarians celebrate by exclaiming to one another *"Chestita Baba Marta!"* ("Happy Grandmother Marta!"). Family, friends, colleagues, and strangers exchange this greeting for good health, good luck, strong families, and happiness. Bulgarians also gift one another with *martenitsa* (singular) or *martenitsi* (plural). These idols symbolize "Mother Nature," though they are generally created and given in pairs representing males and females to epitomize the masculine and feminine fertility of spring. The most common figures seen in *Baba Marta* celebrations are *Pizho* (male) and *Penda* (female). *Pizho* idols are white, while *Penda* idols are red. Each color symbolizes the specific ways in which *Baba Marta* ushers spring into the world. White represents strength and the ability to survive harsh winter, while red signifies menstruation, health, fertility, and conception. In the pre-Christian era, white symbolized universal human nature, as well as the light solar zone. After the advent of Christianity, early practitioners appropriated the color white as symbol of masculinity and Christ-like virtue in an attempt to subvert pagan traditional connotations. Red, however, has long been associated with the feminine in Bulgarian folk culture and represents women in a variety of

Decorations hanging from trees for the Bulgarian spring custom of *Baba Marta*. (Nikolay Dimitrov/Dreamstime.com)

celebrations. For example, Bulgarian brides wore red dresses at wedding ceremonies until Queen Victoria made white gowns fashionable in the nineteenth century.

Traditionally, *Baba Marta* idols are handcrafted from twined wool, silk, or cotton thread, but in recent years artisans have experimented with metal, wood, leather, ceramic, and other mediums to create these timeless fertility symbols. These figures are popular for a similar celebration north of the Danube River in neighboring Romania where the idols are called *mărțișor*. However, Romanians only accept their fertility idols as gifts from men to women. Yet further south, Bulgarians exchange the male and female figures with family, friends, and colleagues regardless of sex. The figures are typically worn on the person, either pinned to clothing or are hung around the neck as an amulet. In the pagan era—and among some Bulgarians today—*martenitsi* were worn for protection from bad spirits, ill fortune, sickness, and the "evil eye" from vengeful or jealous neighbors. The idols also signified new life and the ancient cult of the sun. Today, these talismans are worn until fruit blossoms appear on trees, flowers bud, or a stork is spotted to symbolize that spring has truly arrived south of the Danube River. By wearing *Pizho* and *Penda* figures, Bulgarians are actually pleading that the capricious "Grandmother March" will have mercy on their land and embrace warmth to let life begin anew. Interestingly, Christianity did not and has not affected the pagan meanings attached to the *martenitsi* fertility symbols or the *Baba Marta* celebration; it has only enriched the connotations of the festivities.

Red and white, the colors that are part and parcel to *Baba Marta*, are also a part of the nation's founding legend. Modern-day Bulgarians' ancestors were the

Proto-Bulgars. They were Turkic people whose possible homeland is present-day Sinkiang in Central Asia. In the fourth and fifth centuries, the Proto-Bulgars began moving westward with the Mongolian Huns toward the Middle East and Eastern Europe. Portions of the tribe remained north of the Caucasus and separated into independent tribal units. Byzantine chroniclers are the earliest known historians to refer to "Greater Bulgaria" in records of the seventh century. This region denoted the area from the Donets River to the Black Sea and Sea of Azov, and between the Kuban and Dnieper Rivers. These scholars also noted that Byzantine Emperor Heraclius recognized the Unogonduri tribesman, Khan Kubrat, as the "patrician" ruler of Greater Bulgaria who fostered the state system that united tribes under his rule and allowed his kingdom to flourish.

Bulgarians contend that as the patrician Khan was dying in 651 ACE, he sent his five sons to fetch a bundle of sticks and break the bundle in half. When none of his sons could complete the task, Khan broke each stick individually. This lesson was not lost on any of his sons. Khan Kubrat's children understood that only through unity could their kingdom remain strong and great. According to legend, however, four of the brothers drifted apart and away from their father's lesson. Historical record confirms the sad fates of four of Khan Kubrat's children. Only his son Asparuh carried the Khan's teachings into adulthood. Historical record verifies that when he became a man, Asparuh gathered his portion of his father's tribe and travelled southwest. By uniting with a tribe of western Slavs, Asparuh waged war on the Byzantine Empire, earning in battle and claiming significant portions of the empire's western lands for his own. Byzantine's emperor, Constantine IV, capitulated with a peace treaty between the empire and Asparuh in 681 ACE. This treaty marked the foundation of modern-day Bulgaria and crystallized Asparuh as a Khan.

Bulgarian folklore recounts that Asparuh was indeed a great leader, but that before he conquered his part of the empire, jealous and bitter enemies sought vengeance. To hurt the future Khan, his rivals kidnapped his favorite sister, Houba. After the signing of the peace treaty and the establishment of Bulgaria, the newly named Khan Asparuh sent a message to Houba where she was held captive and implored her to escape to their new kingdom. Houba was the daughter of a Khan who was as cunning and strong-willed as her brother, and she immediately plotted her escape. She deluded her abductors and managed to flee. When she had traveled south all the way to the banks of the mighty Danube River, Houba struggled for a way to discern where the river was safe to cross. Spying a falcon, she coaxed the bird to her and tied a white ribbon around its leg. Houba then let the bird fly so that she could find where the river was the shallowest. Yet before her falcon flew back to her, an arrow from the forest pierced the bird's leg. Houba's captors, enemies of the Khan, had found her. However, the falcon had already discovered the shallow part of the river, and Houba carried her wounded but strong bird and crossed the Danube, eluding capture. The pair found refuge in Bulgaria, the kingdom of Khan Asparuh. Her falcon still had the white ribbon tied to its leg, now streaked with crimson blood from the enemy arrow. Since the day that Houba and her falcon arrived in Khan Asparuh's Bulgaria, red and white have symbolized health, prosperity, and freedom.

Bulgaria's *Baba Marta* celebration is one of Eastern Europe's richest folk culture celebrations. Steeped in legend, the festival of "Grandmother March" harkens to pagan traditions that modern-day Bulgarians revere as winter becomes spring. Greetings, idols, and symbolism abound from March 1 throughout April as Bulgarians commemorate life renewed. However, these ancient rituals allow Bulgarians to remember and practice the cultural folk beliefs of their ancestors. These commemorations also serve to remind them of their great history and rich legends of the founding of Bulgaria.

Misti Nicole Harper

Further Readings

Johnson, Andreas. *Baba Yaga: The Ambiguous Mother and Witch of Russian Folklore.* New York: Peter Lang, 2010.

"Khan Asparuh and His Sister Houba." *Project Martenitza.* http://www.martenitza.org/content/khan-asparuh-and-his-sister-houba. (Accessed on October 15, 2012).

MacDermott, Marcia. *Bulgarian Folk Customs.* London: Jessica Kingsley Publishers, 1999.

"Martenitsa—An Ancient Bulgarian Tradition." *Study English Today.* http://www.studyenglishtoday.net/martenitsa-bulgarian-tradition.html. (Accessed on October 20, 2012).

Petrova, Ekaterina. "Every March, Red and White Strings Welcome Spring in Bulgaria and Romania." *Balkan Travellers.* http://www.balkantravellers.com/read/article/413 (Accessed on October 9, 2012).

Sobol, Joseph Daniel. *The House between the Earth and Sky: Harvesting New American Folktales.* Portsmouth, NH: Teacher Ideas Press, 2005.

"Traditions and Name Days: *Baba Marta* Day (the "Martenitsa" Day)—March 1." *Plovdiv Guide.* http://www.plovdivguide.com/_m1703/Traditions-Namedays/BABA-MARTA-DAY-the-Martenitsa-Day-March-1-503 (Accessed on October 23, 2012).

BABY-NAMING CEREMONIES IN GHANA

In West Africa, baby-naming ceremonies are traditional rituals that have galvanized communities for centuries. While variations of the same custom exist in neighboring Nigeria, Benin, Togo, Cameroon, and Côte d'Ivoire, the traditions of the Akan tribal groups in Ghana have been extensively researched and documented. Members of this large ethnic group participate in multiple communal ceremonies that mark important events in their lives and culture. The first time Akan babies face the entire clan of elders and neighbors is during their naming ceremony; this is the precise moment when they officially come into existence. More specifically, Akan names reflect significant cultural information about the circumstances in which children are born. Moreover, the Akan believe that children's names can contribute to their potential success in life. The closest association of this tradition in the Western world would be baptisms and christening ceremonies performed in religious settings.

Ghana is a country that has only existed as a sovereign nation since 1957. There are over fifty tribal groups with very distinct cultures, languages, and rituals. By far the largest ethnic group is composed of the Akan tribes, which make up almost 50 percent of the national population of 22 million. The different Akan groups speak variations of the Tiwi language, especially in the central and south-ern regions of Ghana. While English is the official national language, Tiwi is often considered to be the most common standard of communication throughout the country. For centuries, the Akan people have managed to retain their culture and language, even though they have suffered excruciating circumstances such as the historical horrors of the slave trade, an extensive diaspora, and forced migration to nearby Nigeria and Côte d'Ivoire. At the start of the twenty-first century, their social organization is still mostly centered around small villages that survive on small-scale farming that manage to keep their communities and customs alive. A crucial component for retaining Akan traditions is to include all its members actively engaged in a close-knit community that helps in collectively raising its children. As part of that custom, the participation of the entire village in the ritual of naming an infant is an experience intended to provide an extended bond for the rest of the baby's life.

Akan families keep newborn babies indoors for the first week after delivery. Both mother and infant remain in the house, and they do not see any visitors dur-ing that period. The day of the week in which the baby was born is of crucial im-portance because it is exactly eight days later that the naming ceremony (*den to*) will take place. It is also commonly referred to as an "outdooring ceremony" be-cause it is the very first time that babies are taken out of the house. Given the pre-carious level of health care available in rural areas, it is rather common for babies not to survive the first seven days of life. Consequently, friends and family do not even attempt to visit the newborn for the first few days. As a result, another related tradition has emerged, perhaps as a realistic copying mechanism; infants who die within a week of delivery are not necessarily mourned by their family or commu-nity because they did not possess an identity—not before being properly named. This is the main reason why the naming ceremony is extremely crucial for the Akan culture.

The Akan tribal groups essentially give their babies three or four names. The first name (*kra den*) is determined by the day of the week on which they were born. The seven-"day" names for males and females respectively are: Monday (*Kwadwó, Adwoa*), Tuesday (*Kwabená, Abenaa*), Wednesday (*Kwakú, Akua*), Thurs-day (*Yaw, Yaa*), Friday (*Kofi, Afia*), Saturday (*Kwámè, Ámmá*), and Sunday (*Akwasi, Akosua*). Sometimes, there are slight variations in spelling and sound. Since light-color skin is a rarity in Ghana, those who look "white" are often called *Akwasi or Akosua* (born on a Sunday), even if they were born on a different day of the week. The reason is that historically, average Ghanaians (during the colonial period) only came in contact with Europeans on Sundays during church services, most of whom were either Portuguese or British. Children also receive a second name (*den pa*) selected by the father, which is a formal name connected to the ancestor clan or an admired person. In the Western world, it is somewhat similar to a fam-ily name. However, the father can select different *den pa* for each of his children. Consequently, siblings might not seem to be related—at least not by name. The baby's third name identifies the order in which children were born in relationship to their siblings: first born (*Píesíe*), second born (*Mǎnu, Máanu,* or *Evelia*), fourth born (*Anan*, *Anané*), and so on. Moreover, children are also given yet another name that reflects babies been born into special circumstances, such as during war (*Bekōe*, *Bedíàkàō*), prematurely (*Nyaméama*), on the farm (*Afúom*), or after a father had died (*Antó*). A recent social phenomenon since the 1980s is the migration of Akan families from the countryside to the urban areas such as the capital city of Accra. This move is often linked to the family's conversion to Christianity. In such cases, new babies born into the new social and religious environment also receive a Christian name on top of the traditional African names. Such agglutination of traditions can sometimes produce people with at least three names but often up to ten names. However, relatives within the same nuclear family might not share a single name at all; all the children often have entirely different names—unless two of them were born on the same day of the week.

The ritual of the naming ceremony is full of symbolism and moral lessons. The joyous event begins early in the morning before sunrise when most members of the community start to arrive at the father's house. Even earlier on that day, the baby is bathed for the first time and then dressed in white clothing. The leader of the ritual is always a family elder (known as *nana*). At the beginning of the gathering, it is customary to have a group singing spiritual songs. Then, one of the elders from the father's family brings the baby into the ceremony and announces the child's name for the first time. Then, the presiding elder begins the ritual with a prayer. Subsequently, the elder gives the infant the first traditional name by stating the common phrase, "You have come to us to stay, and this is your name. You should always respond to it. May you have a long life among this community." Then, he reveals two cups he had previously prepared: one contains water and the other a strong drink such as wine or spirits (known locally as *nsa*). The elder dips his index finger first into the water cup and then places his finger in the baby's mouth while saying "This is water." Then, he repeats the same procedure by softly whispering "This is wine." The general idea is to provide babies with a sample of sweet and bitter tastes on the mouth; it is also intended to impart a moral lesson on the baby to always tell the truth. The liquids are supposed to be a metaphor to avoid confusing two very different things in the future. Then, the elder mixes the remains of the two cups, and they are shared with the parents, who usually offer a toast wishing health and a long life for the newest member of the community. After a final prayer asking for blessings for all the attendees, the baby receives presents and well-wishes. The rest of the day is used for a village celebration of food, music, dancing, and singing.

Examples of three famous Ghanaians at an international level serve to highlight the cultural content codified into their traditional African names. The very first president of Ghana—Kwame Nkrumah—had a name composed of *Kwame* (born on a Saturday) and *Nkrumah* (for being the ninth child being born among his siblings). Second, the former United Nation's Secretary-General, Kofi Atta Annan, has a name with a very distinct meaning: *Kofi* (for being born on a Friday), *Atta* (for being a twin), and *Annan* (for the family name and being the fourth-born son). Another revered Ghanaian in international politics was the elected president who recently died on July 24, 2012 while he was in executive office (John Fiifi Atta

Mills); he had a Christian name (John), was born on a Friday (*Fiifi*), was a twin brother (*Atta*), and his family name was Mills. Their names reveal a legacy of cultural pride and traditions that have managed to survive for thousands of years in West Africa.

Javier A. Galván

Further Readings

"African Names." http://www.afrikannames.com (Accessed on August 20, 2012).

"Akan Naming Ceremony." *The Earth Center.* http://www.theearthcenter.com/templates/firefly/archives/ffarchivesdento.html (Accessed on August 20, 2012).

Levy, Patricia. *Cultures of the World: Ghana.* New York: Marshall Cavendish, 1999.

Serwaa-Fobi, Maame Afia. "Child Naming Ceremonies in Ghana." *All Ghana Data.* http://www.allghanadata.com/?id=36-671-1&t=Child-Naming-Ceremonies-in-Ghana (Accessed on August 20, 2012).

Sheehan, Patricia. *Cultures of the World: Côte d'Ivoire.* New York: Marshall Cavendish, 2000.

Utley, Ian. *Ghana: The Essential Guide to Customs and Culture.* London: Kuperard, 2010.

BABY'S FEET OFF THE GROUND

When babies are born in Bali, they are considered mini-gods. While the people of this Indonesian island commemorate special events with rituals that guide a person from birth until death, the first six months are truly exceptional. Bali's population is almost 90 percent Hindu, but it practices a special blend of Hinduism that incorporates local customs sprinkled with multiple celebrations, rituals, and festivals covering almost every week of the calendar. Since babies are considered to be pure, they receive special attention. At home, the parents create a package containing the umbilical cord mixed with spices, which is then placed at the foot of the crib to protect babies from evil spirits. During the first six months of their lives, the community at large participates in two special celebrations that mark crucial dates in a child's spiritual and social development: one takes place at exactly three months and the other at six months.

From the moment babies are born in Bali, their feet are not supposed to touch the ground for 105 days or three months. Following the Hindu calendar, every month has thirty-five days. During these three months, someone has to carry the baby at all times. The rational is that—in Balinese culture—the ground is considered to be dirty and impure, and it would taint the purity of the baby's soul. Therefore, families go through great lengths to make sure that babies remain clean for this period in which they have a special connection with god. In practical terms, this belief translates into having the extended family (including aunts, grandparents, and neighbors) constantly taking turns to carry the baby.

When babies reach 105 days, a big celebration called *Penyambutan* (Three Months Ceremony) is organized. For the festivities, children are traditionally dressed in yellow and white colors. A village priest (*pemangku*) performs a cleansing ceremony of the house and then blesses the child. Subsequently, he feeds the baby a

A baby's feet touching the ground for the first time at an *Oton* ceremony in Bali. (Dimaberkut/ Dreamstime.com)

small amount of rice, which is the very first time the baby eats solid food. At this point, the baby also receives a name. Then, with lots of anticipation—and cameras ready—the baby is finally permitted to touch the ground for the first time, much to the delight of family members and friends. The parents offer a meal that often includes a roasted pig, which reveals the importance of the celebration.

Balinese babies celebrate their first birthday (*Oton*) when they reach six months of life or 210 days in the Hindu calendar. The temple ceremony is extremely colorful. This is also the first time babies (both boys and girls) get their hair completely cut off and the head shaved as a symbolic measure to represent purity. Since babies are considered little gods during the first twelve months of their lives, they will continue to be pampered until their next birthday, which is celebrated at 420 days or twelve months.

Javier A. Galván

Further Readings

"Bali Ceremonies." http://www.baliholidayisland.com/balinese_ceremony.htm (Accessed on July 25, 2012).

Covarrubias, Miguel, and Adrián Vickers. *Island of Bali.* Jakarta, Indonesia: Periplus Editions, 2008.

Pringle, Robert. *A Short History of Bali: Indonesia's Hindu Realm.* Sydney, Australia: Allen and Unwin Publishers, 2004.

BALUT: EATING DUCK EGGS WITH EMBRYOS

Balut is a fertilized duck egg that contains a partially developed embryo. It is a popular snack or street food prepared primarily in the Philippines but also in other parts of Southeast Asia. It is served primarily late at night, but also as part of breakfast. Balut is a traditional Asian fast food because it is a low-cost snack, and it also has nutrient-rich qualities that contribute to its popularity as a dietary staple. Eating balut also serves several sociocultural roles within the Filipino and other Asian cultures.

Preparing balut takes patience and precision. After the duck eggs are laid, they are sorted for quality. Non-blemished eggs weighing over 65 grams are placed into an incubator, where they continue to develop for fourteen to twenty-one days. Incubation is performed using a balutan, a procedure relying on encasement in parchment or tubes (*taong*) with heated rice husks (*ipa*), or in another type of artificial machine. Eggs must be frequently monitored, often turned two or more times daily. They are also checked every few days for fertility in a method called candling. On the 7th, 14th, 16th, and 18th days, a candle is held up to the egg to view the contents. Infertile eggs or embryos that are no longer developing are removed and repurposed. The process of carefully monitoring the development of balut concludes when the eggs are incubated for the desired length, boiled in salted water for approximately thirty minutes and then served.

The way to eat balut depends on personal preference. One way to eat this unusual delicacy is to season it with salt, and then quickly suck out the veins, feathers, bones, and eyes, taking few to no bites. Another method involves tapping the shell with a utensil and breaking the membrane carefully to sip the encased liquid, all the while continuing to remove the shell. As the parts of the embryo are exposed, they are consumed. Balut is always eaten warm, and it can be accompanied with condiments like vinegar or soy sauce.

Filipinos have multiple reasons for eating balut. Some people believe the eggs have medicinal properties, while others choose it for its low-cost nutritional value. Men often eat balut for its aphrodisiacal qualities; they believe that the food increases sexual stamina and virility. Women, on the other hand, eat balut for its nutrition and also while participating on social gatherings. Among the top female consumers are pregnant women. Balut eggs have higher calcium levels than regular eggs, and they deliver extra nourishment to a developing baby. Both genders participate in a social custom known as *inuman*, where people gather in the evenings to drink and eat finger foods. Balut is a popular staple at *inuman*, believed to help gatherers relax and rejuvenate. In addition to its medicinal and social purposing, balut is further appealing because of its low price. Members of the lower social classes can afford to eat balut, making it available and accessible to all Filipinos.

Dating the history of balut consumption is extremely difficult. When the Spanish arrived in the Philippines in 1521, locals already enjoyed egg dishes such as balut. Pre-dating Western contact, the Philippines and China maintained ongoing communication from 300 ACE. Chinese culture consumes duck eggs, including a delicacy known as century-old duck egg. China had sustained contact with Vietnam, Laos, and Cambodia, other areas where balut is consumed, lending credence to the theory of Chinese influence. The major difference between balut eaten in these areas is the amount of incubation required for the perfect egg. For Filipinos, proper balut is incubated seventeen days. In Vietnam, the eggs, or *hot vit lon*, are ideal at nineteen to twenty-one days, when the embryos are almost completely developed. Cambodians prefer their *phog tea khon* at eighteen to twenty days. Though Chinese influence on balut remains theoretical, scholars uphold cross-cultural contact as a plausible explanation for the food's origin. The preference for balut in Southeast Asian areas having sustained contact with China supports the theory. In most of Southeast Asia and China, however, balut is produced only on a small scale. Mass production and consumption of balut is a uniquely Filipino tradition.

Balut production is both a cottage and larger industry. Some families breed ducks in their backyard to enjoy balut at home, which accounts for roughly 75 percent of all the duck raised in the country. Mass production is often localized to specific areas. In the Philippines, Pateros is known for producing high-quality balut. The town's name comes from the Spanish word *pato*, meaning duck; a *patero* is a person who raises ducks. Located approximately 40 kilometers from Manila, Pateros developed a reputation for high-quality balut eggs in the 1950s. By the late 1970s, pollution contaminated waterways used for duck cultivation, causing production to decline sharply. Many *pateros* were forced to seek employment elsewhere. To revitalize the industry, the Pateros government passed tax breaks to balut producers in 2012.

Balut's popularity outside the Philippines is on the rise. In recent years, San Francisco and New York have hosted balut-eating contests. This dish has also been featured in several cooking shows and reality competitions, and some celebrities have posted videos of their balut-eating experiences online. For discerning foodies, balut is reaching new heights as haute cuisine; in the Philippines and across the globe, it is being reimagined in appetizers, omelet and pastry fillings, soufflé, or even as deep fried delicacies. While balut remains a beloved Filipino staple, more people around the world are learning to eat and enjoy these eggs.

Laura Steckman

Further Readings

Deutsch, Jonathan, and Natalya Murakhver. *They Eat That? A Cultural Encyclopedia of Weird and Exotic Food from around the World.* Santa Barbara, CA: ABC-CLIO, 2012.

Food and Fertilizer Technology Center. "Enhancing the Value of Eggs: How to Make Balut and Century Eggs." *Post Harvest.* July 1, 2001. http://www.agnet.org/htmlarea_file/library/20110716205807/pt2001028.pdf (Accessed on November 13, 2012).

Lambio, A. L. "Duck Production." In *Poultry Production in the Tropics*, 140–159. Quezon City: University of the Philippines Press, 2010.

Magat, Margaret. "Balut: Fertilized Duck Eggs and Their Role in Filipino Culture." *Western Folklore* 61, no. 1 (Spring, 2002): 63–96.

Melican, Nathaniel R. "Pateros Officials Approve Tax Break for Balut Makers." *Philippine Daily Inquirer.* July 24, 2012. http://newsinfo.inquirer.net/234825/pateros-officials-approve-tax-break-for-balut-makers (Accessed on November 13, 2012).

Paska, Paola. "Cracking the Shell: Balut Revealed." *Tangled Noodle.* March 13, 2011. http://tanglednoodle.blogspot.com/2011/03/cracking-shell-balut-revealed.html (Accessed on November 4, 2012).

BARONG DANCE CEREMONY

The people of Bali (Indonesia) believe that good and evil exist in all things, and that it is mankind's duty to keep the two forces in balance. The general conviction is that evil forces that bring misfortune to people cannot be destroyed but can certainly be brought under control. The Barong ceremony is used precisely for this purpose. There are two protagonists in this event. The Barong—a symbol of good and the protector of mankind—watches over the male dancers who are his followers as they clash with Rangda, the evil witch. When the victory of the Barong is threatened, the dancers rush to his assistance by violently attacking Rangda with sacred daggers called *kris*. Rangda retaliates by using magic to reverse their anger. As a result, the dancers fall into trance and stab themselves with their *kris* daggers, but they do not harm themselves because of the Barong's protection. In this way, the balance between good and evil is reaffirmed for the village. When the community is protected by the Barong, the presence of *bataro gade* (the protective spirit of Bali) is present not only in the village but also throughout the entire island.

Part of the Muslim nation of Indonesia, Bali is a small island 2 miles off the west end of Java that has maintained its own form of Hinduism. Agama Hinduism is so closely connected to the culture of the Balinese people that Bali is called the "Island of the Gods." There are many temples throughout the island, and ritual celebrations such as the Barong ceremony take place in these temple compounds.

A Barong Dance Ceremony in Bali. (Santonius Silaban/Dreamstime.com)

The ritual of the encounter between Barong and Rangda is carefully staged and orchestrated as a ceremonial performance. Men of the village act as ushers who outline the stage, take care of the audience and community members, and prevent those in trance from hurting anyone. Men play the roles of the Barong and Rangda (considered mythical beings from the spirit world) by wearing special sacred masks and costumes. Before the ceremony starts, the players are protected through offerings to the gods so that the sorcery and magic of the ceremony will not harm them. The performance builds up to a battle between Rangda—the witch that symbolizes the evil in us all—and the Barong, who is essentially good and will save the village by encouraging community members to fight the inner evilness known as Rangda. Acting in "goodness" the dancers in trance eject the "evilness" concentrated in their bodies. With each thrust of the *kris*, the evil is released. As a result, evil and good are at a balancing point and harmony prevails.

The Barong is similar to the dragons and lions of China and Japan in its duty to protect the community from evil spirits. Like these mythical figures, two dancers animate the Barong; the first dancer forms the forelegs and manipulates the head mask and the second dancer is in charge of the legs behind. This dance requires great coordination since the Barong must be a lively and playful creature, whirling around, snapping its jaws at the *gamelan* (musical orchestra), and swishing flies with its tail. The image of the Barong has bulging eyes, a red complexion, and enlarged wooden teeth, which he can snap. Since he is considered to be white magic, he can conquer but not kill. His sorcery is strongest in his sacred beard, which is dipped in holy water.

The mask of the Barong is made from *pule* wood, which is believed to have magical properties. The hair of the Barong is also made from special materials, including peacock feathers and horse mane. Since this is a mask with a spirit, a proper day must be chosen to work on it. When the mask is completed, special ceremonies are performed to bless it at a major temple and to ask for spirits to descend and give the mask special powers. These final steps make the Barong mask sacred.

One male dancer wears the Rangda mask and costume. Rangda, who is both a widow and a witch, represents darkness and black magic. She rules over evil spirits and the witches who haunt graveyards at night. While she has aspects of Durga—the Hindu destructive female goddess—Rangda is very specific to Balinese culture. Rangda is a frightful vision with huge hair, sharp teeth, and long splintery nails. Her mouth is always open, from which hangs a long flaming tongue symbolizing her consuming fire. Around her neck is a necklace of human entrails. She carries a white cloth in one hand, which is the center of her powerful magic. In addition, the figure of Rangda utters curses while stalking the Barong.

In the actual dance performances, the Balinese masks are empowered with *taksu* or spiritual energy. This unique energy makes the mask a sacred object and also connects the dancer's mind and body to the character of the mask. When the dancers put on the masks (the Balinese use the term *njaloek*, which means "to bear" the mask), they can immediately go into a trance. Trance can be defined as an altered state of consciousness that has been used throughout history by many cultures for purposes of relaxation, healing, inspiration, and also as part of religious and mystical experiences. There are many different paths of going into a trance, including religious rituals, meditation, breath exercises, visual art, music, dance, fasting, or special foods and drugs. The way someone goes into trance is usually associated with a person's religious and cultural traditions. The trance experience is specific to each culture, and it can include contact with supernatural and spiritual beings that give important advice or aid to the community.

In Bali ritual ceremonies, those who experience trance perform an important function for their village. Through the ritual of trance, they provide the link between the everyday environment and the spirit world. Dancers, musicians, and *dalang* (shadow puppeteers), when performing in religious roles, are vulnerable to trance during a ceremony. This altered level of consciousness is a very important aspect of the Barong dance ceremony. In fact, the event is not complete without trance. In temples where nobody goes into trance, this can be a sign that the gods have not accepted the dance offering. Priests ask themselves whether they have done the ritual correctly.

The followers of the Barong (called the *pangurek*) do not wear masks, but they also fall into trance as they try to attack Rangda with their *kris* daggers. Rangda, using her magical white cloth, forces them to turn their weapons upon themselves. The trance dancers' self-stabbing is called *ngurek*. Bystanders (especially priests) sometimes fall into sympathetic trance, obtain a *kris*, and begin self-stabbing. Women can also perform *ngurek*, though not as commonly as men. *Kris* are ritual daggers that can also be spiritual objects. The *kris* have a distinctive wavy blade, and they used to be actual weapons used by court soldiers. Families keep *kris* for generations as symbols of honor, talismans, and sacred heirlooms (*pusaka*). The godly power of the Barong protects the *pangurek* as they attack themselves with their *kris*—and even though they try very hard to wound themselves—the blades bend and do not pierce their bodies.

Dancers are brought out of trance by the Barong who dances among the *pangurek*, brushing them with his beard and by priests who sprinkle holy water on the dancers. It is unusual for *pangurek* dancers to be injured, but they are closely watched and protected by fellow villagers.

This ancient dance ceremony is still an important part of religious life in the rural villages of Bali. However, it is now being threatened because of the impact of tourism on Balinese culture. Tourism is the largest industry of the island. In tourist centers, foreign visitors can buy T-shirts imprinted with the image of the Barong or watch staged performances of Barong and Rangda complete with *gamelan*, dance ensemble, and dancers in trance. These performers are paid to entertain non-Balinese, and they do not carry the same spiritual meaning as ceremonies performed in the villages. Some Balinese elders feel the Barong ceremony performed for money brings evil and bad luck to a village. The sacredness and belief of the battle between good and evil is crucial to the well-being of Bali, and it was not originally intended to be used for any other purpose.

Eve Kikawa

Further Readings

Belo, Jane. *Bali: Rangda and Barong*. Seattle: University of Washington Press, 1942.

Eiseman Jr., Fred B. *Bali: Sekala and Niskala*. Watsonville, CA: The Crossing Press, 1990.

Pringle, Robert. *A Short History of Bali: Indonesia's Hindu Realm*. Crow's Nest, Australia: Allen and Unwin, 2004.

Reichle, Natasha. *Bali: Art, Ritual and Performance*. San Francisco: Asian Art Museum, 2011.

Simmonds, Nigel, and Teltoni, Luca I. *Bali: The Morning of the World*. Hong Kong: Periplus, 1997.

Sullivan, Gerald. *Margaret Meade, Gregory Baateson, and Highland Bali: Fieldwork Photography of Bayung Gede 1936–1939*. Chicago: University of Chicago Press, 1999.

Tafoya, Xochitl. *Ritualizing Barong and Rangda: Repercussions of a Collaborative Field Experience in Kerambita, Bali*. Baltimore: University of Maryland Press, 2009.

BERBER MARRIAGE FESTIVAL

The Berber Marriage Festival in Morocco is a unique event drawing tourists from around the world. The festival, or *moussem* in Arabic, is usually held each September high in the Middle Atlas Mountain Range of Morocco near the southern town of Imilchil. Several Berber tribes take part in the celebration. At this celebration, young men and women meet each other and decide on marriage partners in a collective event with many potential mates. The interaction between the men and women is often fast-paced. It might even be compared to the practice of speed dating in American culture when men and women meet with a number of potential partners in a short period of time to decide who they might like to get to know better. However, in Berber culture this festival leads to a marriage, not just a dating relationship. Often the women are so covered that men cannot see exactly what the women look like. Men may get clues from other men who may know the women. Family members often take part in the event and aid the men and women in making their decisions. The mass nature of the event gives men and women isolated by terrain, winter weather, and widely scattered villages an opportunity to meet a far larger number of potential spouses than if such an event were not held. In fact, this marriage festival is somewhat outside the norm of how most marriages are arranged. The festival is held in conjunction with a holy day honoring a man buried in the area. The *moussem* is also a market event, with many people bringing their wares for sale. Recently, the event has become a large tourist draw as well, and Berber culture is well represented at the event.

The Berber people settled much of North Africa long before the Arabic people moved into the areas. In Morocco, almost one-half of the population is of Berber descent. There is a Berber language widely spoken among the people group, although there are multiple dialects. Several different Berber groups are scattered throughout North Africa. Tribal divisions were, and still are to some extent, led by chiefs. Prior to Islam spreading into North Africa, most Berbers were Christian and Jewish, with many practicing animism. Animism is the belief that spirits inhabit inanimate objects, such as rocks, trees, and mountains. St. Augustine, one of the early church fathers in Christianity, was of Berber background. The Berbers, while largely adopting the religion of Islam, have maintained many unique customs.

Consequently, they have often been discriminated against by Arab-led governments. With many Berbers living in isolated areas, such as the Middle Atlas Mountain Range of Morocco, they have been able to pass down many of their customs despite social restrictions imposed upon them. Berbers refer to outsiders by a derivation of the term Roman, harkening back to the days when they ran up against the Roman Empire.

Berber people always maintained herds of livestock with the men tending the herds and leading them to places of pasture. This activity kept many of the men away from home for long periods of time. Berbers were also involved in growing crops. The women often became skilled at weaving materials from the abundant wool coming from the sheep herds. Berber handicrafts, especially carpets, can be very valuable. The various Berber tribes often have their own unique design for weaving fabric and carpets.

The origin of the Moroccan Marriage Festival is said to go back to a young man name Isli, meaning groom in Berber, and a young woman named Tislite, whose name meant bride. They fell in love and wanted to be married despite the fact that they were from warring tribes. Because the tribes were enemies, their parents would not consent to the marriage. They were said to have grieved themselves to death by crying so much that each formed a lake with their tears. Two lakes near Imilchil bear their names. The lakes are separated by a mountain; so, they were apart even after their death. The warring tribes and grieving parents were said to have been motivated by this event to give their children forever the right to choose their own spouses from that day forward. The choosing of spouses at the festival is thought to be a result of the deaths of Isli and Tislite. The similarities between this story and the story of Romeo and Juliet are striking.

Sidi Mohammed Maghani was a holy man who had blessed marriages during his lifetime. The festival takes place near his tomb. The men who come to the festival wear white turbans and clothing, happy for the opportunity for time with others, especially a potential wife, because many of them live in isolated areas, and they have been further sequestered by time seeking pasture for the livestock. Women are dressed in their best attire, and they have their faces made up, although some will only allow their eyes to be seen because of the coverings.

The Berber Marriage Festival at Imilchil lasts for three days, and it is filled with music, food, trading, selling, and with men and women looking for a husband or wife. Sometimes forty couples will get married in a collective wedding service, and many others may get engaged through the activities. It is often suggested that financial incentives based on tourism entices some couples to take part in the festival. The marriages that take place during the festival may sometimes be the result of previously arranged marriages between families. Those getting engaged will find their families dealing with the legalities and financial issues, such as deciding how much the husband will have to give to the family of the bride. Brides who accept a marriage proposal will often tell the prospective husband that he has captured her liver. The liver is seen as an important organ in the process of romance; when a young lady's liver is captured, it means that she is swept off of her feet. A woman does have the right to reject a young man's offer of marriage. Men and women are also allowed to divorce their spouses. After getting engaged at the festival, some of the weddings will actually take place in their villages and will be surrounded by festivities of their own.

Cultural interpretations suggest that such communal marriages may have resulted from the fact that many could not afford the expense associated with a private wedding. A matrimonial ceremony at the festival provides a way for an inexpensive wedding. The Berber Marriage Festival is held after the crops are harvested. As a result, the crops are often brought to the market held as part of the festival. By marrying off daughters and sons at this event, it can be a thrifty way to have a wedding.

A typical Berber wedding begins with the groom asking his parents for permission. If they agree, then the groom's parents visit the bride's parents to discuss the dowry, the price paid by the groom's family to the family of the bride. A government official is involved to put a marriage contract in writing. The groom then begins the process of obtaining the dowry. If the bride calls off the wedding, she would have to return the dowry. If they are divorced later on, she is entitled to keep the dowry.

On the day of a typical wedding, the dowry is taken to the bride's home, and the items would be checked against the marriage contract. Animals are slaughtered and cooked, and a feast is enjoyed. The wedding typically lasts for three days. On the third night, the couple is allowed to consummate the marriage. It is very important for the bride to be a virgin at the time of the marriage. It would bring great shame on her family if it was determined that she was not a virgin. The next morning, the participants have breakfast, and the people return to their homes, except that the bride's mother stays until the bride leaves to go to the husband's home. The expectation is that all women will live with their husband's families, which then exercise almost complete control over the wife's activities. Often the bride is subjected to verbal and physical abuse from both the husband and his family. The husband can take a second wife if he is able to take care of both wives. In Morocco, the husband must get the first wife's permission before taking a second wife. In this specific social and cultural context, it is legal for a husband to have up to four wives.

Ken Taylor

Further Readings

Dax, Peter. "Seven Brides for Seven Berbers." *The New York Times.* September 3, 1989. http://www.nytimes.com/1989/09/03/travel/seven-brides-for-seven-berbers.html?pagewanted=all&src=pm (Accessed on April 6, 2013).

Goufrani, Muguette. "Berber Wedding Fair at Imilchil." *Africa Travel Magazine.* http://www.africa-ata.org/mc_berbers.htm (Accessed on April 7, 2013).

Hoffman, Katherine E., and Susan Gilson Miller, eds. *Berbers and Others: Beyond Tribe and Nation in the Maghrib.* Bloomington: Indiana University Press, 2010.

Morocco Blog—A Morocco Travel Guide. "Morocco's Berber Bride Festival." http://www.journeybeyondtravel.com/news/morocco-travel/morocco-berber-bride-festival.html (Accessed on April 7, 2013).

Morocco Channel. "Imilchil—A Celebration of Marriage." *Morocco.com*. http://www.moro
    cco.com/blog/imilchil-a-celebration-of-marriage (Accessed on April 7, 2013).
Njoku, Rafael Chijioke. *Culture and Customs of Morocco*. Westport, CT: Greenwood Press,
    2006.

BLACK PUDDING THROWING CHAMPIONSHIP

Children are told not to throw their food, yet in the British town of Ramsbottom
in the county of Lancaster, adults are encouraged to throw food in the annual
World Black Pudding Throwing Championships. Held at the Royal Oak pub,
contestants are given three six-ounce black puddings (blood sausages) which they
throw underarm from a floor surface to knock down Yorkshire puddings (bigger
sausages) from a 20-foot-high platform. This bizarre contest began in 2001, and it
now sees participants coming from as far afield as Hong Kong, South Africa, and
Australia.

The British delicacy known as "black pudding" is a blood sausage that originated
in Europe. It was made famous in 1929, when the "Chadwick's Original Black Pudding" was handmade by a family-owned company known today as the Bury Black
Pudding Company. The closely guarded recipe is based on an unlikely combination of ingredients such as pig's blood combined with barley, oatmeal, rusk, herbs,
spices, and flavorings. This is then shaped into a plump, black sausage which can
be boiled or fried.

The origin of the throwing championship is set in medieval times at the "War of
the Roses," a civil battle between Lancashire symbolized by a white rose and Yorkshire with a red one. When both opponents ran out of ammunition, they resorted
to throwing food instead. Nowadays, in the championship—which takes place
on the second Sunday in September—the black-pudding sausages represent the
town of Lancashire, and the Yorkshire pudding symbolizes the county of Yorkshire. For the competition, the contestants stand on the ceremonial square called
the Golden Grid, which is placed on the ground. Then, a stack of Yorkshire puddings (sausages) are piled on a 20-foot-tall platform. Armed with three six-ounce
black puddings, the contenders have to throw underarm to skillfully topple the
Yorkshire sausages from the platform. Participants vie for the title of becoming the
World Black Pudding Throwing Champion, a trophy, a medal, and a cash prize.

In the early stages of the throwing championship, there was some controversy
concerning the Yorkshire puddings. As an outdoors competition, it is open to the
elements of British weather. Therefore, when it rained, the Yorkshire Puddings
(which are made of flour, milk, and eggs and then baked to regulation size and
weight) absorbed rainfall like a sponge, which increased the weight and made it
difficult to topple the stack. To resolve the problem, frozen Yorkshires were used
in 2002, but they stuck together. Today, the organizers have reverted back to the
original baked Yorkshires with the black puddings swaddled in ladies' panty hose
to prevent splatter and strengthen the sausages.

The eccentric affair is full of pomp and ceremony. It begins with the arrival of
the Golden Grid by steam train which is then paraded through the streets flanked
by Scottish bagpipe players until reaching the Ramsbottom Town Centre. With

over 650 contestants, the competition now enjoys added attractions such as a farmer's market, stalls, trampolines, and the Pudstock Music Festival. All the proceeds from the event are donated to multiple charities. Overall, it is a fun family day in Bury, home to the World Black Pudding Throwing Championship.

Nadia Ali

Further Readings

Black Pudding History. http://www.blackpudding.org/history/ (Accessed on July 18, 2012).

Frew, Elizabeth. *Tourism and National Identities.* Oxon, UK: Routledge, 2011.

Holman, Tom. *A Lancashire Miscellany.* London: Francis Lincoln Ltd, 2010.

Le Vay, Benedict. *Eccentric Britain, 2nd: The Bradt Guide to Britain's Follies and Foibles.* Bucks, UK: Bradt Travel Guides, 2005.

Pilkington, Martin. *Bury Black Pudding Peasant Goes Gourmet.* http://www.lovefood.com/journal/features/13486/ury-black-pudding-peasant-goes-gourmet (Accessed on July 18, 2012).

BLACKENING THE BRIDE

The nation of Scotland has, quite possibly, one of the most unique cultural traditions regarding the marriage of a man and a woman. In Scotland, there are several rituals which are still honored by modern brides in large parts of the Western world. Most are sweet and beautiful customs which serve to honor ancient Scottish traditions, and they are usually performed with dignity and grace. However, there is one specific custom which has gained international attention for being rather odd and decidedly the opposite of the elegance and serious tone of a traditional wedding ceremony. In certain parts of Scotland, before a woman can get married to the man of her choice, she must undergo an interesting Scottish tradition which goes back to ancient times. To many outsiders who happen to witness the event, it would seem a very bizarre practice and perhaps more of an assault than a joyous custom. However, to the people of Scotland, it is a time-honored tradition which celebrates the heritage of Scots and allows some of the austerity of the wedding ceremony to be lifted and replaced by joy, laughter, and a strong sense of community. Blackening the bride, also known as *Reschtach* in the Celtic language, is a Scottish ritual which is designed to be decidedly unpleasant in terms of smell, sights, and cleanliness. It is also designed to cause the bride embarrassment and even a degree of humiliation, all in the name of good fun. Despite its unpleasantness, it has a certain feeling of inevitability, and perhaps there are even those brides who look forward to being blackened.

The blackening of the bride is a pre-wedding ritual wherein the friends and family of the bride-to-be will ambush her at a time when she is busy with other things, conduct a type of faux kidnapping, and place her in a location where friends and well-wishers can each have their turn attacking the bride. During this time, the community will cover her in all manner of disgusting things, such as rotten eggs, old fish sauce complete with fish heads and bones, sticky molasses, rotten milk,

A couple takes part in the traditional "blackening" of the bride in Balintore, Scotland. (Balintore Holiday Homes)

and any other such matter of foul substances. The rule of thumb is that the more rancid the material to hurl at the bride, the better. Everyone who sees the bride is welcome to add to her blackening, even those who are not involved in the wedding ceremony. The entire community takes turns throwing refuse and garbage at the bride-to-be. Following this, the bride will either be walked through the streets, placed in a cage which is attached to a car or truck, tied to a tree, or displayed for the public in some other way. Everyone in town is to look at her, gawk at her, and add to her collection of disgusting smells. All the while, her friends are making noise by banging pots and sticks and shouting to announce the approaching wedding. The bridesmaids make as much noise as possible accompanied by members of the community who decide to join in on the fun. The next act of the ritual in many towns and villages is to cover the bride with feathers that attach to the sticky goo. Finally, the young woman is often led to a body of water and thrown or pushed in.

Interestingly, despite the seeming unpleasantness of being covered in all of this muck, the brides of Scotland understand that this is part of the wedding ceremony in their native land, and few are upset when it occurs. Very few people will adamantly refuse to take part in communities where the tradition continues, and few brides try to avoid the blackening or hide out until they can be wed. The blackening is considered a festive and happy occasion, not just for the bride but for her surrounding community as well. Modern blackening rituals tend to end in pubs or other locations where the bride-to-be and her company can get inebriated, usually preceded by the aforementioned dip in water or a period where the bride is allowed to go home and clean up before being thrown into a body of water.

Brides are not the only ones who can receive a blackening, although they are the predominant targets of the tradition in Scotland. In most villages, historically, only the bride was subject to this ritual, but in places like the Orkney Isles, it was the groom who traditionally received the treatment from his friends and family members. In addition, in the male version, the groom is often stripped, even in winter before the blackening occurs, proving himself more manly and sturdy for being able to stand it. The gender ultimately receives the blackening is wholly dependent on the community and the traditions that have been built into the area. The ritual of the individual community is as important as the blackening itself. In modern times, a bride can be blackened, a groom can be the target of the attacks, or both members of the couple can be blackened together as a bonding experience. Couples who have undergone the blackening ritual together are symbolically connected by the tradition, which is meant to be the first difficulty that they share as a pair. They have shared this moment, and they will reflect upon it in their later years as a reminder of what they are capable of overcoming together. There is also the fact that few people will want to be around the odorous couple until they have cleaned off, allowing them personal time together before their wedding.

There are many theories about why and how this particular tradition started. The mythological explanation states that ancient peoples believed that the blackening of the bride was meant to ward off evil spirits who might try to possess or torment the bride on her wedding day. Thus, this tradition is supposedly used as a ward against any mythical spirits, known as *trows*, and to keep them at bay. Another explanation regarding fairy folk says the ritual was to ward off bad fairies who might go so far as to kidnap the bride and take her away before the wedding. Historical explanations for the custom have it that the tradition goes back to the medieval period when Scotland had another marriage tradition which involved the bathing of the feet and hair of both the bride and groom. This bathing would be the most thorough and careful of their lives and therefore before the wedding the community would make the bride as filthy as possible before her ceremonial washing. Further evidence to this theory is the fact that many blackenings end in a sea, lake, river, or other nearby body of water when the bride is thrown or led to jump into the water. She could therefore be cleaned of the fish, sap, and other rancid substances before she continued with her wedding preparations. Other more prosaic theoreticians say that this ritual is supposed to prepare her for the daily difficulties and humiliations that she will have to face in her married life. In Scotland, it is said that if women (or men man in certain places) can survive the humiliating blackening ritual with their dignity still intact, then they will symbolically be prepared for whatever life throws at them. Nothing can be as bad, as difficult, or as embarrassing as being covered in molasses and then paraded through the streets of your home town.

Most large cities in Scotland in the present time do not practice the "Blackening of the Bride" any longer. This is the case for many of the ancient Celtic traditions which have fallen out of favor as society has progressed. These places have let go a lot of the more individual traditions in exchange for a more modern idea of what is appropriate or inappropriate in terms of honoring their Scottish heritage. As a result, the communities which still hold the blackening are mostly small towns and villages in the countryside of Scotland. Nowadays, occurrences are still been recorded in many parts of Scotland, including Aberdeen, Angus, and Fife. The communities which continue the blackening tradition do so to honor their ancestors, even if it means getting rather messy.

Rachelanne Smith

Further Readings

"Ancient Scottish Traditions." *Destination Loch Lomond.* 2012. http://www.destination-lochlomond.co.uk/images/pdf/old%20customs%20.pdf (Accessed on September 5, 2012).

Bennett, Margaret. *Scottish Customs: From the Cradle to the Grave.* Edinburgh, Scotland: Birlinn Ltd, 2005.

"Culture Ledger." *Word Press.* July 16, 2010. http://www.cultureledger.com/blackening-of-the-bridegroom-scotland/ (Accessed on August 20, 2012).

O'Sullivan, Joanne. "Blackening the Bride and Groom." In *Book of Superstitious Stuff*, 168–70. Watertown, MA: Imagine, 2010.

Sartain, Sheree. "Hen-Night with a Difference: 'Blackening' the Bride." *Women's View on News.* http://www.womensviewonnews.org (Accessed on August 2011).

Towrie, Sigurd. "The Wedding Blackening." *Orcadian Wedding Traditions.* 2012. http://www.orkneyjar.com/tradition/weddings/blacken.htm (Accessed on September 1, 2012).

BLOOD DRINKING

Drinking blood from a cow is a common cultural tradition among the Maasai people of East Africa. They live in an area known as the Great Rift Valley, which is located in southern Kenya as well as northern Tanzania. The group is an indigenous tribe, and it is a part of the Nilotic family of African tribal groups. Around 1500 ACE, the Maasai migrated in mass from Sudan to southern Kenya and northern Tanzania where they are still located today. The Maasai people are often viewed in East Africa as warriors. Despite major growth and development in Kenya and Tanzania, the group has managed to maintain large cattle herds and a pastoral way of life. Consequently, the group is often viewed as a culture from the past, resistant to the continuous growth and change in their area. From that point of view, the Maasai people are often described as proud, independent, and sometimes arrogant herdsmen. The group's unwillingness to change has placed them far behind the rest of other groups in the region in terms of development. It is mostly due to their cultural traditions that the majority of the Maasai people live on Maasai Reserves in both Kenya and Tanzania.

The Maasai are pastoral people, and cows are revered animals in their culture. The Maasai people believe that their rain god (Ngai) gave all the cattle to the Maasai people. Based on this notion, the group believes that if other tribes are found to have cattle, they must have at some point stolen them from the Maasai. While they drink the blood from the cow as a form of nourishment, they take the proper precautions throughout the process to ensure that the cow is not harmed. The Maasai people believe that drinking the blood of the cow is an important component of maintaining their health. Drinking blood is believed to help keep a person's body strong as well as to keep them warm when the temperature is cold. They also believe that drinking a glass of blood has the ability to raise a person's body temperature.

The Maasai people take the blood from the cow early in the morning while the cow is standing in its corral. Members of the community restrain the cow to keep it still. A tourniquet is then tied around the neck of the cow so that the blood is able to pool. Then, another member of the community stands at short range and shoots an arrow into the jugular artery of the cow. On the arrow, there is a ring that is used to prevent the arrow from going too deep and causing serious injury to the cow. As a result, the puncture wound is small. Once the incision has been made, a liter-sized jug called a *calabash* made of a dried gourd is filled. Once enough blood has been drawn, the hole is covered with a mixture of dirt and the cow's own feces so that the wound can heal properly. The Maasai believe that they can perform this procedure on a cow once a month without suffering any damage to its health.

Once collected, the Maasai consume the blood in a number of ways. Sometimes they drink the blood fresh while it is still warm from the cow's body. If it is drunk that way, the cow's blood is considered to be breakfast. Others will wait for the blood to clot and then separate it. In doing so, the blood can now be drank throughout the day. In this instance, the clots that formed can also be cooked and eaten once they have been separated from the blood. In addition, the blood can also be mixed with curdled or fresh milk.

The Maasai also drink blood during special occasions. After giving birth, a woman in the Maasai culture is often given blood from a cow to drink. It is believed that drinking blood following the delivery procedure will help the woman's body to quickly replenish some of the vitamins that she lost during labor. Blood is also given to a man to drink following a circumcision. In addition, sick people in the village also drink it to help them heal, as well as men when they return from a hunting trip. After consuming too much liquor, the elders of the village known as the *ilamerak* often drink blood from the cow to recover from both the intoxication and the feeling of having a hangover.

In the Maasai culture, the men of the village are given the opportunity to take part in a bush retreat known as the *Orpul*. The *Orpul* can last for up to a week. While on the retreat, the drinking of alcohol is not permitted. During this period, the men obtain their nutrition from eating beef, drinking beef-soup broth, and also drinking fresh blood. The *Orpul* commonly takes place during the area's dry season when food such as milk is often scarce.

The Maasai people believe that drinking blood from a cow is helpful because it is rich in protein, and it has been found to be good for the human immune system. Blood is an important part of the Massai's traditional diet. In addition to cow's blood, the diet predominately includes meat as well as milk from the cow.

The Maasai people's diet is also supplemented by a drink called *mursik*, which is made from milk that has been fermented with the urine of a cow and ashes. It is believed by the Maasai that drinking *mursik* can help to lower a person's cholesterol.

In recent years, the act of drinking the blood of a cow is no longer as common a component of the Maasai diet as it once was. This is because the tribe has seen a decrease in their livestock numbers. In order to still make sure that they are receiving the proper nutrients from their food, the Maasai people have begun to supplement their diet and the lack of cow's blood by eating fruits and vegetables.

Dawn Cioffoletti

Further Readings

Bain, Keith, Pippa de Bruyn, Lizzie Williams, and Philip Briggs. *Frommer's Kenya and Tanzania (Frommer's Complete Guides)*. Hoboken, NJ: Wiley Publishers, 2010.

Garine, I. de, and Valerie de Garine. *Drinking: Anthropological Approaches*. New York: Berghahn Books, 2001.

Gupta, Aman. *Human Rights of Indigenous Peoples*. New Delhi, India: Isha Books, 2005.

Maasai Association. "The Maasai People." http://www.maasai-association.org/maasai.html (Accessed on January 23, 2013).

Parkinson, Tom, Matt Phillips, and Will Gourlay. *Kenya*. Victoria, Australia: Lonely Planet, 2006.

Zachary, J. H., and Jean Zachary. *More Amazing True Mission Stories from around the World*. Nampa, ID: Pacific Press, 2005.

Zimmern, Andrew. *Andrew Zimmern's Bizarre World of Food: Brains, Bugs, & Blood Sausage*. New York: Random House, 2011.

BOCHNIA SALT MINE UNDERGROUND RELAY RACE

The Bochnia Salt Mine Underground Relay Race, an annual event held in Poland, holds numerous Guinness records for its distinctive attributes. Bochnia is a small town in the Malopolskie Province, located in the central part of Lesser Poland (or "Little Poland"). The town is situated on the Raba River, 40 kilometers (25 miles) east of Krakow. It stands at the meeting point of historic trade routes north–south and east–west, a position that proved convenient for distributing the mine's salt as well as cloth, Bochnia's other key commodity. The Bochnia Salt Mine, currently the town's primary attraction, was active from 1248 to 1990, making it the oldest industrial plant in Europe. It is also Poland's oldest salt mine. Other landmarks in Bochnia include St. Nicholas Basilica, the Stanislaw Fischer Museum, the Bochnia Academy of Economics, and statues of King Casimir III of Poland (1310–1370) and General Leopold Okulicki (1898–1946).

As one of the oldest towns in Little Poland, Bochnia has a long history, marked with several tragic chapters. It was repeatedly ravaged by fire in 1561, 1709, and 1751. It also sustained heavy damage during the Great Northern War in 1702. During the Holocaust, all but 200 of Bochnia's Jewish residents were killed by the Nazis; the rest of them were held as forced labor in a plant. Although the salt industry had once anchored the town's economy, even that activity came to an end.

As a result, Bochnia had to rebuild and restore itself time and again. Part of that process has required the town to reinvent itself through a transformation from a commercial town into a site for tourism, establishing the hospitality industry of central importance to the town's future.

The Bochnia Salt Mine Underground Relay Race began as a celebration of the Day of the King Casimir. This race takes place each year during early March in conjunction with that observance. The competition involves a relay race that is twelve hours in duration. As a half-marathon, the event has a course that is roughly 22 kilometers (approximately 13 miles) in length. Both professional and amateur runners may register for the race.

This relay race is unique in several respects. Perhaps most notable among these rarities is the fact that the Bochnia Underground Relay Race occurs entirely in an historic salt mine. For this reason, participants do not conduct a road race at ground level. Rather, they descend 212 meters below to traverse the galleries of the one-time mine. On this basis, the Underground Relay Race holds several Guinness records, including both "the deepest underground half-marathon" and "the longest distance to be covered in a relay race underground." In addition, the organizers of the race documents how many total kilometers the participants run in hopes that they will not only beat previous years for distance but also break the existing Guinness record. For example, the 2009 event involved 8,262 kilometers and 508 meters (roughly 5,134 miles) traveled by fifty-five relay teams.

The signature location of this race has a lot to offer its visitors. The decommissioned mine is now functioning as something like an underground town. The facility is owned and operated by the Bochnia Salt Mine Health Resort Ltd. In the context of participating in the distinctive event, runners typically spend an extended period of time within the salt mine, which maintains a year-round temperature of 14°C (57.2°F). Their visit typically involves a two-night stay below ground, sleeping in the mine's largest chamber, a salt room now serving as a sanatorium (subterranean therapy). While there, racers may join a 2.5-hour guided tour of the site conducted at 220 meters (721 feet), complete with a multimedia presentation relating the location's backstory. Other highlights of the salt mine tour include the Passions chapel, chapel of St. Kinga (considered to be the patron saint of salt miners); sculptures; and exhibitions of machinery and mining tools. The mine tour provides some incongruous sightseeing moments. For example, visitors may behold peculiar sights such as underground chandeliers and also experience some of the elements remaining from the mine's 742 years of continuous operation. For example, tourists are afforded the opportunity to slide 140 meters (459 feet) down a ramp that once conveyed the rock salt. They can also ride an underground train or board a boat within a chamber in the mine located 230 meters (754 feet) deep underground, now flooded with saline to form a lake. In addition to the mine itself and the pathways associated with the race, Bochnia also boasts numerous underground amenities, such as a restaurant, football and basketball pitch, and spa. The salt chambers of Bochnia are regarded as a health resort for their air quality and other properties, which its present operators tout as a "therapeutic microclimate." The underground location also hosts dances, plays, concerts, film screenings, and a cycling event known as "The Salt Downhill." Taken together, these attractions make Bochnia's Salt Mine a popular destination for recreational travelers and tourists, with hundreds of thousands arriving each year.

Bochnia has taken several measures to preserve this historic district for generations to come. Since 1981, the mine's historic structures have appeared on the local register of monuments. In 2000, the Republic of Poland's president declared the Bochnia Salt Mine an official monument of historic heritage. Consequently, historic portions of the mine, including its salt caverns, enjoy some legal protections. Efforts are currently underway to place Bochnia Salt Mine on the UNESCO World List of Cultural and Natural Heritage. A 2010 application proposed that Bochnia Salt Mine be added as an extension of its nearby counterpart, the Wieliczka Salt Mine, which joined the list in 1978.

Although relay runners may compete in a great many memorable races, few can match the unusual setting and history associated with the Bochnia Salt Mine Underground Relay Race. Participants can have remarkable experiences there, from sailing the brine to running the underground relay itself.

Linda S. Watts

Further Readings

Official Promotional Website of the Republic of Poland. "Bochnia Saltmine." http://en.poland.gov.pl/Bochnia, Saltmine,12070.html (Accessed on February 14, 2013).

Republic of Poland, Promotional Website. "Underground Relay Race—Running for the Guinness Record." http://en.poland.gov.pl/Underground,relay,race,11541.html (Accessed on February 14, 2013).

Wiewiorka, Janusz, Jrzysztof Dudek, Jozef Charkot, and Malgorzata Gonera. "Natural and Historic Heritage of the Bochnia Salt Mine (South Poland)." *Studia Universitatis Babes-Bolyai, Geologia* 54, no. 1 (2009): 43–47.

BOG SNORKELING

An extraordinary event takes place once a year in Llanwrtyd Wells, Wales—Britain's smallest town. The occasion attracts people from all around the world to partake in a wacky extreme sport known as "Bog Snorkeling." Contestants gather on the side of the Waen Rhydd Bog wearing flippers, a face mask, and a snorkel ready to take the plunge into the bog (dark and mossy wetlands) where they swim predetermined lengths to compete for the fastest time.

The beginning of this strange competition dates back to 1979. Gordon Green was the owner of a hotel in Llanwrtyd Wells who wondered what event could possibly provide the spark to attract tourists to the small town. He found the answer in the surrounding landscape. After careful planning, his ideas became a reality when the first ever bog snorkeling event was held in 1985. Since that year, the annual contest takes place during the August Bank Holiday at the Waen Rhydd Bog which is primarily a wetland site rich in rotting plants giving growth to Sphagnum moss that creates a dark, spongy-like ground. It is here that over 110 contestants travel from across the globe to clinch the title of the World Bog

Snorkeling Champion. For the contest, two man-made trenches 6 feet deep (2 meters) and each 60 yards long are specially dug at the bog. Contestants must swim two lengths but not using a conventional swimming style. With the aid of flippers, a mask, snorkel gear, most of them swim doggy-style with their heads down, and they make the two lengths in approximately five minutes. The event is always held at the same bog every year.

Participants take part in this eccentric affair for multiple reasons. However, the main motivation is that competitors vie for the title of becoming the World Bog Snorkeling Champion and the opportunity to get their name listed in the *Guinness Book of Records*. Competitors pay a nominal entrance fee, and all proceeds are donated to charity by Gordon Green's company Green Events Ltd.

While most people see the event as a fun extreme sport, there are red flags warning those who participate stating that bog snorkeling in trenches that are full of filth are a breeding ground for disease. Weil Disease, in particular, is often associated with stagnant areas where infected animal urine can exist in the water. If this water is absorbed into the body through the mouth or nose, it can lead to life-threatening bacterial infections. While the bog on the hilly terrain is completely flushed out by rains and flood water every year, it is still home to various fish and creepy-crawlies such as leeches, tadpoles, and harmless water scorpions.

Since its inception in 1985, the competition has grown to include categories for women, juniors, and men with an option to dress in a fun costume. It now enjoys corporate sponsorship with bog snorkeling events also being held in Ireland and Australia. It is regarded as an extreme sport that attracts more attention each year as it boosts tourism to Britain's smallest town of Llanwrtyd Wells.

Nadia Ali

Further Readings

Hole, Abigail. *Lonely Planet: Wales.* Oakland, CA: Lonely Planet Publications, 2004.
Liedewij, Loorbach. *Sullivan's List: The 100 Most Amazing Events in the World.* Middlesex, UK: Lightning Publishing Ltd, 2011.
Ripley's Believe It or Not! Hertfordshire, UK: Ripley Publishing, 2004.

BONE HOUSES AND OSSUARIES

Ossuaries, or bone houses, are depositories of the skeletal remains of dead people. The word "ossuary" is derived from the words *os* and, in plural, *ossa*, which is a Latin word for bones. These words first appeared in Roman languages, and they have been featured in English dictionaries only since 1650. Originally, ossuary was a name for a container of skeletal parts, such as the James Ossuary—the wooden box believed to have belonged to the brother of Jesus, but later proved to be a forgery. Later, the word ossuary changed its original meaning, and it began to signify not so much transportable containers but rather architectural forms, ranging from single rooms to whole buildings. While some of the ossuary rooms are rather bare and simple, others display intricate architectural design and artistic creativity. Ossuary in this sense is similar to the charnel, or charnel house, which is derived

A bone house in Hallstatt, Austria, with over 1,200 skulls. (Petitmiaou/Dreamstime.com)

from the Latin word *caro* (literally translated as flesh, but often referring to the remains of the dead).

Ossuaries may appear bizarre to contemporary people, but in fact they were fairly common types of burials for medieval Europe and other earlier cultures. The first and most direct reason for the appearance of ossuaries was the lack of space for other forms of burials, such as coffins, especially in relatively densely populated urban areas. Bodies of the deceased were temporarily buried and then, after several months, exhumed, so as to rebury the skeletal remains of corpses in a separate location. It is for this reason that ossuaries were never featured as possible forms of burial in Muslim countries, because Islam places a ban on the practice of exhumation for whatever reason. On the contrary, the traditions of exhumation and later reburial were nothing out of the ordinary in Zoroastrianism, Judaism, as well as both Catholic and Orthodox Christianity. In addition, in the medieval Christianity, remnants of the people who had led virtuous lives—especially those of saints—were expected to withstand corruption and remain in good condition. Thus, moral firmness was directly linked to the durability of skeletal remains. Many bones of saints were preserved in churches and monasteries as artifacts of special value, and they often attracted pilgrimages from distant followers. Some relics of Christian saints were incrusted inside important objects of material culture, such as swords or large ornamental crosses, and they were believed to enhance the spiritual power of their owners. In some cultures, portable ossuaries were also used to serve as portable repositories for remains of dead ancestors because carrying these ossuaries was supposed to bring spirits of the deceased into closer contact.

Ossuaries of varying sizes can be found in various parts of Catholic Europe. Some of the largest ossuaries are situated in Austria, Czech Republic, Italy, Portugal, and Spain. The most significant Austrian ossuary is situated in the village of Hallstatt, which is located in the Salzkammergut region of the Upper Austria. This location is significant because of the number of collected remnants and due to their chronological scope. The earliest of more than 1,200 skulls preserved in the Hallstatt ossuary dates back as early as the twelfth century, and the most recent addition was made as late as 1995. Most surprisingly, over one-half of all skulls in this Beinhaus (bone house in German) have flower designs on them. The tradition of painting skulls with flowers supposedly originated in the early eighteenth century, and it was actively practiced for considerable period of time.

The largest Italian ossuary is located within the grounds of the church named *Santa Maria della Concezione dei Cappuccini* (translated as Our Lady of the Conception of Capuchins). It is situated in Rome, and it was built between 1626 and 1631. What makes this ossuary distinct from others is that all the remains preserved here belong to friars. One of the six parts of the church, Our Lady of the Conception of the Capuchins, even contains three skeletons held upright against the background of skulls, and they are artistically arranged and clad in monastic habits of the Franciscan order. Some of the other parts of the church also have names directly referring to its purpose, such as Crypt of the Skulls, Crypt of the Pelvises, and Crypt of the Leg Bones and Thigh Bones. In fact, the whole church may be regarded as a huge ossuary with remains of over 4,000 dead, the only exception being the chapel where mass is celebrated.

The suburban town of Sedlec in the Czech Republic is known for the massive amounts of human skeletons found in the ossuary of a small Catholic chapel that is situated below the city's Cemetery Church of All Saints. The best estimate is that it houses between 40,000 and 70,000 sets of human remains. A large number of the bones belong to people who died during the period of the Black Death epidemic that hit this region of Central Europe during the fourteenth century and also during the devastating wars that followed a few decades later during the early fifteenth century. Since so many people had been buried in the cemetery (and they needed the space to bury even more people), the skeletal remains were exhumed in mass, and the bones were placed inside the church. Having so many bones available, local artisans have created works of art out of them, such as chandeliers and regional coats of arms.

The largest ossuary in Portugal is called *Capela dos Ossos*, which is translated as the Chapel of Bones. This chapel is a part of the sixteenth-century church of St. Francis, which is situated in the city of Evora in the southern part of Portugal in the region named Alentejo. The walls and pillars of this interior chapel near the entrance to the church are decorated with parts of about 5,000 skeletons brought there from at least ten different cemeteries from the neighboring regions. In a very peculiar and unusual arrangement, two corpses are hanged on chains from the ceiling; one of them is the skeleton of a small child. Their origins are unknown, but they are popularly believed to be the remains of a man and his son, both of whom were cursed by their respective wife and mother for the man's adultery.

An important function of ossuaries, besides preserving skeletal remains, was also to remind visitors of the transitivity of human life compared to permanence of death. As an indication of this purpose, the Italian ossuary-church *Santa Maria della Concezione dei Cappuccini* features in one of its chapels the following inscription: "What you are now, we once were; what we are now, you shall be." This saying proved able to impress two different and salient visitors such as Mark Twain and Marquis de Sade. In a similar fashion, the ossuary in the church of Santa María in the village of Vamba near the Spanish city of Valladolid greats the visitor at the very entrance with the following text: "As you see yourself, I saw myself too; as you see me, you will see yourself; everything ends in this, think about it, and you won't fall into sin." Likewise, the Portuguese *Capela dos Ossos* was supposedly built with the explicit purpose of inviting Franciscan monks to contemplation on the futility of life in this world, in a spirit of the Book of Ecclesiastes. Thus, the roof of the chapel is adorned with depictions of death, in addition to original skulls and bones, and an inscribed quotation from Ecclesiastes, 7, 1: "*Melior est die mortis die nativitatis* (Better is the day of death than the day of birth)."

Marharyta Fabrykant

Further Readings

Becker, Annette. "From Death to Memory: The National Ossuaries in France after the Great War." *History and Memory* 5, no. 2 (1993): 32–49.

Magness, Jodi. "Ossuaries and the Burials of Jesus and James." *Journal of Biblical Literature* 124, no. 1 (2005): 121–54.

Musgrave, Elizabeth. "Memento Mori: The Function and Meaning of Breton Ossuaries 1450–1750." In *The Changing Face of Death,* edited by Peter C. Jupp and Glennys Howarth, 62–75. New York; St. Martin's Press, 1997.

Peleg, Yifat. "Gender and Ossuaries: Ideology and Meaning." *Bulletin of the American Schools of Oriental Research* 325 (2002): 65–73.

Popovic, Mislav. "Bone Houses." *Traditions and Customs from All over the World.* http://traditionscustoms.com/strange-traditions/bone-house (Accessed on March 23, 2013).

"Portugal's Chapel of Bones." http://www.atlasobscura.com/places/portugals-chapel-bones (Accessed on March 3, 2013).

Trinkaus, K. Maurer. "Mortuary Ritual and Mortuary Remains." *Current Anthropology* 25, no. 5 (1984): 674–79.

Walter, Tony. "The Empire of Death: A Cultural History of Ossuaries and Charnel Houses." *Mortality* 17, no. 3 (2012): 303–4.

BORYEONG MUD FESTIVAL

From both commercial and cultural perspectives, mud is considered a significant resource in Boryeong, South Korea. The coastal city of Boryeong celebrates a summer festival that highlights the beach town's mineral rich mud used in a number of cosmetics in the area. The Boryeong Mud Festival takes place in July, and it attracts over two million people from both Korean and foreign populations. This event is so popular that the festivities are currently considered to be the largest festival in South Korea. Boryeong, the cosmetics company that sponsors the event, transports about 200 tons of beachside mud to the festival site. The festival allows visitors to sample the mud for free in an entertaining way, as the mud is normally highly regulated by local cosmetics companies throughout the year.

Located about 120 miles (193 kilometers) southwest of the capital city of Seoul, Boryeong's Decheon Beach is the site of the festivities, and it features views of South Korea's western coast, multiple islands, and a sandy beach. Other sites of the area include Wonsando Island (a picturesque island off the coast) nearby Mt. Seongju and a coal mining museum with information on mining, mineral samples, and the history of the mining industry in Boryeong. First opened in 1996 as a four-day affair, the festival continued to expand to its current length of ten days, and it eventually became designated as a special festival by Korea's Ministry of Culture and Tourism as its popularity grew.

The festival suffered a setback in 2009 when skin inflammations were reported in 230 children after participating in the festival. Symptoms included itching and rashes, which resulted in researchers conducting tests on mud and water at the event. Reports suggested that the contamination originated in the Daecheon Stream rather than the mud itself. Officials continued on with the event, but only after they instituted more rigorous sanitary protocols and guidelines.

Today the mud festival is a chaotic mix, part Spring Break party, part family day at the beach, and part cosmetics sale. The more raucous side includes mud training courses and games such as mud wrestling and human pyramids. Other events include street parades, fireworks, slides, and mud painting. The event also contains mud massages and exhibitions, as well as sales of various cosmetics.

The cosmetic products based on Boryeong's rich mineral soil include mud packs for skin health and beauty, which are often compared to cosmetology materials from the Dead Sea in Israel. In addition, the peculiar qualities of Boryeong mud also contain variations with yellow earth and white clay—often claimed to promote health. While the mud is the town's main attraction, other local products are also sold. These include Nampo Inkstone and Ungcheon Stone, a glossy black stone used for tombstones and other religious purposes. As part of the celebratory events, culinary produce are also on sale, such as pickled oysters, the sap of painted maple trees (good for stomach ailments), Nampo grapes, and local mushrooms prized for their excellent taste.

Biju Sukumaran

Further Readings

Jiwatram, Jaya. "Good Clean Fun." *Time Magazine.* June 19, 2006. http://www.time.com/time/magazine/article/0,9171,1205425,00.html (Accessed on August 11, 2012).
Shin-who, Kang. "Boryeong Shrugs Off Mud Contamination." *The Korea Times.* July 12, 2009. http://www.koreatimes.co.kr/www/news/nation/2009/11/117_48322.html (Accessed on August 11, 2012).

Weller, Ben. "South Korean Mud Festival Attracts Messy Behavior." *Reuters*. July 16, 2008.
  http://www.reuters.com/article/2008/07/16/us-korea-mud-idUSSEO31940820080716
  (Accessed on August 1, 2012).

BREAST IRONING

Every day, tens of thousands of young girls in Cameroon experience the painful tradition of breast ironing. When girls' bodies start to develop as early as ten years of age, their mothers apply a procedure that involves taking a hot object straight out of the fire to forcefully press the adolescent girl's breast. They use heated wooden pestles, coconut shells, hot stones, spatulas, and even metal hammers to vigorously massage the chest area in order to stunt the girl's physical development. The general goal is to prevent the breasts of pubescent girls from becoming noticeable. Since Cameroonian boys and men believe that a girl with a developing body is ready for sexual activity, mothers try to suppress early signs of sexuality. The practice of breast ironing is intended to protect girls by reducing their sexual attractiveness at an early age and to reduce the potential dangers of sexual harassment and rape. In addition, the family is also trying to prevent early teenage pregnancies that would force thousands of young girls into early marriage arrangements and thus abandoning the dreams of a potential education.

The custom of breast ironing is centuries old in Central Africa, including the current countries of Chad, Togo, and Benin. In Cameroon, it is common throughout the entire country, and it is consistently practiced by all ethnic groups, in all language regions, and by all religions. Cameroon is a country located on the Atlantic coast of Central Africa with a population of nearly 20 million people (2010 estimate). It includes over 200 ethnic groups, and it is socially divided by language and religion. The largest geographical section is made up of the English-speaking groups, and it roughly corresponds with the former British Cameroon colonial territories. The former geographical area of Colonial French Cameroon also left a tangible imprint on the country, especially regarding the use of language and the national education system. Simultaneously, people also speak one or more of the African regional languages, such as Bantu, Fulfulde, Bali, and a variety of pidgin languages. From a religious perspective, demographic data show that the southern part of the nation is mostly comprised of Christian and Indigenous religions, while the northern territories are mostly Muslim. Despite all the existing linguistic, social, and religious diversity in the country, mothers of all groups practice the custom of breast ironing on their young daughters.

Former victims of breast ironing have recently started to speak out against the tradition in the past ten years. They describe the harmful practice as a painful procedure that left them with both physical and emotional scars. For example, Geraldine Mbafor is a thirteen-year-old who narrated her story. While remembering and crying she said "When I was younger, I had just finished my homework when my mother summoned me to the kitchen. She boiled water, and she had put a grinding stone in the water. She then removed the stone holding it with a thick cloth to protect her own hands. She then put the hot stone directly on my breasts and started ironing. I felt so much pain that I started crying. After that, she put something around me called the breast-band. She did this to me for two and a half months" (Child Rights International Network, 2006). The painful experience often has disastrous consequences. Girls often see running away from home as the only solution to their family situation, which then places them in danger of sexual abuse and pregnancy at a very early age.

For centuries, breast ironing used to be a well-kept secret between daughters and mothers. However, it all changed in 2006 when the German Development Agency for Technical Cooperation, or Gesellschaft für Technische Zusammenarbeit (GTZ), conducted a national survey of over 5,000 Cameroonian women regarding the secretive tradition of breast ironing. They interviewed girls and women between ten and eighty-two years old. The study exposed how pervasive the practice really was and how widespread it had become. It revealed that over one million young girls have experienced breast ironing in Cameroon, which is over 25 percent of the entire female national population. While it was once believed that the custom was an uncommon tradition relegated to rural communities, the study also showed that the practice is actually more prevalent in urban areas—such as Yaounde, Bamenda, and Nkongsamba—where mothers were most afraid that their girls would fall victim to sexual abuse and rape. In addition, the study also concluded that there is considerable variation in rates of incidence by geographical areas. Almost 53 percent of young girls in the southern area of Littoral (which are mostly Christian and African religions) suffered breast ironing. In comparison, the northern territories—which are mostly Muslim—had the lowest rate of occurrence at less than 10 percent of young girls. The GTZ survey also highlighted the link between improved nutrition and the practice of breast ironing. For the past five decades, Cameroon has experienced considerable dietary improvements across all ten regions of the country. One of the results has been that healthier girls begin their physical development at an earlier rate of puberty. Consequently, over 50 percent of girls who developed their bodies earlier than nine years of age had their breast ironed by their mothers. When the girls reached pubescent development a little later by age eleven, then the rate of breast ironing was lower at 38 percent. The GTZ study also found an almost even divide regarding support and opposition to the practice: 39 percent of women in Cameroon opposed breast ironing; 41 percent supported it; and 26 percent were indifferent to it.

Doctors from Cameroon and international agencies have warned that the practice of breast ironing exposes young girls to serious health problems. Some of the consequences most often cited include infections, cysts, tissue damage, abscesses, itching, loss of sensitivity, dissymmetry of breasts, blisters, and deficient levels of milk production at later stages of life. International agencies for human rights consider the harmful practice of breast ironing as part of a body-mutilation spectrum that also includes female genital mutilation. Moreover, doctors have also declared that the tradition of breast ironing is a futile attempt to stop physical development, and it is not an effective deterrent for early sexual activity or teenage pregnancy. Instead, physicians urge mothers to talk to their daughters about sex and to openly discuss adequate protection against pregnancy and sexually transmitted diseases, including HIV and AIDS. However, the topic of sex still remains a cultural taboo in Cameroonian mother–daughter relations. The lack of information about sex keeps young girls unaware about adequate protection and makes them more vulnerable to HIV infections in a country with high rates of AIDS.

Since the GTZ report on breast ironing was released in 2006, multiple government and independent agencies have become more active in their medical, legal, educational, and social campaigns against the damaging practice of breast ironing applied to young girls. For example, Cameroon's Ministry for the Promotion of Women and Family has embarked on an ambitious program to educate parents of school-age girls on the health problems and side effects caused by this cultural custom. It has also pursued national legislation to punish such abuses. At the regional level, a grassroots organization called Network or Aunties has also lobbied for authorities to introduce a law banning the detrimental practice. These women belong to over sixty regional associations spread throughout Cameroon that are well coordinated under a parent organization called the National Network of the Association of Aunties, or the *Réseau National des Associations de Tantines* (RENATA). Its membership includes mostly girls who were victims of breast ironing. They have embarked on a national campaign to completely eradicate the practice. Their strategy is to draw public attention to the physical and psychological trauma that the tradition inflicts on young women. Their campaign consists of disseminating information about the negative health consequences associated with breast ironing and the psychological scars that are not always visible but still pervasive. To spread their message, they have partnered with schools, newspapers, clinics, and media outlets to produce radio programs, television commercials, printed leaflets, and newspaper articles. RENATA has certainly earned the respect of official government agencies and the cooperation of international agencies working toward eradicating the harmful custom of breast ironing in Cameroon.

Javier A. Galván

Further Readings

AlertNet. http://www.crin.org/violence/search/closeup.asp?infoID=9218 (Accessed on June 15, 2012).

All Africa. "Cameroon: Campaign Launched to Counter Breast Ironing." *All Africa: Humanitarian News and Analysis.* June 28, 2006. (Accessed on June 13, 2012). http://allafrica.com/stories/200606290001.html

"Cameroon: Breast Ironing of Young Girls, a Harmful Custom." *Women Living under Muslim Laws.* http://www.wluml.org/node/4129 (Accessed on June 15, 2012).

Child Rights International Network (CRIN). "Millions of Cameroon Girls Suffer Breast Ironing." *CRIN Network: Children and Violence.* June 13, 2006.

Epstein, Irving, ed. *The Greenwood Encyclopedia of Children's Issues Worldwide.* Westport, CT: Greenwood Press, 2007.

Gesellschaft für Technische Zusammenarbeit (GTZ). http://www.gtz.de/en/689.htm; New and Updated Website. http://giz.de (Accessed on June 15, 2012).

"Iron Maidens." *Harper's Magazine* 313, no. 1879 (December, 2006): 25–26.

Mabuse, Nkepile. "Breast Ironing Targeted in Cameroon." *CNN World Report.* July 27, 2011.

Sheelan, Sean. *Cameroon.* New York: Marshall Cavendish Publishers, 2001.
"Teenage Girls Undergo Breast Ironing in Cameroon." *Huffington Post: World.* May 25, 2011.
    http://www.huffingtonpost.com/2010/07/23/teenage-girls-undergo-bre_n_656965
    .html (Accessed on June 13, 2012).

BRUSHING TEETH WITH COW'S DUNG ASHES

With a population of slightly over one million, the Nuer people constitute the second largest group in South Sudan—only outnumbered by the Dinka group. They live in a landlocked nation located in East-Central Africa surrounded by Ethiopia, Kenya, Uganda, Congo, and Sudan. The Nuer tribes are essentially cattle herders, and their entire cultural, social, and economic life is based on their livestock. While cows provide basic necessities, such as food, they are also the foundation of Nuer families and society. The entire family owns the long-horn cattle, and they share the responsibility of taking care of them: the women milk them, and the men herd them. At the community level, cows are used for bridal dowries, debt settlements, and payment of fines. The more cows a family owns, the higher social standing they have in their respective communities. Since the Nuer people live on a dry and barren landscape, men have to herd their cattle to far away locations looking for water and pastures. Consequently, they spend a lot of time with their cows: singing to them, sleeping next to them, and decorating their bull horns. Moreover, it is rather common for men to be called by their cow's nickname. While most Westerners can certainly understand the desire for a pastoral life, they are often surprised by the practical aspects of living in close proximity to cows with little water available and questionable sanitary conditions.

The Nuer routinely use cow's urine and dung in ways that are initially repulsive to outsiders. For example, these villages do not have much access to potable water. In addition, living in a hot barren desert, there are no trees available to use as firewood to boil water and sterilize it. Consequently, the Nuer had to adapt to their unforgiving environmental conditions based on a culture of raising cattle. One tangible adjustment is that they use cow's urine to wash their hands; it is even occasionally mixed with milk to drink it. While it may intuitively not sound as a sanitary practice, cow's urine is actually quite sterile and often used as an antiseptic. Therefore, members of the community are unlikely to become sick from its consumption and use. Being surrounded by cattle and living in an extreme ecological region, nothing can go to waste. Every morning, young kids collect the cow's excrement, and they arrange it by small piles on the sun to dry. When dusk arrives, the dried dung is burned in order to create smoke. This practice drives away insects that attack the cattle when they lay down at night. The result, however, is the constant smell of cow's dung and a smoky environment that permeates the village until the next morning. Still, nothing can be wasted. The next day, children gather the ashes of the burned dung and collect it in large clay containers. While performing their task, they like to cover themselves with the ash powder as they are playing around the village. The adults use the ashes from the dung fire to brush their teeth. They use ashes instead of toothpaste, and they use their index finger to function as tooth brushes. While this practice might be expected to generate dental infections or deteriorating hygiene conditions, it is actually very safe. Medical studies of Nuer people arriving at international refugee camps have revealed that—as a group—their dental condition is better than average, especially considering that they do not get routine dental checkups and maintenance.

Javier A. Galván

Further Readings

Heine, Peter. *Food Culture in the Near East, Middle East, and North Africa.* Westport, CT: Greenwood Press, 2004.

Holtzman, Jon D. *Nuer Journeys, Nuer Lives.* Boston: Pearson Education, 2000.

"The Nuer of South Sudan and Ethiopia." http://strategyleader.org/profiles/nuer.html (Accessed on August 20, 2012).

Ryle, John, et al. *Sudan Handbook.* Rochester, NY: James Currey Publishers, 2011.

Willis, Mary S., and Rachel M. Bothun. "Oral Hygiene Knowledge and Practice among Dinka and Nuer from Sudan in the U.S." *Journal of Dental Hygiene* 85, no. 4 (Fall 2011): 306–15.

BULLET ANT INITIATION

The Sateré-Mawé people are an indigenous tribe found on the Brazilian Amazon region, and they practice a unique cultural rite of passage: the bullet ant initiation. This painful ritual is intended to mark the transition of young Sateré-Mawé males from boys to warriors. As part of this tradition, they use the venom of the *Paraponera clavata* (commonly called the bullet ant) to inflict multiple stings on a young man's hand. The ant's name comes from the comparison of the ant inflicting pain that is similar to being shot with a bullet. The community places dozens of these ants inside a glove especially woven for this occasion; the initiates are then expected to insert one hand inside the glove. The ability to withstand this ongoing pain demonstrates the commitment of the young man to be considered a worthy warrior. Essentially, after the rite is completed, the boys transition from childhood to adulthood and enjoy a different status in their community.

The Sateré-Mawé people (also called Maué, Andira, and Arapium) have practiced the bullet ant initiation since early in their history, and they continue to maintain their tradition alive today. Originally living throughout the Amazon, the Sateré-Mawé now hold approximately 788,528 hectares within the Brazilian states of Amazonas and Para, which are both located in the middle of the Amazon River area. The Sateré-Mawé have a relatively small number of tribal members, equaling around 7,000 according to a 1999 estimate. This number takes into account roughly forty-two villages near the town of Andira and thirty-one villages near to town of Marau, both located on the Amazon Basin of Brazil. Many Sateré-Mawé are fully integrated into mainstream Brazilian life and live within urban centers such as Manaus, Brazil, which is the largest city in the deep Amazon area. This interaction has resulted in most Sateré-Mawé men becoming bilingual, and they often speaking both the Sateré-Mawé language (related to the Tupi language, the

Ants used for the bullet ant initiation in Brazil. (Pablo Hidalgo/Dreamstime.com)

historical language of indigenous Brazilians) as well as Portuguese. Although most Sateré-Mawé men speak Portuguese, few women do. Their tribe has faced immense challenges and obstacles for survival due to over three centuries of contact with outsiders, beginning as early as 1669 when Jesuit missionaries founded the Tupinambaranas Mission in the area. Despite their contact with other social groups, the Sateré-Mawé are still actively maintaining their cultural traditions. The bullet ant initiation signifies one of the most important customs within their cultural heritage.

The bullet ant is particularly suited for this rite of passage as its sting is often considered to be the most painful of any Hymenoptera species that also includes ants, bees, wasps, and sawflies. The Schmidt Sting Pain Index was designed to measure the pain of insect bites and stings on a scale of 1 to 4 with a 1 being the least painful and a 4 the most painful. In this range of possibilities, bullet ants receive a score of 4 plus. This scale was developed by Justin Schmidt, a prominent entomologist. In order to develop his rankings, Schmidt inflicted the bites and stings of all the insects on himself. Although this makes the scale somewhat subjective, it is clear that the bullet ant's sting is remarkably painful. Schmidt noted that the pain of a single bullet ant is equal to thirty wasp stings. In fact, the sting is so painful that it inspired its name as many victims describe it as equal to or exceeding the pain of a bullet wound. As a result, the bullet ant's ability to inflict immense pain on its victims makes it a useful technique to mark the transition from childhood to adulthood for the Sateré-Mawé people. The pain from a single sting typically lasts anywhere from three and five hours, and it dissipates over a twenty-four-hour period. The sting is often followed by many adverse reactions, including trembling, perspiration, nausea, and an inability to use an injured arm or leg if stung there. The sting is so severe because the bullet ant's venom is a neurotoxin, and it impedes synaptic transmissions in the central nervous system. The bullet ant administers its sting through a retractable syringe on its stomach. Adding to the pain is the fact that the bullet ant is also the largest ant in the world. Its worker ants can reach sizes of up to 1 inch long (18 to 25 millimeters). Naturally, this immense size causes its sting to be more painful than for average-sized ants. Typically, bullet ants build their nests at the bottom of moist trees, and they are usually nonaggressive, stinging out of defensive tactics rather than as an offensive strategy. Due to the bullet ant's naturally benign nature, the Sateré-Mawé must utilize an artificial manner to get the bullet ant to repeatedly sting the young males.

The Sateré-Mawé people use the bullet ant (which they simply call Tucandera) within their ritual because of its suitability to their purposes. The severity of the bullet ant sting is significant as the boys' ability to endure pain is symbolic of their new role as potential warriors. Not only must the young men undergo this excruciating ritual, but they must also do so without calling out in pain. The actual initiation requires the boys to wear a glove-like wrapping over their hands. Made out of leaves, this glove has many bullet ants (around thirty of them) woven into it with the stingers facing toward the inside of the glove. In order to create the gloves without receiving stings themselves, the glove makers give the bullet ants a natural sedative made from local plants. As the drug wears off, the bullet ants grow increasingly aggressive as they try to free themselves from the gloves. A light coating of charcoal is put over the boys' hands. This is rumored to alleviate some of the stings as it often confuses the ants. However, this is the only protection they receive against the bullet ant stings. Boys are expected to wear these gloves for a period of approximately ten minutes. While the boys undergo this practice, other members of the Sateré-Mawé tribe sing and dance traditional chants and dances to distract the boys from the pain experienced during the ritual. However, the initiation is not completed by simply withstanding the pain once. A series of additional tests, usually totally twenty, are rendered over a period of months or even years before the initiation is considered complete. Only then can a boy be welcomed as a warrior for the Sateré-Mawé tribe. Naturally, this rite is extremely painful, and it results in many adverse reactions caused by a bullet ant sting. However, the idea of wearing a glove full of poisonous ants does not deter potential warriors. Actually, in many cases boys are left without the use of their hands or arms for several hours or even a day after the ritual. This rite of passage is significant to the Sateré-Mawé people not only for its ability to designate the transition from boyhood to manhood but also as a lasting aspect of their way of life despite their extended contact with the outside world.

Matthew R. Blaylock

Further Readings

Blackshall, Steve. *Venom*. London: New Holland Publishers, 2007.

Capinera, John L., ed. *Encyclopedia of Entomology*. Dordrecht, The Netherlands: Springer Science + Business Media B.V., 2008.

Frater, Jamie. *Listverse. Com's Ultimate Book of Bizarre Lists: Fascinating Facts and Shocking Trivia on Movies, Music, Crime, Celebrities, History, and More*. Berkeley, CA: Ulysses Press, 2010.

Hogue, Charles Leonard. *Latin American Insects and Entomology*. Berkeley: University of California Press, 1993.

Lorenz, Sonia da Silva. "Enciclopedia dos Povos Indigenas no Brazil." *Instituto Socioambiental*. http://pib.socioambiental.org/en/povo/satere-mawe/print (Accessed on March 23, 2013).

McAllister, Peter. *Manthropology: The Science of Why the Modern Male Is Not the Man He Used to Be*. New York: St. Martin's Press, 2010.

Morgan, Randy C. "Giant Tropical Bullet Ant, Paraponerea Clavata, Natural History and Captive Management." *Sonoran Arthropods Studies Institute*. http://www.sasionline.org/default.asp?go=antsfiles/pages/bullet/bulletbio.html (Accessed on March 23, 2013).

Robinson, Alex. *Bradt Bahia: The Heart of Brazil's Northeast*. Guilford, CT: The Globe Pequot Press Inc., 2010.

Salzanmo F. M., T. A. Weimer, M. H. L. P. Franco, and M. H. Hutz. "Demography and Genetics of the Satere-Mawe and Their Bearing on the Differentiation of the Tupi Tribes of South America." *Journal of Human Evolution* 14, no. 7 (1985): 647–55.

Stewart, Amy. *Wicked Bugs: The Louse That Conquered Napoleon's Army & Other Diabolical Insects*. Chapel Hill, NC: Algonquin Books, 2011.

Tagliaferre, Lewis. *Lessons from Sedona: A Spiritual Pathway to Serenity and Contentment: Volume II*. Bloomington, IN: iUniverse, 2010.

BURNING OF WITCHES EVENT

In central and northern Europe, people once believed that the spirit world was stronger during certain times of the year. Since the Middle Ages, multiple European countries have observed Walpurgis Night (also known as "the Witches' Sabbath") on April 30. During Walpurgis Night, it is said that ordinary people built bonfires on hills and mountains to frighten witches away. Today, the "Burning of Witches" tradition has endured in Finland and the Czech Republic, but it has morphed into a lively celebration that includes bonfires, food, music, and dancing.

Walpurga (710–779 AD) was an English nun and missionary to the pagan Frankish Empire. Early representations of Walpurga depict her holding stalks of grain; religious scholars have interpreted these images as representations of the older Germanic pagan "Grain Mother." Before Christianity, people believed that the spirit of the grain lived in the crops and that the harvest would make it homeless. Therefore, early farmers would weave straw into animal or human shapes and leave them in their fields to rehouse the grain spirits after the harvest. In Germanic and Scandinavian countries, it was common to weave "old grandmothers" out of straw. Sometimes, people even danced around these figures during harvest festivals. Farmers traditionally kept them until the new planting season, when they would be plowed into the earth or burned. According to the Roman calendar, these events took place in mid- to late April. Such harvest customs were common among Celtic, Germanic, and Nordic pagans, and they persevered into the twentieth century in parts of northern Germany and Scandinavia.

Early Christian missionaries tried to discourage northern pagans from these fertility rites, with little success at first. During the Middle Ages, the Church focused initially on the persecution of heresy, and practitioners of folk magic were usually left alone. During those early trials against heretics, however, ecclesiastical and secular courts recorded claims of secret meetings, orgies, consumption of babies, riding of goats, worship of the Devil, and other phenomena that took place in rural and secluded locales. The church labeled such events of Devil worshipping as "Witches' Sabbaths." By the thirteenth century, accusation of participation in a Witches' Sabbath often lead to excommunication from the church, torture, or burning at the stake. Commonly mentioned dates for "Witches' Sabbaths" in church records included April 30 and May 1 (Walpurgis Night and May Day). These dates have traditionally overlapped with indigenous pagan traditions involving fertility rites, sacrifices, sexual activities, and consumption of hallucinogenic plants and fermented beverages. In the case of Walpurgis Night, the pagans also built huge bonfires to scare predators and evil spirits away from their livestock. Celtic and Finnish pagans believed that running their own animals through the fires would increase their fertility. Witnessing these events, church officials often interpreted such ancestral traditions as Devil worshipping.

In Finland, the "Burning of Witches" tradition on April 30 has become a national celebration. Witch hunt hysteria arrived in Finland during the seventeenth century, much later than in the rest of northern Europe. While the majority of Finns identified themselves as Lutherans, magic and superstition still influenced their everyday lives. The Kingdom of Sweden, of which Finland was a part, did not participate in the religious inquisition taking place in the rest of Europe; torture was against Swedish laws and only used in very rare circumstances. Meanwhile in northern Finland, the pagan Lapps were well known for their shamans and magic. Those parts of Finland occupied by Swedes and Germans experienced witch trials; while approximately 2,000 people were accused of witchcraft, less than 10 percent were actually sentenced to death. In 1809, during the Russian occupation, a strong nationalist movement took place in Finland where many Finns rediscovered—and recorded in writing—their pagan traditions. The "Burning of Witches" is now the eve of May Day (*Vappu* in Finnish), a state public holiday honoring workers and the spring season.

The twenty-first century Finnish "Burning of Witches" event has become an urban celebration. It is the biggest national carnival-style event that takes place in the streets of Finland's towns and cities. *Sima* (a homemade mead), accompanied by doughnuts, funnel cakes, or rosette cookies, are traditionally consumed during the holiday. University students, politicians, activists, and even church officials have raucous parties. In Helsinki, the "Burning of Witches" event has also become known as "Students' Day." Students distinguish themselves by wearing white caps with black visors; they also place a cap on the nude female Havis Amanda mermaid statue. Students distribute two magazines—*Äpy* and *Julkku*—to promote their causes. *Ápy* is often printed on toilet paper or bed sheets and then stuffed in sardine cans or milk cartons.

Unlike in Finland, whose "Burning of Witches" event was originally tied to fertility rites, the Czech *páленí čarodějnic* event focuses on chasing away winter. Czechs believe that the celebration dates back from the Iron Age, when Celtic pagans occupied Bohemia and Moravia. The region known today as the Czech Republic was a crossroads for Celtic, Germanic, and Slavic pagan traditions. Early Christians in this region believed that, during Walpurgis Night, evil powers were at their strongest, and people had to protect themselves and their livestock by lighting fires on hillsides. They believed that witches would fly on broomsticks to the Witches Sabbath, and so the people would also throw burning brooms up in the air to weaken the witches' powers. Nowadays, however, Czechs provide different reasons for the event. First, they believe that the power of witches would weaken with the arrival of warmer temperatures. Second, they believe that setting fires would purge them of any evil spirits that might have been collected inside of them during the dark winter. In the modern *páленí čarodějnic* celebration, Czechs make a "witch" out of old clothes stuffed with straw, and they tie it to a broomstick. A bonfire is lit, and people roast *buřty* (fat Czech sausages), drink beer, play musical instruments, dance, and sing. At dusk, the "witch" is held up and then thrown onto the bonfire. Sometimes an ugly doll is paraded around the village prior to burning. Multiple Czech villages have informal competitions during the holiday to see who can build the biggest bonfire. On that day, children often spend all day finding tree trunks and trash to build a teepee style pyre. In addition to the traditional bonfire (which is illegal within city limits, but overlooked for the holiday), festivities in the capital city Prague include a "Miss Witch" pageant. Other regions include live music, open-air swimming pools, games, broom-burning contests, and opportunities for children to dress up in costumes.

Rachel Wexelbaum

Further Readings

Cravens, Craig. *Culture and Customs of the Czech Republic and Slovakia.* Westport, CT: Greenwood Press, 2006.
Nenonen, Marko, and Timo Kervinen. *Finnish Witch Trials in Synopsis.* May 15, 2001. http://www.uta.fi/yky/arkisto/historia/noitanetti/witchtrials.html (Accessed on July 1, 2012).
Tan, Chung Lee. *Finland.* Tarrytown, NY: Marshall Cavendish Benchmark, 2007.
Toivo, Raisa Maria. *Witchcraft and Gender in Early Modern Society: Finland and the Wider European Experience.* Burlington, VT: Ashgate Publishing Company, 2008.
Tufnell, Blanche O. "Czecho-Slovak Folklore." *Folklore* 35, no. 1 (March 31, 1924): 26–56.

BURYING LLAMA FETUSES

Out of all the Andean nations in South America, Bolivia is the most connected to its indigenous past. Over 60 percent of the current population (based on 2010 census) has either direct Aymara or Quechua roots. This high-altitude territory was historically dominated by two expansionist empires: the Incas and the Spaniards, and they both left a tangible imprint, especially in terms of language and religion. As a result of multiple cultural influences, spiritual life in Bolivia is now a galvanized mixture of Catholic beliefs, indigenous gods, community traditions, witchcraft, and general superstition. The result is a set of hybrid cultural traditions that blend multiple belief systems across most social and economic levels. The custom of burying llama fetuses under the house is best analyzed as a contemporary ritual based on Bolivia's historical and religious heritage.

Daily social and cultural practices in Bolivia are mostly a mixture of European influence combined with Aymara and Quechua social traditions. The indigenous religion was originally a polytheistic system of male and female gods that were holistic in nature. These deities were not found in heaven; instead, they lived in rivers, mountains, fields, and other sacred locations. Out of all the indigenous gods venerated in the past, the one that still commands much devotion nowadays is Pachamama, the goddess of earth and fertility. Many of the modern celebrations in Bolivia coincide with agricultural and harvest seasons, which are directly linked to Pachamama. Her influence is so great, that she is now specifically mentioned in the new national constitution of 2009. The European influence arrived in 1536 when the Spaniards conquered the Inca Empire and took control of the Andean territories. They imposed a monotheistic religion that initially intended to erase all traces of what they called "pagan" gods and rituals. However, it quickly became apparent that these deities were too interconnected to social and community traditions. By the early 1600s, the result was a compromise where a parallel system established two spiritual beliefs that coexisted and complemented each other. Contemporary Bolivians still follow a blend of both spiritual systems; this practice is specially revealed on Sundays.

The Catholic church of San Francisco is the hub of religious life in the capital city of La Paz, Bolivia. Sundays are popular for the multiple mass services offered in three languages: Spanish, Quechua, and Aymara. However, the real action happens in the narrow streets and alleys behind the massive church. This is where the Witches Market (El mercado de los brujos) is located. All along, streets such as Jiménez, Sagarnaga, and Santa Cruz, rows and rows of vendors sell a rare combination of products, herbs, and ingredients needed for fortune telling and as offerings to multiple gods. The market is buzzing with activity every day, but it is especially busy after Sunday mass when the Catholic followers go to the street market to purchase amulets; incense; bundles of plants and herbs; aphrodisiac potions; statues of Ekeko to find a wife or husband; bunches of coca leaves; and spiritual figurines of Pachamama attached to shapes of turtles, frogs, and snakes. However, the most salient feature of the Witches Market is the sale of dried or dissected llama fetuses (locally known as sullus).

The llama fetuses are traditionally buried under the foundation of a new house prior to the construction process. The ritual must also include a special blessing (called cha'lla) offering the fetus to Pachamama, the earth goddess. The dissected fetuses are quite large (roughly 2–3 feet tall), and many of them still have hair. The tradition is so popular that it is estimated that over 90 percent of all homes in

Bolivia have a llama fetus underneath it. In fact, most construction crews send a representative to the blessing ritual because the workers most likely would refuse to work on a house without a *sullu* already buried underneath and the appropriate blessing performed. While there is no specific location where the fetus should be buried, the majority are placed under the foundation that supports the front of the house. The fetus is intended as an offering to Pachamama, who in turn is supposed to protect the construction workers from harm. In addition, the practice is also believed to bring health and prosperity to the occupants of a house. Once the house is completed, however, the owners of the new construction also invite a Catholic priest to bless the house once it is completed—just in case.

The practice of burying llama fetuses before the construction of a new house reveals the deep connections that still exist in contemporary Bolivia between

THE COEXISTENCE OF CATHOLIC AND AYMARA RELIGIOUS BELIEFS

Shop owners at the famous Witches Market in La Paz, Bolivia, always seem to have an abundant display of llama fetuses for sale. The fetuses with hair look almost like cute stuffed animals, but the ones without fur look more like dissected birds with exaggerated jaws, creepy eyes, and sharp teeth. The indigenous vendors explain that when the construction season is about to start, then llama fetuses are in high demand (as well as witch doctors to perform a special blessing before the construction for a new house). These unusual animal fetuses are usually for the regional market, and they are not generally purchased by tourists because it is illegal to take them out of the country. Most shop owners also explain the origins of so many of these fetuses: "when llamas are killed at the slaughter house for meat consumption, they are sometimes pregnant, and the fetuses are set aside to sell at the Witches Market." While this scenario is completely possible, it is rather strange that they all seem to have such an identical predetermined answer. In addition to the traditional hustle and bustle of the market, it is truly enlightening to return to visit the Witches Market on a Sunday morning. At this time, hundreds of Catholic followers first attend Sunday mass with apparent spiritual fervor, but as soon as they step out of the church, they go around the narrow alleys where they carry out consultations with an Aymara religious leader (*yatiri*) who provides spiritual guidance. This apparent contradiction is a wonderful display of how religious orthodoxy is bendable and adapted to the needs of daily life in Bolivia, which incorporates traditions that date back to a period before the arrival of both the Incas and the Spaniards.

Javier A. Galván

historical struggles, community practices, indigenous customs, religious traditions, and a bit of superstition. The amalgamation of Catholic theology with indigenous gods has created a parallel religious path where most Bolivians function without hesitation on a daily basis.

Javier A. Galván

Further Readings

Cramer, Mark. *Culture Shock! Bolivia: A Survival Guide to Customs and Etiquette.* Tarrytown, NY: Marshall Cavendish Editions, 2011.

Galván, Javier A. *Culture and Customs of Bolivia.* Santa Barbara, CA: Greenwood Publishers, 2011.

Morales, Waltraud Q. *A Brief History of Bolivia.* New York: Facts on File, 2010.

Werner, Robert J. *Bolivia in Focus: A Guide to the People, Politics, and Culture.* Northampton, MA: Interlink Books, 2009.

BURYING THE PLACENTA

While Western medicine treats the placenta as mere human waste, many cultures across the world still consider it to be extremely important. It is also treated with superstition based on a ceremony or ritual attached to it. In Nigeria, where there are over 250 ethnic groups—many of them distinct from one another in terms of language, customs, and practices—placenta burying is an ancient tradition where most of these tribes agree in beliefs and practice. In most parts of Nigeria, people believe that evil forces could change the destiny of a child through the placenta if it is not buried or disposed of properly. If a birth takes place at a hospital, most Nigerians hardly ever leave the placenta there. Instead, they insist on taking it home for a proper burial. Most medical facilities usually hand it over to the father or another trusted family member. The placenta of a newborn is regarded as an extension of life, and it is treated with utmost care. At home, the placenta is then washed delicately (like a baby) and carefully buried.

Four of the main tribes in Nigeria (Igbo, Yoruba, Hausas, and Ibani) practice similar traditions related to burying the placenta but with small variations. For example, the Igbo group considers the earth as a symbol of fertility and life. Consequently, it is important for the placenta (or *Alo*) to be buried in a land or property owned by family, both as proof of ownership and as a memorial so that the children know their background and do not abandon their roots. Afterward, a tree is planted at the burial spot as a symbol of a continuous and flourishing life.

The Yoruba tribe calls the placenta *Ikeji-omo*, which literally means "the child's twin or partner." This name is used because when a baby is born, the placenta is still connected to the child. The general belief in Yoruba land is that burying a placenta in a family home or land will ensure that children never forsake their family however far life takes them from home. The placenta can also be buried in a land or property owned by someone influential in Yoruba society who may have no blood relationship with the newborn in hopes that children will have some of the traits and nature of said person—such as being wealthy or highly placed and respected in society during their lifetime. In addition, the Yorubas bury the placenta by placing it in a special clay pot called *shashu*. Then, they bury it in a secret location.

The people of Ibani in Rivers, Nigeria, insist on burying the placenta beside a tree following the belief that the child will live long and be fruitful. Individuals who do not know where their placentas were buried are threatened with lack of progress, becoming barren, and suffering an untimely death. The Ibani even celebrate the annual festival of *Nwaotam* related to the placenta, which tends to escalate the sentiments attached to this vital organ. Ibani women who have their babies at hospitals are usually very anxious of potential complications that may arise if the placenta is switched with that of another newborn.

In contemporary Nigeria, the process of burying the placenta has become less elaborate due to modernization. For example, the Igbos used to believe that the placenta was the dead twin of the newborn and thus gave it an elaborate funeral. Nowadays some of the young parents simply leave it to the hospital where the baby was born to be disposed. However, this behavior is still generally frowned upon. Despite development and progress, a considerable number of young Nigerians continue to treat the placenta as an important cultural tradition. They even send the placenta of their newborn from faraway places across the world where they have migrated to their trusted families in Nigeria for a proper burial.

In modern times, the use of human placentas for commercial cosmetic products has generated recent controversies. For example, the emergence of placenta-based creams and lotions has increased the number of accusations against hospitals in Nigeria for selling placentas to companies (that manufacture these products) but without the proper consent of trusting mothers. Overall, Nigerians also fear that some of these hospitals may use the placentas for ritualistic purposes; consequently, many families are highly reluctant to donate them for scientific or medical research purposes regardless of how transparent the researches appear to be.

It is commonplace for fathers to inquire about the placenta of their newborn from the hospital authorities after birth. If the mother of the newborn baby has disposed of the placenta without the consent of the father (or through means he has not approved of), it may actually create serious marital problems.

TAKING THE PLACENTA HOME FROM THE HOSPITAL

When Nigerian women deliver a child, a large number of hospitals will usually ask the parents if they would want to keep the placenta or leave it to the health authorities. The majority of parents usually still request to take the placenta with them, and it is then wrapped carefully and inconspicuously (usually in a cloth or black polythene bag), still in its state of birth (unwashed) and handed over to the parents or a close family member.

Veronny Odili Okwei

Finally, there is an African cultural tradition that Nigerians definitely do not practice regarding human placentas. Despite reports of some cultures and the new-age fads that celebrate the placenta as nutritious and healthy if ingested, Nigerians do not eat the placenta. That would be highly unusual in Nigeria, and it may be termed cannibalistic or misinterpreted as ritualistic.

Veronny Odili Okwei

Further Readings

Akintunde, Dorcas O. "Dynamism in Culture and Values a Desirable Trend in Combating Vulnerability to HIV/AIDS: The Yoruba experience." In *People of Faith and the Challenges of HIV/AIDS*, edited by Mercy Amba Oduyoye and Elizabeth Amoah, 87–100. Ibadan, Nigeria: Sefer Books: A Circle Publication, 2004.

Lefeber, Yvonne, and Henk W. A. Voorhoeve. *Indigenous Customs in Childbirth and Child Care.* Amsterdam: Van Gorcum Publishers, 1998.

Oluwakemi Oke, Ruth. "Iya-Agbebi, Traditional Birth Attendants in Yoruba Setting and Issues on HIV and AIDS." *Lumina: Interdisciplinary Research and Scholarly Journal* 20, no. 1 (March 2009). http://www.hnu.edu.ph/main/publication/kinaadman/1200309/12 0030911.pdf (Accessed on July 28, 2012).

BUZKASHI, AFGHANI SPORT ON HORSEBACK

Roughly 800 years ago, Genghis Khan and his nomadic tribesmen emerged from the grasslands of Central Asia to overrun most of Eurasia—on the back of the horse. The conquest was efficient and swift because the Mongolians and other regional cultures had developed around the unique attributes and capabilities of an animal that has lived among human beings for over 7,000 years. The domestication of the horse began in the very place where Mongol warriors—equipped with bows, arrows, and whips—began racing across the treeless plains and through mountain valleys to raid, plunder, raze, and possess villages and kingdoms that lay between the Pacific Ocean and Mediterranean Sea, as well as areas in the Arctic and Indian Oceans. Without sustenance from the horse's blood, milk, and meat, or without its strength, speed, and intelligence—or back to sleep on—the Mongol's strategy of conquest could never have been conceived, let alone achieved. The embodiment of horseman was perfected during the Mongol's subjugation of much of the known world which includes an area that is today Afghanistan where horse and man coalesce to play *Buzkashi*, the country's national sport. Only men are allowed to participate in the event as both players and spectators. The most distinctive motion enacted during a match is when a wrestler (player) rides on a horse at high speed and bends down to pick up a decapitated goat from the floor—all the while competing with dozens of players and horses trying to stop him from reaching his goal. To practice this national sport, horses must possess a unique combination of strength, agility, and specialized training.

One minor tactic less admired than the notorious scorched earth effect used by the Mongols to execute their strategy for conquest is *Buzkashi*. The name comes from Dari, a language not spoken by the Mongols but one of Afghanistan's official languages. The word *Buz* means goat, and *Kashi* means either or simultaneously pulling, grabbing, and dragging, a practice the Mongols excelled in while on horseback riding full stride through villages swiping goats and sheep from right under the noses of their foes. The Afghans eventually learned to reciprocate, and they then turned the warcraft into a game, and a brutal one at that.

Most of the time the competition takes place on a vast, barren, boundless field that is given new meaning by the appearance on the ground of the "circle of justice" and, 75 yards away, a small post with a flag. The circle is usually 6 feet wide and drawn with white chalk or delineated by a ring of stones. Around the circle is where the game begins, and in the circle lays the beheaded, de-hoofed, disemboweled carcass of a goat, or sometimes a calf because the skin better resists tearing. Usually the animal is soaked in cold water overnight to make it more durable. The carcass weighs between 60 and 150 pounds. During the reign of the Taliban (1996–2001), a Muslim fundamentalist movement, *Buzkashi* was deemed immoral and more or less banned. However, whenever it was played during this period, the *Buz* sport was made of animal skins sewn together and stuffed with hay.

Toward the circle gallop the *Palawans* or wrestlers on horseback (more popularly known as *Chapandaz*) who are at times divided into as many as three teams of eight to fifteen players; at other times it is a free for all with no teams but more than 100 riding wrestlers. The most basic accoutrements are: headgear being traditional turbans, fur caps or Soviet tank crew helmets made of leather, knee-high animal-hide boots, a bridle and an inconspicuous saddle atop poly-patterned saddlecloths, and a horse whip commonly carried in the mouth.

The best *Chapandaz* deploy nearest the circle where scrums continuously form. These are the men who have been playing for at least a decade, and they are perhaps the descendants of the first players. Communication with their horses (which finally gain the necessary character and experience after a decade of summer pampering and winter competition) is hardly ever lost in translation. Only their leathery toughness and unencumbered competiveness outmatch their acrobatic finesse on horseback. Strength resides in the grip; therefore, the hands are the focal point, particularly for opponents who use the horse whip to dislodge rider from horse and carcass from grip. Hammer punching thighs is considered illegal; still the hands of champions are scarred, knotted, and gnarled.

The game begins the moment a rider reaches down, grabs and lifts the goat carcass, and attempts to makes a dash for the flagpole while others follow in hot pursuit. Once around the flag, the objective is to replace the carcass in the circle of justice while the other riders attempt to prevent this by almost any means necessary. There are not many rules in *Buzkashi*, and there are no official referees—just scorekeepers. However, there are a few promises which these fierce rivals keep, such as no biting, pulling hair, or knifing, even when the opportunities for such tactics abound in the brawl of the scrum where men are yelling, horses screaming, and hooves clacking. Traditional matches can go on for days, but contemporary team now last only a few hours. Either way, each drop of the carcass in the circle is a point. When playing in teams it is not unusual for scores to reach a quarter of a century since teamwork involves blocking out opponents' access to the carcass carrier or pulling him along by grabbing his horse's reins.

Spectators like to stay close to the action but still remain a safe distance from the swarm which can in a moment of momentum close that gap. Sometimes patrolmen with sticks or rifles will try to steer the spectators away, but, like the *Chapandaz*, devotees can be knocked down and trampled; they can have their bones broken, or find themselves in a tussle which may lapse into a bout of rock throwing. In some places such as in Mazar-a-Sharif, Afghanistan, the hearth of *Buzkashi*, rudimentary grandstands have been set up. In Kabul, shipping containers become seating areas which surround the official playing field, giving it the look of an arena. After Friday Muslim prayers, pandemonium begins to build towards the field. As spectators choose their vantage points, young boys with wads of cash in their hands rush around the more formal gallery to collect wagers, while those already settled-in share cigarettes and red-dyed hardboiled eggs in relative safety.

Afghans participate in two forms of *Buzkashi*: *Tūdabarāy* which means "coming out of the crowd" and *Qarajāy* meaning "black place." The former is more traditional; therefore, there are no formal teams or boundaries, and it reinforces a sense of community among villagers who play to celebrate special occasions such as weddings or birth of a son. *Qarajāy* has become a sport for professionals, but it also carries political and economic implications. Its promoters hope the sport will soon be accepted by the International Olympic Committee. In the meantime, regional tournaments are taking place in various Central Asian countries with teams entering even from India and Pakistan.

Qarajāy became prominent during the latter part of King Mohammed Zahir Shah's rule over Afghanistan which lasted from 1933 to 1973. Festive matches were first arranged to commemorate his birthday, then eventually for public holidays. By 1977, government sponsorship had propelled *Buzkashi* into a well-organized national sport. However, the tradition all but vanished by 1979 when the country fell into a civil war that has been raging now for over thirty years. Yet, war also has financed its renaissance. Over the past ten years, the United States along with its allies have been fighting in Afghanistan while simultaneously supporting a campaign for nation building. Large amounts of money have been sloshing around one of the poorest countries in the world, some seeping into the pockets of businessmen, politicians, and local bosses (*Khans*) who have informally channeled it into *Buzkashi*.

The government of the Islamic Republic of Afghanistan along with the urban nouveau riche has made Kabul the capital city of *Buzkashi* where the sport is the most organized, controlled, and seemingly professional. Teams with uniforms vie for cash prizes and recognition while the Afghanistan Buzkashi Federation, a new quasi-government body, looks on as informal advisor.

Outside of Kabul, particularly in the north, tradition and professionalism converge to create a version of the *Qarajāy* sport that illuminates the political culture of Afghanistan. In some sense, the *Khans*, local bosses, are high-stake event planners, but their regional political clout is pegged to the tournaments they arrange. First, they must have the financial resources to support such an event. Second, they must be able to garner support from tribal elders and leaders and other *Khans* in effect reinforcing alliances and seeking political patronage. Such grand events which begin with the pre-tournament ceremony of *Tū'īs* demand cooperation among a large number of people. A smooth-running tournament with minimal protest and extracurricular violence reflects positive leadership qualities. Third, the host's stable of horses must stand a good chance at winning. For this to happen, they buy top-of-the-line breeds from Kazakhstan and Kyrgyzstan for $50,000and upwards each. It should be noted that most Afghans live on less than $1 a day. When a *Chapandaz* (wrestler on horseback) scores, he immediately reaps the benefits of his sponsor's wealth and prestige by riding over to pick up luxurious prizes. When the tournament is over, the carcass may be given to the poor who enjoy the goat meat tenderized by *kashi*.

Kenneth Whalen

Further Readings

Azoy, G. Whitney. *Buzkashi: Game and Power in Afghanistan.* 2nd ed. Long Grove, IL: Waveland Press, 2003.

Frankenheimer, John. *Les Cavaliers* [*The Horsemen*]. United States: Columbia Pictures, 1971. http://www.youtube.com/watch?v=O5gufMm3l6U (Accessed on December 1, 2012).

Hoffman, Carl. "Rider in the Storm." *ESPN: The Magazine.* September 11, 2011. http://espn.go.com/espn/story/_/id/6944843/afghanistan-national-sport-buzkashi-evolves-post-9–11-world-espn-magazine (Accessed on November 1, 2012).

CAMEL RACING

Camel racing is a well-organized sporting spectacle with large stadiums built specifically for these events, intense media coverage, and enormous financial investments and prizes, as well as elaborate festivals with the pageantry of music, poetry, and national pride. In a manner similar to horse racing, jockeys ride the camels around a track or predetermined course at speeds of up to 65 miles per hour. However, there is a crucial difference: camels are sometimes also raced by robotic jockeys. These specialized robots were recently developed in response to serious concerns for the welfare of jockeys since they were often children. What once were unorganized, small-scale competitions between friends using family animals now feature governing bodies with detailed rules and regulations; performance-enhancing drug testing; and scientifically bred, fed, and trained camels. Though a majority of the largest and most prestigious races are located in the Arabian Peninsula, North Africa, and many countries in the Middle East, this exotic custom can also be seen in other regions with a desert habitat, including parts of Asia and Australia. The main reason for the growth of the sport is an attempt to preserve and celebrate the cultural heritage of nomadic people who relied on camels for their livelihood and survival for centuries.

Nomads are people without a permanent home who often live a pastoral life herding livestock, sheep, goats, camels, cattle, horses, or donkeys. This is a tradition that dates back for centuries. For nomadic tribes, camel races have been informal parts of weddings and other local celebrations with no set schedule, at no set time of the day, of no standard distance, and the winners did not receive any prizes. It was only until the oil boom of the 1960s that took place in the Middle East and beyond that camel racing evolved into a major sporting event. The huge influx of oil money allowed many of the nomadic groups of people to settle into urban living. Instead of being crucial for survival, camels were then used for entertainment through organized racing. Once the sport grew in multiple locations throughout the Middle East, it slowly spread to places such as Australia where there are now several major races held. In fact, camel racing has become a tourist attraction and source of cultural pride that is promoted by governments as an attraction for sports tourism.

Nowadays, camel racing draws large crowds and passionate interest for a season that stretches from October to April. There are as many as eight divisions for various age, sex, and different breeds of camel. Distances can vary, but 6.2 miles (10 kilometers) is a common distance for mature male camel competitions, and younger camels often run shorter distances. While in Australia as few as five or six camels might compete in a single race, it is quite common to see in the Middle

East a group of thirty camels in the same race. Interestingly, fans at the stadiums only get to see the beginning and ending of the race in person and must rely on television coverage in the stadium and the public address announcer's narration. The stadiums specifically built for this sport often use architecture to honor the past by imitating nomadic tent structures, but they also include luxurious VIP seating. Different types of seats and areas reveal the socioeconomic class structure that is often present in Middle East societies. For example, members of ruling families and wealthy merchants are often the camel owners in the Middle East. However, the evidence of such class divisions is not as great in Australia or Mongolia.

While not all areas that practice camel racing are necessarily Muslim, Islamic law prohibits gambling on camel races as is commonly done on horse racing worldwide. However, Islamic law does allow for prize money to be awarded to the winners. As the prestige and prize money grew, so did the incentives to find an unfair advantage. Some of the ways people attempted to cheat included giving the camels performance-enhancing drugs and using electric shocks on both the camel and the jockey. In many countries, race winners are not actually celebrated until the results of the camel's laboratory results are returned showing that the camel did not have any illegal substances in their blood. Also, electric shock devices have been banned, and evidence of the use will result in disqualification and serious penalties from governing bodies.

One of the most serious controversies surrounding the sport of camel racing is the common practice of using child jockeys. While the ancient races had camel owners riding their own camels, modern races and the large prize money and prestige led owners to seek out the lightest jockeys, which in turn resulted in the use of children. It was not uncommon to see young kids as young as five years old who were forced to ride camels at up to 60 miles per hour. This dangerous practice was linked to many serious injuries, including paralysis and even death for the child jockeys. While horses can be fitted with weight-bearing stirrups, camels cannot. This makes smaller and lighter jockeys even more important for those seeking a competitive advantage. One of the most disturbing practices reported was that child jockeys were sometimes abducted and forced to perform as jockeys in camel racing. In other cases, the families of young boys were lured with false promises of jobs and high pay—neither of which usually materialized. Moreover, child jockeys often faced verbal and physical abuse, including intentional malnutrition to keep their weight down. As a result of international outcry against this practice, age and weight minimums were enforced more regularly, and robotic jockeys were developed specifically for this sport. According to *New Scientist*, a Swiss company was reportedly paid US$1.3 million to develop the robotic jockeys, which have been sold for roughly US$5,500 each since 2005 (Knight 2005). The remote-controlled robots have mechanical legs for balancing and mechanical arms for directing the camel's reins. The result is the current competitive sport of camel racing that attempts to retain a link to the cultural heritage of desert nomadic groups but with a touch of modern technology to avoid child abuse practices.

Charles H. Wilson Jr.

Further Readings

Khalaf, Sulayman. "Camel Racing in the Gulf: Notes on the Evolution of a Traditional Cultural Sport." *Anthropos* 94 (1999): 85–106.

Knight, Will. "Robot Camel Jockeys Take to the Track." *New Scientist.* July 21, 2005. http://www.newscientist.com/article/dn7705-robot-cameljockeys-take-to-the-track .html?full=true&print=true (Accessed on May 18, 2013).

McGeehan, Nicholas. "Spinning Slavery: The Role of the United States and UNICEF in the Denial of Justice for the Child Camel Jockeys of the United Arab Emirates." *Journal of Human Rights Practice* 5, no. 1 (2013): 196–24.

Oman Ministry of Tourism. "Camel Racing." http://www.omantourism.gov.om/wps/por tal/mot/tourism/oman/home/experiences/activities/camel (Accessed on May 18, 2013).

Tinson, A., K. S. Kuhad, Rajesh Sambyal, A. Rehman, J. Al-Masri, and T. K. Gahlot. "Evolution of Camel Racing in the United Arab Emirates, 1987–2007." In *Proceedings of the International Camel Conference: "Recent Trends in Camelids Research and Future Strategies for Saving Camels."* Issue 16–17, 144–50. Rajasthan, India: College of Veterinary & Animal Science, February 2007.

CAMEL WRESTLING

Camel wrestling is a traditional sporting event in rural western Turkey involving two trained male camels competing for dominance. The sport is steeped in local rituals and occurs frequently as an integral part of a carnival or tournament. Camel matches emulate other sporting events with trainers, coaches, officials, rules and regulations, and spectators. Wrestling events take place during camel mating season, usually during the winter months. Two bulls are led into a ring, or area cleared for the match, while a female in estrus is paraded by to stimulate the camels' natural instinct to fight over the potential mate. The males are then allowed to wrestle for a period of ten minutes. Referees declare a winner based on which camel makes the other retreat, scream, or fall; a fourth way to win requires an owner to forfeit the match, a tactic employed to preserve the health of the animal. The most common, desirable fighting camel is a *Tülü*, which is a hybrid breed—the offspring of a female, single-hump Dromedary camel (*Camelus dromedarius*), and a male double-humped Asian Bactrian camel (*Camelus bactrianus*)—bred especially for fighting.

Historians and researchers believe that camel wrestling is at least 2,400 years old. While there is no way to verify this claim, the fact that the sport is built around natural mating behavior suggests that fighting for dominance is as old as the camel breed; at some point after domestication, people learned to utilize the animals' instinctual behavior in programmed sporting matches. Persian and Mughal art provides evidence that people observed camels wrestling more than 2,000 years ago. A stone amulet from Margiana, dated to the second millennia BCE, depicts two camels biting each other. Organized camel fighting is featured artistically much later; one famous miniature painting featuring a camel match is attributed to well-known Persian Islamic artist Bihzad ca. 1525. Though dating camel wrestling origins is difficult, using ancient artwork makes it possible to gauge that people observed natural camel behavior more than 2,000 years ago, eventually turning the animal's proclivities into a sporting event. The artifacts suggest early nomadic

A camel wrestling match in Mugla, Turkey. (Aydindurdu/Dreamstime.com)

groups were the first to work closely with the beasts and to devise camel matches, pre-dating the arrival of Islam in Turkey around the seventh century. Camel wrestling can, therefore, be considered an indigenous Turkic cultural tradition.

More recent documentation demonstrates that the sport has grown in popularity over the past 200 years. The first recorded public camel wrestling festival occurred in the Turkish Hidirbeyli village, Aydin Province, about 200 years ago. After that time, travel writers from the nineteenth century describe camel fighting as a favorite pastime of the Turks, depicting events as both colorful and savage. The sport was popular during the late Ottoman Empire until the 1920s; in fact, the Turkish National Aviation league used camel matches to raise funds to enable the government to purchase airplanes during that decade. However, as the empire collapsed and the Turkish state was established, the new government heavily discouraged camel wrestling as it interfered with the European notion of a modern state. In the 1980s, the country experienced a military coup that encouraged the revival of camel fighting matches as a celebration of traditional Turkish culture.

Today, there are approximately thirty annual camel wrestling events held across Turkey. Owners acquire most of their fighters from Iran and Afghanistan, two countries known for breeding solid wrestling stock. When the male camels reach ten years of age, they are eligible to fight in a tournament. For each match, camel owners bring their entries a day or two prior to participate in the festivities in their entirety, with programming that often includes a camel beauty pageant. Each camel is given a name, either from the owner, from the spectators, or from a popular cultural icon such as a television character. Cheerful Outlaw is an example of one named camel entered at Selçuk in 2011; during the 2012 wrestling season, Çilgin Özer (Crazy Özer) was considered an unbeatable champion. A name is significant not only as an identifier for the camel but also because that name is written on a *peş*, a small cloth hung behind the ornate saddle, preceding the word *Maşallah*, an invocation for God to protect it during the fight. The day before the camels wrestle, they are elaborately dressed. In addition to wearing the saddle and protective clothing, the beasts are often covered in colorful decorative rugs and bells. Once the camels are adorned with their traditional costumes, owners also don festive clothing, usually consisting of pointed caps and distinctive scarves worn over jackets, trousers, and long leather boots. Together, owners and camels participate in a march, caravan-style, through the streets to the tune of drums and *zurnas*, special instrumental horns. Customary music follows traditional Zeybek style; historically, the Zeybeks were considered a bandit community that upheld its own cultural traditions, including the rhythms featured at camel tournaments. During the tournament, the camels and their owners are considered celebrities. By evening, the parade turns into a large festival for the owners and spectators where everyone gathers together to sing regional songs, and to enjoy food, drink, dancing.

The wrestling event starts the next morning. Spectators and vendors arrive early to claim good seats, and by 10:00 A.M. the arena grounds are flooded with people enjoying themselves, cheering, hearing the drums and *zurnas*, and listening to the master of ceremonies. Some spectators place bets on possible winners to add to the day's excitement. Ironically, most onlookers will celebrate the day eating camel sausage, the most typical snack served at this event. As excitement in the audience builds, the *cazgir* (the main announcer) will broadcast each camel's name and recite a poem about it. As the camels are paired to fight, the *urgancılar*— rope handler—will lead the adversaries into the arena after their mouths have been muzzled to prevent biting. Once in the arena, there are multiple officials and referees to ensure all competitors adhere to the established rules. Each match is timed to protect the animals. Different camels will choose multiple wrestling tactics, which may include striking the other's head, twisting necks, and using forelegs to push the adversary down. After time expires, the referee will declare the winner or call a tie.

The wrestling event itself is often limited to one day, though traditional rituals can follow that evening, on succeeding days, and at other points throughout the year prior to the next annual local tournament. Some camels and their owners will make a circuit of the region's annual matches throughout the season from November to March. Every festival has slight differences, with rules and regulations varying across western Turkey. Apart from Turkey, localities in Iran, Afghanistan, and Pakistan also sponsor camel wrestling activities.

Presently, the future of camel wrestling is uncertain. For many rural Turkish communities, camel wrestling festivities are viewed as a significant expression of identity and culture. Ancient Turkish nomads relied on camels as a means of transport and of nourishment, and many modern Turks view the sport as an exhibition of the historic bond forged between people and animal. From this vantage point, rural villagers see camel fighting as a preservation of their cultural heritage and believe that the tradition should be perpetuated. However, financial costs threaten the sport's decline. Some Turkish experts report that the cost already makes the sport a rich man's endeavor; a new fighter can cost US$12,000, and a prize-winning camel is valued at roughly US$30,000 in addition to training, boarding, and transportation costs. Adding to the financial difficulties associated with camel owning, animal rights groups are vocal about how the treatment of camels is inhumane, and they fiercely advocate abolishing the practice. The struggle between the villagers' desire to retain the sport as a cultural treasure and external pressures to force its abolition will be quite challenging, and it will depend on multiple factors, including government support and the ability to attract international tourist dollars for assisting in preserving the camel wrestling tradition.

Laura Steckman

Further Readings

Adamova, Adel T. "The Iconography of a Camel Fight." In *Muqarnas, Volume 21—Essays in Honor of J.M. Rogers an Annual on the Visual Culture of the Islamic World*, edited by Gülru Necipoglu, Doris Behrens-Abouseif, and Anna Contadini, 1–14. Leiden, The Netherlands: BRILL, 2004.

Aydi, Ali Fuat. "A Brief Introduction to the Camel Wrestling Events in Western Turkey." SOAS Camel Conference. May 24, 2011. www.soas.ac.uk/camelconference/file75386 .pdf (Accessed on November 20, 2012).

"Camel Wrestling." *Bodrum Info*. February 9, 2012. http://www.bodruminfo.org/en/camel-wrestling.html (Accessed on December 9, 2012).

Christie-Miller, Alexander. "Turkey: Tradition of Camel Wrestling Making a Comeback." *Eurasianet*. January 27, 2011. http://www.eurasianet.org/node/62784 (Accessed on December 9, 2012).

"Duel of the Dromedaries: Afghan Camels in Wrestling Showdowns to Celebrate Persian New Year." *Daily Mail Online*. April 1, 2011. http://www.dailymail.co.uk/news/article-1371992/Duel-dromedaries-Afghan-camels-wrestling-showdowns-celebrate-Persian-New-Year.html (Accessed on December 9, 2012).

Knight, Charles. *Sketches in Natural History: History of the Mammalia*, Vols. V and VI. London: C. Cox, 1849.

Scott, Alev. "Camel Wrestling on Turkey's Aegean Coast." *The Guardian*. March 23, 2012. http://www.guardian.co.uk/travel/2012/mar/23/turkey-holidays-camel-wrestling-aegean (Accessed on December 11, 2012).

CANDOMBLÉ RELIGION AND ANIMAL SACRIFICE

Candomblé is considered the second largest religion in Brazil—only after Catholicism. It consists of a polytheistic pantheon based on African gods (*Orixás* in Portuguese and *Orishas* in Spanish). This Afro-Brazilian religion is mostly rooted on the spiritual beliefs of former African slaves from the Yoruba territories (Sudan and Nigeria) mixed with Catholic influence. One of its salient characteristics is that almost every ceremony must begin with an animal sacrifice, including goats, pigeons, ducks, and chickens. While the Brazilian syncretic religion of Candomblé is often compared to Cuban Santería, the former uses a much wider array of animals as part of its rituals. Animal sacrifice is used as a special bond for practitioners to communicate with their gods. Priests or priestesses offer the animals in honor of *Exú*—he is the messenger to all the deities in Candomblé. The general belief is that the essence of the sacrificed animal actually "feeds" the gods, who in turn reciprocate by helping the follower's requests for healing sicknesses, resolving financial difficulties, and clarifying personal relationships. During the early 1900s, Candomblé used to be a forbidden religion in Brazil, but it is now widely accepted and interwoven into daily life. It is estimated that there are now almost 2 million practitioners, not only in Brazil but also in Colombia, Venezuela, and Panama. As a result, Candomblé is no longer a secretive religion; most houses of worship (*terreiros*) even accept outsiders to attend—as long as they are respectful of its traditions.

The genesis of Candomblé rituals can be traced back to the slavery period in Brazil (1452–1888). In 1452, Portuguese slave traders started importing African slaves to fulfill their labor needs. The largest number of slaves arrived at the northeastern territories (the current state of Bahia), which explains why this region currently constitutes the largest population of African descent in the nation. While slaves were often separated from their regional groups in order to avoid potential rebellions, they still maintained their spiritual traditions based on multiple gods and a respect for nature. Slaves were forced to convert to Christianity—even if they did not really understand that they were being baptized Catholic. What they did, however, was create a parallel correspondence between their Yoruba deities and multiple Catholic statues. The result was that they prayed to Catholic saints in front of Portuguese priests, but they were actually worshipping their own Yoruba gods. For example, they disguised Goddess Iemanja as the Catholic representation of the Virgin Mary, and the powerful god of Xangó was paired with St. Peter. The origins of the Candomblé religion itself emerged in the Bahia region along the northern coast. Nowadays, it is quite common to hear drumming sessions in the city of Salvador de Bahia where multiple Candomblé ceremonies take place on small gathering places (locally known as *terreiros*), which are spread throughout the city.

Brazil has the infamous record of being the last country in the Americas to abolish slavery in 1888. At that time, however, Candomblé was associated with illiterate, poor, and backward members of society. It has also been linked to other names of Afro-Brazilian religions—such as Batuque, Umbanda, and Macumba—which are all variations of different syncretic religions mixing African traditions with Catholic beliefs. During the early twentieth century, the rituals that included animal sacrifice, drumming sessions, euphoric dances, and apparent spiritual possessions were considered part of devil worshipping. However, Cleusa Millet (1931–1998) became a priestess from the Bahia region who is recognized for adapting Candomblé and transforming it into a respected religion. By the 1970s and early 1980s, it was already widely accepted into all levels of society. While contemporary Brazil certainly has a strong African influence, Candomblé also appeals to other ethnic groups.

From a comparative point of view, Candomblé has crucial differences with other mainstream religions. For example, it does not have a central administration (such as the Vatican for Catholicism). It is also mostly an oral tradition that is not based on a sacred scripture (such as the Christian Bible, the Jewish Torah, or the Islamic Koran). Overall, Candomblé followers are known as holy people (povo-do-santo). Their places of worship are rather small compared to European Gothic cathedrals or impressive churches. Instead, Candomblé's temples are of three basic types: casas (houses), roças (plantations), and terreiros (yards). A terreiro is an open square similar to an interior courtyard. Since there is no central control of the religion, most terreiros are individually owned by the priest or priestess, and the members of a congregation refer to each other as "family." Another crucial difference is that Candomblé is mostly anchored around women. Most traditional Candomblés are matriarchies, and the head of the family (or congregation) is usually a woman priestess (mãe-de-santo) and only occasionally a male priest (pai-de-santo). They are both referred to as babalaos (similar to the term used in Cuban Santería). The tradition of including women as priestesses emerged during the slavery period (1492–1888) when the men were always working, and the female slaves were able to tend to the routine requests of the religious followers. Since women obtained freedom in larger numbers than male slaves, the first Candomblé center founded outside of a slave plantation was established by three manumitted female slaves in 1830.

Candomblé practitioners believe in a Supreme Being called Olodumaré or simply Olorum. Directly under him, there are multiple Orixás (deities) assigned to rule and keep balance between the material and spiritual worlds. Orixás can be best viewed as intermediaries between humans and Olorum. Each Orixa governs unique elements of the natural world, such as mineral qualities, earth fertility, water, wind, metals, fire, oceans, and animals. One of the basic tenants of Candomblé is that every person is connected to a specific Orixa at the time of birth. These deities, however, cannot exist in a tangible and visible form. Instead, they can be called upon by using music and rhythms that are specific relevant to each Orixa. Priests and priestesses carry out consultations to find out which is the most appropriate Orixa regarding a potential solution to spiritual and physical problems. They usually throw four small shells to the ground and then interpret the desires of the Orixás based on how the shells landed on the floor.

Most Condomblé ceremonies begin with an animal sacrifice. According to priests and priestesses, a total of twenty-nine animal species are used in sacrificial rituals. However, there is a direct relationship between the color, gender, and behavior of the animals selected and the specific Orixa to whom the animal is going to be offered (Leo Neto, et al. 2009, 1). Goats, chickens, and pigeons are the most common animals used for sacrifice because they are easily accessible, and they have less legal environmental restrictions. Other amphibians, reptiles, shell fish, and birds are also used depending on the Orixa to be addressed. Wild animals such as yellow-footed tortoises are occasionally sacrificed, but their use is much more restricted. In addition, the specific animals determine how they will be killed. For example, pigeons are considered sacred messengers to the Orixás;

consequently, they cannot be killed with a knife. Instead, the priest uses blades of sedge grass—which are extremely sharp—to strangle and decapitate the animals. The religion offers only the vital parts of an animal (e.g., the heart, the liver, genitals, gizzards, flippers, paws, tail, ribs, and the head) to multiple deities. They are usually cooked with oil—and sometimes honey—before being offered. The practice of offering animal body parts is in contrast to Cuban Santería, which usually only offers the blood of an animal to the Orixás. It is important to highlight that only male priests are allowed to perform animal sacrifices. This restriction is based on the notion that women are considered to be "givers" and not "takers" of life. After the animal sacrifices are completed, the gods (Orixás) are summoned by playing drum percussion music, euphoric dancing, and spiritual signing. The priests and priestesses must be extremely careful when calling on the Orixás because each deity has its own influence, favorite colors, special food, animal associations, and symbols.

Candomblé sessions offer a social component where people eat, pray, and socialize in a setting that seems less restrictive than traditional church gatherings. In contemporary Brazil, Candomblé priest and priestesses are extremely inclusive by extending their ministry to groups of people who have been traditionally marginalized by mainstream religions in Brazil. Such approach—together with the lack of sufficient Catholic priests—have contributed to the religion's unprecedented growth in the twenty-first century.

Javier A. Galván

Further Readings

Astor, Michael. "Brazil's Once-Banned Religions Gain Followers." *Los Angeles Times.* January 25, 2005. http://articles.latimes.com/2005/jan/02/news/adfg-brazil2 (Accessed on July 25, 2012).

"Candomblé in Salvador de Bahia, Brazil." http://www.bahia-online.net/Candomble.htm (Accessed on July 24, 2012).

Capone, Stefania. *Searching for Africa in Brazil: Power and Tradition in Candomblé.* Durham, NC: Duke University Press, 2010.

Edwards, Todd L. *Brazil: A Global Studies Handbook.* Santa Barbara, CA: ABC-CLIO, 2008.

"Federação Internacional de Umbanda e Candomblé." http://www.fietreca.org.br (Accessed on July 20, 2012).

Leo Neto, Nivaldo A. *et al.* "From Eshu to Obatala: Animals Used in Sacrificial Rituals at Condomblé 'terreiros' in Brazil." *Journal of Ethnobiology and Ethnomedicine* 5, no. 23 (August 2009). http://www.nbci.nlm.nih.gov/pmc/articles/PMC2739163 (Accessed on July 23, 2012).

Omari-Tunkara, Mikelle S. *Manipulating the Sacred: Yoruba Art, Ritual, and Resistance in Brazilian Candomblé.* Detroit: Wayne State University Press, 2005.

Vincent, Jon S. *Culture and Customs of Brazil.* Westport, CT: Greenwood Press, 2003.

CANNIBALISM

Cannibalism is defined as the consumption of one's own species. Human cannibalism is also known as anthropophagy. There are two types of cannibalism described in literature: endocannibalism (eating the flesh of dead people from the same community), and exocannibalism (eating the flesh of dead people from other communities). In contrast to other animals, human beings rarely practiced cannibalism to satisfy their hunger, except at the time of severe famines. Across cultures, homicidal cannibalism was practiced as a matter of revenge, punishment, and cult-related human sacrifice, while necro-cannibalism was carried out as a mortuary ritual and spiritual experience. Cannibalism as a mortuary ritual was practiced for a variety of reasons, an example being the Bimin-Kuskumin tribe of Papua New Guinea who would do so to honor the deceased and obtain their strength, or the Fore tribe of Papua New Guinea who would do so to help the soul of the deceased person to settle in their new body. This endocannibalistic mortuary ritual contributed to the transmission of Kuru—incurable encephalopathy caused by a human prion. Kuru was endemic among Fore people until 1950, when the route of transmission was established, and the mortuary cannibalism ritual ceased. In the review of academic literature, there are two salient cultural groups whose practices have been studied extensively: the Aghori religious sect of India, and the Korowai people of Papua New Guinea.

Cannibalism among India's Aghori religious sect comprises eating remnants of corpses, either raw or cooked. This cult-related ritual was (and still is occasionally practiced by members of the Aghori caste with many aims, including to worship the Indian deity called Shiva) intended to overcome disgust, obtain supernatural powers, increase longevity, and prepare themselves for a direct after-death passage to Shiva without the process of reincarnation. Aghoris retrieve floating river-buried bodies, and they also take the unburned remnants of unclaimed bodies from the cremation grounds. They do not kill people specifically for their rituals nor do they steal the bodies from the families; killing and stealing are prohibited by their customs. Prior to consumption, the Aghori people sit on the corpse and meditate, dedicating the soul of the deceased person and some of their flesh to their deity, simultaneously gaining control over the deceased's soul.

Other ritualistic behaviors of the Aghori caste include body smearing with cremation ashes and using bowls made of human skulls and decorated with human bones. These bowls are used as eating and drinking utensils and as ritual vessels. Consumption of human and animal urine, feces, and vomitus was also reported. According to the rules of the Aghori sect, followers should live a free life and should not be attached to earthly matters. Aghori do not marry and do not have families. Some men mutilate themselves by smashing their penises to prevent them from producing offspring and to avoid sexual urges, jealousy, and revenge. Some Aghoris perform ritual sex, which is commonly group sex with a prostitute at the time of her menstrual bleeding. Withdrawal is usually practiced prior to ejaculation.

Aghoris walk naked and live in caves surrounding cremation grounds. Other Indians consider them as outcasts. In the caste hierarchy, the Aghori caste is positioned lower than the Indian lowest cast. Hindus believe that Aghoris do not belong to their religious denomination because of their meat and alcohol consumption practices, which are juxtaposed to vegetarianism and alcohol abstinence.

Aghoris' most famous pilgrimage place is Baba Kina Ram's temple in Varanasi, a city located in the state of Uttar Pradesh and regarded by Indians as holy. This place, at the time of religious festivals, attracts a lot of tourists, researchers, and media correspondents.

British authorities prohibited the practice of human corpse consumption in India. In historical literature, there are occasional court reports of cannibalism and human corpse dragging and cutting until the late1890s. Contemporary researchers have found it difficult to interpret whether Aghori cannibalism is a myth or a reality. Anthropologists, who spent years living among modern-day Aghoris and pretended to practice some of their behaviors, said that they have never witnessed cannibalistic rituals. They have suggested that necro-cannibalism could still be secretly practiced within this sect. In 2005, a short ethnographic film titled, *Feeding on the Dead*, depicting a corpse-eating ritual by Aghori pilgrims heading to Varanasi, confirming earlier suggestions of their modern-day cannibalism practices. This film was broadcast worldwide on BBC, MSNBC, and National Geographic Channel. Contemporary cultural anthropologists and psychologists have explained Aghori behaviors as symptoms of a culture-bound psychosis induced by alcohol and drug consumption.

Another cultural group that has been studied regarding its traditions of cannibalism is the Korowai people of Papua New Guinea. Among this tribe, cannibalism was practiced mainly as an act of punishment for witchcraft. Korowai is a small tribal group in Papua New Guinea, located at the southeastern part of Papua Province. Korowai people believed that a witch could eat human flesh from inside without the victim knowing what is happening. Behind any illness, accident, misfortune, or death, Korowai people suspected a prior weakening of the human body resulting from witchcraft. The prosecutors would take the person suspected of witchcraft, who was usually male, to another clan where he was executed and his body eaten. In return, the villagers expected the body of a witch from that clan to be sent to them at some point in time.

The prosecutors were usually relatives of the recently deceased community member. It was usually dying people who revealed their suspicious concerns or direct accusations about other villagers. The relatives usually waited for a good moment to catch the suspected witch. This moment was described as unexpected and surprising to the witch, his family, and his relatives. However, family members of the witch and the prosecutors would not participate in the cannibalistic ritual.

After consumption of the witch's body, the bones were placed between the tree branches around the village to be visible to everyone who passed by. The relatives of the witch were prohibited to have any relations immediately or even in the long term with the people who consumed the body, for fear that reconciliation may turn these people into witches. The prosecutors usually offered a bride from their kin to the executed witch's kin, in order to reconcile and to establish a positive relationship through childbearing.

According to Korowai belief, the consumption of a witch's body had a similar effect upon the witch as the original witchcraft actions that led to the weakening and death of their victim. Korowai people believed that a witch who has strong powers might cause a victim's death by eating his or her heart from the inside. Witches who are not so strong may only cause an illness or misfortune by damaging a victim's other internal organs. Consequently, the ritual of eating a witch's body was even more meaningful, by revealing a witch's actions that were conducted invisibly.

Nowadays, confirmed acts of witchcraft among Korowai people are punished with public humiliation by village courts and with financial implications, compulsory community works, and imprisonment by national courts. Although there were some occasional reports of killings and torture of people suspected of witchcraft in contemporary Papua New Guinea, cannibalism as a form of punishment was not reported. This practice decreased rapidly with changing religious morals and death-related rituals after the Christianization of the country since the1950s. With the outlawing of witchcraft and sorcery—and the restriction of illegal witch punishment and false accusation in witchcraft by the country's Sorcery Act 1971 and Criminal Code Act 1974—cannibalism as a form of punishment for witchcraft was no longer practiced in Papua New Guinea.

Victoria Team

Further Readings

"Aghori, Aghorapanthi, Augar, Aughar." In *Encyclopaedia of Religion and Ethics: Volume 1. A—Art. Part 1. A—Algonquins*, edited by James Hastings and John A. Selbie. Adamant Media Corp., 2005. http://www.worldcat.org/title/encyclopaedia-of-religion-and-eth ics/oclc/184910182/viewport?bib_key=ISBN:1402166273 (Accessed on November 30, 2012).

Barrett, Ronald L. "Chapter 6. Death and Nondiscrimination." In *Aghor Medicine: Pollution, Death, and Healing in Northern India*, edited by Ron Barrett, 138–66. Los Angeles, CA: University of California Press, 2008.

Favazza, Armando R. "Self-Injury and Eating Disorders." In *Bodies under Siege: Self-Mutilation, Nonsuicidal Self-Injury, and Body Modification in Culture and Psychiatry*, 43–56. Baltimore: The Johns Hopkins University Press, 2011.

Mathews, John D., Robert Glasse, and Shirley Lindenbaum. "Kuru and Cannibalism." *The Lancet* 292, no. 7565 (1968): 449–52.

PACE, Papua Heritage Foundation. "Life Up in a Korowai Tree House." http://www .papuaerfgoed.org/en/Life_up_in_a_Korowai_tree_house (Accessed on November 30, 2012).

Parry, Jonathan. "Death and Digestion—The Symbolism of Food and Eating in North Indian Mortuary Rites." *Man* 20, no. 4 (1985): 612–30.

Parry, Jonathan P. "The End of Death." In *Death in Banaras*, 250–70. New York: Cambridge University Press, 1994.

Porten, Mariya "Holy Cannibalism. The Aghori of India." In *Tuscer Geographica* 7, no. 6 (2011). http://www.enewsbuilder.net/tusker/e_article002109245.cfm?x=b11,0,w (Accessed on November 30, 2012).

Stasch, Rupert. "Giving Up Homicide: Korowai Experience of Witches and Police (West Papua)." *Oceania* 72, no. 1 (2001): 33–52.

Whitfield, Jerome T., Wandagi H. Pako, John Collinge, and Michael P. Alpers. "Mortuary Rites of the South Fore and Kuru." *Philosophical Transactions of the Royal Society of London B: Biological Sciences* 363, no. 1510 (2008): 3721–724.

CARNAVAL DO RIO DE JANEIRO

The energetic Carnaval do Rio de Janeiro in Brazil is one of the most famous carnivals in the world, with the city itself sometimes dubbed the *Carnival Capital of the Globe.* This vibrant musical event is mostly known for its colorful competition between samba schools, and it is a pre-Lent celebration, which begins on Friday and ends on Fat Tuesday. Although for some people the Carnaval do Rio is primarily a hedonistic and frivolous tradition, this celebration is considered to be one of the most important symbols of Brazilian identity and national culture.

The lively Carnaval do Rio de Janeiro has deep roots, as do other pre-Lent celebrations of this type, in pre-Christian seasonal festivities of joy, dance, and merrymaking—such as Greek festivals in honor of Dionysus as well as Roman Saturnalia and Bacchanalia. These festivities were later incorporated into the Roman Catholic tradition, losing on the way some of their features. By the 1500s, the celebrations brought by the Portuguese to Brazil had the form of brutal *entrudos*—chaotic, violent festivities, probably not involving street dancing nor music, during which water, mud, flour, or other substances were thrown at other people. *Entrudo* was formally outlawed in 1857, though it probably did not wither away before the 1860s.

Music became a crucial component of carnival in the 1800s. Masked balls, copied from those in Paris, appeared in Rio de Janeiro around the 1840s, and they dominated the city's festivities for the next few decades. These balls were soon followed by parades organized by the parading societies of elite men (on horseback, decorated floats, and with military bands). Cariocas (people from Rio) unable to participate in masked balls or parades soon took to the streets and celebrated the pre-Lent festivities in their own manner. Dancing became celebratory and

Samba dancers at the Carnaval Do Rio de Janeiro. (King Ho Yim/Dreamstime.com)

inclusive of the masses. Groups such as *Congos* (black men and women parading in a mobile pageant), *Ze Pereiras* (marching to drums), *cordões* (males dancing to African rhythms), and *ranchos* (which are sometimes credited for being the first to introduce themes in their parades) appeared in the following decades. By the 1890s the street carnival environment had become common. What was probably the first contest between street dancers was organized (and covered) by the newspaper *Gazeta de Noticias* in 1906. By this time most groups already had some features of the present-day samba schools (e.g., color-schemes). Soon other groups emerged, such as the *blocos* (looser carnival groups).

Contemporary samba schools (*escolas de samba*) are associations of people which prepare for the Samba Parade; they are probably the most important institutions during the carnival. The first group to call itself a "samba school" was Deixa Falar ("Let Them Talk") in 1928. Composers belonging to this group are also credited with transforming the Rio de Janeiro samba into a specific format, which later spread through other samba schools. Among the next schools to be formed were some of the most famous and long-lived: Estação Primeira de Mangueira (first appearance in 1929) and Portela (since 1935, with its roots in a group founded in 1923). Today, there are over seventy samba schools in Rio, most of which are located in *favelas* (poor slums) and working-class neighborhoods. Their source of funding is very diverse, including supporters who donate money from some questionable activities (including drug-dealing and illegal lotteries). Samba schools are organized into six leagues (Special Group, Group A, B, C, D and E): the three highest-ranking groups actually participate in the parade during carnival in the *Sambódromo* stadium, while the other three perform on the streets.

Initially, the street carnival and samba schools performed away from the city center. It was only in the mid-1930s that the nationalist President Getúlio Vargas officially endorsed the parades, and the carnival won the sponsorship of the city. Soon the parade came to take place downtown on Presidente Vargas Avenue, with grandstands assembled every year. In 1968, the first *samba-enredo* (a theme samba) musical record was released. It was only in 1984 that the present venue of the parade (the famous *Sambódromo* stadium) was built. It is located away from the city center, at the actual birthplace of samba rhythms.

Samba is today probably the most popular carnival music in Rio. However, until the 1960s, melodical *marchas* (*marchinhas*) were equally, if not more, popular. The first *marcha* "Ó abre alas" was created by Chiquinha Gonzaga in 1899 for the *cordão Rosa de Ouro*. It is known as the first song to be written specifically for carnival. In the 1930s and 1940s, many now classic *marchas* and sambas were composed. *Marchas* remain popular among the bands (*bandas*) which today perform in the streets.

The Rio (Carioca) carnival starts with the delivery of the key of the city to King Momo—the symbolic figure from the Greek mythology—who, according to the legend, settled in Rio de Janeiro after being expelled from Olympus. Other important figures during the carnival are the Queen of Carnival (chosen in a contest) and the Princesses of Carnival (the first and second runners-up). The carnival encompasses various events, such as Samba Land (which revives the atmosphere of Praça Onze, where the first official parades took place), various balls, street parties, street band processions, and multiple rehearsals. However, it is the parade of the Special Group that attracts most attention. The other three parades in the *Sambódromo* are Samba Schools in the Access Group, Children's Samba Schools, and the Champions Parade.

The preparations for the annual Samba Parade begin months in advance. Each samba school, some of which sometimes bring together thousands of people, relies on strong collaboration and commitment from most of its members. After the theme of the year (*enredo*) is chosen, the samba song (*samba-enredo*) is selected, and later recorded and released. Outstanding costumes and elaborated, richly decorated floats are designed by the school's *Carnavalesco* (carnival designer), many of whom are well known in Rio and have their own style. Rehearsals for the parade begin in December, long before the event. The parade itself is an approximately ninety-minute show, which is the final stage of several months of preparation.

Starting in the mid-1930s, as a consequence of public funding, the school themes mostly evolved around national symbols and heroes. Later, Brazilian folklore and literature became popular. Since the 1980s, the themes have often addressed national issues and problems (e.g., ecology, poverty, and discrimination). Nowadays, the samba schools may choose any theme they consider interesting or important.

The Samba Parade takes place in the *Sambódromo*, which was designed by Oscar Niemeyer, the renowned architect of Brasília—Brazil's capital city. This 700-meter long *passarela* was designed as a straight runway flanked on both sides by stands for several thousand people. However, until recently the project had only been partially

---

KING MOMO, A LEGENDARY FIGURE IN CARNAVAL

Every year, the city of Rio de Janeiro selects a king for the famous carnival, a position with the name *Rei Momo* in Portuguese. This local tradition dates back to 1933. Usually, the person selected to be the king is a tall and fat man displaying rather large physical characteristics. The appearance of the king at the carnival marks the official beginning of the festivities. The selection of such a king, however, is not limited to the carioca city. There are other King Momos selected for other carnivals celebrated in other parts of Brazil, such as the cities of Santos, Belem, and Salvador. In other Latin American countries, such as Panama, Uruguay, Curaçao, Argentina, and Colombia, the respective carnivals also have representations of Rey Momo.

Javier A. Galván

completed, due to the buildings of the Brahma beer company located on one side of the runway. In preparation for the 2016 Olympic Games, after a consensus was reached between the city and the company, the buildings were demolished and the *Sambódromo* underwent renovation. The new venue is symmetrical, following the initial design. After the reconstruction of the whole area, the capacity increased to accommodate roughly 90,000 spectators. It will be the venue of the opening ceremonies of the 2016 Summer Olympic Games, and it will host the Archery events at the Olympic and Paralympic Games, as well as the Olympic Marathon.

The samba schools that compete in the *Sambódromo* are the finest of all the samba schools in Rio de Janeiro. The Special Group consists of the twelve best, most spectacular samba schools. The schools are judged in ten categories: Percussion Band (*Bateria*), Samba Song, Harmony, Flow and Spirit, Theme of the Year, Overall Impression, Floats and Props, Costumes, Vanguard Group, and the Flag Carrying Couple. The school that scores the lowest is downgraded to Access Group A, whereas the champions of Access Group A are promoted to Special. The parade itself is thoroughly organized and well prepared. Different sections of each school have their specific tasks and costumes. The floats (drawn by the school members, since no motorized floats are allowed) carry beautiful samba dancers, usually scantily dressed, as well as special guests. During the parade, only percussion and friction instruments can be used.

The Carioca carnival has spurred various opinions and interpretations. The positive view of the carnival as a symbol of national identity and social leveling, on the one hand, is contrasted with the arguments that the appropriation of Afro-Brazilian samba constitutes a theft and exploitation of black culture. Also, the construction of the *Sambódromo* is sometimes seen as the moment when the authentic, public, street Rio carnival disappeared, while an organized, commercialized, televised, tourist attraction was born.

Carnival parades have also occasionally sparked controversies on other grounds. For example, in 1989 the Beija-Flor samba school had to cover up a float on which the Rio statue of Christ Redeemer was presented as a homeless person. In 2008, the Viradouro samba school was barred from featuring a Holocaust float. In 2010, the same school provoked a heated debate on the participation of children in the celebrations, when a seven-year-old girl danced as a drum corps queen.

While the celebrations held in Rio de Janeiro receive most of the international attention, there are other important regional carnivals in South America that are held during the same period. For example, the carnival held in Oruro (Bolivia) and the celebratory parade held in Barranquilla (Colombia) are so elaborate that they were incorporated to the UNESCO Representative List of Intangible Cultural Heritage Events of Humanity.

Anna Kaganiec-Kamieńska

Further Readings

Chasteen, John Charles. "The Prehistory of Samba: Carnival Dancing in Rio de Janeiro, 1840–1917." *Journal of Latin American Studies* 28 (1996): 29–47.

Costa, Haroldo. "Carnaval: From the Ticumbís, Cucumbís, Entrudo and Carnival Societies to Current Days." Embassy of Brazil in Kuala Lumpur. http://www.brazilembassy.org.my/cultural/pdf/revistaing11-mat6.pdf (Accessed on October 28, 2012).

Malkin, Bonnie. "Holocaust Float Banned from Rio Carnival." *The Telegraph*. February 1, 2008. http://www.telegraph.co.uk/news/worldnews/1577274/Holocaust-float-banned-from-Rio-Carnival.html (Accessed on November 2, 2012).

McGowan, Chris, and Ricardo Passanha. *The Brazilian Sound. Samba, Bossa Nova and the Popular Music of Brazil*. Philadelphia: Temple University Press, 1998.

Olsen, Dale A., and Daniel E. Sheehy, eds. *The Garland Handbook of Latin American Music*. New York: Routledge, 2000.

Palmer, Colin A., ed. *Encyclopedia of African American Culture and Culture*. 2nd ed. Farmington Hills, MI: Thomson Gale, 2006

Rio Carnaval 2013 Homepage. http://www.rio-carnival.net (Accessed on November 1, 2012).

"Rio 2016 Olympics." http://www.sambadrome.com/rio-carnival-sambodromo/2016-olympics/ (Accessed on November 1, 2012).

"Seven-Year-Old Rio Carnival Queen Breaks Down in Tears during Parade." *The Telegraph*. February 15, 2010. http://www.telegraph.co.uk/news/worldnews/southamerica/brazil/7240358/Seven-year-old-Rio-Carnival-queen-breaks-down-in-tears-during-parade.html (Accessed on November 2, 2012).

CARRYING FLAMING TAR BARRELS

The custom of carrying flaming tar barrels occurs in various parts of the British Isles. One of the most celebrated instances occurs in Ottery St. Mary in Devon, England, on the 5th of November each year (unless the 5th falls on a Sunday). This specific date is also known as Bonfire Night in England, and it marks the anniversary of the Gunpowder Plot of 1605, which was an unsuccessful attempt to blow up the Houses of Parliament in London (and thus the Protestant King, James I, and his government) by a gang led by Guy Fawkes. The plotters wished to return England to the Catholic faith. To make their point well known, they hid thirty-six barrels of explosives in the cellars of the Houses of Parliament, but their scheme was rumbled, and all the gang members were apprehended and executed. While the exact origins of the Ottery St. Mary custom are unknown, it is most likely that the tradition is in some way connected to the Gunpowder Plot. Other reasons suggested for the procession of Burning Tar Barrels include the fumigation of cottages and as a warning of the approaching Spanish Armada in 1588.

The Ottery St. Mary procession includes seventeen barrels ranging in size from small (to be carried by boys), medium (to be carried by women and youths), and large (to be carried by men) transported on the shoulders of participants known as Barrel Rollers from early afternoon until late at night. The barrels are set alight at various public houses and hotels around the town until the final barrel is brought into the town square at midnight. Though the custom is held only one day out of the year, the build-up to the festival takes place over twelve months. Throughout course of the year, the townsfolk select barrels to be used in the procession. The inner surface of the barrels is coated in coal tar which is ignited with straw and paper on the day of the procession. In 2009, the survival of the celebration was endangered after spectators were injured when a metal can—possibly an aerosol—was thrown into a flaming barrel. Ottery St. Mary also marks Bonfire

Night with the annual Rolling of the Tar Barrels in which eight flaming barrels are rolled through the town and released down a hillside after the town's bonfire has been lit. Another Devon location, Hatherleigh, hosts a similar ritual. Each year on the Friday nearest to November 5, blazing barrels are pulled on sledges through the town in order to be added to the local bonfire.

Another notable Bonfire Night tradition involving flaming tar barrels occurs in the Sussex town of Lewes. This Bonfire Night celebration is particularly spectacular attracting up to 60,000 visitors each year. While organizers suggest the rite may date back to pagan times, it is most likely that the festival commemorates the burning at the stake of seventeen Protestants by Queen Mary I on the town's High Street. For centuries the festival was a riotous event—so much so that in 1832 authorities sought to ban the celebrations as they objected to the

A young man carries a burning barrel through the streets at the Ottery Carnival. (Clive Chilvers/ Dreamstime.com)

lighting of bonfires and rolling of flaming tar barrels through the town. In 1838, local magistrates confronted revelers on Cliffe Bridge, thereby initiating the annual custom of throwing a flaming tar barrel into the River Ouse.

The carrying of a flaming barrel is also at the heart of an annual Scottish festival called the Burning of the Clavie, the Gaelic word for casket. Each year on January 11, the Scottish fishing village of Burghead holds this unique fire festival in order to welcome the New Year. The festival dates back to the 1750s, and it marks the replacement of the Julian calendar with the Gregorian calendar in Britain. This change resulted in eleven days being deducted from the length of the year—something that angered many British people who rioted in order to demand the return of their missing eleven days. The inhabitants of Burghead however decided to make the best of the new calendar by celebrating New Year twice—once on January 1 (the start of the Gregorian calendar) and again on 11, which would be the first day of the year according to the Julian calendar. Therefore, in the evening of every January 11, a burning Clavie is carried around the village followed by a large crowd of spectators. The Clavie consists of a barrel set atop a long pole. The barrel is then filled with peat and tar-soaked staves (the pieces of wood used to make the sides of barrels) and set alight. The Clavie is then transported through the village carried on the heads of various villagers. The first person to carry the Clavie is the Clavie King, and he is accompanied by seventeen villagers known as the Clavie Crew; these are villagers who have attended the ceremony before and who wear clothes scorched from carrying the burning Clavie in the past.

At the start of the evening, the Clavie is extremely heavy; however, as the Clavie burns, it becomes lighter. Consequently, the villagers are able to transport the Clavie to the ramparts of a Pictish fort on Doorie Hill where the barrel is wedged firmly into a stone pillar, refueled, and then allowed to burn itself out. Once the fire has burned through, the ashy remains of the Clavie roll down the hillside where the glowing embers are eagerly gathered by onlookers since possession of a piece of the Clavie is reputed to bring good luck to the owner for the coming year.

Victoria Williams

Further Readings

"The Burning of the Clavie." Visitor Centre Burghead. http://www.burghead.com/clavie
.html (Accessed on October 18, 2012).

"Centuries-Old Ottery Tar Barrel Race at Risk after Insurance Rose 1150 Per cent." *The Telegraph.* November 6, 2010. http://www.telegraph.co.uk/news/uknews/8113814/Cen turies-old-Ottery-tar-barrel-race-at-risk-after-insurance-rose-1150-per-cent.html (Accessed on October 14, 2012).

"History of the Lewes Bonfire Celebrations." *Lewes Bonfire Night Celebrations.* http://www
.lewesbonfirecelebrations.com/the-lewes-bonfire-celebrations/ (Accessed on October 14, 2012).

Official Website for the "Ottery St Mary Tar Barrels." http://www.otterytarbarrels.co.uk/
history.html (Accessed on October 14, 2012).

Simpson, Jacqueline, and Steve Roud. *Oxford Dictionary of English Folklore.* Oxford: Oxford University Press, 2000.

Wakefield, Lorraine. "Burning of the Clavie, Burghead, Moray." *Travel Scotland.* http://
www.scotland.org.uk/magazine/burning-of-the-clavie-burghead-moray (Accessed on October 18, 2012).

CHEESE ROLLING COMPETITION

On the last Monday in May, the United Kingdom observes its Spring Bank Holiday. At 12:00 P.M. sharp, thousands of people gather to watch a wheel of cheese being rolled down Cooper's Hill in Gloucestershire, England, in an event known as the annual "Cheese Rolling and Wake." Dozens of men and women follow an 8-pound wheel of cheese rolling down the steep hill in hot pursuit using a variety of forms of locomotion: running, walking, tumbling, tripping, and sliding down on their haunches. Children participate as well, but in a series of much safer, uphill races. This cheese-chasing ritual has taken place continuously for at least 200 years, with the first recorded race occurring in 1836.

Some historians speculate that the event has its origins in Celtic fertility rituals, while others claim that it may have been a medieval way of ensuring land rights for commoners who resided on the hill. The most promising suggestion is that the "wheel" of cheese is linked to the wheel motif of Celtic and Druidic sun worship. Since the fourth century BCE, Celts in Roman Europe had been rolling flaming wheels downhill as part of Midsummer rituals, meant to strengthen the power of the sun and ensure a good harvest. A similar practice was noted in England nearly 1,000 years later on Midsummer's Eve—only 10 miles from Cooper's Hill, the present-day site of the annual cheese rolling event.

The novelist Thomas Hughes, who hailed from the nearby town of Oxford-shire, reported on races being held as part of the festivities on Whit Monday in 1857. That religious holiday has been observed as the Spring Bank Holiday since 1965. This celebration took place exactly on the same day as the Cooper's Hill race, thereby indicating a continuity between the two traditions. During the Ox-fordshire races, men would chase wheels or wheels of cheese interchangeably; the prize, however, was always a wheel of cheese. Throughout the nineteenth century, cheese rolling was just one of many attractions that occurred during the Cooper's Hill parish festival; it was locally known as the "Wake" from which the current event takes its name of "Cheese Rolling and Wake."

The Wake took place for nearly 100 years, surviving well into the 1930s. Coun-try traditions slowly lessened in popularity after World War I (1914–1918), es-pecially as many rural inhabitants migrated to cities to find employment. During World War II (1939–1945), and for many years afterwards, cheese was one of the items which were strictly rationed in Great Britain. From 1941 to 1954, the cheese-rolling tradition continued to be practiced, but a wooden cheese was used in place of a real one. It had a niche that contained a very small portion of real, ed-ible cheese, though the winners were not allowed to keep either item.

Today's participants in the cheese rolling competition are eligible for prizes. Current custom mandates that the winner of each race be awarded the wheel of Double Gloucester cheese they were chasing. The runner-up in the men's and women's races receives 10 pounds, with 5 pounds being awarded to the third-place winner. Since 1988, the 8-pound wheel of cheese has been provided by Smart's Farm of Churcham, which still uses traditional handmade methods to pro-duce its cheeses.

The hill used for the competition is so steep that the entrants do not actually begin the race standing due to its natural geographical inclination. Instead, they remain seated at the starting line before the beginning of the race, and they push themselves off a ledge to go after the rolling cheese. Given that the cheese can reach speeds of up to 70 miles per hour, it is never actually caught by any of the participants, and so the de facto "winner" is simply whoever reaches the bottom of the hill first.

Injuries are commonplace among the participants and sometimes among spec-tators. In fact, the event is considered so dangerous that not even the thirty-odd inhabitants of the town of Cooper's Hill will risk harm by taking part in it them-selves. Nevertheless, they also frown on the media's tack of sensationalizing the event by focusing on the negative aspects of the town's tradition. The highest number of wounded competitors on record was in 1997, when thirty-three people suffered from all manner of scrapes, bruises, and broken bones. As a rule, competitors are more prone to injury, but bystanders and observers are also at risk. The fast-moving cheese may bounce off course, or the downhill racers may careen into those watching from the sidelines, which makes it dangerous for both competitors and spectators.

THE ULTIMATE CHAMPIONS OF CHEESE ROLLING COMPETITIONS

The most celebrated champion of the cheese rolling competition held in Gloucestershire, England, is Stephen Gyde. He has been the winner of twenty-one cheeses in a period of fourteen years, which gives him the status of a local celebrity. He won all these awards—more than anybody else in the history of the sport—in a period between 1978 and 1991. He came back to compete in 1993, 2004, and 2006, but he never won the top awards ever again.

Among the competitions reserved for ladies, there is a tie among three women: Rosemary Cooke, Amanda Turner, and Dionne Carter. All of them have won three cheeses each. However, they never competed against each other because they have earned their awards in different decades: Cooke in the 1950s, Turner in the 1980s, and Carter between 2004 and 2006.

Javier A. Galván

Officially, the event has been cancelled since 2010, mostly due to issues related to health and safety. The main concern for the event organizers and the local authorities has been overcrowding, which prohibits ambulance crews from reaching those who might need medical attention. Even though the number of participants is fairly small—about twenty in each of the five downhill races—the sheer quantity of spectators keeps increasing. Rough estimates place the number of attendees at around 5,000, though three times as many have attempted to attend. While the competition has been officially banned, local residents of Gloucestershire have staged their own unofficial events in recent years.

Despite the concerns with safety and overcrowding, the cheese-rolling competition continues to increase in popularity. Cooper's Hill attracts not just local but also international spectators, who travel to witness this singular tradition. As of 2012, it is unclear whether the races will ever be officially reinstated. However, steadfast local residents have sought to carry on the tradition. They will ensure that the annual rolling of the Double Gloucester takes place, and if the cheese is there, then no doubt daring enthusiasts will be there to chase it.

Erin Pappas

Further Readings

Bleacher Report. "The Nine Most Unusual Popular Sports in the World." http://bleacher report.com/articles/82123-the-nine-most-unusual-popular-sports-in-the-world (Accessed on September 4, 2012).

Daeschner, J. R. *True Brits: A Tour of Great Britain in All Its Bog-Snorkeling, Shin-Kicking, and Cheese Rolling Glory.* New York: Overlook Press, 2005.

Jeffries, Jean. "Cheese-Rolling in Gloucestershire." http://www.cheese-rolling.co.uk/index1.htm (Accessed on June 30, 2012).

Official Website of the Cheese Rolling Competition. "Cheese Rolling." http://www.cheese-rolling.co.uk/index1.htm (Accessed on September 5, 2012).

SoGlos.com. "Gloucestershire Cheese Rolling." http://www.soglos.com/sport-outdoor/27837/Gloucestershire Cheese-Rolling (Accessed on August 15, 2012).

CHESS BOXING CHAMPIONSHIPS

As the name implies, chess boxing is a hybrid sport that combines the mental challenges of chess with the physical exertion of boxing. The sport was founded by a Dutch performance artist named Iepe Rubingh who had grown up playing chess and began boxing in his twenties. The inspiration for combining the two activities, however, came after Rubingh read *Le Froid Equateur* by the French cartoonist Enki-Bila, which discussed the fictional sport of chess boxing. According to Rubingh, the ultimate goal of the sport is to create an avenue to help both individuals and the general society to control aggression. As he said in one interview, "You fight in the ring, not in a bar or in the streets. And you wage war on the chessboard, not in the Middle East."

A match of chess boxing consists of eleven rounds which include four minutes worth of chess, three minutes of boxing, and a one-minute break. The match can be won with either a technical knockout or a checkmate. In the event of a tie, the winner will be declared based on their results in the other event. In other words, if

Two fighters sitting to play chess at the Chess boxing championships in Berlin, Germany. (Paul Prescott/Dreamstime.com)

the tie is declared in chess, the winner will be decided on their points accumulated in boxing. Alternately, when there is a tie in boxing, the player using the black pieces in chess will be victorious. In order to ensure the athletes are equally versed in both aspects of the competition, the regulations require that participants are physically fit and also score at least 1,800 on the Elo chess ranking system, which equates to one level below expert on the United States Chess Federation scale used in the United States.

The first chess boxing match most likely took place in an art gallery called Platoon. The first official match occurred several months later on November 14, 2003, at the Paradiso in Amsterdam. This bout featured founder Rubingh and his friend, billed as "Iepe the Joker" versus "Luis the Lawyer" with Iepe winning on a technicality, as Luis took too long to make his chess move. The sport grew quickly, with fights featured in Tokyo in 2004, and the first European Chess boxing Championship being held on October 1, 2005, at the Autosalon Ost in Berlin. The Berlin match coincided with the opening of the very first Chess Boxing Club in the Mitte district of that city. Currently the World Chess Boxing Organization holds three to four championship fights annually held at multiple international locations.

Behavioral therapist Andrea Kuszewski has been one of the most vociferous proponents of chess boxing citing the social benefits which the sport could provide. She stresses that the skills which the sport instills—specifically the aspect of task switching—provide a sense of emotional training. This type of skill set could be used in helping to modify behavior in adolescents and young adults. Kuszewski makes it clear that this type of behavioral training could produce more tangible results than previous Band-Aid approaches to childhood aggression and school bullying. In the meantime, the sport of chess boxing continues to increase in both numbers and popularity.

Bob Tiegs

Further Readings

Kuszewski, Andrea. "Chess Boxing Is Fighting for Good Behavior." In *The Best Science Writing Online 2012*, edited by Jennifer Oullette, 180–86. New York: Scientific America, 2012.

World Chess Boxing Organization. http://wcbo.org/content/index_en.html (Accessed on September 2012).

CORPSE HIGH-PLATFORM EXPOSURE

Large numbers of people worldwide practice a ground burial when they contemplate providing a final resting place for their loved ones after death, but many indigenous cultures still incorporate natural exposure of the deceased body into their funerary practices. In parts of Australia, Aboriginal groups continue to practice burial methods based on corpse high-platform exposure. These burial traditions involve the ritualized placement of a corpse in an elevated platform and leaving it there until the flesh disintegrates. The general belief is that the body is placed within the broader environment, and natural elements (weather, sun, and small animals) aid in the process of decomposition. After some time has passed, the bleached bones are readied for their secondary and final burial. Generally, platform exposure is enacted because it is related to specific religious beliefs coupled with environmental realities that may limit alternate options for funeral practice. Instances of platform exposure are not as common as they once were in Australia, but it continues to be a funerary option for some indigenous populations that occupy Australia today.

Australia is a 7.6 million square kilometer (2.9 million square miles) island-continent surrounded by the Indian Ocean, the Pacific Ocean, and several seas. The geography of Australia is vast and characterized by a range of habitats from alpine and subtropical rain forest to expansive deserts. Australia is the flattest and driest inhabited continent on earth; the semi-arid lands that make up the largest portion of the continent are collectively known as the "outback." Human habitation patterns repetitively favor settlement in the east due to more temperate geography and climate. Over 22 million people live in Australia today and about 2.5 percent (or 500,000 people, ca. 2011) identify themselves ethnically, culturally, or biologically as Aborigines (on the mainland) or Islanders (Torres Strait). Although not as common today as it once was, Aborigine groups in Northern Australia have commonly made use of corpse high-platform exposure to dispose of the dead for millennia.

It is estimated that indigenous populations have inhabited Australia for the better part of 60,000 years. When European colonization began in Australia in the eighteenth century, native populations were observed as highly nomadic, hunter-gatherer societies that engaged in a complex oral culture with sophisticated social tribal structures. Their spiritual values are based on reverence for the land and belief in *Dreamtime*. Traditional Australian indigenous people embrace all phenomena and life as part of a vast and complex system or network of relationships, which can be traced directly back to the ancestral connections to the earth that surrounds them. The religious world of Australian Aborigines is thought to be inhabited by ghosts of the dead and spirits who control multiple aspects of the natural world. Engaging in complex ritual actions are thought to placate the ever-present spirits. The idea that in death the spirit leaves this world and returns to its birthplace to be reborn is prevalent in its association with *Dreamtime,* and ritual practices observed during burial help to attain a favorable return.

Many types of burial practices coexist within regions of Australia and among various tribes, which can be tricky for an onlooker to decipher. Burial and disposal practices can be roughly divided into seven major types: abandonment, carrying of corpse or bones, cremation, cannibalism, burial, platform exposure, and secondary disposal. It is extremely common to see several types of burial rituals practiced in conjunction with one another. Burial traditions often vary depending on the deceased's age, sex, and status. High-platform exposure involves placing the corpse upon an elevated structure (such as a scaffold or platform in a tree), and leaving it there until the flesh decomposes and disintegrates from the bone.

The major distribution for platform exposure has historically been practiced in Queensland, Central Australia, the Northern Territory, and northeastern Western Australia—although scattered occurrence has been noted in New South Wales, Victoria, and southeastern Australia. Platform exposure is one of the most honorific types of burial in these regions. This is discerned because the practice is often reserved for adults of active status, particularly men. Platform exposure almost always incorporates at least one of the other major burial types, and there is immense variation in the practices documented among and between numerous tribes and locales. Alternate burial practices and rituals will occur either before or after the platform exposure itself—most often, secondary disposal.

Secondary disposal is redisposition of the skeletal remains subsequent to the initial or main funeral ceremonies, in this case platform exposure. Aspects of secondary rites can be a significant part of the burial, or simply practical. The end result is that the bones are interned at a secondary burial site, often a rock shelter ossuary or buried in the ground, depending on what the terrain allows or local custom dictates. Some groups prepare the bones in various ways prior to secondary disposal. East Kimberley tribes, for example, carefully clean, paint, and wrap the bones in tidy bundles tied with human hair before the remains are placed in an ossuary. Other groups divide skeletal remains and intern each group at separate, specifically designated sites. Site choice often reflects spiritual beliefs about the land that have been structured through the *Dreamtime,* and they are associated with familiar spiritual and totem beings. Ancestral connection is paramount, and some Aboriginal groups will carry bones of the deceased or bone relics on their person for stretches of time before final secondary disposal can take place.

One of the most controversial aspects of platform exposure is that it can be difficult to gain a full understanding of when and where it continues to exist. Though evidence shows that platform exposure is still practiced in Australia, it has been largely eclipsed by ground burial as it is commonly understood in a Christianized, European, and American context. Australian Aborigines face many of the same problems that First Nations groups face in North America, such as disputes related to land rights and ownership, loss of traditional cultural systems due to forced assimilation, and social disruption due to extended political disenfranchisement. Despite increases in numbers of people in Australia who identify themselves as Aborigines since legislation was passed in the 1990s to somewhat recognize their collective and individual rights, only a relatively small percentage adhere to the ancient religious and spiritual practices of their Aboriginal cultures—such as high-platform exposure.

Stephanie L. Hamilton

Further Readings

Attwood, Bain. *Telling the Truth about Aboriginal History*. Sydney, Australia: Allen and Unwin, 2006.
Broom, Richard. *Aboriginal Australians*. 3rd ed. Sydney, Australia: Allen and Unwin, 2001.

Davidson, D. S. "Disposal of the Dead in Western Australia." *Proceedings of the Philosophical Society* 93, no. 1 (1949): 71–97.

Macintyre, Stuart. *A Concise History of Australia: Cambridge Concise Histories.* Cambridge: Cambridge University Press, 2009.

Monroe, M. H. "Aboriginal Mortuary Rites: Disposal of the Body." *Australia: The Land Where Time Began.* http://austhrutime.com/aboriginal_australia.htm (Accessed on December 13, 2012).

COW JUMPING INITIATION

The cow jumping initiation is a rite of passage for young adult males of the Hamar people. They are an Omotic community located in southwestern Ethiopia and live in an area known as the Omo River Valley. This unique initiation custom is the final step in a series of ritual acts. Following a successful cow jumping, a young man would be embraced as an adult member of the Hamar community and allowed to be married.

The Hamar people live a pastoral lifestyle in which cows playing a major role in their communities. Examples of this tradition can be seen in both the names of the Hamar and in the cow jumping initiation. All members of the Hamar tribe are given three names: a human name, a goat name, and a cow name. In addition, the cow jumping challenge is used as a tool to determine whether a young man is ready for marriage. In order to be married in the tribe, all young men must

Ethiopian boys apply face paint for the cow jumping initiation ritual. (Michele Alfieri/Dream stime.com)

successfully complete the cow jumping initiation. This cultural event is commonly known as "jumping over the bull." The Hamar, as well as other nearby tribes, see the cow jumping initiation as an important part of the pastoral culture.

The initiation begins as follows: when a young man of the village announces that he would like to marry a girl of his choice, he must first successfully complete the jumping challenge before the girl's parents can give him permission to marry their daughter. The initiation itself is preceded by an extremely important ritual. During this time, the women of the village—specifically the jumper's sisters and female relatives—provoke the *maz*, or the adult males who have previously completed the jump. As a result of their challenging behavior, provoking the men's anger, the *maz* then beat the women on their bare backs with sticks. As a result of such beating, the women end up with open wounds that will most likely leave scars. These wounds and eventual scars are important to the Hamar women. They are seen as the mark of the true women within the tribe. The women of the village who take part in provoking the *maz* give prior consent and are happy to be a part of this ritual. If the sister or relative of the jumper is whipped, they know that if they were to ever fall on hard times and need help, they can turn to the male relative who took part in the initiation that day. This is because it is believed by the Hamar community that if a female relative takes a beating on the day of the young man's initiation, he is indebted to her for the pain that was inflicted upon the woman. The scars that the female relative received from the beating remain as living proof that the man owes her a huge personal favor.

For the initiation, the girl's family selects thirty cows for their daughter's suitor to jump over during a public event. The cows that are chosen by the girl's family must be castrated males. The young man must stand up on top of a cow as it moves. Then, he must successfully jump on top of another cow as they are running. While completing the jump, the young man is completely naked with the exception of cords that he is allowed to wear across his chest. The aspiring man must complete the jump four times, twice in each direction. He is able to complete the jump with the assistance of his male friends, *maz*, who have successfully completed such initiation previously. It is the job of the *maz* to attempt to hold the cows moving slowly to keep their friend from falling. By holding the cattle, the *maz* are able to limit potential physical injury to their protégé when completing the jump. The challenging activity is complicated because the young man must successfully complete the four jumps without once tripping or falling.

If the jumper is unable to complete the cow jumping initiation, it is viewed as a bad sign. As a result, he will not receive permission to marry. He is, however, given a chance to attempt the initiation again the following year. On rare occurrences, it may be determined that the young man was unable to complete the cow jumping initiation because of strong winds. If this is agreed upon, he is then given a second chance to successfully complete the cow jumping challenge within the same year. If he succeeds in completing the entire task of four jumps the second time, then he will be given permission to marry.

Once the young man has successfully completed the cow jumping initiation, he would then be considered as a *maz*, an adult member of the Hamar community.

Upon this successful completion, he is deemed ready for marriage. In exchange for the girl's hand for matrimony, her family will traditionally receive cattle. Following these events, the couple will spend two months betrothed. During this time, they will perform acts that place emphasis on the role of the cattle in the everyday lives of the Hamar. The betrothed couple will share a drink of blood and milk. For this drink, the blood is taken from the neck of the cow, and it is then mixed with cow's milk to be drunk by the couple. In the Hamar tribe, a man who has successfully completed the initiation is viewed as both wealthy and strong by the community, and he is allowed to marry up to four women.

The cow jumping initiation is scheduled each year to take place at the end of the harvest season in Southwestern Ethiopia usually between July and September. Outsiders visiting the area and Hamar people from nearby communities are both permitted to attend the initiation. However, it is advised that anyone who plans to visit the Omo Valley area should only do so with the accompaniment of a local guide and a vehicle that is equipped with four-wheel drive capabilities to handle the rough and uneven terrain.

This Hamar initiation of cow jumping has its roots in traditional African cultures. Today, the event still draws from both the social evolution and the oral tradition of the community in which the initiation is taking place. However, in present day, the cultural ritual is not as common as it once was. The cow jumping initiation is no longer widespread throughout Africa. It is, however, still common among the Hamar people as well as other tribes in the lower Omo Valley, including groups such as the Tsamai, Aavii, Banna, and Bashada.

Dawn Cioffoletti

Further Readings

"Hamar." *Ethiopianet.* http://home.planet.nl/ . . . romei017/ethiopianet-peoples-section-hamar.htm (Accessed on January 23, 2013).

Janssens, Frank. "Jump the Cattle." *Demotix.* http://www.demotix.com/news/459054/jump-cattle#media-458972 (Accessed on January 23, 2013).

Rough Guides (Firm). *Make the Most of Your Time on Earth: The Rough Guide to the World.* London: Rough Guides, 2010.

Uhlig, Siegbert. *Encyclopaedia Aethiopica 3 He—N.* Wiesbaden, Germany: Harrassowitz, 2007.

DAY OF THE DEAD: *DÍA DE LOS MUERTOS*

Death is simply a transition to another life. Such were the beliefs of pre-Hispanic Mesoamerican peoples. While cultures across the world practice a variety of rituals to honor their dead, people in Mexico and Mexicans/Latinos in the United States continue the rituals of their ancestors by setting up altars or *ofrendas* (offerings) for their dead in their homes or at their local cemetery. The belief is that, once a year, departed loved ones return to unite with the living ones. In Mexico, the practice of making offerings to the dead goes back at least 3,000 years. Ancient cultures believed in the afterlife. To make the journey more pleasant, the departed were often buried with food or with their pet animal to guide them along. *The great beyond* (*Mictlán*, the place of death) could be a paradise with butterflies and acrobats, or it could be a frightening place. However interpreted, Mesoamericans accepted death as a very natural phenomenon. To this end, images of skulls permeated everyday life: Skulls were carved on stone walls, they were painted in codices, and skulls were made of obsidian and quartz stones and then offered to multiple gods. The Aztecs even composed poetry that acknowledged death by stating: in the universe, life requires death, and death requires life.

Day of the Dead activities incorporate both pre-Hispanic and Catholic beliefs and practices. Since the Spaniards conquered the Aztecs in 1521, two religious systems fused and gave rise to a syncretic religion that today still reflects a spiritual *mestizaje* (blending). Prior to the Spaniards, Aztecs prayed to a variety of deities, including Miclantecuhtli, god of death. Today's offerings to the dead seem to have their origins in gifts made to the goddess of death, Mictecacihuatl, who was honored during the ninth month of the solar calendar. She is often also referred to as the "Lady of Death," and she is brought to life by women who decorate their faces and impersonate her, referred to as *Catrinas*. Today, people continue to bring her offerings of flowers and food.

In the Catholic religion, November 1 is known as All Saints Day and November 2 as All Soul's Day. Consequently, efforts were made to unify pre-Columbian days of honoring the dead with Christian days essentially doing the same, yielding what we know today as the Day of the Dead. November 1 is set aside for remembering deceased infants and children, while November 2 is for honoring deceased adults. Geographically, Day of the Dead rituals tend to be practiced more in central and southern Mexico, especially in areas that are able to adhere closer to their native traditions. Two states especially known for their practices are Michoacán and Oaxaca. People who have immigrated to the United States have long brought with them their funerary beliefs and rituals. Today, we observe a growing increase

A vendor's display of souvenir skulls in Michoacán, Mexico, 2013. (Courtesy of Leonardob0880)

in the celebration of the Day of the Dead, maintaining core elements from Mexico and yet, oftentimes transforming their content and context according to the specific community.

The key belief of the Day of the Dead is that departed family members will visit their homes on the evening of November 1. They will leave their place of rest (identified as Mictlan or purgatory) to visit their loved ones and partake in the essence of the food and the ambiance. The altar can be set up anywhere in the home but with sufficient space for numerous family members to come together. The altar table is decorated with a nice tablecloth, perhaps one stitched, crocheted, or decorated by the women of the house, or sometimes a special colored cloth might be laid out such as a purple cloth, which is a color closely associated with death.

While every altar is unique, certain essential items, such as flowers, pictures, food, candles, incense, bread, water, skulls, and specialty items, need to be displayed. Located both on the altar and surrounding it are marigolds, the official flower of death, known as *cempasúchits* or *zempoaxochitls* in Spanish. An essential element of the display is of course the picture of the departed family member or friend, for they are the ones who will be visiting that evening. If an actual picture is not available, a drawing or illustration of them will suffice.

Food is the primary element of the offering; after all, the dead are coming to partake in a feast organized just for them. The deceased's favorite foods are presented, often including the most traditional of Mexican dishes such as tamales and mole (a mixture of chili sauces and chicken). After a long journey, the deceased will also undoubtedly be thirsty; so, it is important to offer their favorite beverages such as beer, tequila, or hot chocolate. *Pan de muerto* (meaning, "bread of the dead") needs to be set on the table, and it is reflective of European influence since there was no wheat in Mexico until the Spaniards arrived. The bread might be in

Traditional makeup for the Day of the Dead celebration in Mexico. (Zepherwind/Dreams time.com)

the shape of a small round loaf, sweet, decorated with dyed red sugar to represent blood, or the bread might be elongated, shaped in the form of bones. *Pan de muerto* is usually sweet, although some communities prefer salted bread.

The Christian aspect of the *ofrenda* is reflected in the crosses, rosaries, and sacred images of Christ scattered throughout the display, or the deceased's patron saint may take center stage. Candles are lit throughout the night to guide the souls to their final destination; there is generally one for each departed person, and an extra one for a lost soul. The ambiance of death is reinforced through the use of incense. An *ofrenda* would not be complete without the display of skulls, which are typically made of sugar. The space above and around the altar is enhanced with stringed *papel picado* (tissue paper with cut-out designs, known in Spanish as *papel de china*). The brightly colored flags display skeletal/death designs that reinforce the funerary ambiance. Lastly, items that reflect the unique personality of the deceased should be visible; for adults, it might be cigarettes if they smoked or a CD of their favorite music; and for children, their favorite toys. It is tradition that the family stays up all night waiting "for the dead to arrive" at midnight. While the practice of setting up an *ofrenda* and arranging food for the dead may be pre-Hispanic in origin, the prayers said throughout the night are certainly Catholic.

An important part of the Day of the Dead rituals is setting up offerings at a cemetery and keeping vigil all night on November 1. A few days before, the tomb of the deceased is cleaned up and made ready for gifts. Women and children bring armloads of marigold flowers to decorate the tomb, and they often design a marigold "cross" on top. Again, the favorite foods of the family member are placed on top of the tomb. Throughout the night family members sit and kneel, pray, chant, sing, each attending to their loved one. Though they may not be seen, the expectation is that the departed loved ones will be there, among family members, and the living are here to celebrate their life and death.

In addition to altars and cemetery visitations, some towns add to the Day of the Dead festivities by offering *comparsas*—theatrical performances representing the return of the dead. Other activities allow for local men to don women's clothing, or allow locals to break social behavioral rules upheld the rest of the year, or simply provide an opportunity to dress up in all sorts of macabre costumes. These festivities mock death and display the creativity of the living.

Over decades, Mexicans have immigrated from urban centers and rural communities to the United States, and while a majority of Mexicans are located in the Southwest, Mexicans and Latinos are found throughout the United States. San Francisco, California, and San Antonio, Texas, are some of the major centers in which Day of the Dead activities are carried out. For example, local museums may sponsor Day of the Dead displays or altars and invite the community to learn how to make sugar skulls and *papel picado*. Local vendors sell an assortment of skulls, skeletons in tombs, or offer face painting for the children. School districts sometimes offer Day of the Dead activities as part of their Halloween activities, making sure to de-emphasize the religious aspects of the day. Community centers often commemorate the day by inviting local Aztec dancers to perform. Catholic

THE ISLAND OF JANITZIO AS THE HEART OF "DAY OF THE DEAD" CELEBRATIONS

The state of Michoacán is one of the most traditional locations for the Day of the Dead celebrations in Mexico. More specifically, Lake of Pátzcuaro gets a large number of visitors from around the world to witness the traditional celebrations that take place at night. However, the focus of the events is actually on the island of Janitzio, located right in the middle of the lake. Making the trip by small boats is an unforgettable experience. When traveling at night from the shores for the twenty- to thirty-minute ride to the island, the lake is completely dark. The only markers to guide the boats are a set of tall wooden stakes that have been placed sticking out of the water coated with tar on top of them. At night, these poles are lit with fire that lasts a few hours. These amber-color rudimentary lights make the transportation to the island a very spooky, scary, and somewhat spiritual experience. Upon arrival, the scene offers a feast for the senses with smells of food and incense, sights of bright-color flowers, the sweet and soulful sounds of amateur musicians, and the taste of *pan de muerto* (bread for the dead).

Javier A. Galván

churches hold processions to the local Catholic cemetery or at the cemetery itself. Mexicano/Latino neighborhoods occasionally organize parades with colorful altars, clothing, face paint, and artwork displays. Contemporary rituals and festivities sometimes honor collective groups of individuals, such as people who have died of cancer, lost military veterans, forgotten women of the Mexican Revolution, or those who have died crossing the U.S.—Mexico border. Ultimately, the Day of the Dead rituals and festivities are an opportunity to honor the deceased and for family and community members to strengthen their relationships.

Angelina F. Veyna

Further Readings

"Dia de los Muertos." http://diadelosmuertos.yaia.com/historia.html.(Accessed on July 15, 2013.)

Grose, Robin. "Los elementos de la ofrenda de Día de los muertos." http://comidamexi caa.about.com/od/HistoriaYCultura/tp/Los-Elementos-De-La-Ofrenda-. . . (Accessed on July 20, 2013.)

Haley, Shawn D., and Curt Fukuda. *Day of the Dead: When Two Worlds Meet in Oaxaca.* New York: Berghahn Books, 2004.

Martinez, Manuel Luis. *Day of the Dead: Dia de los Muertos.* Mountain View, CA: Floricanto Press, 2009.

Moss, Jean. *The Day of the Dead: A Pictorial Archive of Dia de los Muertos.* (Dover Pictorial Archive). New York: Dover Publications, 2010.

Palfrey, Dale Hoyt. "November 2: The Day of the Dead." http://www.mexconnect.com/ articles/1972-november-2-the-day-of-the-dead (Accessed on July 5, 2013).

Williams, Kitty. *Day of the Dead.* Layton, UT: Gibbs Smith, 2011.

DIABLADA DANCE, DANCE OF THE DEVILS

The *Diablada* Dance, or "Dance of the Devils," is an extremely colorful, religious-cultural dramatization of the battle between good and evil that today is performed only in a few selective parts of South America. This elaborate performance is a modern cultural adaptation of the classic *auto sacramental* (or religious dramatization) held during Roman Catholic holy day celebrations. Another possible sources for these dances are the early medieval English mystery plays, which also featured dramatizations of biblical stories in tableaux with dance and song. Perhaps the best known of the auto sacramental authors was the great Castilian playwright Pedro Calderón de la Barca (1600–1681) who wrote literary masterpieces, such as *Belshazzar's Feast* and *The Divine Orpheus.* These religious dramatizations were extremely popular in the seventh century ACE but their appeal dwindled considerably. By the tenth century, auto sacramentals were performed only in churches of the Spanish-speaking world.

From a cultural perspective, South America's *Diablada* Dance processions date back over 300 years to colonial times when the Spanish landowners gave their workers a day off to celebrate the New Year. During the colonial era (mid-1500s to early 1800s), various pagan beliefs were blended with new Christian Catholic traditions. Later, new iconography was added and revised. Moreover, the celebrations

A dancer wearing a devil costume for the Oruro Carnival in Bolivia. (Edurivero/Dreams time.com)

adopted an additional meaning during the Latin American wars of independence. Multiple South American countries today have their own versions of *La Diablada* in their major festivals. In Ecuador, the annual procession of *Diablada*—or the Dance of the Devils—is observed by townspeople and tourists on the streets of Pillaro (near the capital city of Quito) with great pomp and glory on January 6. In Chile, the "Dance of the Devils" occurs during the feast of Our Lady of Carmen of La Tirana every July as part of honoring the patron saint of Chile, the Virgin of Carmen (Albrecht 2007, 175).

Perhaps the largest and most well-known *Diablada* Dance is the one held in Oruro, Bolivia, a city with a population of roughly 230,000 people located 122 miles (or 197.5 kilometers) southeast of the capitol La Paz. The regional celebrations take place before Lent, which is the Catholic time of fasting and repentance preceding Easter. It draws millions of tourists annually. Overall, it is the most well-known and popular holiday dance in Bolivia, and it is probably the most elaborate dance in Bolivian folklore. The annual carnival reveals strong Incan heritage that honors the Virgin of Socavón (Virgin of the Mineshaft). The carnival also celebrates the pre-Columbian god of the underworld. The colorful festive event has been called one of the richest expressions of folklore: "a masterpiece of oral and intangible human heritage," according to a 2001 UNESCO declaration (Bustamante 2009, 58).

Despite its current popularity, there is no complete agreement about when and where the Oruro carnival actually began. One of the most accepted theories is that it started in Copacabana as a celebration for the Virgin of Copacabana. In fact, the devil's dance was not a part of the carnival until 1789. A legend about *La Diablada's* beginning tells that a thief named Chiru-Chiru living near a mountain with a silver mine would light candles before the image of Virgin of Candlemas and ask for her protection. After he robbed a poor family, however, the Virgin withdrew her protection, and soon he was badly injured. Nevertheless, she took pity, and she cared for him until he died. When his body was found, the townspeople discovered a large image of the Virgin on the wall above his head, and they deduced that the Virgin was the protector of miners. They changed her name to the Virgin del Socavón (Virgin of the Mineshaft), and they promised to honor her during a carnival by composing songs and doing prayers for her. However, the people worried that honoring the Virgin might anger a bad legendary spirit named Supay (the spirit of the underground) who they had worshiped since the seventeenth century. Believing that Supay would give them much ore to mine if he was pleased or only mining mishaps if he was unhappy, the people decided that they would please him by dressing like devils in his image and dancing *La Diablada*. At that time, the Spanish colonial authorities added this drama to try to inject Christianity into the carnival. They especially desired to stop the people's worship of spirits such as Supay, who they equated with the devil. However, the Spanish never succeeded in completely eliminating these indigenous cultural elements from the carnival (Royal Geographical Society 2005, 78).

Today, the *Diablada* dance performance is an essential part of the Oruro festival. The festival begins with a procession of colorfully decorated Indian miners through the streets behind sixty mules and oxen filled with silverware and household objects. The miners symbolically offer this silver and china—that were once made to Inti, the Inca god of the sun—at the Roman Catholic Church of the Virgin of the Cave, patroness of Oruro tin miners. The celebration of the Mass itself is solemn with no dancing and only the music of the church's choir. Then, after a blessing by the priest, *La Diablada* begins.

The characters that are represented in the *Diablada* Dance have a long history among the Bolivian population. First, an Indian cast in the role of Lucifer (who wears a mask and a red velvet cloak) dances into the area in front of the church's front doors. Holding his scepter, Lucifer proclaims in a mixture of Spanish and indigenous languages that he is the Prince of Darkness. He then proves his point with a series of very impressive leaps and uproarious shouts. The Archangel Michael (dressed in white and pink colors) responds by coming forward. In the name of god and the seven virtues, he challenges Lucifer. Seven devils—notable for their terrifying lizard masks and costumes with sharp horns, bug eyes, and drooling fangs—follow and challenge St. Michael. The devils include Envy, Sloth, and Lust. Finally, *La Diabla* (the she-devil and strongest of the netherworld) slithers in. Despite the she-devil's efforts, Michael outdances and outpreaches all the devils. He lastly throws Lucifer to the floor and stomps him, proclaiming the victory of god and virtue. Michael then leads the devils into the church, where they take off their masks and sing "Our Mother, here we are, your little children devils." After that, they all leave the church in a unified procession.

Subsequently, the dancers perform around town for the carnival's three days and nights of street parties, dancing, feasting, and fireworks. During these events, thousands of masked and costumed dancers and musicians perform well-choreographed numbers. The celebration is an enormous affair that includes forty to fifty different dance companies that in turn have between 40 and 300 members each. The dance groups (e.g., morenadas and diabladas) that have been made famous at Oruro have become part of a national system of dance groups across Bolivia that perform at various festivals, such as the Virgen de Copacabana in Lake Titicaca. The more professional groups have trumpets, tubas, and other brass instruments along with bass and snare drums, cymbals, and various percussion instruments. These amateur, university, and professional dance groups are a combination of Bolivian folklore culture and intensive religious devotion (Albrecht 2007, 176; Díaz-Barriga 2003, 248).

In the festivals of other Bolivian cities and towns, other dramatic dance performances have been added. One of the most traditional dances is *la morenada* ("Dance of the Black Slaves"), which also goes back to the colonial era, and it has servants mocking the social dances held in the viceroyalty's ballrooms. Another dance drama, *las caporales*, depicts the sacrifice made by enslaved Africans, originally brought to Bolivia by the Spaniards to work in the silver mines of Potosí. This dance also honors the Virgin of Socavón (patroness of miners) for coal for their fires, or the Virgin of Candelaria (Canary Islands in origin). The dance groups' musicians sometimes play pop songs, including rhythmic dance numbers from various countries and even "Yellow Submarine" by the Beatles (Jefkin-Elnekave 2004, 22; Albrecht 2007, 177).

In contemporary Bolivia, most people combine cultural and religious elements of their Spanish heritage with indigenous traditions. While over 80 percent of Bolivians are Christian, many also believe in Ekeko (the Indian god of abundance). It is rather common to have people who see no contradiction whatsoever in belonging to two religious traditions simultaneously. Today, many Inca and Roman Catholic holidays are officially observed, often in combination.

Modern Catholicism in most countries retains the particular national culture's pagan symbols. In Bolivia, this reflects the country's history. When the Spanish arrived in Bolivia in the sixteenth century, they allowed the Indians to keep their community organization, but forced them to work for the Spanish (e.g., in the silver mines) in exchange for "protection" and conversion to Christianity. When Bolivia finally gained its independence from Spain in 1825—led by Simón Bolívar (1783–1830)—its people continued their ancient blend of multiple cultural traditions.

William P. Kladky

Further Readings

Albrecht, Robert. "The Virgin, the Princess, and the Goddess: A Field Report and Analysis of Pagan and Christian Symbolism in a Roman Catholic Religious Celebration of Northern Chile." *Atlantic Journal of Communication* 15 (2007): 171–93.

Bustamante, Fernando. "Pageantry in Oruro." *Americas* 61 (2009): 58.
Díaz-Barriga, Miguel. "Materialism and Sensuality: Visualizing the Devil in the Festival of Our Lady of Urkupiña." *Visual Anthropology* 16 (2003): 245–61.
Graf, Christine. "Carnaval Time in Bolivia." *Faces* 25 (2008): 13.
Jefkin-Elnekave, Debbie. "Bolivia." *PSA Journal* 70 (2004): 21.
Royal Geographical Society. "Mountain Life in Bolivia." *Geographical Archive* 77 (2005): 76–81.

DIPO WOMANHOOD CEREMONY

The Dipo Womanhood Ceremony is a sacred female puberty rite celebrated annually around Easter (usually in April) by the people of Manya and Yilo Krobo, in the regions of Krobo-Odumase and Somanya in southeastern Ghana. While the age group of the participants varies, it is generally for girls between twelve and sixteen years of age. In this part of Africa, every Krobo girl is expected to go through this ritual in order to be truly recognized as a Krobo woman. The Dipo ritual has been called a crucial element of Krobo society. This cultural tradition has been practiced since the eleventh century, and it is one of the most famous ceremonies in Ghana. As a result, it draws a considerable number of tourists to the area.

While the Dipo tradition dates back for centuries, there is considerable disagreement about its true origins. One version is that circumcision and other rituals were performed for teenage boys, who then were dressed with beads and paraded around the community, concluding with a feast in their honor. Women with female children grew jealous of this custom, and they coordinated an initiation celebration for girls alone. Another version is that Dipo was begun by the ancient priestess Nana Kloweki ("Klo" meaning the Krobo, "we" for people, and "ki" indicating a first-born child), who was a goddess incarnated into human form and accompanied the Krobos in their migration (Boakye 2010, 25–26). Both versions are still popular today.

A typical Dipo ceremony lasts five days, though it may vary considerably throughout regions of Ghana. Originally, it involved a complete year in isolation. In order to participate in the ritual, only the qualified girls go to the house of the traditional chief priest to prepare for the rite. At first, family members attend, to be later joined by other people from the community and tourists. The priest is assisted by ritual mothers, who are mostly female relatives. On the first day, the girls are paraded in public (naked above the waist), and their heads are shaved leaving only a small amount of hair. The exposure of the upper body signifies that these girls are now moving into the adulthood stage of their life and ready to become wives. A raffia ribbon is tied around their neck to signify they are now Dipo girls (*Dipo-yi*). They are then allowed to cover their breasts with a wax-print cloth except when a ritual is being performed. This is the beginning of the girls' symbolic seclusion from the community (Boakye 2010, 33; Steegstra 2002, 204).

The next two days of the Dipo celebration are very ritualistic and full of symbolism. On the second day, all the initiate girls are given a ritual bath in a nearby stream. Family members sometimes give the girls dirty linen to wash. Throughout the event, girls are not allowed to speak at all. Upon returning to the priest's house, a priestess sprinkles chalky water and a red camwood substance on their faces. Maize and sugarcane are placed three times on their lips before they can eat them. The girls then taste foods like sugarcane and peanuts. After the ritualistic meal, the rest of their head hair is shaved. Libations are then poured, two local ones, including palm wine and a foreign drink, such as Schnapps. This "tri-libation" is done to ask the gods to bless the girls. Next, a castrated goat from each parent is slaughtered, and its blood is used to wash the feet of all the girls participating in the ceremony. On the third day, to wash away any bad omen that might prevent the girls from having babies, the chief priest directs them to sit on stools covered with a white cloth. A clay solution is used to make symbolic marks and designs on their bodies. The slaughtered goat's intestines are then wrapped around the girls' shoulders, and they are taken to a shrine where they sit three times on a sacred stone (called Tekpete).

On the fourth day of the festivities, the priestesses (ritual mothers) teach the girls what is needed to be a good Krobo woman (e.g., grooming, conduct, dance, and seduction). Tribal marks are made on their hands to show they have passed the rite, and they are fully accepted as women in the community. Subsequently, elephant skin is tied around the head to ensure fertility. Throughout these steps, the mothers of very young girls hold their hands when they perform some of these tasks.

On the fifth (and final) day of the Dipo ceremony, the girls display their beau-tiful beads—which have been passed down for generations and signify affection, prosperity, protection, and spirituality. They also dress in silk or *kente* (hand-woven) clothing, while singing and dancing the Klama dance. The Krobo people are histor-ically very good makers of Ghanaian beads, and Krobo is the biggest bead market town in Ghana (Gyan-Apenteng 2004, 44). The girls then thank all their friends and family members, receive gifts, and are sent home amid drumming, dancing, and jubilation.

There are many symbolic elements in the Dipo womanhood ceremony. The red-loin cloth worn by initiates during most of the ceremony symbolizes men-struation, a sign that a girl is capable of conception. The white cloth—worn only at some times, such as the visit to the stone—is a sign of fertility, purity, and holi-ness. Other Dipo activities have symbolic meaning, such as requiring the girls to stand on the antelope skins. It is believed that by doing so they will go mad if they are pregnant (Boakye 2010, 50).

The Dipo ceremony today is sharply criticized as being old-fashioned and sex-ist, which often leads to controversial debates. Some aspects of the rite such as the exposure of initiates' breasts and washing their feet with the blood of a goat have been criticized as offending "the twenty-first century's sense of women's dignity [and] abuse of human rights and freedoms of the girls involved, amounting to more or less maltreatment of a child." As a result, a number of Christian girls do not participate in Dipo (Boakye 2010, 5–6; Steegstra 2002, 224). Since roughly half of the Krobo girls in this part of Ghana are Christian, nowadays, the timing of this rite has been affected. For Christian baptism, it is believed that a puberty initiation had to precede baptism. This was because baptism was seen as a means of washing away their sins after initiation. In this view, Dipo was considered as something sinful needing the cleansing of baptism (Steegstra 2002, 222). While the debate continues between the need to conserve ancient cultural traditions versus adapting to contemporary views on human rights, the Dipo womanhood ceremony continues to be practiced in Ghana, but it is increasingly becoming a regional custom performed for tourism.

William P. Kladky

Further Readings

Boakye, Priscilla Akua Boakye. "A Rite of Passage among the Krobos of Eastern Region, Ghana." Master's Thesis, University of Tromsø, Norway, 2010.
Gyan-Apenteng, Kwadwo. "Ghana Says It with Beads." *New African* 425 (2004): 44–46.
Steegstra, Marijke. "'A Mighty Obstacle to the Gospel': Basel Missionaries, Krobo Women, and Conflicting Ideas of Gender and Sexuality." *Journal of Religion in Africa* 32 (2002): 200–30.

EATING HUMAN PLACENTA

The placenta is a vascular organ that is the main life support system of the developing fetus in utero. It assists with the nutrition and breathing of the developing baby. Poets have described it as the tree of life. In many parts of the world (including North America) after giving birth, some women consume the raw placenta, a custom that is known as placentophagia. The term *placenta* derives from the Latin word for "cake," and it may also be interpreted to mean "pleasing" and "gratifying." Its taste has been compared to that of steak tartar, kidneys, or liver.

Multiple cultures have developed a variety of methods to prepare the placenta for human consumption. In addition to eating it raw, another common practice includes swallowing capsules of dried, ground, placenta tissue. First, the placenta is dried either in an oven or by keeping it under the sun. In traditional societies, it is often wrapped in a piece of cloth and hung to cure in a cool, dry place. Later, it is ground into a powder with a mortar and a pestle or a coffee grinder. The powder can be kept for up to three years. In addition to eating it raw or swallowing it in capsule form, some people boil the placenta, and they use the broth for various remedies. Yet, another popular method is to steam the placenta at a low temperature, which is believed to enrich it with energy.

In the United States, multiple cookbooks that contain placenta preparation recipes exist. For example, adding placenta powder to lukewarm beer or champagne is often believed to stimulate breast milk production. Placenta soup (which may also include ingredients such as poultry, vegetables, spice, and herbs) is a common recipe, and it is also thought to help new mothers with enhanced milk production.

In terms of who actually eats placenta in the United States, Mark Kristal, a neuroscientist at the University of Buffalo, reports that the first recorded cases of placentophagia began in the 1970s when a number of adults living in communes shared placenta stews. Today, a subset of middle-class, college-educated American women in their thirties are either eating placenta or having supplement pills prepared. Such women claim that the supplements help with increasing breast milk production, lowering rates of postpartum depression, acting as a uterine tonic, and replenishing nutrients they have lost during pregnancy.

A great number of rationales have been presented for eating human placenta. It is believed to have mood-enhancing effects, such as creating feelings of euphoria for the person consuming it. Placentas contain hormones that inhibit stress and release endorphins. The organ is commonly described as helping in increasing a

Bags of dried human placenta for sale in China. The placenta is eaten for medical purposes. (Hellobobo/Flickr.com)

new mother's breast milk production due to its high levels of oxytocin. Consuming placenta has also been linked to new mothers regaining their energy and healing quickly after giving birth. It is also thought to provide hormones that protect against heart attacks and strokes.

Cross-culturally, the consumption of placenta is rather common. In the 1500s, a piece of the placenta was usually added to the southern German mother's first postpartum meal, as it was believed to speed up the delivery of the afterbirth and to reduce bleeding. In Java, Indonesia, women consume placenta to increase fertility. In Morocco, it is also thought of as a cure for infertility. Hungarian and Chinese women eat a bit of placenta to speed up the process of delivering a child; and in Italy, parts of the organ are eaten to prevent pain after birth.

Human placenta, prepared in different manners, has been used as a medical remedy for hundreds of years. Certain placenta cells can become cells of other body parts; similar to what occurs with stem cells, so the potential use of placenta cells for medical research is quite innovative. Health remedies developed from placenta powder were commonly produced and sold by European pharmacies until the late 1800s. Dried placenta is believed to help fight epilepsy, and until 1835, European pharmacists sold dried placenta from a first-born child for this purpose. In Thailand, Vietnam, and Korea, placenta hormones are used in folk medicine to treat badly healing wounds and for blood circulation disorders. Placenta powders, extract injections, and emulsions have also been found to help reduce swelling in fingers and legs. The Chinese have used placenta in folk medicine for over 1,400 years; it is thought to help with infertility, asthma, arthritis, as well as liver and immune system issues. Placenta injections have been used in Germany to treat different types of cancer, AIDS, and multiple sclerosis. In Mexico, eating placenta is thought to help women recover from depression and hormonal changes caused by hysterectomies. It is also provided to women going through menopause to help prevent hot flashes, mood swings, and palpitations.

Contemporary Western scientists find the existing research to be tenuous in supporting the extensive claims that have been made in advocating the use of ingesting placenta. While placentas do contain high levels of iron, vitamin B-12, and other hormones, there is no conclusive evidence linking these nutrients to increasing strength in a new mother. Additionally, if the placenta is prepared by being cooked, significant amounts of the potential nutrients evaporate.

The use of placenta is also believed to help stimulate tissue growth and remove wrinkles. Consequently, the use of this organ in cosmetic products began to emerge in the United States in the 1940s. In addition, during the early 1990s, hair care products containing placenta were linked to premature sexual development in African American girls. Outside of America, placenta material has been used in facial creams sold in France, while plastic surgeons in Japan offer placenta extract shots to help reduce wrinkles.

In an interesting popular culture event, placentophagia was depicted on a British cooking show called *TV Dinner* in 1998. In one episode, a London couple celebrated their granddaughter's birth by preparing and eating the baby's placenta to pay tribute to various world customs. They fried the afterbirth with garlic and shallots; then it was flambéed and pureed; and it was finally served as pate on focaccia bread for family members and friends. The Broadcasting Standards Commission received a number of complaints after the episode aired, and it ruled that the program had breached a cultural taboo since many citizens found watching the show to be disagreeable.

The history, uses, and meaning of ingesting placenta vary widely by nation and era. Yet, even though it is not a mainstream practice in the United States, placentophagia does not appear to be a ritual that will disappear anytime soon.

Sharla A. Blank

Further Readings

Abrahamian, Atossa. "The Placenta Cookbook." *New York Magazine*. August 21, 2011. http://nymag.com/print/?/news/features/placenta-2011-8/21 (Accessed on July 24, 2012).

Enning, Cornelia. *Placenta: The Gift of Life—The Role of the Placenta in Different Cultures, and How to Prepare and Use It as Medicine*. Oregon: Motherbaby Press, 2007.

Field, Mary. "Birthrites: Healing after Caesarean, Placentophagy." *Midwives Chronicle and Nursing Notes*. November 1984. http://www.birthrites.org/placent.html (Accessed on February 9, 2014).

Long, E. Croft. "The Placenta in Lore and Legend." *Bulletin of the Medical Library Association* 51, no. 2 (1963): 233–41.

ENDOCANNIBALISM

Endocannibalism is the practice of consuming dead members of a close social or family group. It stands in contrast to exocannibalism, which is the eating of outsiders and people with no social or family relationship to the cannibal. While in the modern era cannibalism carries with it a connotation of savagery or at best desperation (such as in the case of the Donner Party in the American West), the roots of most examples of endocannibalism lie in the consumption of human remains as part of traditional cultural rituals or funeral rites dating back to hundreds of years. In the funeral rites of the Fore people of Papua New Guinea, the process is a means to respect and honor the dead rather than a cultural permissiveness for the consumption of human flesh for sustenance, survival, or other reasons. As a result, the terms "funerary cannibalism" and "compassionate cannibalism" have also been used to describe the rituals and customs associated with this tradition among the Fore cultural groups. Endocannibalism provides practicing cultures a way to cope with grief, a method through which the positive qualities of the deceased may be inherited, or a way to return the life force of the departed to the rest of the people in the social group. Other cases of such rituals tap into fears over a spirits' fate in the afterlife. As endocannibalism did not require the killing of outsiders through violence or war, and it was an essential element of the process of death in the cultures that practiced it, cases of endocannibalism have continued to be performed well into the twentieth century.

Tangible examples of endocannibalism can be found across the world. Although many variations exist, the practices of the Fore in Papua New Guinea are generally representative of many elements of the funerary aspect of such traditions. For the Fore people, the consumption of dead members of the tribe was a way to show both grief and a deep and abiding affection for the deceased. The act of cannibalism was seen as a means to take the flesh of a loved one (and by extension the very essence of the dead) into the bodies of the living members of the tribe, a postmortem fate that was viewed as comforting and inherently compassionate to the Fore. They believed that in this manner the spirit of the dead would live on within the bodies of the tribe. Burying the body underground only consigns the dead to oblivion, as the corpse and the spirit would simply decay into the earth rather than continue on living among the tribe members.

When a member of the Fore society died, the women of the tribe were responsible for preparing the body for consumption. The deceased was cut apart, with the larger bones broken open for the marrow and the skull cracked to expose the brain. In some cases, the deceased would have clearly indicated which body parts were to be eaten by specific people. Women along with children ate most of the remains, with the brain and spinal cord considered particularly special. Sexual organs were reserved for close relatives of the opposite sex. Men often only ate a small amount of flesh. Most of the entire body was eaten by the tribe and family members, with the exception of teeth, the bile sack, and other inedible portions. Whatever body parts remained, such as bone pieces, were then burned at the end of the ritual meal, and the calcium-rich ash was sprinkled on other food for further consumption.

The Wari people of the Brazilian Amazon region also have a custom of funerary cannibalism, which illustrates the diverse belief systems and different methods behind the practice. In the case of the Wari, immediate family members did not partake in the process of eating the dead due to their belief that the transmission of bodily fluids connected people as one individual. Close relatives would be in essence eating themselves, an action which was anathematic to the Wari. Instead, relatives asked other members of the tribe to honor social obligations and take part in the consumption of the dead. Family members from distant areas were called to gather, and all the possessions of the deceased were burned and destroyed. As it could take some time for the entire required social group to assemble, the body of the deceased would often begin to decompose. The decomposing flesh was still cooked and eaten, even if it was difficult for the Wari to consume the rotten human remains. After the body was consumed, all remaining traces of the deceased were eradicated by burning the parts left over from the funerary feast as well as the implements used in the preparation of the body. In the belief system of the Wari cultural heritage, the destruction of worldly belongings and the act of endocannibalism allowed the spirit of the dead to accept death and proceed to the afterlife.

The endocannibalistic funeral rituals of the Yanomani people of the Amazon differ in the way the body is consumed. Similar to the Wari people, the Yanomani tribes seek to cut all ties between the deceased and the physical world to prevent the spiritual energy of the dead from troubling the tribe. A dead member of the Yanomani is burned as thoroughly as possible in a ritual meant to remove the vital power of the deceased. This practice allows the spirit to obtain eternal rest. As this energy is thought to be strongest within the bones, a week after the cremation, the bones are crushed into fine powder. The soft powder is then distributed among family and friends who organize special meals during which the powder is blended into other food and then consumed. Endocannibalism thus gives the Yanomani a means to free the dead from the forces that would hold it to the physical world in their view of their physical environment and the afterlife.

While death rituals are the most notable and elaborate examples of endocannibalism, other reasons for the practice exist. Reports indicate that the Korowai people of Papua New Guinea believe that mysterious deaths among their people are the result of witchcraft. When a Korowai falls ill, the perpetrator is believed to be a male witch called a *khakhua* living in secret among them. The witch is thought to slowly eat away at the insides of his victim. At the moment of death, the victim of witchcraft is able to name their killer. The family of the victim then kills and eats the *khakhua* as an act of revenge. The Korowai do not practice other forms of cannibalism, since the *khakhua* is seen as something other than human. As the witch is still a member of the Korowai tribe, the act is technically classified as endocannibalism. On a related tradition among the Junkun tribal groups of West Africa, a new leader will eat the heart of the previous tribal chieftain. This specific form of endocannibalism involved only the tribal leader, and it served to set the leader apart from his people.

Due to the sensitive and often private nature of death rituals within endocannibalistic cultures and the problems encountered by researchers in traveling to isolated areas, there exists a large degree of uncertainty regarding the reported practices of cannibalism. For a time, there was spirited academic debate over whether ritual cannibalism truly existed, or if it was the creation of overzealous missionaries or publicity-seeking explorers. The use of nearly the entire body in both endocannibalism and exocannibalism has contributed to the difficulties encountered by scientists as very little material evidence remains to be studied.

The impact of the modern world on even the most remote parts of the earth has brought unavoidable change to traditional cultures. As a result, the practice of any kind of cannibalism has declined with the expansion of centralized governments and the imposition of restrictions upon the people under their jurisdiction. Among the Fore people of Papua New Guinea and the Wari tribal groups of the Brazilian Amazon region, endocannibalism ended with the strict enforcement of laws concerning the treatment of the dead. Due to their relative isolation, the Korowai are thought to be the only practicing endocannibals left. Aside from the modern social stigma attached to cannibalism, the neurological disease Kuru is believed to have been spread among the Fore by the consumption of infected individuals. Yet, despite the repulsion it evokes in most regions of the world, endocannibalism served an important function within the culture of the societies that practiced it, often serving as an expression of true concern for the fate of the deceased people among the tribal members.

Daniel Fandino

Further Readings

Hollingshead, Iain. "Tales of Cannibalism from the South Pacific." *The Telegraph.* October 11, 2011. http://www.telegraph.co.uk/travel/travelnews/8831702/Tales-of-cannibalism-from-the-South-Pacific.html (Accessed on March 24, 2013).

Metcalf, Peter. "Wine of the Corpse: Endocannibalism and the Great Feast of the Dead in Borneo." *Representations* no. 17, Special Issue: "The Cultural Display of the Body" (Winter, 1987): 96–109.

Raffaele, Paul. "Sleeping with Cannibals." *Smithsonian.com.* September 2006. http://www.smithsonianmag.com/travel/cannibals.html (Accessed on March 28, 2013).

Travis-Henikoff, Carole A. *Dinner with a Cannibal: The Complete History of Mankind's Oldest Taboo.* Santa Monica, CA: Santa Monica Press. 2008. http://users.rcn.com/salski/No18–19Folder/Endocannibalism.htm (Accessed on March 24, 2013).

FANTASY COFFINS

The country of Ghana, located on the Gold Coast of West Africa, is known for elaborate funeral celebrations and processions. One of its unique cultural aspects is the use of fantasy coffins, which are large realistic depictions of popular objects carved out of wood and painted in bright colors. Loved ones are laid to rest in specially crafted coffins in the shape of an object symbolizing the life of the deceased. Farmers are buried in an onion or a cocoa pod (one of the main crops of Ghana). Fishermen's coffins can take the shape of a tuna or a pirogue, the wooden boats found along the entire coast of Ghana. A good mother can be buried in a hen-shaped coffin. A successful businessman can be buried in a white Mercedes Benz, which is the most popular choice for a coffin as it symbolizes wealth and good fortune. Fantasy coffins are made in several workshops across the whole greater Accra region of southeast Ghana. Some of the most famous and successful coffin makers are Daniel Mensah and the two brothers Cedi and Eric Adjetey Anang; they operate multiple carpentry workshops. While most of the fantasy coffins are used for funerals, a few of them are occasionally sold to galleries and art museums. Coffin makers have also been known to make miniature coffins for tourists to take home in their suitcases.

Ghana was the former British colony known as the Gold Coast; it became independent in 1957, but the Europeans left a tangible print in local customs. Europeans have had a presence in Ghana since 1471, when the Portuguese began trading gold and built forts along the coast to protect their interests. The Catholic Portuguese were the first inhabitants of the coast to use coffins to bury their dead. Although Ghana is a small country, it is well known for its traditional arts and crafts. Ghanaian craftsmen are celebrated for their creativity and technique, and they are famous for such products as kente cloth, adinkra stamps, brass weights for gold, pottery, basket weaving, and woodwork.

While the Ashanti are the largest ethnic group of Ghana, it is the Ga people, situated around the capital of Accra in the southeastern coastal region, who are the creators of the fantasy coffins. Custom coffins are not an ancient tradition but rather a contemporary creation. The coffins were first built in the 1950s in rural villages where traditional beliefs are still practiced. Now, they have become part of Ghanaian funeral culture.

The attraction of fantasy coffins can be explained by the history and religious beliefs of the Ga people. The Ga carried their chiefs in *palanquins*. One chief had his palanquin (a litter he sat in carried by four men) made in the shape of a cocoa pod. Before he could use it, he died. The royal court decided that he would be buried in the cocoa pod-shaped palanquin. Others began to honor their dead in the same way. Honoring the dead is crucial to the Ga tribes due to their belief that death is not the end. Instead, a person's life continues in the next world in the same way it did on earth. When a person dies, his or her soul remains closely linked to his or her body for three days. The soul then wanders freely for a year until the celebration of the final rite (*faafo*) when it crosses the river into the world of shadows. A person has the same social status in this shadow world as he or she had in life. The coffins, which symbolize the dead person's profession in life, help continue with his or her earthly profession in the afterlife.

As the dead become ancestors, they are considered to be much more powerful than they were as living human beings. They can now influence the fortunes of their living relatives. Families do everything they can to ensure that a dead person will be helpful and sympathetic toward them. They want to appease any angry or vindictive feelings the ancestor might have toward his family. The more powerful and wealthy a person was in life, the more the family needs to make sure the dead have been treated to a proper funeral that reflects the status they held while they were alive.

Ghana is now predominantly a Christian country, and the only fantasy coffin acceptable to the church is the Bible. The other fantasy coffins are not allowed to enter the church; they only travel from the deceased's home to the cemetery. The church is also keenly aware of multiple traditional rituals sometimes performed at the burial site, but it does not condone them.

In Ghana, many families purchase expensive coffins due to the necessity to show proper respect to the deceased. They also spend large amounts of money on elaborate funeral celebrations. Younger people are buried at less expense, but the amount spent on a funeral is usually greater than the amount spent on health care when the person was alive. Everyone in the community is expected to attend the funeral, which can last several days, and they usually will contribute financially to the cost. Donations and the donor are explicitly announced during a part of the funeral at the deceased's house. People donate money to funerals, and they expect that in the future their own funeral will be just as lavish an event. Even with the donations, funerals are still a financial burden on families. The cost of the event includes the morticians, the fantasy coffin, musicians, meals, and libation for hundreds of guests. Sometimes families have to sell property or assets to pay for the funerals—even to the point of incurring a large debt. Religious leaders have protested against the extravagance of such funerals and have demanded they be curtailed. However, Ghanaians continue to believe that, through the funerals, they are showing their true regard for their deceased family members and respect for ancestors who will be helping them in the future.

Eve Kikawa

Further Readings

Blauer, Etlagale. *African Elegance*. South Africa: Struik Publishers, 1999.

Salm, Steven J., and Toyin Falola. *Culture and Customs of Ghana*. Wesport, CT: Greenwood Press, 2002.

Secretan, Thierry. *Going into Darkness: Fantastic Coffins from Africa*. London: Thames and Hudson Ltd, 1995.

FATTENING ROOMS

Despite the dangers of obesity, and in sharp contrast to slim being a standard of beauty in many Western societies, the Efik tribe of Nigeria popularly lauds the plump woman as the definition of beauty, allure, wealth, and fertility. Consequently, the culture of fattening prospective brides and first daughters of families in preparation for marriage has become a traditional rite of passage into womanhood. As with other societies in the world, different Nigerian ethnic groups have many forms of traditional practices in preparing their women or maidens for marriage. This is to ensure that the girl will be a well-mannered woman who brings her family joy and pride in the way she keeps her home, cares for her family, and carries herself. Overall, Efik culture frowns at slim women and celebrates rotundity as a model of beauty and coming of age. Other cultures in Nigeria that practice fattening include—but may not be limited to—Ibibio, Okrika, and the Anaang tribes. To accomplish such purpose, young Efik Nigerian women are segregated in a special "fattening room" for weeks and even months at a time being constantly fed high doses of complex carbohydrates; in addition, these girls are strongly discouraged from any physical activities.

The culture of fattening rooms (traditionally known in Efik language as *Nkuho*) is said to originate from past centuries when the Efiks lived among Egyptians, and they adapted this custom, which was usually also linked to the ritual of female circumcision. Originally, a female who was to be admitted for *Nkuho* had to undergo female circumcision as a preliminary step. However, this practice is now considered somewhat barbaric, and it is mostly skipped. The ritual of female circumcision is referred to as *Mbobi* in the Efik language, and it always precedes the segregation of the woman into the fattening room. Circumcision was usually performed for three main reasons: as a distinct mark of Efik womanhood, as a check for promiscuity, and also to enhance the erotica by "beautifying" the genitalia. In traditional Efik society, chastity is a virtue that is praised. A good deal of importance was placed on preserving a girl's virginity until marriage and being a faithful and dutiful wife. To discourage early sexual activity, folklore and songs were composed and popularly sang about women who had multiple sexual partners or were wayward for entertainment. As a deterrent to others who were into immoral sexual vices and other detrimental behavior, girls who submitted themselves for circumcision were seen as virtuous women who did not lead promiscuous lives. A girl who was married and found a virgin by her husband on her wedding night brought great pride and joy to her parents and family, and it gave them credence in society by serving as proof that they did a good job of raising her. Moreover, the prevalence of widespread superstitions that predicted doom, barrenness, and an unfulfilling life for an uncircumcised Efik woman also helped the practice thrive, and since no woman particularly enjoys stigma, most felt it was safer to submit to *Mbobi*. The general belief was that the physical risks and pains involved in circumcision were far lesser than the social consequences for staying uncircumcised.

Originally, the process of fattening a girl in a *Nkuho* typically lasted anywhere from six months until up to a year, depending of the financial ability of her family and the presence of a suitor who is expected to give material and financial support to his future wife. However, modernization has really affected this timing, as women have been known to undergo *Nkuho* for as little as three weeks. The reality of contemporary social and economic conditions in Nigeria requires that cultural practices be adapted to the current environment.

After girls have completed the preliminary step of circumcision, they are ready to begin the tradition of entering a fattening room (*Nkuho*). In the next step, a girl is bathed carefully by elderly women who may comprise her aunts and other village women but not her mother. Before entering the water, virgin girls below the age of puberty who are assigned to a fattening room are supposed to make sure that the bath place is devoid of a green insect that is believed to bring ill luck and defeat the benefits and aims of *Nkuho*. The ceremonial bath is then usually performed in a secluded part of the family house, and only a few select females are allowed entry. The girl is then kept away from the public eye for the entire period of fattening until her coming out. Men are strictly forbidden from seeing her or interact with her—not even her fiancé—until the end of the ritual. Only a few of her best friends who are females may visit her to keep her company.

A woman who has been admitted to the long process of fattening rooms is typically fed about six meals daily of starchy carbohydrates and other classes of food,

FATTENING ROOM REALITY TELEVISION, AFRICAN STYLE

For the Efik people in the Calabar region of Nigeria, a full-figured woman is more desirable for marriage than someone with a thin body. Based on this tradition, EbonyLife Television based in Lagos, Nigeria, recently launched a reality show titled *Fattening Room* in the Summer of 2013; it became an instant hit with extremely high ratings in over forty-six African countries. The show follows the process of fattening up six girls from different countries: Ghana, South Africa, Nigeria, Kenya, Botswana, and Zambia. The variety of cast members reveals that this traditional cultural practiced is not limited to Nigeria, but it is rather extensive in multiple countries of sub-Saharan Africa. The show became successful based on the premise of taking an ancient tradition and giving it a modern twist. Even men are incredibly interested in this reality program, mostly because the process of how this cultural practice was actually done has always been carried out in secrecy.

Javier A. Galván

such as cassava; rice; yams; beans; plantain; fish; meat; and traditional meals like ayan ekpan, ekpan kukwo, and other pepper soups. The entire menu is aimed at making her figure fuller. She is served these meals frequently and is encouraged to eat them consistently. After eating so much every day, she is expected to rest and take long naps. Her cutlery and bath essentials are not to be shared with anyone, and she is to sit on a special stool made exclusively for her. Moreover, strenuous activities and/or any type of physical exercise are expressively forbidden. Although civilization has modified some aspects of this ritual, many parents of daughters and prospective brides—particularly those who have attained puberty—continue to ignore the financial expenses of *Nkuho* and still participate in the ritual. The cost is extremely high to provide all the food, pay the personnel to cook and prepare the food, and pay people who provide constant care for the girl at every hour of the day. As a result, some fathers feel socially inadequate if they cannot afford to sponsor their daughters through the fattening process.

The ideal of a round female figure has become so accepted that nowadays other women in Nigeria—who are not from tribes that practice fattening—have been known to willingly submit themselves for *Nkuho* because fat is still regarded in parts of Nigeria (and a large part of Africa) as a sign of affluence and allure. Many of these nontribal women describe *Nkuho* as having similarities with spa treatments in the sense that the recipient of the ceremony is physically groomed and treated to lavish massages with herbs, native chalk, and special oils to aid the fatting process, proper blood circulation, and a brighter skin. However, a spa is not half as intrusive as the fattening rooms, which also offers very particular lessons and training in home-keeping, intimate massages, child care, cooking traditional meals, satisfying her husband sexually, and how to cope with the future in-laws. As part of the fattening process, women are also advised on how to be upstanding members of society, and they are taught traditional folklore and dances such as *Ekombi*, which is a special wedding dance a girl is expected to perform on the day she comes out of the fattening room, on completing *Nkuho*.

Once women complete the rite of passage based on the fattening rooms tradition, the family may send out invitation cards, inviting guests comprising family, friends, and well-wishers for a coming-out party (coming out of the fattening room). In cases where there is an acceptable suitor, the event will result in an elaborate wedding. Most Efik men in Nigeria support their wives to go through *Nkuho*, and they are happy to receive her on her coming-out day because the pervading theory is that thick hips are useful for child bearing, and most Efik men in Nigeria love more flesh for cuddling. Naturally, since most of these coming-out parties are also marriage ceremonies, they turn out to be very lavish affairs. Traditional culinary delicacies like Atama, Afang soup, and Ekpan Kukwo are usually served at the occasion.

For the wedding, the new full-figured woman is dressed traditionally in bright and elaborate attire, with her hair decorated and beaded, in a stylish up do, with fancy hair combs stuck in. As part of the festivities, there is a short procession where the bride is escorted by young girls who are dressed in similar traditional costumes, amid cheers, singing, and dancing. As part of the celebration, a special dance called *Abang* (meaning 'pot') is performed at the event, in reference to the rite of passage she has completed that has made her as round as a pot. At the marriage ceremony, there are eating, dancing, and merriment with generous gifts and presents showered on the happy couple amid prayers and good wishes.

Veronny Odili Okwei

Further Readings

Blankson Ikpe, Eno. "Human Sexuality in Nigeria: A Historical Perspective." *Understanding Human Sexuality Seminar Papers*. Lagos, Nigeria: Africa Regional Sexuality Resource Center. July 29, 2004. http://www.docstoc.com/docs/34892784/Human-Sexuality-in-Nigeria-A-Historical-Perspective (Accessed on September 7, 2012).

Oloruntoba-Oju, Taiwo. "Body Images, Beauty, Culture and Language in the Nigeria African Context." *Understanding Human Sexuality Seminar Papers*. University of Ibadan Nigeria: Africa Regional Sexuality Resource Center. September 13, 2007. http://www.arsrc.org/publications/uhsss/index.html (Accessed on September 7, 2012).

Simmons, Ann M. "Where Fat Is a Mark of Beauty." *Los Angeles Times*. September 30, 1998. http://articles.latimes.com/1998/sep/30/news/mn-27869 (Accessed on September 7, 2012).

Tiemoko, Richmond. "Preliminary Findings on Youth, Sexuality, and Marriage in Selected African Countries." *Sexuality in Africa Journal* 3, no. 1 (2006): 11–13. http://www.arsrc.org/downloads/sia/mar06/jan06.pdf (Accessed on September 7, 2012).

Tobe, Eteng, Ikpi. "Socio-Cultural Determinants of Sexual Behaviors and Trafficking in Children and Adolescents in the South-South Geo-Political Zone of Nigeria." Doctoral Dissertation in Sociology, University of Zululand, South Africa, Department of Sociology Faculty of Arts, June 2009.

FEMALE GENITAL CUTTING AND MUTILATION

In modern times, Western governments have begun to discuss whether the alteration of human genitalia is a human rights violation. Most Westerners have heard of male circumcision, frequently practiced as a religious rite by Jews, Muslims, ethnic groups in eastern and southern Africa, and some Pacific Islander cultures. A significant percentage of secular Western parents—particularly those in the United States—believe in the necessity of male circumcision for medical reasons. The Western world is less familiar, however, with the practice of female genital cutting (FGC), often called "female circumcision" or "female genital mutilation" (FGM) by those who are against the practice.

FGC is the collective name assigned to traditional rituals involving partial or complete removal of the female external genitalia. These rituals predate Muslim, Christian, and Jewish religious practices. Historically, the first specific mention of FGC appeared in an ancient Egyptian hieroglyphic text ca. 2400 BCE, in which God Uha notes his circumcision along with 120 men and 120 women. Ancient Greek historian Herotodus noted FGC among the Phonecians, Hittites, and Ethiopians in the fifth century BCE, and Agatharchides of Cnidus (a later Greek historian) described female circumcision as a common Egyptian practice in the second century BCE. Early Romans and Arabs had also adopted the practice, perhaps from their Egyptian subjects.

In ancient Egypt, people believed that gods as well as people were endowed with masculine and feminine "souls," revealed through their genitalia. Ancient Egyptians believed that the feminine soul of a man lived in his foreskin, and that the masculine soul of a woman lived in her clitoris. When children reached a certain age—and were ready to take part in adult male or female society—they had to rid themselves of their respective non-male or non-female properties. This belief was accomplished through male and female circumcision. Only a girl who experienced FGC could claim to be a woman ca-

A former circumciser displays the tools for the trade (a knife and herbs) in Senegal. (AP Photo/ Alexandra Zavis)

pable of sexual activity and reproduction. Historians have also suggested that FGC originated in the patriarchal family system, where a woman could have only one husband while a man could have several wives. FGC restricted women's sexuality for the preservation of the male lineage.

During the nineteenth century, physicians in English-speaking countries believed that FGC, or "clitoral excision," would cure lesbian practices and lesbian inclinations, as well as "hypersexuality," hysteria, and anxiety. Up until 1935, American medical reports described clitoral excision and removal of the inner and outer labia to curb female masturbation, particularly in mental hospitals. This practice lasted in British hospitals until the 1940s.

Theories that drove Western doctors to perform clitoral excision and labioplasties remain alive and well in nations where FGC is still prevalent. In the cultures of such countries, the clitoris is perceived as an "aggressive" organ, threatening the penis and potentially endangering the infant during labor. It is also believed that the clitoris will grow into a penis-like organ if it is not removed, and that removal of the clitoris will protect the girl from strong sexual urges, saving her from temptation and thus preserving her chastity. In truth, due to the pain experienced during the procedure and healing process, a woman would think twice before having sexual intercourse, as penetration would literally tear her open. The scars that result from FGC are physical evidence of a girl's virginity, an absolute requirement for marriage in some cultures.

The World Health Organization has identified four specific classifications of FGC:

Type I: Removal of the clitoral hood, almost always accompanied by removal of the entire clitoris (clitoridectomy);

Type II: Removal of the clitoris and inner labia;

Type III: Removal of all or part of the inner and outer labia, and usually the clitoris, and the fusion of the wound, leaving a small hole for the passage of urine and menstrual blood. This fused wound is opened for intercourse and childbirth.

Type IV: Other harmful procedures to the female genitalia for nonmedical purposes, such as pricking, piercing, incising, scraping, stretching, burning, or scarring. Procedures such as hymen removal, tightening the vagina, and cutting vaginal walls are included in this category.

According to the World Health Organization, between 100 and 140 million women around the world have experienced FGC; furthermore, it is estimated that three million girls and women still undergo the procedure every year. Approximately 85 percent of women who go through FGC experience Types I or II, and 15 percent experience Type III. In Somalia, Sudan, and Djibouti, Type III is the most common procedure. The age when girls undergo FGC varies from region to region. In Yemen, girls most commonly experience FGC as early as two weeks old; in Egypt, girls undergo FGC anywhere from five to fourteen years old. In most countries that practice FGC, the practice is completed before the girl reaches puberty. It is customary for mothers to arrange for the procedure, and for an older woman known as a *gedda*—or traditional circumciser—to carry it out. FGC may also be done by the girl's grandmother. Most of these traditional arrangements involve no anesthetic or sterilization of cutting instruments. Traditional practitioners have used multiple devices such as razor blades, knives, scissors, cut glass, sharpened rocks, and fingernails to cut the genitalia; then, they traditionally use agave or acacia thorns to stitch the wound. Wealthier families may pay for a nurse, midwife, or doctor to perform the procedure with local anesthetic and sterile medical equipment. In Nigeria and Egypt, the local male barber frequently performs the procedure.

FGC often results in serious medical problems for women; immediate complications include urinary retention, urinary infection, wound infection, septicemia, tetanus, increased risk of hepatitis, and HIV when unsterile and reused instruments are employed. Although UNICEF has stated that the number of girls and women who die from the procedure remains unknown due to lack of records and negative reports, Nigerian midwife Comfort Momoh estimates that 10 percent of girls and women die shortly after the procedure due to infection, hemorrhage, or shock. Long-term complications from FGC include incontinence, chronic vaginal and pelvic infections, cysts, preeclampsia, and either irregular painful menstruation or lack of menstruation altogether. Women who undergo FGC are more likely to have Cesarean operations than women who do not have the procedure, and FGC increases the risk of infant mortality. The spread of HIV and AIDS in Africa is sometimes also partially attributed to FGC, due to the exchange of blood.

The World Health Organization has documented FGC in twenty-eight African countries and Yemen. Non-government organizations (NGOs), Muslim women's groups, and anti-FGM organizations have also documented FGC in all Middle Eastern countries and among the Muslim populations in Malaysia and Indonesia. The practice is most prevalent on the African continent's equatorial band, particularly in those countries that make up "the horn" of Africa. More than 80 percent of women in Somalia, Djibouti, Ethiopia, Eritrea, and Sudan have endured FGC. In most cases, these women from the Horn of Africa have also experienced infibulation, which involves the complete removal of internal and external labia as well as the clitoris. Somali model Waris Dirie and writer Ayaan Hirsi Ali have played a major role in informing the Western world about FGC in Somalia through their books, films, and public presentations; over 90 percent of Somali women have experienced FGC, and most frequently infibulation.

FGC is practiced by Christians, Muslims, Ethiopian Jews, and animists, but the Western world associates the procedure mostly with Islam. While female circumcision is noted in the Koran, it is identified as an "honorable" practice for women and not required as male circumcision. Islamic religious scholars from around the world have issued *fatwas* (a religious decree announced by an Islamic leader) for and against the practice, and the governments of Egypt, Djibouti, Eritrea, Kenya, Nigeria, Senegal, Tanzania, Uganda—all nations with significant Muslim populations—have outlawed the practice. However, due to severe social pressures, women continue to perpetuate the FGC tradition. In many cases, FGC is a steady income stream for women who perform the procedure; their opportunities to earn income through other means may be limited due to religious or legal restrictions.

THE UNITED NATIONS BANNED FEMALE GENITAL MUTILATION IN 2012

February 12, 2012, is an important day for the rights of women worldwide. On this date, the 194 member nations of the United Nations General Assembly passed a significant resolution to end the harmful practice of female genital mutilation (FGM). It was a unanimous vote of approval. This decision urges the member states to enforce violations but also go beyond simply criminalizing the practice. The UN urges countries to also offer services for girls and women who are victims of this practice, as well as to create locally based activities that directly address this tradition with the goal of changing social norms. In addition, nations are encouraged to provide enough funds for programs that protect girls and women from violence related to FGM.

Source: http://www.unwomen.org/en/news/stories/2012/12/united-nations-bans-female-genital-mutilation

Javier A. Galván

The World Health Organization, NGOs, and others who wish to abolish FGC have developed strategies to discourage people from engaging in the practice. Community meetings that include cross-generational workshops, male–female discussions, musical productions, and hiring respected local women to teach women and girls in their communities about the harmful effects of FGC have proven successful. In some countries, communities have replaced FGC with a substitute ritual that does not harm the genitals. Although the World Health Organization reports a decline in new FGC cases, activists and academic researchers believe that the tradition is just as strong as before, but going underground, and being practiced on girls at even younger ages. Meanwhile, an increasing number of women have sought asylum in countries where FGC is illegal, while other immigrants from FGC-practicing regions sometimes wish to continue this practice. This controversy has pushed Western healthcare workers to learn more about FGC in order to help women who have experienced the procedure, as well as to educate immigrants about the danger of the practice and its legal implications. As of 2012, U.S. federal law has declared that the practice of FGC on anyone younger than eighteen years is a felony punishable by fines or a prison term. This legal restriction, however, does not necessarily stop parents from sending their daughters out of the country during school vacations in order to perform the procedure.

Rachel Wexelbaum

Further Readings

Horowitz, Carol, and J. Carey Jackson. "Female 'Circumcision': African Women Confront American Medicine." *Journal of General Internal Medicine* 12, no. 8 (August 1997): 491–99. http://www.ncbi.nlm.nih.gov/pmc/articles/PMC1497147/ (Accessed on August 26, 2012).

McVeigh, Tracy, and Tara Sutton. "British Girls Undergo Horror of Mutilation Despite Tough Laws." *The Guardian.* July 25, 2010. http://www.guardian.co.uk/society/2010/jul/25/female-circumcision-children-british-law (Accessed on August 26, 2012).

Momo, Comfort. *Female Genital Mutilation.* Oxon, UK: Radcliffe Publishing Ltd, 2005.

UNICEF. *Female Genital Mutilation/Cutting: A Statistical Exploration.* 2005. http://www.unicef.org/publications/files/FGM-C_final_10_October.pdf (Accessed on August 26, 2012).

von der Osten-Sacken, Thomas, and Thomas Uwer. "Is Female Genital Mutilation an Islamic Problem?" *The Middle East Quarterly* 14, no. 1 (Winter 2007): 29–36. http://www.meforum.org/1629/is-female-genital-mutilation-an-islamic-problem (Accessed on August 26, 2012).

Wasunna, Angela. "Toward Redirecting the Female Circumcision Debate: Legal, Ethical, and Cultural Considerations." *McGill Journal of Medicine* 5, no. 2 (2000): 104–10. http://www.medicine.mcgill.ca/mjm/v05n02/v05p104/v05p104.pdf (Accessed on August 26, 2012).

Webber, Sara, and Toby Schonfeld. "Cutting History, Cutting Culture: Female Circumcision in the United States." *The American Journal of Bioethics* 3, no. 2 (Spring 2003): 65–66.

World Health Organization. *Female Genital Mutilation.* http://www.who.int/topics/female_genital_mutilation/en/ (Accessed on August 26, 2012).

FERIA DE LAS FLORES, FESTIVAL OF FLOWERS IN MEDELLÍN

The famous Feria de las Flores (also known as the Flower Festival) is celebrated every year in the city of Medellín, Colombia. This international celebration was founded and established by Arturo Uribe, a member of the National Board for the Office of Development and Tourism of Colombia. The first flower festival was first established on May 1, 1957; however, the following year the festival date was changed to the month of August to coincide with the patriotic festivities linked to the independence of Antioquia, Colombia. The festival is a five-day affair composed of a pageant, an antique automobile show, a Paso Fino horse parade, and multiple musical concerts. It also includes a prominent exposition of flowers displayed at the Metropolitan Cathedral.

Social traditions carry valuable significance in every culture, and the Feria de las Flores in Medellín provides a great source of pride for all Colombians. The flower parade also marks the date for the complete abolition of slavery in this South American nation. It is a wonderful way to celebrate the end of an oppressive institution that brought significant pain and suffering for decades and centuries. The festival actually did not start as the flower festival. For many years, men and women carried flowers on their backs up steep hills to represent the slaves who were used as *silleteros*, porters used by colonial officials to carry them and their belongings across the Quindio pass in the Colombia Andes.

With time, the festival evolved into the great parade that it is now with a rich cultural and international flavor. During the week-long parade in the month of August, Colombia attracts tourist from all over the world. They represent a diverse mix of people from the United States, Australia, Europe, neighboring countries in South America, and the surrounding areas near Medellín. In terms of tourism spending, the month of August is one of the most profitable periods for the region and Colombia in general. Tourists take pleasure on the different activities that the town has to offer, such as a trail ride through town on horses, orchid competitions, a legendary music festival, and the parade of the *silleros*, except that the *silleros* now carry bundles of flowers in baskets up a steep hill. The celebration of the Flower Festival in the month of August could be equivalent to the Fourth of July celebration in the United States, but the most salient difference is the length of time (one week) of the festivities in Colombia.

This colorful lively cultural event kicks off with an amazing fireworks show along with a dog and mascot walk, and the National Trova Festival, which is a renowned series of concerts based on jazz music. The celebrations also continue with a Classic and Antique car parade, the Sanalejo Market, the colorful Orchids, Flower and Birds Expo, the National Equestrian Fair, and the famous Humor City, which is a great show of comedians and good humor for the entire family. In addition, the event includes a fantastic orchestra festival, a horse ride through town, a caravan of *chivas* (goats), popular and folk music concerts, children activities, and various cultural displays. Finally, the festival ends the same way as it started, with a great fireworks show to end a week-long celebration of the Feria de las Flores.

The preparations of the festival take practically the entire year. Once the festival is over—and all the committee members involved have taken a much-deserved break—they go back to planning the festival for the upcoming year. Every year, the committee in charge of the festival strives to make it grander and better than the year before. They do it by planning on better performances and more spectacular shows to help attract more tourists to their beautiful country to experience this cultural tradition that they have upheld for so many years. They plan everything down to the smallest detail: they have to plan what kind of performances they should have and what type of flowers will be used to represent their great tradition. Overall, this unique parade and festival is intended to reflect the cultural pride of the Colombian people.

Every culture has traditions and customs that represent its national heritage and culture, and people usually love to it share with the world. These traditions are what make every culture unique to its land and its surroundings. In addition, travelers are constantly looking for new experiences. In the case of Medellín, La Feria de las Flores is a great way for Colombians to expose their beautiful tradition to the world. Sharing all the beautiful flowers found and grown in the region is the best way to maintain a tradition that has been ongoing for several years, and the popularity of the Feria de las Flores in turn ensures its continuity.

To be a traveler, people need to have an open mind and be willing to try new experiences. The festivities in Medellín, Colombia, have a mesmerizing effect due to the beauty that thousands and thousands of flower displays offered throughout the city in a celebratory environment. La Feria de las Flores is a cultural tradition rooted in national history and pride, and people from Medellín hold it dear to their hearts. By being active participants in the parade, musical performances, and community gatherings, the local people ensure that their tradition will never die. Moreover, the Feria de las Flores allows Colombians to reach out to the world and invite an increasing number of international visitors to share in their colorful and musical annual celebration.

Alejandra Tapia

Further Readings

Cathey, Kate. *Colombia—Culture Smart: The Essential Guide to Customs and Culture*. London: Kuperard Publishers, 2011.

Discover Colombia, Official Visitors Guide. http://discovercolombia.com/medellin (Accessed on January 6, 2013).

Knight, Dave. *Medellin, Colombia: Including Its History, the Festival of Flowers, Candelaria Church, Plaza Cisneros, and More*. New York: Earth Eyes Travel Guides, 2012.

Official Website for the Feria de las Flores Festival and the City of Medellin. http://feriad elasflores.medellin.travel/ (Accessed on February 15, 2013).

FIESTA DE SANTIAGO Y VEJIGANTES

The *Fiesta de Santiago Apóstol* (Festival of Saint James the Apostle) has been celebrated in Loíza, a municipality on the northeast coast of Puerto Rico, at least since the first half of the nineteenth century. The exact origins of the *fiesta* are vague. The popular belief is that it has its roots in the sixteenth-century Spanish culture, combined with African elements. However, as has recently been put forward, the Loíza Festival seems to be—like many other festivities—a blend of various "universal" aspects of human rituals and celebrations and some more specific cultural elements and performances. The *fiesta* combines religious and secular elements, which include masses and *novenas*, on the one hand, and popular music, drumming, masks, and costumes as well as house parties on the other hand. During the festivities, popular food and drinks are sold.

A *vejigante* mask and outfit used in Ponce's carnival. (Courtesy of Javier A. Galván)

The central part of the *fiesta*, which is celebrated around the end of July, is the processions for three images of Santiago, which are held on three consecutive days beginning on July 26. The festival is, however, a mixture of religious ceremonies and colorful folk festivities, which include the participation of four principal types of characters: *caballeros* (knights or gentlemen), *vejigantes* (devils or diablo tricksters), *las locas* (cross-dressed crazy women), and *los viejos* (old men). They accompany the saint during the processions, dancing in front of the carried image and the devotees. After the processions are over, dancing, merry-making, feasting, and drinking continue into the night. The typical genres of music that accompanies the festival are *bomba* and *plena*. The main location for this celebration is the town of Loíza. The cultural tradition is so strong that many emigrants from Loíza residing in the United States return to Puerto Rico to participate in the *fiesta*. In recent decades, the festivity has also grown in popularity among tourists.

The community of Loíza is home to a predominantly black community, which has retained its traditional character due to its ethnic homogeneity and relative isolation from other communities. The town is an early settlement, in which blacks quickly came to form the majority of the population. In 1719, Loíza was the seventh largest town on the island. In 1910, the municipal capital was moved south to the barrio Canóvanas, a prosperous ward with a significant white population, while isolated Loíza Aldea was left stagnant. The official separation of the municipalities of Loíza and Canóvanas took place in 1971. Recently, the town has struggled with unemployment and a high crime rates as well as financial problems. Hoping to develop tourism, it has been promoted as a "Capital of Tradition." The *fiesta* of Santiago has become an important element of the *loiceño* identity and the

image of Santiago forms part of the municipality's emblem. The *fiesta*, which originally lasted for three days, has now been prolonged to ten days.

Although since 1645 the official patron saint of Loíza has been San Patri-
cio (St. Patrick), it is Santiago who finds here his faithful devotees. There are
various hypotheses concerning the origin and significance of the festival of
St. James. The cult of St. James the Moor-Slayer (*Matamoros*)—a Christian warrior fighting against the Moors—was important in Spain during the Reconquest
(*reconquista*) of the Peninsula. In Latin America, *Santiago Matamoros* was transformed into *Santiago Mataindios* (the Indian-Slayer)—fighting against the Indians. The Spanish dance-drama of Moors and Christians (*danza de Moros y
Cristianos*) brought to Latin America came to depict the fight between the Spanish (good) and the Indians (bad). In fact, today *la danza* is found throughout
in the region, under a variety of names (e.g., *danza de la conquista*, *danza de
los Moros*, and *danza de Santiago*). The cult of Santiago may have taken root in
Loíza due to the constant need of defending the settlement against the attacks
of Indians and European corsairs. Also, the two main characters of the Loíza
festivity—*vejigantes* and *caballeros*—are sometimes identified as *Moros* (the evil)
and *Cristianos* (the good).

The findings of the early research on the origin of the festival conducted in the
1940s and 1950s were dominant for about four decades and had a great influence
on the popular beliefs about the *fiesta*. They described the festival as a combination
of Spanish culture and the African Yoruba traditions of the slave population. According to this hypothesis, Santiago was identified by blacks with the African god
of war (Shangó). The fact that the most faithful devotees of Santiago are among the
black population may support the syncretism hypothesis.

The Yoruba influence thesis has recently been contested by other scholars, who
have pointed to the Bantu—not Yoruba—origin of the early slave population in
Loíza. Recent research also stresses (Iberian) carnival traditions (e.g., *diablitos*, carnival's alternative hierarchies of power or bladders carried by medieval fools) and
the "universals" of festive performance (e.g., cross-dressing, dancing, and self-
decoration) rather than the syncretic fusion of European and African elements.
Vejigantes and *caballeros*, thus, appear as carnivalesque figures, ethnic caricatures,
who only happen to exhibit similarities to *Moros y Cristianos*.

During the Festival of Saint James, the Apostle's three different images of Santiago take part in the processions—*Santiago de los Hombres* (Santiago of the Men),
Santiago de las Mujeres (Santiago of the Women), and *Santiaguito or Santiago de los
Niños* (Santiago of the Children). The latter is believed to work miracles for the
powerless. The first day of the processions, July 26, is dedicated to *Santiago de los
Hombres*; however the other two images join in the parade. The procession goes
from the center of Loíza to the ward of Medianía, accompanied by a colorful parade of *vejigantes*, *caballeros*, and other characters. When it reaches the neighborhood of Las Carreras, where *Santiaguito* is believed to have appeared beneath the
cork tree, a traditional race of horsemen with flags takes place. Then the procession makes the journey back, leaving all three images back with their *mantenedoras*
(keepers or guardians). The second day belongs to *Santiago de las Mujeres*, which

is joined in the parade only by *Santiaguito*. On the last, usually the most attended, day of the processions *Santiago de los Niños* reigns alone.

Four different types of character participate in the celebrations. *Losvejigantes* are believed to represent the evil, the Moors. The very name *vejigante* is derived from the Spanish word for "bladder" (*vejiga*). During the celebrations, *vejigantes* traditionally carried inflated dried cow (or goat) bladders on a stick and chased children and women. Today balloons or paper bags are commonly used. The most typical *vejigante* costume is a loose garment made of brilliantly colorful and patterned fabric, with batwings. The typical Loíza *vejigante* mask is made of a painted coconut shell, with horns. The masks display exaggerated features, interpreted to be African. *Vejigante* is the most typical character of the festival and has become internationally famous.

Los caballeros (knights, Spanish gentlemen) wear pale-faced and blue-eyed masks made of wire mesh. Their costumes pretend to be rich, sometimes with flowers in their hats. *Los viejos* (old men)—the third type of characters that appears during the festival—wear ragged clothes and cardboard masks, while *las locas* (cross-dressed crazy women)—the fourth type—have their faces blackened, and breasts and buttocks exaggerated. They carry cans and brooms. *Las locas* tease and flirt with the spectators. Today they are often played by transvestites.

Other variations of the *Fiestas de Santiago y Vejigantes* are also found in Ponce—Puerto Rico's second largest city—during the pre-Lenten carnival celebrations in February. As in Loíza, *vejigantes* in Ponce wear brightly colored costumes. The richly painted masks with horns and sharp teeth are, however, made of papier-mâché and not of coconut shells.

The festival of Santiago Apóstol de Loíza is also celebrated in the United States. Most of the emigrants from Loíza reside in New Haven, Connecticut, where the celebrations have been organized since 1977 by *Fiestas de Loíza en Connecticut en Honor al Apostol Santiago*. The *fiesta* is also celebrated in New York's East Harlem. Many people also visit Puerto Rico to celebrate the *fiesta* in Loíza. Nonetheless, the *loiceños* who are not present in the town are also honored on one of the days of the *fiesta*.

Anna Kaganiec-Kamieńska

Further Readings

Alegría, Ricardo E. "The Fiesta of Santiago Apostol (St. James the Apostle) in Loíza, Puerto Rico." *The Journal of American Folklore* 69, no. 272 (1956): 123–34.

Fiestas de Loiza en Connecticut in Honor al Apostol Santiago (FLECHAS). http://www.flechasct.org/ (Accessed on November 5, 2012).

Galván, Javier A. *Culture and Customs of Puerto Rico.* Westport, CT: Greenwood Press, 2009.

Harris, Max. "Masking the Site: The Fiestas de Santiago Apóstol in Loíza, Puerto Rico." *The Journal of American Folklore* 114, no. 453 (2001): 358–69.

Hernández Hiraldo, Samiri, and Mariana Ortega-Brena. "'If God Were Black and from Loíza': Managing Identities in a Puerto Rican Seaside Town." *Latin American Perspectives* 33, no. 1 (2006): 66–82.

The Puerto Rican Festival and Parade of Rhode Island Inc. http://www.puertoricanri.com/statefestivals.htm (Accessed on November 5, 2012).

The Puerto Rico Online Encyclopedia (PROE). http://www.enciclopediapr.org/ing/ (Accessed on November 11, 2012).

Sargasso, 2006–07, II. "Re/Visions of Santiago Apóstol: Art, History, and Cultural Criticism." University of Puerto Rico. http://ufdc.ufl.edu/UF00096005/00020/3 (Accessed on November 10, 2012).

FIESTAS DE QUITO

The annual Fiestas de Quito is a week-long series of festivities that take place in the capital of Ecuador to celebrate the anniversary of the date the city was founded. It is a combination of events, including a marathon, dance parties, card games, bull fights, dances, theater performances, exhibitions, concerts, a beauty contest, and other cultural activities designed to attract people of all ages. The contemporary city of Quito, officially named San Francisco de Quito, has a population of over two-and-a-half million people, and it is situated in the north-western part of Ecuador close to the Equator line, which gave the country its name. The Historic Center of Quito is the part of the city where all major events of the Fiestas de Quito take place. This historical location is an architectural gem that was one of the first cultural heritage sites to be declared by UNESCO in 1978 into its registry of important global cultural locations.

The festival is held to celebrate what is regarded as the date when the capital city was founded; the official date is considered to be December 6, 1563. Nevertheless, the city itself had existed much earlier. It was first inhabited by the local tribe of the Shyries, and it later became part of the Inca Empire during the fifteenth century. The year 1563 is accepted as the official date of the city's founding because this is the year when the Spanish colonizers (203 in number and led by Sebastian de Belancazar), after a bloody conquest against the Incas, entered the city to rule for the succeeding three centuries as part of the Spanish Empire in the Americas. The first celebration of the founding of the Spanish Quito was held in 1934, to mark the fourth centenary of the city. Unlike the contemporary festival, it lasted for only one day: December 6. The event was patronized by the Archbishop of Quito, who, for the first time ever, allowed local monasteries and convents to open the doors of their museums to the general public. Despite its heavy coverage in the newspapers of the period, the celebration had not been continued until 1958. It was during that year that a local journalist named Don Caesar Larrea made a popular appeal to revive the celebration. Since then, the festival started to take its contemporary shape, with some key activities becoming repeated annually up to the present days.

The first event in a series of celebrations of the Fiestas de Quito is the beauty pageant that results in electing the *Reina de Quito* (the Queen of Quito). Then, the start of the festival is announced in the Plaza San Francisco (St. Francis Square) with an announcement made by the mayor of the city. Once the festivities get on their way, it becomes apparent that it features a diverse multitude of festive activities combining vigor traditionally associated with Latin American carnival, remnants of Spanish heritage, and unique local forms of celebration.

One of the most characteristic features of Fiestas de Quito is the *chivas*, which are specially decorated open-side buses that make slow tours around the historical center of Quito every night during the week of celebrations. Surprisingly enough, these buses are made of local wood, to mark their uniqueness and to celebrate the ancient history of the Ecuadorean capital. Throughout the festival, these buses are usually full of passengers, who enjoy the music of a live brass band performing from the top of the bus, sing together, proclaim their admiration for the city, and even dance on top of these slow-moving buses. Somewhat in a contrast to the slow *chivas* buses, the festival also features a traditional *Maratón de Últimas Noticias*. This is a ride in wooden go-carts, and the participants are usually children from different districts of the city. The event takes place along the Olmego Street, and the steepness of the street throughout the whole 10-kilometer (6.3 miles) distance makes carts reach rather fast speed, contributing to the general excitement of the *fiestas*. The overall festive mood is maintained by another specific feature of the celebration: *canelazo*, which is a hot cocktail with cinnamon. This drink, together with many other traditional dishes of Ecuadorean and Spanish cuisine, is served in the many restaurants and clubs of Quito.

Music is a crucial component of the Fiestas de Quito. Both in clubs and on the streets, many concerts take place simultaneously throughout the week. Quite frequently, these musical events are reported to be the most popular and the most-attended parts of the fiestas. The two music styles featuring most prominently are mariachi songs and flamenco dances. Mariachi is a sort of urban folk music that appeared in Mexico in the early twentieth century, and it is believed to have originated from wedding songs (hence the word mariachi derived from the French word "marriage"). Flamenco is a traditional southern Spanish dance to the accompaniment of singing and guitar playing. The combination of these music styles in Fiestas de Quito reflects open and broadly Hispanic, rather than purely local, flavor of the festival.

Other interesting and essential parts of the celebration include the quarente, or *cuarenta* (translated as "forty") card tournament. Although *cuarenta* is a traditional Ecuadorean card game, it is most often played during the festival. It can be played both individually and in teams; in general terms, it is based on "capturing" opponents' cards by matching values. Players can enter both individually and in teams, and the annual tournament held during the *fiestas* never ceases to attract the best cuarenta players of Quito, but it is also interesting to newcomers who are just curious to learn the game.

One of the most prominent—but lately also the most controversial features of the Fiestas de Quito—is the bullfighting festival. Quito's bullfighting event is called the Jesus of Great Power, and it takes place at the *Plaza de Toros* (translated literally as "the Square of Bulls"). This venue was originally designed as a bull ring, but it is used for this purpose only once a year as a part of the festival. This *corrida* (bull run) is probably the most recognizable of all Spanish traditions, and as such it is the most obvious display of the Spanish roots of Ecuadoreans. It was partly for this reason that bullfighting was considered to be the most prestigious and elite part of the whole week-long, activity-packed celebration. For this reason, it attracted not only top bullfighters but also crowds of festively dressed spectators, and it now generates an estimate of US$15 million in revenues every year. The number of bulls killed annually during the festival's bullfighting is between forty and sixty. In 2011, local authorities decided to place restrictions on the technical procedures of bullfighting. First, only a third from a former number of weapons, such as *banderillas* (decorated sharp sticks used by a type of toreadors named banderilleros), was allowed to remain in use. Second, the bull was no longer permitted to be killed within the bull ring. In the year 2012, however, for the first time in the history of the Fiestas de Quito, the traditional bullfighting was excluded from the program of the festival. The government announced the decision shortly before the start of the week of celebration, and it caused numerous protests from the organizers. The reason for this drastic decision, however, was the outcome of the previously held national referendum. The special ballot took place in Ecuador on May 7, 2011. It featured a large array of questions related to political, social, and cultural issues, such as the regulation of media content. However, the most controversial and hotly debated issue proved to be the proposed ban on killing animals for entertainment (i.e., in the course of bull fights and cock fights). Eventually, the question had to be changed from a total ban to a decision restricted to a municipality. In Quito, unlike some smaller towns, the ban on killing animals in spectacles was approved by a considerable margin. Despite the loss of one of its former distinctive features, the Fiestas of Quito of 2012, same as in earlier years, made for a week of fervent celebration, requiring not so much top-down regulation as enthusiasm and exuberance.

Marharyta Fabrykant

Further Readings

Cañizares-Esguerra, Jorge, et al. "City Fragments Space and Nostalgia in Modernizing Quito, 1885–1942." Doctoral Dissertation in History, University of Texas at Austin, 2005.
Capello, Ernesto. *City at the Center of the World: Space, History, and Modernity in Quito.* Pittsburgh: University of Pittsburgh Press, 2011.
Capello, Ernesto. "Imaging old Quito." *CITY* 10, no. 2 (2006): 125–147.
"Fiestas de Quito." http://www.vivatravelguides.com/south-america/ecuador/ecuador-overview/holidays/fiestas-de-quito/ (Accessed on March 1, 2013).
"Fiestas de Quito—Founder's Day in Quito." http://www.ecuadorexplorer.com/html/fiestas_de_quito.html (Accessed on March 1, 2013).
"Fiestas de Quito—Toasting to the History and Character of the Capital." http://www.volunteeringecuador.info/travel/the-fiestas-de-quito-toasting-to-the-history-and-character-of-the-capital.html (Accessed on March 1, 2013).
"Get Ready for Fiestas de Quito." http://www.lan.com/onlyinsouthamerica/2012/11/get-ready-for-fiestas-de-quito/ (Accessed on March 1, 2013).
"Quito Folklore, Quito History and Community in Quito." http://www.getquitoecuador.com/quito-folk-community/index.html (Accessed on March 1, 2013).
Stevenson, Robert. "Music in Quito: Four Centuries." *The Hispanic American Historical Review* 43, no. 2 (1963): 247–66.

FINGER AMPUTATION AT FUNERALS

The Dani are an ethno-linguistic group who live in the isolated highlands of Papua New Guinea. For centuries, they have practiced a unique funerary ritual that involves the amputation of the fingers of female relatives after the death of male family members. During early explorations to the region, Europeans and Americans were shocked to witness these cultural practices. It was not until recently that the custom was officially outlawed by the government. In order to examine the Dani finger amputation, it is crucial to understand the complex relationship between the Dani belief in spirits and their practice of ritualized warfare.

The Dani live a remote habitat on the western half of New Guinea in what is now the Indonesia province of Papua. They occupy one of the most isolated places on earth called the Baliem Valley, also known as the Grand Valley. This region was thought to be uninhabited until tribal members were spotted by an airplane during the Archbold Expedition in June of 1938. Even after their identification, they remained relatively isolated due to the remoteness of their villages and a lack of resources in the area that would be of value to outside interests. The Dani are composed of several tribes based on kinship, and they are differentiated by four unique linguistic groups: Lower Grand Valley Dani, Mid-Grand Valley Dani, Upper Grand Valley Dani, and the Western Dani. There are approximately 270,000 people who speak the Dani language or a variation of it. Population estimates also include those who can trace their family lineage back to the Dani; however, other estimates suggest that there are only about 50,000 Dani still living

A Dani woman with amputated fingers in West Papua, Indonesia. (Ulet Ifansasti/Getty Images)

their traditional lifestyle. The latter are groups of predominantly small-scale farmers who primarily cultivate yams in addition to raising pigs. Other traditional food sources that are regularly gathered in the Baliem Valley include bananas, sorghum, and cassava. Today, in addition to farming, the Dani participate in eco-tourism by allowing small groups of tourists to hike into the highlands to purchase "authentic" Dani goods and witness firsthand how these indigenous people still maintain many aspects of their traditional lifestyle.

The Dani have a religious system that is based on ancestor worship and magic. For the Dani, the spirits of their ancestors rule most aspects of their daily lives. Many of the rituals, ceremonies, and even their warfare are often done to appease the spirits of their deceased ancestors. Disgruntled spirits can cause negative events to occur to individuals or even entire communities. This traditional belief makes it extremely important that all members of the community regularly honor the spirits, which may be lurking in the nearby forests and homes. Bad harvests, illness, injuries, and general misfortune are often attributed to the unsatisfied spirits of the Dani. It is the desire to appease the spirits that drives the need for the Dani to regularly engage in warfare with neighboring communities.

The intent of warfare among the Dani does not hold the same objectives that it derives in Western societies. Overall, there is no a desire to conquer neighboring populations and acquire their resources, but instead warfare serves a religious purpose. It is through the yelling, chanting, and spilling of blood during warfare that the Dani let the spirits know how much the living are doing to honor their ancestors who have passed. Warfare also serves as a mechanism to socially bond surrounding communities and distant kin groups, who usually side with one of the teams of combatants. The usage of wooden spears, elaborate body decorations, and a causal sporting atmosphere more comparable to a game of dodge ball seems pervasive among the ritualized practice. Combat is often ceased when one of the members of either group suffers a serious injury, or for numerous other justifications, such as smoking breaks, bad weather, and encroaching too far into one another's tribal lands. War almost always stops upon the death of a single member of the opposing group at which time the deceased individual is often carried away by their tribe for a funeral ritual. If an individual is fatally wounded and the body not recovered, the opposing tribe may bring the body back to their village and then consumes it along with a traditional feast of pigs and yams for the participants. It is through this feasting associated with warfare that members of the community increase their social status and honor their deceased ancestors by generously donating pigs and yams to the celebration.

When a male is killed during warfare, female relatives willingly perform finger amputation as part of the funerary ritual. The dead body is brought back to the village where members of the community prepare it by cleaning it, rubbing it with oils, placing it on a wooden throne, and decorating the body with beaded strings of shells. The body is then paraded to the center of the village accompanied by song, dance, and a long procession. The beaded shells are removed from the body and distributed to members of the family beginning with those closest to the deceased. Subsequently, the body is placed on a funeral pyre and cremated. During the cremation, female relatives often cover their faces and bodies in ash. In addition, strings are wrapped tightly around the fingers of female candidates who will undergo amputation to help numb them. After a half hour of the fingers being bound, they are cut off with a traditional bamboo or stone blade. Once removed, the fingers are cremated and the ashes are placed in a bag and then moved to a sacred location in the family house for storage. It is believed that finger amputation serves to demonstrate the dedication to the deceased, and it also serves to keep their spirits satisfied by taking a part of their family with them to the afterlife. Furthermore, it is suggested that the finger amputation ceremony serves as a symbolic sharing in the pain of the death of their kinsmen. While the practice has been outlawed in Papua New Guinea, many women in Dani communities still bare the visible effects of this form of ritualistic amputation.

Mario Robertson

Further Readings

"Disappearing World." *New Guinea.* http://disappearing-world.com/en/deyatelnost/novaya-gvineya (Accessed on August 30, 2012).

Gardner, Robert. *Dead Birds* (film). Documentary Educational Resources, 1963.

Gardner, Robert. *Gardens of War: Life and Death in the New Guinea Stone Age.* New York: Random House, 1968.

Heider, Karl G. *The Dugum Dani: A Papuan Culture in the Highlands of West New Guinea.* New York: Aldine Publishing, 1970.

Heider, Karl G. *Grand Valley Dani: Peaceful Warriors, Case Studies in Cultural Anthropology.* 3rd ed. Independence, KY: Wadsworth Publishing 1966.

FIREWALKING

Although firewalking is often performed in public (and it has become a popular event at various venues for entertainment and confidence-building training), it is originally part of religious rituals, spiritual healings, and martial arts. This ritual has been performed since 1200 BCE by various tribes and cultures. However, a reliable historical record suggests that the initial practice took place 4,000 years ago in the region of what is now known as India. It was carried out by two Brahmin priests who competed to determine who could walk the longest distance on top of hot burning coals. Other reports indicated that the ancient Roman citizens would be rewarded with tax exemption if they successfully demonstrated the ability to overcome the pain when they walked on fire. In contemporary practices, the most impressive firewalking festivals (or *Thimthi*) are held in India, Bali, Fiji, and Singapore.

The ritual of firewalking can now be observed in almost all continents. In Africa, the Kung Bush men tribal dance around a fire is a powerful healing rite—a ceremony that also includes rolling on the fire. In Indonesia, families celebrate the coming of age for their seven-year-old daughters in the island of Bali by performing a firewalking ceremony. The Kahunas in Hawaii allow hot moltenlavato be hard enough to hold their body weight before walking over it. Other countries

Firewalking at a Shinto ceremony. (Sean Pavone/Dreamstime.com)

and regions have practiced fire immunity and firewalking rituals, including Brazil, Burma, China, Egypt, Bulgaria, Australia, Fiji, Hawaii, Indonesia, Japan, Malaysia, India, Haiti, New Zealand, Singapore, Spain, Pakistan, Thailand, the Philippines, Trinidad, South Africa, Sri Lanka, and Tibet.

The majority of people who perform firewalking rituals in the aforementioned countries are mostly former Hindu residents who migrated from South India to these countries. The firewalking ritual is called the *Thimthi* festival (variants of the name also include *Theemidhi* and *Theemithi*). In India, the celebration is usually conducted in the Aippasi month on the Tamil calendar, which falls on the months of October and November in the Gregorian calendar. This ceremony is to honor the Goddess Draupadi, who is highly honored as an incarnation of Goddess Mari, also known as the "Mariamman." Tradition tells of a story of an epic war in which the grand finale occurs when Goddess Draupadi walks on fire (a process known as *Theemithi*) to prove her virtuosity and chastity by her adherence to dharma.

Multiple Hindu traditions take place before the actual firewalking ceremony is held. For example, a week before the ceremony, Hindus pray to Goddess Priyachi; people ask for blessings and fortune from her during the festival. During this period, it is also typical to remember a symbolic marriage ceremony between Arjuna and Draupadai. Arjuna is an archer who is often called Jishnu, or the unbeatable. Two days before the *Thimthi* festival, there is a big parade procession using a silver chariot specifically made to remember memorable epic wars.

A crucial part of the firewalking rituals is the symbolic sacrifice of Hijra. The participants in this ceremony bring boxes of milk and practice two important traditions: *Kumbiduthandam* (looking face down after every step) and *Angapirathatchanam* (rolling around the temple area). They use the milk to wash a statue of Goddess Mariamman. This practice offers believers the feeling that they have also washed away their sins.

The firewalking celebration itself is done after the fire pit was prepared the night before the final day of the festival. The enactment of this event includes the *pandaram* (chief priest) first walking across the fire with the *karakam* (a sacred, decorated pot) with the Goddess Mariamman inside is thus tested anew. If her devotees are as pure as the goddess herself, then they will also be able to cross the coals unharmed. The first walking group includes other priests who take a pot of *Karagam* (sacred water) on their head. Then people follow the priest to walk on top of the hot fire to demonstrate the power of their faith or to fulfill certain promises. The *Theemithi* firewalking ritual usually begins at dawn at roughly 4:00 A.M. and it is always on Monday before the celebration of Diwali (the Festival of Lights). The complete custom of firewalking traditionally ends at about 11:00 A.M.

The firewalking ceremony is also conducted on the island of Bali in Indonesia. The regional name there is the Trance Dance in which the Dance of Spirits appears to invite the gods to enter the body and create a state of trance. The ceremony is influenced by pre-Hindu beliefs that the holy spirits will pass the dancers, and they have healing powers to help in the process of curing illnesses. Celebrations of firewalking in Bali are conducted in the fifth or sixth month of the Balinese traditional calendar. They selected these months because they believe that in those months, disease and natural disasters are more frequent. There are six variations of *Sanghyang* (*trance*) dance that accompanies the firewalking festival. During the prominent *Sanghyang Jaran* dance, a man or a priest who is in the state of trance performs a dance that provides an image of a riding toy horse. He dances around the fire made of burned coconut husks. The sound of music provides part of the trance. Participants dance in a ritual they had never learned before. If they were asked, they could not remember what they had actually done during the ritual. However, those Hindu believers who dance in *Shangyang* have respectable status in their society.

The firewalking festival has also been performed all over the islands of Polynesia in the South Pacific for centuries. In Fiji, the festival is conducted in four places known as Dakuibeqa, Dakuni, Soliyaga, and Rukua. They are located on the small island of Beqa, which is only a few kilometers from Fiji's capital Suva in the main island of Fiji, Viti Levu. The distinguishing element of firewalking in Fiji is that the ceremony is performed using hot stones. In addition, firewalking here is an ancient tradition. According to the local legend in Beqa Island, a young man Tunaiviqalita was given by god the power to walk barefoot over hot stones because of his bravery, heroism, and loyalty to his community. He then passed that god-given gift of walking on fire to his bloodline in the Sawa Tribe on Bega Island. His descendants are today, as promised by god, still able to walk on hot stones without any ill effects. The descendants of Tunaiviqalita are in the villages of Rookwa,

Dakubeqa, Dakuni, Soliyaga, and Naceva. However, given the lack of economic opportunities in the area, these descendants now often perform the firewalking customs at hotels in Fiji. In this tradition, walkers on the fire should practice two major taboos for two weeks before the show. The taboos are that they cannot have sexual relations with women and should not eat any kind of coconuts. The failure to follow these rules can result in serious burns. At the time of the performance, the firewalkers walk on hot coals for several meters and surprisingly their feet are not burned.

In Singapore, the firewalking festival is performed by people from South India in similar practices almost the same as the *Thimiti's* ritual. Hindu priests lead the procession followed by many Hindus and non-Hindus from Srinivasa Perumal Temple at approximately 10:00 P.M. headed to Sri Mariamman temple, which is the oldest and largest Hindu temple in the area. After walking about 4 miles, they arrived at the Sri Mariamman temple, and here the priests start the ceremony by walking through the fire from wood coals upholding pots containing holy water called *karakattam* on their head. The main priest is then followed by male devotees who practice firewalking in order to fulfill personal vows and to prove their faith. Among the devotees, there are also non-Indians and non-Hindus. In 1997, for example, 2,500 people took to the streets following the ritual of firewalking and 10 percent of them were Chinese. Around a few weeks earlier, more than 20,000 people attended a remission of sin ceremony. It has also become one of the most interesting events in Singapore in early November that attracts many visitors.

While the custom of firewalking is rooted in ancient traditions and spiritual beliefs, it has recently been used in workshops and seminars as part of confidence-building exercises. In such settings, it no longer follows a religious foundation, but rather a purpose of personal growth. However, methods of firewalking have been extensively studied, and researchers have offered scientific data proving that many people can do it without being harmed.

Patit Paban Mishra and Abubakar Hara

Further Readings

Babb, L. A. *Walking on Flowers in Singapore: A Hindu Festival Cycle*. Singapore: Department of Sociology, University of Singapore, 1974.

"Fire Walking at the Theemithi Festival in Singapore." http://www.travelandbeyond.org/2011/10/18/firewalking-in-singapore/ (Accessed on November 13, 2012).

"Firewalk." http://www.happinessquest.com/firewalk.html (Accessed on November 13, 2012).

"History of Firewalking." http://www.firewalking.com/firewalk_history.jsp (Accessed on November 13, 2012).

Lipsner, J. *Hindus: Their Religious Beliefs and Practice*. London and New York: Routledge, 1994.

"Rokwa Village Firewalking in Fiji." http://www.fijibure.com/rookwa/fire.htm (Accessed on November 15, 2012).

Willey, David. "Firewalking Myth vs Physics." University of Pittsburgh. http://www.pitt.edu/~dwilley/Fire/FireTxt/fire.html (Accessed on November 10, 2012).

FOREHEAD-CUTTING INITIATION

The transition from childhood into manhood is often celebrated with both religious and secular ceremonies throughout the world. In African traditional societies, rites of passage also demonstrate a level of a boy's bravery and maturity. In South Sudan, the Nuer tribes constitute the second largest group in the country with a population of slightly over 1 million; they are only outnumbered by the Dinka group. They live in a landlocked nation located in east-central Africa surrounded by Ethiopia, Kenya, Uganda, Congo, and Sudan. Since the Nuer tribes are spread across multiple countries, they do not have a centralized authority. Instead, they remain connected but loosely organized as autonomous villages with historical ties to interlinked clans. Nuer groups rely heavily on cattle to sustain their pastoral lifestyle. In fact, their entire social, cultural, and economic life revolves around cattle. While livestock provides basic necessities such as food, they are also the foundation of Nuer families and society. Everyone in the household has specific tasks to take care of the cows: the men herd them, the women milk them, and children clean after them. When Nuer boys are ready to obtain adult status in their villages, they must go through a painful and bloody scarification ritual to demonstrate their courage. Once they experience this rite of passage, their new status will allow them to receive cattle and consequently advance their social standing among the large clan. In general, Nuer boys participate in a forehead-cutting ceremony when they are twelve to sixteen years old. The initiation ritual involves a community elder cutting multiple parallel lines (usually six of them) across the forehead by using a razor or a sharp knife. The incisions become identifiable facial scars (locally known as *gaar*) that reveal association with a specific tribe in the area.

The scarification ceremony is highly ritualized, and it is usually coordinated to coincide with the harvest season. All the preparations begin the night before when all the eligible boys gather to socialize with music and dance. At this point, the initiates are referred to as *parapol*, which in the local Nuer language means "someone who stopped milking." At this evening gathering, boys usually arrive with their heads already shaved since it is required for the formal event. On the day of the ceremony itself, they attend a brief blessing for spiritual purification. Then, they are taken to an outdoor location where the ritual will actually take place. They line up to sit on the ground facing west; with their legs crossed, they wait for the sun to rise behind them. Then, an initiator arrives to perform the forehead-cutting ritual. Meanwhile, the boys must remain seated in a row. When the initiator gets closer to each boy, he yells out his name and also acknowledges his known ancestors within the clan. Then, he firmly grabs the boy's head and uses a sharp blade to cut lines across the forehead with steady movements and without hesitation. The incisions are deep; they often touch the skull bones on the forehead. The entire procedure is performed without any kind of anesthesia. As the blood drips down the boys' faces, they are not allowed to show any sign of weakness, pain, or regret. Since the event is performed in front of the entire village, any flinching, squirming, moaning, or screaming would be interpreted as cowardly and would bring excessive shame on the entire family. As a coping mechanism, it is common for the initiates to stare straight ahead and continuously repeat the name of their ancestors. The scars created during the ritual are permanent, and they follow patterns that identify specific tribes or clans. Nuer boys usually receive six parallel lines across the forehead. Members of the Dinka tribe in Sudan also display parallel lines, but they follow a V-pattern on the forehead. It is also common (but less prevailing) that Nuer women receive forehead scars. However, they are usually not very long but rather a series of dots forming a pattern on the forehead.

Once the cutting marks are completed on each boy, they remain seated (and continue bleeding) until the initiator finishes the procedure on all the initiates participating in the ceremony. Then, the initiator quietly leaves the ceremonial site, but there is still much work to be done. After the scarification lines are finished, boys simply tilt their heads down to let the blood drip down. Once the entire scarification ritual has been completed, the boys' fathers are allowed to clean the blood from their son's mouth, cheeks, and eyes, but not the forehead because it has to be covered with a natural leaf to aid in the healing and scarification process.

When the ritual component of the celebration is over, the social festivities begin, and Nuer boys enjoy a new status in society. The post-cutting celebratory gathering involves music, food, and dancing in a joyous event that can last up to three days. At this point, the new adults in Nuer society receive an ox. Given that the Nuer people derive so much value from their livestock, such gift becomes the boys' most valued possession. After the initiation, they no longer have to perform the tedious chores they used to carry out as younger boys. Instead, they are presented with a spear and a shield, which represent the tools of a warrior who can take care of his own cattle. Consequently, they will probably spend a lot of time with their newly acquired companions: singing to them, sleeping next to them, and decorating their bull horns. In addition, their new standing in Nuer society makes these young adults now eligible to marry, and they can begin searching for a suitable wife.

Javier A. Galván

Further Readings

Diagram Group. *People of North Africa.* New York: Facts on File, 1997.

Holtzman, Jon D. *Nuer Journeys, Nuer Lives.* Boston: Pearson Education, 2000.

Hutchinson, Sharon. *Nuer Dilemmas.* Berkeley: University of California Press, 1996.

International Rescue Committee. *The Lost Boys of Sudan.* http://www.rescue.org/lost-boys-sudan (Accessed on August 20, 2012).

"The Nuer of South Sudan and Ethiopia." http://strategyleader.org/profiles/nuer.html (Accessed on August 20, 2012).

Ryle, John, et al. *Sudan Handbook.* Rochester, NY: James Currey Publishers, 2011.

G

GOOSE DAY

In Britain, it has long been the tradition to eat a goose fed on the stubble from the fields after harvest on September 29 (or Michaelmas Day) that is, the Feast of St. Michael and All Angels. This is the traditional date by which the harvest had to be completed. Families typically ate a goose to protect against financial hardship in the coming year and recited a proverb: Who so eats goose on Michaelmas Day shall never lack money his debts to pay. The origins of the tradition are unclear. One suggestion is that the custom dates back to an ancient Celtic rite during which a fowl was sacrificed in order to increase the fertility of the crops over the next year. Another theory has it that Queen Elizabeth I was eating a goose when she was informed of the defeat of the approaching Spanish Armada and vowed to eat a roast goose every year on Michaelmas Day and decreed that roast goose should be served on September 29 (the anniversary of the Armada's defeat) every year as a symbol of remembrance and thanksgiving. However, written references associating geese with Michaelmas pre-date the reign of Elizabeth I, and so it is likely that the ritual of Goose Days date back to pre-Christian times. Another possible reason for the eating of geese on this day is that rural tenants had to pay their rent at Michaelmas, and they often brought a goose to their landlord on the day their rent was due with a view to making the landlord lenient. The goose was ripe for the slaughter at this time of year having been fed on harvest stubble and so any landlord receiving a well-fed goose as a gift may well have warmed to his tenant's pleas for kinder rental terms. Consequently, so many geese were plucked at this time of year that the word "gossamer" (meaning fine cobwebs that hang in the air) is derived from the Middle English word goose-summer, thereby highlighting that during the transition from summer to autumn the air hung heavily with goose feathers.

Yet another possible reason for Goose Days was that Michaelmas was the time of year when rural folk needed new jobs, the harvest having been collected. Thus, Michaelmas Fairs were established. These were markets at which country-dwellers could job-hunt and so many geese were sold at these Michaelmas Fairs that the markets became known as Goose Fairs. Goose Fairs were often associated with sacred ancient sites, though in Christian times this religious element was suggested by the traditional marking of a market square by a stone cross. Domestic geese were vital to the rural economy, and fairs were allowed to set their own rules. However, common to all fairs was the rule that traders must not buy goods on the way to market and subsequently sell them for a profit. Those who committed this offense were said to have "forestalled" and faced heavy fines for doing so. For instance, on October 13, 1375, it was recorded that twenty-two geese were forfeited by the sheriffs of London because the geese had only just reached Holborn on their way to a fair in the city of London when they were forestalled. As was the custom, the geese had been made to walk to the market with their original owners and such a long trek from countryside to city gave ample opportunity for traders to be intercepted and goods forestalled.

The distances covered by the geese-traders are suggested by the fact that the ancient traders' track Sewstern Lane in Stamford, Lincolnshire, continues to the site of England's most famous Goose Fair in Nottingham around 40 miles away. King Edward I awarded Nottingham the charter for the market in 1284; by the mid-sixteenth century, the market was known as the Goose Fair. The event originally began in September on St. Matthew's Day, and it saw over 20,000 geese traded. The geese had to walk into the fair via the famous Roman road known as the Fosse Way, then take Sewstern Lane, and then enter the eastern side of the town via the Goose Gate. From this point, the geese walked on toward the Old Market Square. D. H. Lawrence wrote the short story "Goose Fair," which opens with a description of weary geese waddling into the market town and Arthur Spooner painted *The Goose Fair* (1926), which depicts one of the last times the fair was held in the center of Nottingham. The fair has also been commemorated on a postage stamp issued by the British postal service.

The Goose Fair has a long history and has experienced a number of changes over the years. However, the Goose Fair has not been held continuously every year. In 1646, the fair was cancelled due to an outbreak of plague and no fairs were held during World Wars I and II. In addition, the fair no longer takes place in the centrally located Old Market Square, In the 1920s, the fair moved to its current location at Forest Recreation Grounds on the outskirts of the town. Also, in the nineteenth century, the fair's duration was decreased from eight days to three only to be increased again to four days at the start of the twentieth century. Today, the fair starts on the first Thursday of October, it lasts three days, and it is no longer a trade event but rather features games and funfair rides.

Another famous Goose Fair is located in the Devonshire town of Tavistock. This fair, which began in October 1105, continues to this day and inspired the folk tune "Tavistock Goosey Fair Song." Another Devon fair, Coley Goose Fair takes place on September 28.

Victoria Williams

Further Readings

BBC Nottingham. *History of Goose Fair.* September 4, 2008. http://www.bbc.co.uk/nottingham/content/articles/2005/09/15/goose_fair_history_feature.shtml (Accessed on November 26, 2012).

Chambers, Robert, ed. *The Book of Days: A Miscellany of Popular Antiquities in Connection with the Calendar.* Vol. II. London: W&R Chambers, 1832.

Historic UK. 2012. http://www.historic-uk.com/CultureUK/Michaelmas/ (Accessed on November 15, 2012).

Kear, Janet. *Man and Wildfowl.* London: T&AD Poyser Ltd, 1990.

GURNING

The term "gurning" refers to a rural British custom that evolved into a face-making contest. Gurning involves the practice of twisting one's countenance into an intentionally ugly face. Gurning dates back at least to the nineteenth century. Although accounts of gurning's history vary, a commonly accepted version is that this activity had its origins in a practice of taunting an individual who was regarded as the "village idiot." Villagers subjected this person to mockery and physical indignities, in return for which he would be furnished with beer to drink.

Over time, this gurning ritual inspired a public competition during which contestants strive to make the ugliest facial expression possible. The sport of "pulling faces" has closest ties with the community of Egremont, Cumbria, a former mining town located outside the Lake District in England. Situated just 5 miles from the Sellafield nuclear power plant, Egremont is second only to Chernobyl as a nuclear disaster site, having sustained a major reactor fire in 1957. Egremont hosts the World Gurning Championship on the third Saturday each September. The competition culminates a week of events known as the Crab Fair, a yearly festival that dates back to 1267. The fair's name refers to crab apples rather than to crustaceans, and so it is likely a vestige of a harvest celebration.

Gurning champion Tommy Mattinson with Queen Elizabeth II in 2008. (AP Photo/Arthur Edwards/The Sun/pool)

Egremont's Crab Fair offers a host of unusual attractions for residents and visitors alike. In one such tradition, known as "The Greasy Pole," participants scale a 30-foot pole coated in lard, attempting to secure a prize in the form of a leg of lamb fastened to the pole's apex. In another event central to the Crab Fair, the "Parade of the Apple Cart," festival organizers board the cart and pelt onlookers with apples. Spectators attempt to catch or deflect apples. In still another element of the Crab Fair, Cumberland Wrestling, competitors don long underwear, topped off with embroidered shorts and tank tops. Also popular at the festival are clay pipe-smoking contests, won by the first person to consume the quantity of tobacco provided to participants.

Toward the end of the Crab Fair, a panel of judges presides over the World Gurning Championship, during which men and women compete separately for the title. Each contestant puts his or her head through a leather horse collar (known as a braffin) then snarls before the crowd. Participants have up to one minute in which to achieve this effect. Highest scores go to the most extreme transformations of appearance. Competitors considered ugly to start with will not prove as competitive as those who shift a visage from handsome to hideous.

The emphasis of the gurning competition remains on facial distortion, so elasticity of the muscles in the face is of central importance. Some participants remove their dentures to accentuate their ugly faces, and at least one has had his or her teeth removed for this purpose. Many entrants appear annually to vie for the ugliest face, and some have given names to their signature looks. For example, one well-known gurner, Peter Jackman, refers to his distinctive grimace as the "Bela Lugosi," named after the horror film actor. While Egremont's contest is the most celebrated gurning event, other communities throughout England also hold similar matches.

Linda S. Watts

Further Readings

Daeschner, J. R. *True Brits: A Tour of Great Britain in All Its Bog-Snorkelling, Shin-Kicking, and Cheese-Rolling Glory.* New York: Overlook Press, 2004.

The Official Site of Egremont Crab Fair and Sports. "History of the Egremont Crab Fair." http://www.egremontcrabfair.com/history.html (Accessed on March 16, 2013).

Shuel, Brian. *National Trust Guide to Traditional Customs of Britain.* Exeter, UK: Webb and Bower, 1985.

HAXEY HOOD GAME

The Haxey Hood Game is a unique calendar custom that takes place on January 6 (or the 5th should the 6th fall on a Sunday) each year in the Lincolnshire village of Haxey, England. The ritual was first recorded in 1815, though, according to local legend, the tradition began in the fourteenth century when the silk hood of a local aristocrat—Lady de Mowbray—blew away as she was riding to an Epiphany church service on the hill that separates Westwoodside from Haxey. Thirteen local men chased to retrieve the hood as they believed whoever returned the clothing to her Ladyship would be well rewarded. Eventually one man prevailed, snatching the hood from his opponents. However, as he approached the lady, he was overcome by shyness enabling another man to snatch it from him and present it to her instead. The Lady found the men's behavior entertaining and vowed to present half an acre of land to each of the thirteen men on condition that the villagers would reenact the antics each year.

In its contemporary form, the Haxey Hood Game takes on a riotous nature, and the contest between the regular drinkers of the village pubs causes streets to close for traffic and shop windows to be covered to prevent breakages. The game's main players are based on the event's original participants with the men who chased the hood represented by players called Boggins. The Boggins perform stewarding duties and, starting on New Year's Eve, collect money from neighboring pubs to both defray the cost of staging the game and donate to local charities. A player known as the Fool represents the man who was too shy to hand the Lady her hood, and the man who took advantage of this bashfulness is known as the Lord of the Hood. The latter's costume is pink and includes a top hat adorned with flowers and pheasant feathers. To symbolize his importance, the Lord of the Hood carries a wand made of thirteen osiers woven in a traditional pattern.

The game begins in the morning with contestants drinking in their respective pubs and thereby entering into combative mood. The players sing traditional English folk songs such as "John Barleycorn," "The Farmer's Boy," and "Cannons (Drink England Dry)." At about 12:30 P.M. on the day of the game, the Lord of the Hood accompanied by the Fool and the Chief Boggin carries his wand around the village, stopping at each pub in turn. Each landlord gives the players free drinks as a token of good luck and to try and ensure that the hood will reach his pub first. The Fool's face is decorated with ceremonial markings at the first pub allowing him to kiss any woman he desires.

At around 2:00 P.M., the Boggins assemble at the gates of the village church, and the Fool tries to run away from the Boggins only to be caught and brought back to the church. Once he is returned, the Fool climbs atop a mounting block called the Mowbray Stone, which is situated opposite the church and around which straw has been piled. The Fool then recites the rules of the game, which include orders not to cause physical injury. While the Fool speaks, the straw is set alight in a tradition known as Smoking the Fool with the aim being to see how long the Fool can speak before he is overcome by the smoke and flames from the fire and is forced to quit the mounting stone. This is a tamer version of the traditional Smoking in which the Fool was suspended over a fire and swung back and forth until he nearly suffocated. The Fool was then dropped into the fire from which he had to escape or burn. Next, the Lord of the Hood leads the villagers to a field located equidistant between Haxey and Westwoodside where the game is traditionally held. The Lord of the Hood carries a heavy cylinder, about 18 inches long, which is made of leather-covered rope sealed at each end. This tube represents the Lady's hood.

To start the game, twelve pieces of rolled-up sacking are thrown into the crowd by the Boggins. These tubes represent hoods, and village children try to catch a tube and swop it for sweets or coins. Other villagers who catch these smaller hoods must keep hold of them and carry them away, passing the Boggins who are stationed around the edge of the field. If they are tackled by an opponent, the participant must throw the hood into the air again unless their tackler is a Boggin in which case the player is said to have been "boggined" and must return the caught hood to the Lord of the Hood who relaunches it. After this family-friendly portion of the day is completed, the Lord of the Hood signals the start of the more boisterous rugby-like game. Many male drinkers from the opposing pubs form teams and join in a dense scrum known as the Sway. The men's aim is to get the leather-bound Hood into their pub by pure physical force, though no running, kicking, or throwing is permitted. The Sway may take many hours to reach a pub as it has to pass through the village. Once the Sway is under way, the men's wives and girlfriends join in to add strength to the teams. Victory can be achieved only by the landlord of a participating pub placing his hand upon the hood. The landlord then provides free drinks to all players. The winning pub owner pours beer over the hood and suspends it from two special hooks behind the bar where it remains until New Year's Eve when it is collected by the Boggins for use in the next game.

Victoria Williams

Further Readings

Alexander, Marc. *The Sutton Companion to British Folklore, Myths and Legends*. Stroud, UK: Sutton Publishing, 2005.

Simpson, Jacqueline, and Steve Roud. *Oxford Dictionary of English Folklore*. Oxford: Oxford University Press, 2000.

Wheewall, Adam. "Haxey Hood: 700 Years of Tradition." 2012. http://www.wheewall.com/hood/index.php (Accessed on November 7, 2012).

HOLI, **THE INDIAN FESTIVAL OF COLORS**

Holi, the festival of colors, is celebrated by Hindus in *Phagun* (the spring season from February until March in India). Primarily celebrated in the Indian subcontinent, the festival is also observed in countries with a significant Indian Diaspora population. The celebration marks the beginning of spring as the season of joy and hope, and it bids adieu to the gloom of winter. It is celebrated on the last full moon of the lunar month. As a celebration of good harvests, fertile land, and the plentiful colors of the season, the festival is celebrated with gaiety and enthusiasm. *Holi* has multiple local names and traditions across India, but the linking thread between all celebrations is the spirit of joy, love, and devotion. The most salient characteristic of this unique festival is the use of bright-color powder (simply called *colors*) that people throw at each other in a celebratory environment.

As one of the major festivals of India, the enthusiasm for the celebration of *Holi* could be seen in big cities, small towns, and countryside villages of India. *Holi* is also an official national public holiday. Weeks prior to the festival, Indian markets are flooded with heaps of hues of *abeer* and *gulal* (bright-color powder), *Mitaees* (Indian sweets), and *pichkari* (color-throwing instruments). The participants hold bonfires and smear each other with wet and dry colors. This celebration generally lasts for two days; on the eve of the first day known as *Choti Holi* (minor *Holi*), *Holika Dahan* (a huge bonfire commemorating burning of demoness Holika) is held at various cross roads and prayers are offered; the very next day, *Badi Holi* (major *Holi*) is celebrated with colors. The ambience is filled with various shades of bright colors. The festival is celebrated with colors, food, and music. People often forms *Tolees* (groups) and moves from one colony to other throwing colored powder at relatives, friends, neighbors, acquaintances, and even strangers. To avoid any kind of tension, people often shout the slogan: "*Bura na mano Holi hai*" (Do not feel offended, it is *Holi*). Streets and lanes get filled with people running, singing, giggling, and splashing colors at each other. Apart from throwing bright colors, water balloons have also become very popular recently. People generally wear white clothes so that all the different colors (e.g., hot pink, canary yellow, and fluorescent green) are clearly visible on the participants. Amid the fun and frolic of the festival, special culinary delicacies such as *gujiya*, *malpuas*, *puranpoli*, and *dahibadas* are served. Drinks such as *Thandai* mixed with *Bhang* (intoxicant) are also an indispensible part of the *Holi* celebration. This unique holiday has become the epitome of love, harmony, and brotherhood.

Holi is an ancient festival and might have begun before the Christian era. According to a popular belief, the festival originated in the Indian region of Bengal where it was celebrated as the *Gaudiya Vaishnava* festival. In addition, there is a reference to the festival in the seventh-century Sanskrit drama *Ratnavali*, and it is also found in ancient religious texts such as Jaimini's *Purvamimamsa Sutra* and Kathaka's *Grhya Sutra*. The Veda and Purana people of India have also found a detailed description of the festival in their texts titled *Narad Purana* and *Bhavishya Purana*. Furthermore, the festival also finds reference in sculptures, paintings, and murals on the walls of old Indian temples.

The *Holi* festival has religious importance as it is essentially a representation of the victory of good over evil. The festival is also a commemoration of various religious events of Hindu mythology, and it has numerous legends associated with it. According to Hindu mythology, the demon Hiranyakashipu was granted a unique wish by god, and he almost became immortal. Upon receiving such power, he became ignorant, and he tried to show his supremacy by ordering his pupil to worship him. Furthermore, he proclaimed himself to be as great as god. Contrary to his behavior, his own son Prahlad was a staunch worshipper of Lord Vishnu (one of the main gods of the Hindu trinity). Although he was threatened by his father, he never gave up. As a result, Hiranyakashipu tried to kill his own son. He asked his sister Holika (a demoness) to enter in a massive fire with Prahlad in her lap. His sister Holika had a special power that made her immune to fire. Lord Vishnu protected his devotee Prahlad who had a miraculous escape from the fire, and the demoness Holika was burned alive in the fire. According to another Hindu legend, an ogress named Dhundi (the trouble-maker of the Kingdom of Prithu) was chased away by children on the day of *Holi*. As a commemoration, children play pranks on the occasion of *Holika Dahan*. In another legend called Pootana, an ogress tried to kill Lord Krishna in his infant days by feeding him poisoned milk. The ogress was an agent of Krishna's evil uncle Kansa. Lord Krishna killed the orgess by sucking her blood. A regional tradition from southern India provides yet another important legend related to *Holi*. In South India, people believe that Kaamdeva (the god of love) shot his powerful love arrow on Lord Shiva to revoke his interest in the world, but Lord Shiva—in a fit of anger—opened his third eye and turned him into ashes. Later, on the request of Rati (Kaamdeva's wife), Lord Shiva restored him back. All these legends essentially depict the triumph of good over evil, which is the philosophy behind the festival of colors.

The *Holi* festival is celebrated in different ways across India. The vibrant and colorful festival of *Holi* holds a lot of significance for the people of *Braj Bhoomi* (Mathura, Vrindavan, and Barsana) as the area is associated with Lord Krishna. The celebration of *Holi* in the area is quite different from other parts of India. The boisterous festival of colors is also related with the eternal love of Lord Krishna and Radha. In the Indian region of Braj, the festival lasts for sixteen days. In order to commemorate Lord Krishna's playfulness, men from Nandgaon (the land of Lord Krishna) come to play *Holi* with girls of Barsana, but instead of colors, they are greeted with *Laathis* (long sticks). The men protect themselves with shields and try not to get caught. As part of the festivities, they shout with enthusiasm, chant names of Radha and Krishna, throw colors, and sing *Holi* folk songs. Another linked tradition practiced during the *Holi* celebrations is the *Dahi-Handi* competition (buttermilk and pot). First, a pot is filled with buttermilk and is then hung high on a public street. Then, young boys known as *Govindas* try to break the pot by making human pyramids in order to reach it. The girls try to stop them by throwing colors on them. This tradition commemorates the pranks of stealing butter by Lord Krishna and his friends.

In multiple areas of India (especially in the Kumaon region), the *Holi* festival is a musical affair. Various songs based on the ragas of Indian classical music are

CELEBRATING THE INDIAN *HOLI* FESTIVAL OF COLORS IN UTAH

The small town of Spanish Fork, located in Utah, holds the largest celebration of the Indian *Holi* Festival of Colors in the United States. Over 50,000 people from surrounding states attend this event usually held in March. The reason is that this town is the site for the Sri Radha Krishna Temple, one of the largest Hindu temples in the country. People are asked to bring white clothing, and the use of bright color powder creates an extremely colorful spectacle. The atmosphere includes a lot of Hindu music, and most people refrain from consuming drugs or alcohol. The celebration is promoted as a happy event that brings together people from all races, genders, age groups, and social backgrounds.

Javier A. Galván

sung. *Khari Holi* (standing *Holi*) is celebrated in rural areas of this region. The participants wear their traditional attires, and they sing *Holi* songs and dance to the tune of traditional musical instrument such as *Dhol* and *Hurka*. The celebration of *Baitkhi Holi* (sitting *Holi*) starts in the campus of temples, where *Holi* singers sing classical *Holi* songs. The festival in this area is mostly played with eco-friendly colors made from flower extracts and water. In the Bengal region, *Holi* is known as *Dol Yatra* or *Dol Purnima*, and it involves an elaborate musical procession. The participants wear traditional attires, sing devotional songs, throw colors, and dance in the procession. In Panjim, the capital city of Goa, a huge procession is carried out. Dramas based on mythological and religious themes are performed by multiple cultural groups. In other states such as Maharashtra and Manipur, *Holi* is celebrated for many days. In Maharashtra, the color celebrations take place on *Rangapanchami*, the fifth day after *Holi*, whereas in the northeastern Indian state of Manipur, *Holi* merges with a local festival called *Yaosang*. In the latter celebration, participants burn huts made of hay and twigs. On full moon night of Lamta, they perform a traditional group dance known as *Thabal Chongba* based on folk songs and performed to the euphoric rhythm of drums.

While the *Holi* festival is an exuberant and exciting celebration during the day, the evenings are much more calm and composed. At night, people visit their friends and relatives, exchange sweets, and hug each other conveying *Holi* wishes. The festivities also serve as a community event with the general purpose of unifying people. In many Indian towns and cities, a *Holi-Milan* (*Holi* get-together) is organized, and people from different religions and castes forget their differences and come together. The carnival of colors is celebrated all over India with enthusiasm and joy. Over the ages, the festival has moved away from being a religious festival toward becoming a more secular festival. The *Holi* Festival of Colors allows different groups of people from different strata of society come together to get drenched in the colors of life.

Haris Qadeer

Further Readings

BBC "Holi" *Religions.* September 30, 2009 http://www.bbc.co.uk/religion/religions/hinduism/holydays/holi_1.shtml (Accessed on October 16, 2012).

Lall, R. Manohar. *Among the Hindus: A Study of Hindu Festivals.* New Delhi: Asian Educational Service, 2004.

Maheshwari, Krishna. "Holi." *Hindupedia.* March 20, 2011. http://www.hindupedia.com/en/Holi (Accessed on October 5, 2012).

Mukundchandras, Sadhu. *Hindu Festivals (Origins, Sentiments & Rituals).* Ahmedabad, India: Swaminarayan Aksharpith, 2005.

Shekar, H. V. *Festivals of India: Significance of Celebrations.* Louisville, KY: Insight Books, 2000.

Sivananda, Sri Swami. "Holi." *Hindu Fasts & Festivals.* WWW Edition: 2000. http://www.sivanandadlshq.org/download/hindufest.htm#_VPID_8 (Accessed on October 5, 2012).

HORMIGAS CULONAS, EATING BIG-BUTT ANTS

Insects are known in many cultures worldwide as a plentiful, nutritious, and protein-rich food source. In the Department of Santander in Colombia, *hormigas culonas* (literally, "big-butt" ants) are collected for nine weeks during the rainy

Jorge Raúl Díaz prepares *hormigas culonas*, a culinary delicacy, in Bachira, Colombia. (AP Photo/ William Fernando Martinez)

season to be roasted and eaten. Only available in specific regions and seasons, these oversized ants are known as a potent aphrodisiac with life-enhancing qualities, and they have been a seasonal delicacy in Colombia for centuries. Roasted "big-butt" ants are traditionally given away at weddings or shared at community gatherings, but they have come to fetch a high price as their popularity soars domestically and their availability increases abroad through Internet and specialty sales in Canada, Europe, and the United Kingdom.

Located at the northern part of South America, the geographically diverse country of Colombia has been a constitutional Republic since 1886, and it is currently inhabited by over 46 million people (ca. 2011). The nation gained its independence from Spain in 1819, after over 300 years of Spanish conquest and colonization. Pre-Columbian indigenous populations were mainly hunter-and-gatherer societies who engaged in trade between regional powers headed by *caciques*. A central region known today as the Department of Santander was home to several indigenous groups, including the *Guanes*. In Santander, the regional customs related to *hormigas culonas* have been adapted from their indigenous inception through all subsequent eras of colonialism, immigration, independence, and conflict. There are definite social aspects associated with the culinary custom of eating these unusual ants, which perhaps originated as part of complex *Guanes*-mating rites. *Hormigas culonas* are a representation of the reproductive power of the land and its people. As such, they are a popular gift given at weddings and often consumed as a snack shared by those who collect and prepare them each year. Today, these tasty treats are more popular than ever and roasted *hormigas culonas* are consumed beyond the hillsides of Santander by locals, tourists, and remote clientele as they are alternately given away, sold at roadstands, and exported overseas.

Hormigas culonas (*Atta laevigata*) are a cockroach-sized, leaf-cutter species of ant that are known for their mandible strength and for being a substantial pest to the farmers of Santander. The towns of San Gil and Barichara are the centers of production for *hormigas culonas*, and the practice of eating these ants is simply part of life for most locals. The long-held tradition of consuming such oversized ants is a source of pride for the region of Santander, and stylized images of giant ants can be seen on transit signage, lottery tickets, and T-shirts. Most of those who collect the ants do so out of tradition or because they are a substantial crop-pest. However, they are also tasty to eat and can be sold for profit to various vendors during a nine-week period that traditionally follows Easter. Due to their short season of easy availability, *hormigas culonas* fetch a consistently high price. For example, "Color de Hormiga" is an extremely popular restaurant in the town of Barichara that provides the gourmet culinary experience year-round, even though the price to acquire their main ingredient is much higher during the delicacy's off-season. Distribution of *hormigas culonas* extends to the regional capital city of Bucaramanga and the national capital of Bogota where small packages of the tasty snack are widely available during harvesting season. Cyberspace provides another outlet for sales to markets beyond Colombia, and the export of these unusual ants to individuals and specialty food shops worldwide has increased dramatically over the past decade. High-priced, chocolate-covered varieties of these ants can be purchased at Harrods of London and other luxury venues worldwide, where they can reach prices of up to U.S. $8 for a half dozen.

Leaf-cutter ants, like *Atta laevigata,* collect plant matter to sustain their massive nests that house up to 8 million inhabitants and stretch as far as 26 feet (8 meters) underground. During the rainy season, the queens—full of unfertilized eggs—leave the nest for one or two days annually to mate with likewise compelled drones over a nine-week period (late March to early June). Scores of ants are eaten by predators as they make their nuptial flight, and thousands more are collected by farmers to be subsequently roasted and consumed. The ants come out of their nests in swarms, but collection is not necessarily easy because each queen is guarded by hundreds of soldier ants that are biologically engineered to protect her by delivering bites with their strong mandibles. Locals wait at every nest for the largest winged specimens to emerge. These are captured and held in smooth-walled, escape-proof containers for later preparation and sale.

The preparation of *hormigas culonas* follows a simple process that has not really changed for decades. The ant's head, wings, and legs can be gently removed from the coveted abdomen and thorax prior to or after cooking. The ants are seasoned in batches following one of two traditional ways: tossed with spices in large bowls or soaked in wine or saltwater brine. Once seasoned, the ants are roasted in wok-like skillets or ceramic pots for about forty-five minutes per 1 pound (450 grams). Overall, *hormigas culonas* are said to possess a smoky flavor and a pleasant aroma that perfumes the entire mouth as they are consumed. The actual taste of these insects is often described as "bacon-like" or "nutty," with a moist center surrounded by a crunchy exterior.

EATING BUGS FOR NUTRITIONAL VALUE

Eating bugs and insects is a culinary practice that goes way beyond Colombia; it is rather common in other parts of Latin America, Asia, Africa, and Australia. While the practice of actually cooking bugs might initially sound unusual, insects actually have a recognized high nutritional value. In Mexico, the state of Jalisco produces agave worms that are rich in protein, and the state of Oaxaca offers roasted grasshoppers as a tasty snack served with spicy chili powder and lemon juice. The latter is rich in calcium. In multiple parts of Thailand and Cambodia, it is quite common to see crickets on the menu of street vendors; they are often prepared into cookies and soups. In many parts of Africa, the use of caterpillars is not very strange for dinner; they are usually dried and then fried in hot oil. However, people who consume bugs and insects around the world offer a few common suggestions and warnings: Do not eat poisonous insects, do not eat bugs that are already dead, and do not eat bugs with a strong bad smell (it is usually a defense mechanism for them to protect themselves from predators).

Javier A. Galván

The most controversial aspect related to consumption of *hormigas culonas* is the conservation status of the ants themselves. The people of Santander often say that if they do not eat the ants, the ants will eat them! Although *hormigas culonas* are a seasonal delicacy that focuses primarily on the collection of breeding queens, the ants are intensely prolific breeders with a relatively short lifespan, which means that they tend to exist in very large numbers. Despite their massive numbers, some worry that the custom of eating them as snacks is progressively depleting ant populations in the region. Fluctuating environmental factors and interspecies competition also reduce the numbers in ant populations, which regional experts estimate to be at one-sixth of what they were twelve years ago. Likely due to the rise in export numbers of the delicacy over the past five to ten years, government agencies in Colombia are providing incentives to those who are advancing husbandry practices to deliberately propagate the tasty "big-butt" culinary delicacy.

Stephanie L. Hamilton

Further Readings

Andrews, Brian. "Colombia's Hormigas Culonas." *NTN24 News.com.* April 24, 2012. http://brianandrews.ntn24.com/2012/04/colombias-hormigas-culonas/ (Accessed on September 20, 2012).

Goodman, Joshua. "Crunchy, Big-Butt Ants Entice Gourmands." *Associated Press.* August 14, 2006. http://dsc.discovery.com/news/2006/08/14/ants_ani.html?category=animals&guid=20060814113000 (Accessed on September 4, 2012).

LaRosa, Michael J., and German R. Melia. *Colombia: A Concise Contemporary History.* Lanham, MD: Rowman and Littlefield Publishers, Inc., 2012.

Montoya-Lerma, et al. "Leaf-Cutting Ants Revisited: Toward Rational Management and Control." *International Journal of Pest Management* 58, no. 3 (2012): 225–47.

Venezuela, David. "HORMIGAS CULONAS—Canal TRO." *YouTube.* May 3, 2011. http://www.youtube.com/watch?NR=1&feature=endscreen&v=S9bGlirn0Yc (Accessed on September 20, 2012).

INFIORATA FESTIVAL, FLOWER-PETAL TAPESTRIES

The *Infiorata* (also known as the Flower Festival) is a celebration in Italy that consists of creating intricate and colorful tapestries on the streets completely made of flowers to acknowledge the Catholic celebration of Corpus Christi and the processions that are organized to commemorate the event. This tradition was born in Rome during the first half of the seventeenth century as an expression of floral decorations for religious holidays.

Throughout history, religious traditions have provided powerful spiritual foundations to bring communities together. For example, one religious tradition that Catholics follow worldwide is Lent, a custom celebrating the forty days and forty nights that Jesus Christ spent in the desert. Another regional tradition that Catholics follow (especially in Italy) is to participate in the preparations for *Infiorata*, or Flower Festival. Most people in Italy believe that the creation of flower-decorated pictures was born in the Vatican Basilica by Benedetto Drei, the head of the Vatican Floreria and his son Peter, who had used "flowers frondati and minuzzati to emulation dell'opere mosaic" on June 29, 1625, during the feast of Saints Peter and Paul, who are the holy patrons of the city of Rome.

The colorful event of *Infiorata* takes place every year in small towns throughout Italy in the months of May and June. However, multiple towns in the southeast part of Sicily attract some of the most creative talent for this event. This island in the Mediterranean has developed a reputation for displaying the most intricate flower carpet designs in all of Italy. Every year, returning and new artists spend weeks creating their pictures before the *Infiorata* takes place. Artists typically use soil to outline the amazing pictures on the pavement. Once they have completed the outline of their vision, the real work begins. They use different types of flowers to give their creations amazing colors. They use mostly flower petals, but they also incorporate all the parts of the flower (stems and leaves) to decorate the streets. All the pictures displayed by the artists over the months of May and June are based on religious themes, such as saints and biblical scenes.

The *Infiorata* is a religious flower festival that is well visited by many tourists from around the world; however, it did not become as popular overnight as it is now. The first time that anyone saw the *Infiorata* creations was in 1625, but the celebration did not return as a yearly tradition until 1778, the year in which a carpet covered the entire path for a procession dedicated to the feast of Corpus Christi. After that year, *Infiorata* became an annual festival, and it was established to take place on the ninth week after Easter.

Catholics consider religious traditions to be extremely important. At a global stage, they celebrate Easter, All Saints Day, the Day of the Dead, Christmas, and the Three Wise Men. There are also many regional holidays that are celebrated by each country. The *Infiorata* is one of those regional Catholic traditions that reflect the specific cultural mosaic of Italy. The historical context of this cultural tradition has been kept alive for almost 400 years, and it still continues to attract both regional and international visitors who admire the creative talent of the Italian artists who use the streets as their canvas and flowers as their medium to express religious fervor.

Alejandra Tapia

Further Readings

Bakerjian, Martha. "Infiorata—Flower Art Festivals in Italy: Flower Petal Tapestries and Mosaics for Corpus Domini." *About.com Italy Travel.* http://goitaly.about.com/od/festi valsandevents/qt/infiorata.htm (Accessed on January 24, 2013).

Official Website for the Annual Infiorata Cultural Celebration. "Infiorata: Patrimonio d'Italia." http://www.infiorata.it/ (Accessed on February 25, 2013).

INTI RAYMI, FESTIVAL OF THE SUN

Each year in late June, people from around the world gather in the ancient high Andean city of Cusco, Peru, to witness and participate in a celebration with its origin in one of the greatest civilizations of human history, the Inca. The Festival of the Sun (known as *Inti Raymi* in the Quechua language) was the most significant, sacred, and solemn ceremony of the year for the Inca Empire. It marked the end of the agricultural harvest and the beginning of the new year. An elaborate religious ritual was staged to worship the sun and express gratitude for the benevolence bestowed upon the Inca. However, the conflict between Inca and Catholic religious doctrines caused the *Inti Raymi* celebrations to be halted in 1572. Nearly four centuries later in 1944, Faustino Espinoza Navarro—in combination with the Peruvian Quechua Language Academy and the American Art Institute in Cusco—revised the festival as a spectacular indigenous theatrical performance for a modern audience.

Calendrical ceremonies play an important role in the cultural context of most societies. Some holidays, particularly those associated with religious traditions, have a close relationship to naturally occurring astronomical phenomena. In traditional folk cultures, the movements of the sun and moon often play a profound role in the rhythms of life. Because planting and harvesting cycles, length of daylight periods, and the seasons are all tied to celestial movements, calendars throughout history have cited these motions with special days. Perhaps two important annual astronomical cycles are the two days known as the summer and winter solstices. The Northern and Southern Hemispheres of the earth experience opposite seasons, for example, winter in the Northern Hemisphere occurs during summer in the Southern Hemisphere and vice versa. The summer solstice is the day on which

Dancers participating in the *Inti Raymi* (Festival of the Sun) in Cusco, Peru. (Danilo Mongiello/ Dreamstime.com)

the sun remains above the horizon for the greatest number of hours, providing the longest period of sunlight in the year. It is also the day on which the sun reaches its highest angle in the sky from the horizon. The winter solstice is the shortest day of the year, and the sun is at its lowest angle in the sky. Calendrical ceremonies around the world are related to these two days, but for folk cultures with strong animistic traditions, the two solstices play a central role in society, and such was the case of the Inca.

Before the Spanish conquest in the late 1400s, the Inca Empire stretched along the Andes Mountain range from the modern countries of northern Chile to southern Colombia. Their rise to dominance in the region occurred rapidly through the 1400s and sprang from the center of the Incan world, the city of Cusco, a name that means "bellybutton" in Quechua. The Inca believed that they were at the center of the body of the celestial world and that all else stretched out toward the extremities. Their rapid rise to power combined with their ability to subjugate many of the neighboring indigenous people of the Andes can be attributed to multiple factors, but the Inca themselves understood their primacy as being directly connected to their religion and spiritual pantheon. Tributes to their deities were infused with religious orthodoxy. Such tributes focused on particular days within the year, and they were directed toward the spirits of such physical phenomena as the moon, rainbows, and thunder. The sun held the most elevated place within the Incan pantheon, and they celebrated *Inti* (the sun god) with the greatest and most solemn festival of the year. Their ceremony was held in Cusco a few days after June 21, the winter solstice. Although the ancient Incan system of writing (*quipú*) using a series of cords and knots is enigmatic and does not give a description of the *Inti Raymi* festival, eyewitness accounts from both Incas and Spaniards have provided some insight into the grandeur of the original celebration.

Every year on June 21, the direct rays of the sun reach their most northerly point on earth (lat 231/2° N), the line known as the Tropic of Cancer. This is the first day of winter in the Southern Hemisphere, and it signaled the start of *Inti Raymi* and the beginning of the new year, although the primary festivities actually began three days later on June 24. Because the sun was regarded as the creator and sustainer of life on earth (and because the winter solstice was tied to the rhythmic cycle of planting and harvesting), this festival was the apex of Incan religious ceremonies. In the days leading up to *Inti Raymi*, the Inca people entered a phase of mourning for transgressions committed during the previous year. All fires were extinguished in Cusco for three days before the elaborate festivities, and the nation began fasting and abstaining from sexual interactions. The sins of the world were transferred into a black llama, which was then driven out of Cusco, while the people confessed their own sins aloud. Throughout the empire, similar scenes were replicated. At dawn on the morning of June 24, the Sapa Inca, the national leader who represented the earthly manifestation of the sun god itself, alone but surrounded by the mummies of his ancestors, awaited the arrival of the first sun rays at Coricancha (now the Church of Santo Domingo, which was built atop the foundation of the former Incan temple). This was the Sapa Inca's moment to be alone and commune with the sun god. Simultaneously, the rest of the people would assume a reverential squatting position at sunrise, acknowledging the greatness of their god. When the dawn light appeared, the Sapa Inca would raise a goblet filled with fermented corn-based brew *chicha* for the sun to drink. It all occurred in total silence, but as the sun moved higher in the sky, a corresponding crescendo of chanting emulated the solar movement. As the sun moved toward its zenith, the chanting increased in volume, and as the sun descended, the chants diminished. After the sun rose, the Incan leader was carried in his litter on a procession of nobility, military officers, and ordinary citizens from Cusco to the *Inti Raymi* ceremony in the hills outside the city, a place known as Sacsayhuaman. Being the descendant and representative of the sun, the Sapa Inca would officiate at this second stage of the festival. All participants dressed in their finest clothes, and they wore robes, furs, animal skins, feathers, or masks indicative of their rank. Because the rising sun paints the sky red, both the people and the route were dressed in rich red draperies. Carried along in the procession were the remains of the royal mummified ancestors. A llama was then sacrificed to the sun. The animal's organs were removed, held up to the sun god, and examined for omens used to augur the events of the following year. Depending on the Sapa Inca's interpretation, more animals might be sacrificed hoping for a more auspicious future. The remains of these first animals were burned for consumption by the sun and their ashes spread on the festival grounds. As the ceremony progressed, many more animals were killed to feast upon. *Chicha* beer was also distributed to the people to symbolize both the successful harvest and peace among the population. As these festivities concluded, the people returned to the city and continued the celebration for nine days. At the conclusion of the *Inti Raymi* festival, the Inca leader broke open the dirt on a land parcel to symbolically commence the new year's planting season.

After the Spanish conquistadors took over the Inca Empire in 1535, *Inti Raymi* managed to survive in near-full extravagance for almost four decades. However, in 1572, the Spanish authorities considered Incan religious rites as paganism, and they cancelled the Festival of the Sun. This initiated a 372-year hibernation of the greatest of ancient Incan ceremonies.

Beginning in 1944, Cusco once again welcomed the winter solstice with a version of the *Inti Raymi* festival derived from written eyewitness accounts dating from the period surrounding the Spanish conquest of Peru in the early 1500s. Great care is taken to maintain the dignity of the indigenous peoples and the authenticity of the ceremony, while simultaneously adjusting some of the aspects of the original ritual that could be shocking to the sensibilities of many people today. In addition, while *Inti Raymi* was a religious festival of intense solemnity for the ancient Inca, the modern version takes on a much more celebratory character, with the exception of the rites conveyed on June 24 at Sacsayhuaman. As before, the ceremony begins at Coricancha near dawn with a man representing the Sapa Inca speaking to the sun in Quechua, but without the accoutrement of the mummies of the Incan royal family. In this modern version of *Inti Raymi*, a Catholic Mass is celebrated simultaneously in the nearby cathedral, and it is considered a part of the observance. The assemblage then moves to the ancient fortress of Sacsayhuaman outside of Cusco with the indigenous actors wearing elaborately ornamented costumes much as their ancestors would have worn 500 years ago. This contemporary version of the Festival of the Sun includes a symbolic rather than actual sacrifice and disemboweling of a llama. The Sapa Inca still conducts prognostications of the future based on signs and omens read through the diagnoses of the internal organs of the animal. The consumption of *chicha* and indigenous music are integral parts as well. Added to the contemporary *Inti Raymi* are the vendors who sell food, drinks, and souvenirs. Fascination with the contributions and culture of the ancient Inca has allowed the modern Festival of the Sun to grow to be the second largest celebration in Latin America, filling Cusco in late June with both indigenous people and tourists from around the world.

William F. Courter

Further Readings

Brundage, Burr Cartwright. *Lords of Cuzco, a History and Description of the Inca People in Their Final Days.* Norman: University of Oklahoma Press, 1967.

Carrasco, Fernando. "*Inti Raymi*: The Sun God Festival of Cusco, Peru." *The Travel World.* May 20, 2011 www.thetravelworld.com/2011/05/20/inti-raymi-the-sun-god-festival-of-cusco-peru/ (Accessed on January 2, 2013).

Cobo, Father Bernabe. *Inca Religion and Customs.* Austin: University of Texas Press, 1990.

Garcilaso de la Vega, El Inca. *Royal Commentaries of the Incas and General History of Peru, Part One.* Austin: University of Texas Printing Division, 1966.

Hamre, Bonnie. "Inti Raymi, Festival of the Sun." *About.com.* http://Gosouthamerica.about .com/od/perartandculture/a/IntiRaymi.htm (Accessed on January 2, 2013).

Hemming, John. *The Conquest of the Incas.* London: MacMillan, 1970.

Mann, Charles C. *1491, New Revelations of the Americas before Columbus.* 2nd ed. New York: Vintage Books, 2011.

JERUSALEM ICE FESTIVAL

In the spring of 2012 (between March 6 and the end of May), the ancient city of Jerusalem played host to its first International Ice Festival. The festival was inspired by a similar winter event in the northern Chinese city of Harbin that has been held intermittently since the 1960s, the Harbin International Ice and Snow Sculpture Festival. Along with similar events—Japan's Sapporo Snow Festival, Canada's Quebec City Winter Carnival, and Norway's Ski Festival—Harbin's festival is one of the largest in the world. Jerusalem is one of the most recent examples of exported versions of these events appearing as temporary tourist attractions in places that lack true Arctic cold weather. Consequently, these cities have to create or duplicate a cold environment (and then sustain it artificially) throughout the duration of the festival. Israel's hope is to create a new attraction that will eventually become an established tradition, which will in turn also increase tourism and generate economic activity in Jerusalem.

Since its inception, the expectations for the first ice festival of its kind in Israel were set at a high level. For this purpose, approximately three dozen ice-carving artisans from Harbin (China) were brought to Jerusalem to share their expertise, the same way they have done previously in Washington, D.C., Macau, and several southern states in the United States. These sought-after artisans have won over a thousand prizes, and China's Ministry of Culture selected Heilongjiang Province's Ice Sculpture as one of China's "Outstanding Cultural Exports and Items" in 2010. Once they arrived in Jerusalem to build the ice sculptures for the ice festival, the entire site took approximately one month to construct, since the ice must be carved carefully, and the walls and sculptures need to be constructed one block at a time.

Jerusalem's inaugural ice festival of 2012 was held in an outdoor area adjacent to the Old Railway Station which was artificially cooled to about −10°C/14°F to maintain the integrity of the ice sculptures. Coats were distributed at the entrance to keep visitors warm. Entering through an ice rendition of the Jaffa Gate in the Old City of Jerusalem, other iconic sites of historical interest were touched upon and created as large ice sculptures: the walls of the Old City dating from Ottoman times, the Tower of David, the Israel Museum, the Mifletzet ("Monster") slide, the Montefiore Windmill, and the Jerusalem Light Rail.

The ice festival was designed as a family attraction to include people of all ages. Family activities included a fairy tale world, biblical stories complete with a rendition of Noah's Ark, an ice bar for adults, ice skating, storytelling, and live acrobatic performances. Children were able to use specially designed ice slides to move between the colorful displays. The massive ice sculptures take a different appearance when they are exposed to natural light during the day as opposed to the colorful displays at night. According to the designers, the rainbow varieties of tinted ice are made possible with nothing more than food coloring, though lights and lasers are also used to bring the translucent ice to life.

The event was sponsored by the Jerusalem Municipality, with production duties overseen by the city government-affiliated Ariel Company. Ariel's director cited the Harbin traditions as the paramount example of the art, and the Chinese responded by sending their finest artisans to Israel for this inaugural event. Yet, the logistical efforts of bringing the Chinese team to Israel were stupendous, with thousands of e-mails and phone calls being sent, translated, and responded to over the course of months. Local artists assisted the Harbin team by exchanging plans and sketches that integrated native culture with the foreign ice-carving traditions.

Locals and tourists alike were extremely pleased with the results. One notable exception was an equipment malfunction in April that caused the exhibits to be closed temporarily, which threatened to melt the ice sculptures. Despite this technical difficulty, Jerusalem's mayor visited the event on no less than six separate occasions. Due to the success of the Jerusalem Ice Festival of 2012, the Chinese artisans from Harbin have already signed a five-year contract to re-create the festival through 2017.

Erin Pappas

Further Readings

"Harbin International Ice and Snow Festival 2012." *Boston.com.* http://www.boston.com/bigpicture/2012/01/harbin_international_ice_and_s.html (Accessed on August 21, 2012).

"Jerusalem Freezes Over for Its First International Ice Festival." *GoJerusalem.com.* http://www.gojerusalem.com/discover/article_1645/Jerusalem-freezes-over-for-its-first-International-Ice-Festival (Accessed on August 10, 2012)

Klochendler, Pierre. "Chinese Ice Festival Melts Jerusalem Hearts." *Asia Times Online.* April 4, 2012. http://www.atimes.com/atimes/China/ND04Ad01.html (Accessed on August 21, 2012).

Tourist Israel. "Jerusalem Ice Festival, March–May 2012." http://www.touristisrael.com/jerusalem-ice-festival-march-april-2012/3840/ (Accessed on September 5, 2012).

JUMPING OVER BABIES, *EL COLACHO*

Every year in mid-June, depending on the date of the Corpus Christi festival, Spaniards in the town of Castrillo de Murcia in Burgos, Spain, bear witness to a startling event: a man in a bright red and yellow costume running and leaping over infants who have been placed lying down on the street. The event, which dates back to 1620, is the tradition of *El Colacho*. The drama that unfolds during this multiple-day unusual celebration is a blend of Catholic and pagan rituals; it represents the classic struggle of good versus evil. As part of this elaborate theatrical performance, *El Colacho* is actually a character dressed as a masked devil that hurls insults at people and whips them with a horsetail attached to a stick. His enemies are a

A man representing the devil (*El Colacho*) jumps over babies in Murcia, Spain. (AP Photo/ Israel Lopez)

group of people belonging to the pious character known as *el Atabalero*. The *Atabalero* group of people is typically all dressed in black, and they march with drum rhythms announcing the coming of Christ. The climax of the event is the staged flight of the devil *Colacho* as he flees and leaps over babies as they rest lined up on mattresses on the street. According to ancient tradition, when the *Colacho* jumps over the infants, he absorbs the sin they were born with and takes it with him.

Fewer than 300 people live in Castrillo de Murcia year round, but during this event, the population of the small town more than doubles. The number of babies left on mats to be jumped over is unpredictable, but it is steadily growing each year. Traditionally, only children from families in the village participated, but more recently people have brought infants from as far away as the United States to take part on this unique tradition. In 2008, *El Colacho* jumped over 110 babies, and the number seems to be increasing each year.

The actors in the ceremony are the members of a secret society known as the Brotherhood of the Santísimo Sacramento de Minerva. Aside from *El Colacho* and *El Atabalero*, there are other characters who are also essential to the story: the *Colacho*'s Butler, the *Atabalero*'s Butler, a Secretary, and an undetermined number of costumed admirers. All the members of the *Atabalero*'s procession dress in dark somber colors, and *El Colacho* wears his bright outfit and mask until the final jump. Each year, the expectation is that different local people portray the characters of *Colacho* and the *Atabalero*. In addition, local youth usually fill the streets to run in the path of *El Colacho* and hurl insults at him. They play this role in hopes of warding off bad omens for the rest of the year. As a response to their insults, *el Colacho* whips them with his horsetail on a stick or with cowhide. Behind the masked devil, the entourage of the *Atabalero* marches to the beat of a fiercely pounded kettledrum and *terrañuelas* (large castanets). *El Colacho* tries to interfere with the prayers of the faithful by constantly distracting them and yelling insults at them. In preparations for this unique event, the residents of the small town of Castrillo de Murcia decorate the fronts of their houses, and they also set up altars with flowers and water for people in the parade.

Although the event, which is a blend of Spanish folklore and religion, is undoubtedly theatrical, some in Castrillo de Murcia have spoken publicly against minimizing its religious significance. Members of the Brotherhood of the Santísimo Sacramento de Minerva, clad in their heavy dark costumes in the heat of summer, perform their duties stoically. The mayor of the small town encourages visitors, but he has asked them to remember that this festival celebrates Christ, and not to forget the original intent behind the party. At the start of the festival mass, the host (a sacrament symbolizing the body of Christ) is carried under a canopy by clergy, and it is accompanied by a procession of people singing Eucharistic hymns and holding banners. However, priests in Spain have been asked by Pope Benedict XVI to distance themselves from the event, which is said to be pagan in origin.

While the sight of a mattress full of babies on the street is indeed remarkable and unusual, some residents of Castrillo de Murcia warn not to take things too seriously. For them, this festival is just an occasion to celebrate with their neighbors, with the hundreds of gawking tourists, and to enjoy the novelty of hosting the only baby-jumping devil festival in the world. In addition, it happens to bring the much-needed income to this small town in Murcia.

Michelle E. Houle

Further Readings

Bonuccelli, Domenic. "Baby-Jumping: The Work of the Devil?" *Lonely Planet.* November 20, 2009. http://www.lonelyplanet.com/spain/travel-tips-and-articles/18856 (Accessed on July 12, 2012).

Judd, Xav. "Cleansing Evil Spirits at El Colacho Baby-Jumping Festival." *Metro.* May 25, 2012. www.metro.co.uk/lifestyle/travel/900084-cleansing-evil-spirits-at-el-*colacho*-baby-jumping-festival. (Accessed on October 28, 2012).

Lior, Noa, and Tara Steele. *Spain the Culture: Lands, People, and Cultures.* New York: Crabtree Publishing Co., 2001.

Meancy, Marian. *Spain—Culture Smart: The Essential Guide to Customs and Culture.* London: Kuperard Publishers, 2006.

"Pictures from El Colacho Festival 2012." *Odd Stuff Magazine.* June 15, 2012. http://odd stuffmagazine.com/pictures-from-el-*colacho*-festival-2012.html (Accessed on November 4, 2012).

Stanton, Edward F. *Culture and Customs of Spain.* Westport, CT: Greenwood Press, 2006.

JUNKANOO BAHAMAS FESTIVAL

The Caribbean islands are known for their colorful spectacle of carnival where masqueraders take over the streets and dance to the vibrant musical sounds. The Bahamas is no exception with its unique festival known as "Junkanoo." Thousands of people flood the pre-dawn streets of Nassau, dancing to energetic drums that set the pace accompanied by a grand brass band in an artistic expression of celebration. Music plays a big part of Junkanoo with the use of traditional African instruments such as goatskin drums and cast iron cow bells called *kalik*. Recently, brass instruments have made their way into the festivities creating a great sound that blends the melodies of the vibrant percussion drums.

The festival dates back to the eighteenth century when the Spaniards brought African slaves to the island to work on the cotton plantations. During the Christmas season, the slaves were usually allowed a three-day vacation. It was during this period that one of the slaves (a former tribal chief by the name of John Canoe) insisted that they be allowed to celebrate Christmas following African customs. Therefore, for these three days—starting early in the morning—the island erupted in a very rich, old-rooted masquerade street party. The slaves celebrated the pure joy of their limited "freedom" by jubilantly leaving the plantation behind and visiting fellow slaves. This culminated in a vibrant street party where they flocked to the roads where they danced dressed in fancy costumes, played celebratory music, and created a carnival atmosphere named Junkanoo in the honor of the former tribal chief John Canoe.

These festivities continued with a strong influence of African traditions through the years until 1948, when the Bahamas Development Board organized the festival as a viable and marketable tourist attraction. Since the 1950s, it has been formally coordinated to include distinct bands and costumes, a parade route, and designated judging areas with corporate sponsorship for prizes and cash awards. It has evolved into a key tourist attraction, and it is now a national symbol of the Bahamas. There is even a museum dedicated to the festival. Nowadays, Junkanoo is held on separate days, December 26 (Boxing Day), New Year's Day, and on the Bahamas Independence Day on July 10. The festivities get underway after midnight in the wee hours of the morning and usually conclude at dawn. The parade is locally termed as the "rush," which conjures up the image of a crowd surging forward.

Thousands of masqueraders gather in Nassau to form troupes that portray a yearly theme, such as "nature." The common topic is then interpreted by designers who use cardboard as the base for the costumes. Tradition states that in constructing the costumes the less use of cloth the better. Consequently, they use layers upon layers of pasted colored crepe paper, which is sometimes completed with foil, beads, glitter, and feathers to add that razzle dazzle effect. Larger elaborate costumes are made on a framework that rolls along on wheels and can weigh anything from 100 pounds and up. These costumes are judged in their own category and receive individual prizes. There are popular troupes such as the Valley Boys, Roots, One Family, and Saxons who join rivalries in competition for cash prizes and various titles such as the "Best Costume" or "Most Colorful." The troupes dance down the stipulated masquerades street route and past various judging points to accumulate points that are tallied to give an overall winner of the highly sought after trophy for the "Best Junkanoo Group."

The biggest Junkanoo festival takes place on Bay Street in the city center of Nassau, Bahamas. The public is encouraged to buy tickets for the grandstands that provide much-needed covered seating along the route, allowing spectators to marvel at the colorful spectacle in comfort. Onlookers can also jump with the parade on Shirley Street where they enjoy the rush of Junkanoo first hand, without a ticket and getting prized photos. Visitors can also catch it out of season at the Junkanoo Expo on Prince George Wharf. Given the wide popularity of the celebratory event, Junkanoo is no longer restricted to the island of the Bahamas; similar parades are organized on associated islands such as Grand Bahamas, Bimini, the Abacos, the Exumas, and Harbour Island.

As with all big competitions, the Bahamas Junkanoo celebration has generated controversy. Since the formal judging of the parade began, so did the cries of injustice and parade rigging. The point system awarded by the judges is based on factors other than just the visual effect of the costumes, dance, and music. For example, one of the biggest categories for judging is about the timing of the band to start on the parade route at the stipulated time and place. Another controversy relates to how the festival got its name. The most popular belief is that it was named after African descendant John Canoe who insisted that slaves celebrate Christmas the traditional African way. The other belief is that the essence of Junkanoo is actually a masquerade parade in which participants hide their identity (thus, making them unknown people), which in French is translated to *gens inconnu*. However, the biggest controversy took place during 1933–1947 when the festival was actually banned from Bay Street under a law known as the 1899 Street Nuisance Prohibition Act. The ban lasted for fifteen years but die-hards paraded on other streets until 1948 when the ban was lifted.

Since 1983, Junkanoo has been portrayed as an important component of national culture. It is the essence of Bahamian traditions and has successfully been duplicated in other parts of the world. Promoted as the quintessential Bahamian event, it captures ancestry, vibrant colors, and costumes in an explosion of culture, which highlights the vitality of African drum music and the exuberance of the traditional Junkanoo dance. In recent years, Junkanoo has also been celebrated in Florida (as a smaller festival on the beach), and Canada considers it a vibrant part of its Caribana festival.

Nadia Ali

Further Readings

Bethel, E. Clement. *Junkanoo: Festival of Bahamas*. Oxford, UK: Macmillan Caribbean, 1992.

Carroll, B. Anthony. *The History of Junkanoo, Part 2: The Individual Junkanoo Participants and Performers (1940–2005)*. London: Author House, 2007.

Kuss, Melina. *Music in Latin America and the Caribbean: An Encyclopedic History.* Austin: University of Texas Press, 2008.

Rommen, Timothy. *Funky Nassau: Roots, Routes and Representation in Bahamian Popular Music.* Berkeley: University of California Press, 2011.

Thompson, Krista. "Junkanoo Rush." *Caribbean Beat* no. 82, November/December 2006. http://www.caribbean-beat.com/issue-82/junkanoo-rush (Accessed on July 20, 2012).

KAPPAROT RITUAL

The Kapparot ritual is a ceremony carried out by a group of Jewish followers, especially ultra-Orthodox Jews, just before Yom Kippur (Day of Atonement), which is the most sacred day for Jews. During the ritual, the participant waves a live chicken over his or her head. Appropriate prayers are then repeated. As the people repeat the phrases and prayers, they recognize an atonement for their sins with the chicken being the substitute for them. The sins of the person are said to be symbolically transferred to the chicken. The ritual is not viewed as a sacrifice, since sacrifices are not allowed except in the Jewish Temple, and that building was destroyed almost 2,000 years ago. A man will wave a rooster, and a woman will wave a hen. If a woman is pregnant, sometimes three chickens will be used: a hen for the woman, and both a rooster and a hen for the baby so that the baby is covered whether it is a boy or a girl. The person must then watch the chicken be slaughtered. After being killed, the chicken is made available to the poor for consumption. In some locations, there might be a collective Kapparot ritual with large numbers of people coming together with a Jewish group arranging for the presence of the required number of chickens. Sometimes the chickens are slaughtered in another location and then donated to the poor.

The Kapparot ceremony is not mentioned in Jewish scriptures. The practice originated in medieval times, and there is no clear understanding of its exact origins. A possible precursor to the ritual is mentioned in early writings in which a small seedling of some kind is waved over the head seven times and then thrown into a river on the Jewish New Year. This was referred to as making atonement for sins. There are similarities between this ceremony and the use of a scapegoat in earlier Jewish practice. In the Torah (the holy book of Judaism), instructions are given for choosing a scapegoat. Once the goat is chosen, a Jewish priest lays hands on it, and it is released into the wilderness to make atonement for the sins of the people. Atonement refers to sins of people being forgiven through a specific activity that satisfies God. Earlier traditions show that the scapegoat is taken into the wilderness and pushed off a cliff. The scapegoat is thought of as bearing the sins of the Jewish people. The use of a chicken in the Kapparot process of atonement is likely related to the concept of the scapegoat, even though there is no scriptural basis for such specific practice. This tradition is sometimes viewed as an extralegal practice carried over from a proper temple custom. One of the terms for man in Hebrew is *gever*. In the closely related language of Aramaic, spoken widely by Jewish people before the destruction of the Temple in 70 ACE, *gever* means rooster. It is believed that the connection between these terms may have led to the use of chickens in the ceremony as a substitute for people. The fact that chickens were relatively inexpensive may have also led to the adoption of this bird in the ritual. Another factor in choosing the chicken may be that chickens were never approved for sacrifice in the temple. This would help solidify the fact that the Kapparot ceremony was not a sacrificial ritual. Chickens are to be white and should not have any defects. If chickens are not available, then other kosher fowl can be used instead. However, doves and pigeons could not be used since they were approved sacrifices in the temple.

The Kapparot ritual can be performed during the ten days between *Rosh Hashanah* (the Jewish New Year) and *Yom Kippur* (Day of Atonement). The ideal time is early in the morning on the day before Yom Kippur. One of the ideas behind the killing of chickens is to make people realize that they deserve the faith that is actually happening to the chicken. The general belief is that people deserve punishment for their sins. The chicken symbolically takes the punishment that the person deserves. Those who practice this ritual point out that there is no magic in the ceremony. Most of them simply point out the symbolic nature of the imagery involved.

While the general idea is that one chicken is to be used per person in a family, there are provisions that allow one chicken to be used for the whole family if their finances are such that using multiple chickens would cause hardship. When two or more people use the same chicken, then they should perform the ceremony at the same time. A chicken that has previously been used by another person cannot be reused in another ritual. The prescribed words and prayers are said as the chicken is swung over the head three times. An adult may hold the chicken for a child, and in some cases, someone else will hold the chicken for another adult. At the point that the prayers are said and the chicken revolves around the person's head, then the sins are believed to be atoned (forgiven) already. A few practitioners suggest that participants should rest both hands on the bird during the procedure. This practice highlights even more the practice of using a scapegoat in Jewish tradition. The chicken is then slaughtered, ideally in the presence of the participant. For this part of the ritual, there are specific requirements about the kinds of knives used. Improper knives can render the slaughtered animals nonkosher. The properly slaughtered birds are then given to the poor to eat, or the equivalent amount of money is given to the poor. Groups of Orthodox Jews think that the giving of animals for food that have borne the sins of people is not a good practice. Such believers offer money instead.

Throughout the centuries, there has been rabbinic opposition to the practice. Rabbinic refers to Jewish teachers who teach and write on Judaism. Many leading rabbis have long seen the practice of Kapparot rituals as contrary to mainstream Jewish teachings. They also point out that there appear to be pagan aspects of the practice. The ceremony is practiced more among ultra-Orthodox Jews who follow some of the traditions that are outside the mainstream of Jewish practice.

In addition to the opposition from multiple mainstream Jewish leaders, the Kapparot ritual is opposed by many animal rights activists and by Jews who are offended by the slaughter of chickens. Organizations such as People for the Ethical Treatment of Animals have staged many demonstrations against the practice. In addition, many videos of the ritual chicken slaughter have been posted online in an effort to arouse opposition to the practice. One court in Israel even ruled that the killing of chickens in Kapparot violates animal welfare laws. Many Jewish leaders have also expressed support for using alternatives instead of chickens. They point out that Jewish religious laws prohibit inflicting needless suffering on animals. Some point to the fact that chickens often have to be transported long distances in cages without food and water. They can also be exposed to harsh weather while in their cages. The swinging of chickens over a person's head is another facet of the ritual that is seen as causing suffering. Multiple contemporary websites protest the use of chickens and encourage other ways of conducting the custom of Kapparot.

In the tradition of the ritual, there is an allowance for the use of money in the place of a chicken. The money is swung over the head using virtually the same words, and then the money is donated to the poor. This is often done using a bag of coins. Alternatively, a fish can also be used in place of the chicken. The outcry against the use of chickens is joined by encouragements to use one of these substitutes. For example, Rabbi Shlomo Zalman Auerbach who was an expert on Jewish law and who led a Jerusalem *yeshiva* (school teaching Jewish scriptures and traditions) came to the conclusion that the use of chickens was a violation of the prohibition of cruelty to animals. This opinion led him to end his use of animals in the Kapparot ritual.

Ken Taylor

Further Readings

Brody, Shlomo. "Must One Perform the 'Kapparot' Ritual with a Chicken?" *The Jerusalem Post Magazine.* September 23, 2011. http://www.jpost.com/Magazine/Judaism/Must-one-perform-the-kapparot-ritual-with-a-chicken (Accessed on April 8, 2013).

Federman, Eliyahu. "Use Fish Not Chicken for Kaparot." *The Jewish Press.com.* September 23, 2012. http://www.jewishpress.com/indepth/opinions/use-fish-not-chicken-for-kaparot/2012/09/23/ (Accessed on April 8, 2013).

Fishbane, Simcha. "The Ritual of Kapparot." *Jewish Journal of Sociology* 50, no. 1/2 (2008): 67–75.

Goldrich, Lois. "Ancient Ritual Still Draws a Crowd: Hundreds Expected to Attend Kapparot Ceremonies." *New Jersey Jewish Standard.* September 21, 2012. http://www.jstandard.com/content/item/ancient_ritual_still_draws_a_crowd (Accessed on April 8, 2013).

Hagerty, Barbara Bradley. "Swinging Chicken Ritual Divides Orthodox Jews." *NPR: Weekend Edition Saturday.* September 26, 2009. http://www.npr.org/templates/story/story.php?storyId=113179433 (Accessed on April 8, 2013).

Schwartz, Richard. "The Custom of Kapparot in the Jewish Tradition." *Jewish Virtual Library.* http://www.jewishvirtuallibrary.org/jsource/Judaism/kapparot.html (Accessed on April 8, 2013).

KONAKI SUMO, CRYING-BABY SUMO COMPETITION

Most celebrations and holidays in Japan are deeply rooted in tradition, religion, sports, and social life. The Crying Sumo (*Konaki*) or Sumo of Tears (*Nakisumo*) event is an annual Japanese competition for babies under one year of age. It involves

Two babies compete in the Crying-Baby Sumo Competition in Tokyo, Japan. (AP Photo/Koji Sasahara)

professional sumo wrestlers, babies, a Buddhist priest, and lots of enthusiastic parents with cameras at hand.

While the main festival takes place at the Sensoji Temple in Tokyo during the month of April, it is also celebrated in most of Japan's districts throughout the year. Similar festivities are also held at the Ikiko Shrine in the city of Kanuma-ski of Tochigi in September, at the Yamajioji Temple in Shimotsu-cho of Wakayama in October, and at the Saikyoji Temple in Hirado in February. The tradition dates back to the 1600s, and it is believed to have originated to honor a child priest who lived at the Sensoji Tokyo temple during that time.

Sumo wrestling is a serious affair in Japan. It is a 2,000-year-old sport that became one of the main professional spectator sports (besides baseball) since the early 1700s. In contemporary Japan, it is also widely practiced in high schools, universities, and amateur leagues. The tradition of Konaki Sumo involves real sumo wrestlers, but they are not the main attraction. Instead, babies steal all the attention of the audience (and the cameras). The wrestlers are dressed in their traditional fighting attire, and the babies (both boys and girls) wear head bandanas and silk robes with bright colors such as red and royal blue. The juxtaposition of the oversized wrestlers holding tiny delicate babies offers an interesting contrast that photographers appreciate. The role that sumo wrestlers play in the competition is to hold the babies up facing each other and the local priest. Then, the big-proportioned wrestlers begin scaring the babies by yelling at them and making ugly faces. The first baby to cry is declared the winner. If the two opposing babies cry at the same time, the sumo wrestlers and the priest intensify their efforts to make them cry even more. The baby who yells out the loudest is then announced as the undisputable winner. However, every once in a while, there are babies who refuse to follow the rules, and they simply do not cry. Much to the amusement of the audience, babies either stay quiet, fall asleep or even start giggling at the sumo wrestlers' scaring tactics.

The tradition of the Crying-Baby Sumo Competition (*Konaki Sumo*) is based on a Japanese proverb stating that "crying babies grow fast" (*naku ko wa sodatsu*). It is widely believed that the louder the babies cry, the healthier they will be in life. In addition, their high-pitch yelling sounds are also believed to spook the evil spirits away. Overall, the festivities provide a celebration for families and tourists to enjoy throughout the year.

Javier A. Galván

Further Readings

"Bizarre Festivals of Asia." http://www.dyscario.com/travel-and-places/10-of-the-most-bizarre-festivals-of-asia.html (Accessed on July 2, 2012).
"Japan Festivals." http://japan-fest.info/ (Accessed on July 2, 2012).
Kamachi, Noriko. *Culture and Customs of Japan.* Westport, CT: Greenwood Press, 1999.
Shilling, Mark. *The Encyclopedia of Japanese Popular Culture.* New York: Weatherhill Publishers, 1997.

KRAMPUS AND CHRISTMAS

Krampus is a mythical, horned, goat-like creature that derives from a European Alpine legend. In dark contrast to Saint Nicolas—who travels around the world on Christmas Eve to give gifts to good children—Krampus (the Christmas demon) accompanies Saint Nicolas in order to warn and punish children who misbehave. He usually carries a whip or switch with him in order to carry out his punishments. Krampus also resorts to stealing the bad children's presents. Even worse, he will kidnap all the particularly naughty children, taking them back to his lair to devour them for Christmas dinner. The legend of Krampus originated as pre-Christian Germanic folklore, and it continues as a modern tradition during Christmas time in a myriad of European Alpine countries.

Krampus's appearance varies by description, but he is often described as being shaggy, goat-like with hooves and horns, usually black or brown in color, and as having a long pointy tongue. Some legends have him bearing chains and bells that he whips around in order to frighten children. His cloven hooves and long tail are also noticeable features, as well as the bundle of birch-twigs he wields with vigor toward the naughty children.

The legend of Krampus is rooted in pre-Christian pagan tradition, and it also mirrors some characteristics of the half-goat satyrs in ancient Greek mythology. In Germanic folklore, Krampus was a mystical creature who lived in the European wilderness. There are many legends about wild men that derive from the Alps of central Europe. The stories were mainly about incubus—male demons that had intercourse with sleeping women—and such stories were largely based on older

A Satanic wooden mask used for the Krampus in Austria. (Andreas/Dreamstime.com)

fertility rites. The birch switch he carries has a pagan phallic significance, and the chains (though reminiscent of older pagan traditions) may have been introduced in a Christian attempt to "bind the Devil" (Bruce 1958). The influence of Christianity in the region eventually set the pagan legends apart as evil, thus solidifying the story of Krampus as the wicked counterpart to Saint Nicolas. Some folktales describe the dark-haired, dark-faced Krampus as Saint Nicolas's evil twin brother. While Saint Nicholas dispenses gifts to the well-behaved children, Krampus gives out bags of coal and bundles of birch. Along with the possibility of being kidnapped and devoured for dinner, children would have to worry about Krampus frightening them with rusty chains and bells, whipping them with a switch, throwing them in a barrel or sack to be drowned, or being taken back to hell where his lair awaits.

Krampus is referred to by various names, depending on the region of Europe. The origin of the name Krampus comes from the German *krampen*, meaning "claw." Throughout Austria, Krampen is referred to as *Klaubauf*. In southern Austria, the devil is also referred to as *Bartl* or *Bartel*, *Niglobartl*, and *Wubartl*. Outside of Austria related creatures go by *Pelzebock* and *Gumphinckel*. For example, in southern Germany Krampus is called *Pelznicke*; in Hungary he is known as *Krampusz*; in Slovenia he is called *Parkelj*; and in the Czech Republic he is known as the *Čert*. In general, the regions of the south central Alps call him *Badalisc*.

Different traditions commemorating the hairy creature are practiced throughout many European countries. *Krampusnacht* (Krampus Night) is celebrated on December 5, the evening before Saint Nicholas Day on December 6. Villages in the Alps celebrate *Krampusnacht* by dressing up in costumes made out of sheep-skin. They wear horns, sharp teeth, and carry a switch, chains, or a bundle made of twigs. People dressed as the long-haired devil celebrate by heading out to the streets and frightening young children and adults alike. *Krampuslauf* is a parade of frequently inebriated celebrants dressed up as the beast. A sweet liquor, Krampus schnapps, is often offered to the participants of the parade as they pass by observers during the *Krampuslauf* tradition. Usually, the parade or run takes place on December 5; though in larger cities, there may be numerous runs throughout the Christmas season. In Germany, women will sometimes dress up as the goddess spirit Frau Perchta. According to Jacob Grimm—the nineteenth-century author and editor of the popular *Grimm's Fairy Tales*—Frau Perchta is responsible for Krampus as a "guardian of beasts," similar to her spirit equivalents in other Alpine regions. She usually appears in German folklore during the twelve days of Christmas. She was known to reward good children by placing a small silver coin in their shoe, but she also punished the bad children by cutting open their stomachs, removing their entrails, and then replacing them with stones and straw.

Krampus appears in various forms, and as part of differing celebrations, throughout central Europe. Another tradition honoring Krampus is *Krampuskarten*. Similar to the Valentine's Day tradition of exchanging cards, Europeans have been exchanging *Gruß vom Krampus* (Greetings from the Krampus) cards featuring the hairy beast since the 1800s. The cards range from being stoically serious to crudely humorous, usually including rhymes and poems. The cards often illustrate an ominous-looking Krampus gazing menacingly over the shoulder of an unsuspecting child. Other examples portray Krampus shoving little children in barrels getting ready to whisk them away to his lair, or chaining them up so he can get a taste of what might become his Christmas dinner. A sample of more humorous versions show the black-haired, horned devil gawking at the breasts of a voluptuous woman or standing behind a camera taking pictures of unsuspecting women in their bedrooms. Older versions of Krampus cards tend to represent the shaggy beast as a terrifying and evil creature ever ready to wield his bundle of birch, whereas newer versions portray a friendlier, charming version of Krampus usually depicted as an elf-like creature. Postcards representing Krampus are also sent during the Advent season, and his image is often represented on cartons or tins that hold candies or other holiday treats. In Styria, Austria, along with exchanging Krampus greeting cards, people also practice the exchange of *ruten*, the birch carried by Krampus. Bundles of gold-painted birch are hung on the walls of family homes year-round as a form of decoration. These golden bundles also serve as a reminder for children to be well-behaved throughout the year so they do not have to endure the wrath of Krampus and his rusty chains.

Popular Austrian Christmas markets of the larger cities usually include a more humorous tourist-friendly version of Krampus as opposed to the more frightening devil; however, the tales of more fearsome Krampus are extremely popular in the European countryside. Smaller Austrian towns have started extending the former one-night celebration into festivals or *Krampusfest* lasting for an entire weekend. In southeast Austria, small villages celebrate *Kränchen*, which is a community event held indoors. *Kränchen* is typically held on the Saturday either before or after December 5 in a village facility that can accommodate a large number of villagers. Local organizations will sometimes sponsor *Kränchen*, and they use it as an opportunity to raise money for charity. The *Kränchen* is usually celebrated with music and drinking until the Krampuses arrive. After arriving, the costumed instigators then run around the facility with birch switches whipping those unfortunate celebrants who cannot get away fast enough. Eventually, the participants playing the role of Krampus remove their masks, and they join the rest of the community in the festivities.

Modern celebrations surrounding Krampus are gaining popularity throughout Europe, and they have recently made some appearances in the United States. Though North American Krampus festivities are rare, the more traditional German communities or the northern United States—particularly the Pennsylvania Dutch—celebrate a hybrid version of the Krampus tradition. In these communities, the creature similar to Krampus is referred to as *Belsnichol*. *Belsnichol* simultaneously represents both Saint Nicholas and his evil companions, and he usually travels alone. This character manages to combine the frightening aspects of Krampus with the benevolent features of Saint Nicholas. With Krampus traditions spreading to new markets around the globe, it seems that the festivities surrounding Krampus will continue to be practiced throughout the Alpine regions of Europe and beyond for years to come.

Stefanie A. Babb

Further Readings

Beauchamp, Monte. *Krampus!: The Devil of Christmas.* San Francisco: Last Gasp, 2010.

Bowler, Gerry. *The World Encyclopedia of Christmas.* Toronto: McClelland & Stewart Ltd, 2000.

Bruce, Maurice. "The Krampus in Styria." *Folklore* 69, no. 1 (March 1958): 44–47.

Haid, Oliver. "Christmas Markets in the Tyrolean Alps: Representing Regional Traditions in a Newly Created World of Christmas." In *Festivals, Tourism and Social Change: Remaking Worlds*, edited by David Picard and Mike Robinson. Buffalo, NY: Channel View Publications, 2006.

Scott, Delilah, and Emma Troy. *The Upside-Down Christmas Tree and Other Bizarre Yuletide Tales.* Guildford, CT: Lyons Press, 2010.

KUMBH MELA SPIRITUAL PILGRIMAGE

Kumbh Mela is considered to be the largest religious gathering in the world. As an illustration, the pilgrimage held in Allahabad, India, in 2013 (from January 14 to March 10) attracted over 80 million visitors (Daniel 2013). The festival is usually held between January and February despite the cold temperatures. It is a peaceful gathering in contemporary India where tens of millions of Hindu followers congregate for fifty-five days to bathe in a sacred river during the most auspicious days of the massive celebration. The festivities are held every three years in a rotation pattern in one of four possible locations in India: Haridwar, Nashik, Ujjain, and Allahabad (also known as Prayag). Each of these four locations has at least one large river where the gathering takes place: the Ganges River at Haridwar; the Godawari River at Nashik; the Shipra River at Ujjain; and the meeting point of the Ganges, Yamuna, and Saraswati Rivers at Allahabad. As a result of the rotation system, the Kumbh Mela celebration only takes place in each location every twelve years, but the one held in Allahabad is the largest of them all. Moreover, the Maha Kumbh Mela is held only in Allahabad every 144 years. It is a massive celebration that brings people together (including Hindu saints, gurus, and monks) moved by faith where they can pray for salvation and wash their sins away by bathing in one of the sacred rivers. Millions of followers also come hoping that the attending gurus offer blessings and spiritual wisdom. For devoted Hindus, this is a memorable once-in-a-lifetime experience.

A Hindu follower at Kumbh Mela 2013 held in Prayag, Allahabad, India. (Courtesy of Rajeev)

The primary goal of the pilgrimage is the ritual bath on the river banks. Multiple Hindu groups follow specific traditions. For example, one of the most notorious sects are the *sadhus* followers who wear saffron-color sheets to cover themselves and display their skin covered with ashes; the *naya sanyasis* do not wear any clothes, and they bathe completely naked, even during the extremely cold temperatures in January and February. While these groups receive most of the visual attention of the media, there are millions of average Hindu devotees (mostly from rural areas) who make the arduous pilgrimage from their villages to the religious site. During Kumbh Mela, however, there are other activities held, such as discussing religious doctrine, singing spiritual songs, feeding millions of poor people, offerings for the ancestors in the afterlife, and gatherings of saints and leaders to establish specific religious positions related to contemporary social issues. This congregation brings together so many religious leaders because it is considered the most sacred gathering for Hindu followers.

The history of the Kumbh Mela celebration dates back for centuries as travelers mentioned in their journals events regarding river festivals in India. A Chinese Monk named Xuanzang wrote about it during his visit to India in 629 ACE. Centuries later, Mark Twain also wrote about it during his travels throughout Asia in 1895. In contemporary India, most media venues offer comprehensive coverage of the event in multiple formats, including television, radio, Internet, blogs, twitter, and other communication media. The celebration is based on Hindu mythology. Most devotees have learned the legend of a battle between demons and gods that took place in heaven when they were fighting over a pitcher holding the nectar of immortality. They fought for twelve days and twelve nights, which is equivalent to twelve years in human terms. During the dispute, four drops of such nectar fell to earth and landed on the four places in India where Kumbh Mela has been celebrated for centuries. The actual location for the religious celebration is determined by the position of the Sun in relation to the Moon and the planet Jupiter. Those calculations also determine the most auspicious days to bathe in one of the rivers to maximize the influence of such celestial elements.

The preparations for this event represent a logistical challenge to most local governments as well as health officials and law enforcement agencies. For example, the city of Allahabad prepared for months in 2013 and organized a temporary city on the sandy river banks of the Ganges. In order to manage the enormous crowds, the city made arrangements for more than 40,000 temporary toilets, created a large network of pipes for drinking-water infrastructure, scheduled additional trains and transportation, set up fourteen temporary rudimentary hospitals, employed over 30,000 police for security, coordinated 243 doctors working twenty-four hours a day, and provided a large flotilla of trucks bringing food for millions of people (Pandey 2013). During the celebration, meat and all types of liquor are strictly forbidden. For the high-tech Hindu followers, there is even an app for smart phones to help the devotees navigate their way to the holy rivers. The city also coordinated a vast number of volunteers who helped the weak and the elderly at the river with their ceremonial bathing ritual. They also provided assistance to the crowds by moving the people who had finished bathing in order to make space for more Hindu followers.

In recent years, city officials and social welfare agencies have noticed important social patterns and concerns. For example, health officials at Allahabad have issued warnings against drinking the water due to the potential pollution of the rivers. A more serious concern is that an increasing number of Indian families use the large crowds of the celebration to take their elderly relatives and then abandon them there; the majority are elderly widows. The general reason is that family members no longer want to look after them or support them. City leaders have reported that dozens of elderly people are abandoned at the religious gatherings, and city officials now anticipate such occurrences (Spinney 2013). Overall, the Kumbh Mela celebration has always attracted millions of followers from all regions of India, but in the past twenty years, it has also been attended by large numbers of foreigners who also follow Hinduism.

Javier A. Galván

Further Readings

Daniel, Frank Jack. "Millions of Hindus Take to the Ganges at Maha Kumbh Mela." *Reuters.* Allahabad, India. January 14, 2013. http://in.reuters.com/article/2013/01/14/india-allahabad-ganga-maha-kumbh-mela-idINDEE90D05Q20130114 (Accessed on September 7, 2013).

Kumbh Mela Official Website. http://kumbhmelaallahabad.gov.in (Accessed on September 6, 2013).

Narain, Badri, and Kedar Narain. *Kumbh Mela and the Sadhus—The Quest for Immortality.* Varanasi, India: Pilgrims Publishing, 2010.

Pandey, Geeta. "Kumbh Mela: Eight Million Bathers on First Day of Festival." *BBC News, India.* January 14, 2013. http://www.bbc.co.uk/news/world-asia-india-21017217 (Accessed on September 7, 2013)

Spinney, Laura. "At Largest Religious Festival, Some Abandon Elderly; At the Maha Kumbh Mela in India, Families Ditch Older Relatives in the Crowds." *National Geographic.* February 22, 2013. http://news.nationalgeographic.com/news/2013/02/130223-cul ture-travel-religion-india-maha-kumbh-mela-world-women-widow-hindu-festival/ (Accessed on September 6, 2013).

KUNG MUSICAL HEALING CEREMONY

The Kung (also called as !Kung or Bushmen) people of southern Africa were at one time in history the dominant native people of southern Africa. Their territory once included areas of Mozambique, Botswana, Swaziland, Namibia, Angola, Lesotho, and South Africa. When they were first encountered by Dutch explorers in the seventeenth century, they numbered about 300,000. By the 1970s, their numbers had been drastically reduced to less than 50,000. Nowadays, the multiple Kung groups have significant linguistic variations among them; consequently, they are also known by several names, including Basarwa, Sho, San, and Khwe. As a collective group, they are regionally known as the San people. In modern times, the Kung groups now live mostly in Botswana and Namibia. These people from the Kalahari desert used to live a nomadic lifestyle as hunters and gatherers. However, during the 1990s, multiple governments provided options for them to switch their nomadic traditions into a farming lifestyle. The result has been a significant increase in their numbers, which reached a population of almost 100,000 at the beginning of the twenty-first century. Despite the government efforts to provide small agricultural settlements for them, for the Kung groups, this is still an extremely difficult and arid environment where survival is difficult, water is scarce, and diseases often spread quickly throughout the region. As a result, the relief of suffering and the treating of illness are primary needs for this community. In this regard, music and dance are essential elements of their cultural traditions since they serve both as a source of healing and as a source of survival.

Throughout history, multiple traditional cultures have attributed music and dance with special healing powers, and their ceremonies usually involve a connection to one of their gods. In the belief system of the Kung people from southern Africa, illness and discomfort are caused by a "creator god" who in turn sends good and evil to the community through a series of lesser gods and messengers. Therefore, an illness is considered to be a supernatural event, and treatment requires the Kung leaders to contact and influence supernatural beings. They accomplish such connection to their higher power through the Kung healing ceremony. This spiritual ritual dance is performed once or twice per week, and it typically lasts from dusk to dawn. This is called the *!kia* dance. At its climax, the *!kia* generates the "n/um" energy which is believed to reside in the stomach.

During this spiritual ceremony, music plays a crucial role in the healing process. Music is required to summon the spirits in order to precipitate the trance state necessary for healing. The local medicine man must achieve a trance state for the ceremony to work, for in this way he will come into contact with the spirits and thus drive illness out of people. The healing power is believed to exist within the actual songs performed, and so the order and form of the overall ritual must be strictly followed.

Every member of the community participates in the Kung musical healing ceremony. The ritual begins as the women of the community sit around a fire, and they begin clapping and singing. Each singer adds a melodic fragment, typically sung in what sounds like unclear syllables but which actually have great meaning to the participants. Their multiple contributions create composite melodies that are in fact the product of the community as a whole and not necessarily of any individual alone. Outsiders who have witnessed this healing ceremony state that the music is unlike anything they ever heard before. While the women sing, the men dance around them in single file in a well-choreographed pattern while wearing rattles on their legs. The dancing part of the ceremony can go on for hours. The music and dancing gradually cause the men to enter trace states, and since about half the males are considered to be medicine men, there are many in the community who have the power of healing. Eventually, one entranced medicine man will approach a sick member of the community.

There are two stages of the healing process. In the first, the illness is captured from the afflicted member by the medicine man and driven out. This is done as the medicine man uses his own perspiration (a product of the dance) to anoint the sick member. He then lays his hands upon the sick member and performs a massage in order to draw the sickness away into his own body. Once he is in contact with the spirits (especially the secondary god and his "messengers"), the medicine man demands that they take the illness by hurling it at them. He then drives them away through the use of insults and hurled sticks. Through the process of healing one member of the community, the medicine man manages to heal the entire community.

Multiple religious and cultural traditions throughout the world include rituals in which their members reach a trance state. However, the !Kung musical healing ceremony practiced in Botswana and Namibia is unique in that the trance state is achieved not through hallucinogenic drugs but through the power of the songs to draw the community together. This, in turn, inspires dances with stronger fervor and calls to the spirits. This ceremony is thus a unique example of the power of music to strengthen a community, effect transformation, provide spiritual nourishment, and create healing.

Kevin Wozniak

Further Readings

Adhikari, Mohamed. *Not White Enough, Not Black Enough: Racial Identity in the South African Coloured Community.* Cleveland: Ohio University Press, 2005.

Gill, Victoria. "Africa's Genetic Secrets Unlocked." *BBC World.* May 1, 2009. http://news.bbc.co.uk/2/hi/science/nature/8027269.stm (Accessed on February 22, 2013).

Hast, Dorothea E., James R. Cowdery, and Stan Scott. *Exploring the World of Music: An Introduction to Music from a World Music Perspective.* Dubuque, IA: Kendall and Hunt, 1999.

Khoi San Peoples. "Survival of the !Kung People in the Kalahari Desert." *African First Peoples: The Bushwo/men.* http://www.khaisanpeoples.org/indepth/ind-survival.htm (Accessed on February 22, 2013).

Peoples, James, and Garrick Bailey. *Humanity: An Introduction to Cultural Anthropology.* Beverly, MA: Wadsworth Publishing/Cengage, 2011.

LAND-DIVING CEREMONY

The ritual of land diving is performed by men of different age groups living on Pentecostal Island, which is part of an archipelago in the Republic of Vanuatu in the South Pacific. The colorful ceremony is performed in the southern part of the island, and it is regionally known as both *Gol* (in Sa language) and *Nanggol* (in the Bislama language). Following regional customs, the highlight of the event is when men defy death by jumping head first from tall wooden towers with multiple diving platforms (between 66 and 100 feet high or 20 to 30 meters) specifically built for this annual ceremony; they only wear two thin tree vines (called *lianas*) tied around their ankles. On their way down, the divers reach a falling speed of almost 45 miles per hour (or 75 kilometers per hour). They do not use any safety equipment to mitigate the potential danger of death, or at least serious injuries, such as head concussions, broken arms, or crushed vertebrae. They dive straight down toward the floor below; there is no water, air mattresses, special nets, or any cushions to protect the jumpers. They simply tilt their head down and fold their arms across their chest in order to cover themselves. The objective is to slightly touch the ground with their shoulders without getting their head smashed in the process. The Guinness World Records has labeled this indigenous tradition as the precursor to the recently popular bungee jumping adventure. However, the people of Vanuatu who practice this ritual are not seeking simply an adrenaline rush. Instead, land diving reveals their historical and cultural connection to the land. In fact, they believe that the higher the diver jumps, the most likely a bountiful harvest will follow that year.

The Republic of Vanuatu was an Anglo-French territory for much of the twentieth century, and it obtained its independence in 1980. However, the custom of land diving existed prior to the arrival of the Europeans, and it has two possible origins: as a rite of passage for young men and as a harvest ritual. The tradition does not have a specific date to document when it was established, but it has been practiced for centuries in Vanuatu. Since its inception, it was recognized as a rite of passage for young men to prove they were worthy of adulthood status in the community. An ancient local legend narrates the story of Tamalie, a man whose wife left him because he often abused her. When he went looking for her, he found her hiding atop a tall Banyan tree. He then climbed the tree to take her back home. Fearing for her life, she tied tree vines (*lianas*) around her ankles and jumped off the tree. Tamalie believed that his wife had committed suicide rather than returning to her routine life. As a result, he became so despondent that he also leaped off the Banyan tree. However, he did not tie any of the vines around his body and died upon hitting the ground. His wife, however, survived due to the strength and elasticity of the vines she had used, which kept her from hitting the ground. The remainder of the men in the village took immediate steps to protect their male-dominated society and to avoid similar incidents in the future. Consequently, they started to train for land-diving activities, slowly increasing the height of their jumps, while also learning and perfecting the use of tree vines for the most appropriate length and resistance. Along the way, the village elders also prohibited women from taking part on this new tradition ever, though ironically, a woman was the first person in Vanuatu to jump from a tree at high altitude. Nowadays, the preparations for the land-diving ceremony are extremely elaborate, and women are strictly prohibited from witnessing any of the rituals taking place behind the scenes. Women still play a role in the festivities, but it is mostly limited

A boy jumping from a platform as part of the Land-Diving Ceremony on the Island of Pentecost in the South Pacific. (Johnjewell/Dreamstime.com)

to performing choreographed dances and providing emotional support for the men participating in the jumping ceremony.

The physical center of the land-diving ritual is the wooden tower (*nagol*); everything happens around it. It takes roughly twenty men between two and four weeks to build it using local tree trunks and sturdy branches. During that period, men go into seclusion prior to the event and even refrain from all sexual activity. The day before the jump, most men settle all their affairs—just in case they die. The night prior to diving, they sleep at the foot of the tower in order to keep malevolent spirits away. The morning of the event, between ten and fifteen participants wash their bodies in a spiritual ritual and then rub oil on their bodies. Occasionally, they wear necklaces made of animal teeth and tusks as decorations. The event starts early in the morning when the younger divers begin jumping from the lower platforms. This is part of their training, and it is a venue to prove their bravery. The highlight of the day is when the most experienced divers climb the tower, make a brief speech, and then leap from the highest platforms at almost 100 feet high (33 meters). An adventurous experience of this type has inherent dangers, and divers have died during these events. For example, Queen Elizabeth visited the island in 1974, and she witnessed a diver leap to his death. While international spectators often request permission to jump from the wooden tower during the festivities, the local organizers of the event now refuse to allow foreign visitors to participate on the jumping activities due to potential liability concerns.

The contemporary version of the land-diving ritual takes place between April and May every year. The events are carefully coordinated with the yam harvest, which is a crucial staple food on the islands of Vanuatu. In addition, the *lianas* tree vines have the best natural elasticity during this time of the year. Local land divers have accumulated a vast amount of knowledge about *lianas* over the centuries; their lives depend on such information. For example, they know that if vines are too dry, they might simply snap. The vines also have to be studied carefully regarding the correlation they have with the specific weight of each diver. There is no one-size-fits-all. If the vine is too long, or the weight of the diver is not calculated proportionally to the vine, the result could be serious injuries or death. The tradition has expanded beyond a rite of passage to prove strength and bravery toward a celebration of fertility that reflects the regional respect for the land. The custom is now mostly viewed as a ritual performed for anticipating an abundant yam harvest. When divers perform the dive well, they are supposed to touch the ground (very lightly) with their shoulders, thus blessing the land.

A thrill-seeker from New Zealand (A. J. Hackett) witnessed the ritual of land diving in Vanuatu in 1986, and he had the vision of turning it onto a mainstream attraction. He then went home to adapt the adventurous experience by incorporating modern-world safety equipment, including mountaineering-strength ropes, helmets, and climbing harnesses. For a year, he perfected the jump. Then, in 1987, he performed an illegal jump (albeit certainly impressive) from atop the Eiffel Tower in Paris. The event attracted much international publicity, and it catapulted bungee jumping as a popular attraction not only in New Zealand but also worldwide.

While bungee jumping has increased in popularity worldwide, land divers in Pentecostal island still practice their ritual the way they have done it for centuries and without any safety equipment. Nothing has changed; they even continue to build their wooden towers using the same rudimentary methods learned over the years. However, the land-diving ritual of Vanuatu has become world famous, and it now attracts thousands of international tourists. The commercialization and exploitation of this cultural tradition has certainly been criticized and widely discussed in both academia and indigenous affairs councils at international levels. However, the local elders of Vanuatu decided that allowing spectators to witness the ritual would generate much-needed revenue, which can actually be used to maintain the tradition alive.

Javier A. Galván

Further Readings

Jolly, Margaret. "Kastom as Commodity: The Land Dive as Indigenous Rite and Tourist Spectacle in Vanuatu." In *Culture, Kastom, Tradition: Cultural Policy in Melanesia*, edited by L. Lindstrom and G. White, 131–46. Suva, Fiji: Institute of Pacific Studies, 1994.

Kal, Müller. "Land Diving with the Pentecost Islanders." *National Geographic Magazine* 138, no. 6 (1970): 799–817.

Lee, Mike. "Land Divers of Vanuatu." *ABC News.* http://abcnews.go.com/WNT/story?id=130132&page=1 (Accessed on August 20, 2012).

National Geographic Society. "Land Diving in Vanuatu." http://video.nationalgeographic.com/video/places/regions-places/australia-and-oceania/vanuatu_landdiving (Accessed on August 14, 2012).

Ronca, Debra. "How Land Diving Works." *How Stuff Works.* http://adventure.howstuffworks.com/land-diving.htm (Accessed on August 20, 2012).

Tabani, Marc. "The Carnival of Custom: Land Dives, Millenarian Parades, and Other Spectacular Ritualizations in Vanuatu." *Oceania* 80, no. 13 (November, 2012). http://www.questia.com/read/1G1–243121571/the-carnival-of-custom-land-dives-millenarian-parades (Accessed on August 20, 2012).

LITTLE DEVILS FESTIVAL, *LOS DIABLITOS*

Every year, thousands of people in the town of Boruca, Costa Rica, participate in a festival that celebrates the strength and resilience of the native Boruca population: the *Fiesta de los Diablitos.* The Festival of the Little Devils is a vibrant and colorful tradition that occurs yearly in two Costa Rican indigenous communities: Boruca and Rey Curre. Other names often used to make reference to the Boruca people include Borunca, Brunca, Brunka, and Burunca. The celebration in Boruca runs for three days (from December 31 until January 2) and the festival in Rey Curre is celebrated in February. During the festival, the Boruca people celebrate a victory over the Spanish conquistadors. While the indigenous group fought furiously against the Spaniards in multiple battles, the real triumph actually being celebrated is that the Boruca culture survives despite the efforts of Spanish colonialists to extinguish their traditional way of life. The ritual celebration involves a cast of culturally significant characters dressed in masks and elaborately designed costumes.

In preparation for the *Fiesta de los Diablitos* in Costa Rica, Boruca men spend time designing, carving, and painting intricate masks from Balsa wood and cedar. The masks generally feature large, colorful, grotesquely distorted faces of humans or animals, which are usually adorned with horns. These masks represent ancestral spirits sacred to the Boruca—the *Diablitos.* The nickname is thought to have come from a disparaging term for the Boruca used by the Spanish conquistadors, perhaps due to the fact that the Boruca had not been baptized in the Catholic faith. In addition to the masks, men wear garments made of *gangoche* (a fabric similar to burlap) sacks, thin strips of wood, fur, feathers, and banana leaves. One of the most traditional masks represents a massive bull's head. This is the largest mask out of all the masks used in this celebration, and it is stuffed with dried leaves so that it burns well at the end of the celebration. Traditionally, the bull has represented the Spanish conquistadors who dominated multiple indigenous civilizations. However, in contemporary times, it has come to symbolize any threat to the cultural integrity of the Boruca people.

The festival commences when an elder of the tribe signals by sounding a conch shell at the top of a sacred hill. During the festivities, most of the gathered participants drink liquor made from fermented corn called *Chicha,* which is usually drunk directly from a hollowed *guacal* gourd. The men dance in a "fight" for three days; they weave in and out throughout the community and into peoples' houses and yards. Some use their masks in a manner similar to protective gear used in organized sports such as football. Such staged fights, heavily affected by the growing intoxication level of the *Diablitos*, carry the risk of injury to participants. Due to the potential danger of injuries, some of the elders in this traditionally patriarchal culture prefer that women do not take part in the stages rough events. Although women do not customarily participate in the dance, they are certainly involved in all the preparations for the festival. At the end of the choreographed fight and dance, the balsa wood bull is set on fire at a public location.

In addition to the Little Devils and Bull, there are other characters involved in the elaborate dance performances. While musicians play regional instruments that include skin drums, violins, and reed flutes during the performance, other performers known as "herders" serve as intermediaries between the audience and the performers; they are in charge of coaxing the Little Devils into action. On the last day of the festival, a performer playing the role of the "Matador" kills the bull, and another participant acting as the "Butcher" enacts the cutting-up of the bull meat.

The traditional festival of *Los Diablitos* provides members of the Boruca tribe with an opportunity to commemorate their moral triumph over the Spaniards. It also celebrates their strength, resilience, and identity as a people. Traditionally, the masks remained unpainted, but due to the growing interest in this cultural festival, mask sales have become an important source of revenue for this indigenous group. According to recent accounts, at the end of the festival, participants may sell their used masks for roughly US$100. As demand continues to grow for these items, the number of artisans and the quality of craftsmanship has increased due to the expanding commercial interest. New masks can now cost as much as $300 or $400.

The ancestors of the Boruca people lived in chiefdoms along the Pacific coast of Costa Rica. Like other indigenous people of the region, the Boruca used to live on a subsistence economy. Indigenous groups lived in chiefdoms, and they were ruled by *caciques* (chiefs). During the 1500s, the Spaniards arrived to claim Costa Rica for Spain. The Spanish conquistadors killed and enslaved a large number of Indian tribal members, including the Boruca, who fought against colonial subjugation. Conquered peoples suffered greatly from both the direct torture and cruelty inflicted by the conquistadors, as well as the exposure to fatal diseases for which they had no immunity. The chiefdom of the Boruca people was considered completely conquered by 1563. Subsequently in 1629, the village of Boruca was established as a railway station stop along the route for Spanish mule trains. For nearly 200 years, Costa Rica was a colony of Spain, and it finally achieved its independence in 1821. Land rights were awarded to indigenous people in Costa Rica in 1939. At present time, the Boruca indigenous people live on the Boruca reservation in the Puntarenas Province, located in the cantón (township) of Buenos Aires.

In 1983, a women's organization (*La Asociación de Flor*) was formed to address a number of substantial economic problems that challenged their community. At that time, Boruca lacked access to secondary education, families suffered from food insecurity, and rates of infant malnutrition were on the rise. By capitalizing on the public interest in the *Fiesta de los Diablitos*, the group successfully generated interest in Borucan crafts, including festival masks and handwoven textiles.

The indigenous group now plays a crucial role in promoting tourism, especially by arranging accommodations for students, visitors, and festival spectators.

Today, the *Fiesta de los Diablitos* is a significant tourist attraction that draws a large number of spectators from all over the world each year. The festival and its masks, which symbolize and celebrate the respect Borucan people have for their ancestors and their culture, have now become a means to promote and support the culture and traditions they cherish.

Michelle E. Houle

Further Readings

Helmuth, Chalene. *Culture and Customs of Costa Rica*. Westport, CT: Greenwood Press, 2000.

Koutnik, Jane. *Costa Rica—Culture Smart: The Essential Guide to Culture and Customs*. London: Kuperard Publishers, 2012.

Levin, Matt. "'Little Devils' Game." *Tico Times*. January 6, 2012 http://www.ticotimes.net/layout/set/print/Current-Edition/Top-Story/News/Little-Devils-Game-honors-Boruca-past_Friday-January-06–2012 (Accessed on August 29, 2012).

Rojas, R. Uriel, "Fiesta o Baile de los Diablitos." *Southern Costa Rica*. http://www.southerncostarica.biz/Buenos-Aires/cat-events-parties/Fiesta-o-Baile-de-los-Diablitos/341/ (Accessed on October 14, 2012).

Yoder, Kelli. "'Devil' Masks Infuse Economy, Preserve Culture for Indigenous Tribe." *CNNi Report*. January 24, 2012. http://ireport.cnn.com/docs/DOC-736016 (Accessed on September 2, 2012).

LIVING WITH THE DEAD

In South Sulawesi, Indonesia, the Tana Toraja people perform elaborate funeral rites to assist the spirit of their dead relatives to transition to the afterworld called *Puya*, the land of souls. The Toraja groups do not believe that the spirit of the dead person immediately leaves the body upon death; therefore, the spirit needs help transitioning into its next life. Until a sufficient amount of funds have been collected to produce an elaborate funeral ceremony, the corpse of the dead relative is kept inside the home, or *tongkonan*, of its family members. This is only a temporary solution. During this period, the family lives with the corpse, and they refer to their relative as sick and not necessarily dead. The family will even serve the "sick" corpse three meals a day with the rest of the family. When the funeral finally takes place—sometimes months or even years after the person died—it can last for days, have thousands of attendees, and be very expensive. After the funeral, the spirit of the deceased relative finally leaves its body, and it begins its long journey to *Puya* where all the souls reside.

The Toraja people, an agricultural-based society in rural Sulawesi, are fascinated with death, and they spend their lives preparing for the afterlife. Unlike in most societies, funerals are the most important ceremonies of the Toraja. The richer and more important the individual, the more elaborate and expensive is the funeral ceremony thrown for them by their family. More influential families will hire funeral planners, dancers, and "mourners." The Torajans traditionally believe that the death is a gradual process that can take days, months, or years, for the soul to reach *Puya*. Torajans also believe that as the soul travels to the afterlife, it needs the fundamental provisions that it enjoyed on earth. During this waiting period, the corpse is kept inside the home, or *tongkonan*. The embalmed body is wrapped in several layers of cloths and placed inside a casket. The *tongkonan* are the beautifully carved and painted ancestral homes of the Torajans. The first *tongkonan* was said to have been built in heaven before the first ancestor of man descended to earth. The *tongkonan* are at the center of Torajan social ceremonies and cannot be bought or sold—they can only be passed down through the generations. While the corpse remains in the house, it is treated as if it is alive and only sleeping.

When enough funds have been procured, the funeral finally takes place. Funerals are usually scheduled to coincide with a period after the harvest but before the sowing of seeds. In this part of Indonesia, it occurs typically between July and September. The funeral ceremony is a community event, and it allows for anyone to participate, even curious tourists. The family, with the help of villagers, build a tower in preparation for the ceremony. This is where the family will distribute the meat of the sacrificed water buffalo and pigs. These sacrifices take place so that the animals can accommodate the deceased relative on their journey. The number of water buffalo that is sacrificed depends on the status of the deceased, but the number can run in the hundreds. Before the ceremony begins, the family sometimes holds a Christian funeral service for the deceased, as many Torajans have converted to Christianity during the Dutch occupation of the early twentieth century.

The day before the public ceremony, community members and relatives from Toraja and around the world begin to gather. The formal procession called *Ma'Passa Tedong* begins on the first day. During this procession, family and community member offer gifts of buffalos, pigs, rice, and drinks to the family members of the deceased person. This is a formal process in which all contributions are meticulously registered so that debts can be considered repaid. By the evening, the large coffin is carried by hundreds of people to the funerals grounds. The funeral site is called *rante*, and it is a large grassy field where rice barns, shelters for guests, and other specific funeral structures are built by the family before the ceremony. Once the coffin arrives, the tradition of buffalo and cock fighting begins while attendees place bets on the winners. On the following day, the family decides how many buffaloes are to be slaughtered. The buffaloes are killed in public by simply slitting their throat. Only after the first buffalo is killed is the person considered officially dead, and his or her soul is finally able to leave the body. The most prized buffalo is the spotted or albino buffalo, *tedong bonga*, which can be very expensive and hard to obtain. Attempts to breed the unique animals have failed, and therefore the albino buffalo remains rare. The meat of the buffalo is then distributed to all the attendees, including foreigners and tourists. The funeral ceremony also includes music, singing, dancing, drinking, and wailing. On the day of burial, *Ma'Kaburu'*, the coffin is carried by hundreds of people, and it is followed by sometimes thousands of people in a ceremonial procession to the cliffs. The dead body is not buried, but it is interred in hanging graves high up on the rocks or in cliff caves.

There are several types of graves in Toraja. The *Batu Lemo* grave is carved into the side of the cliff, and the body is wrapped in cloth and then placed inside of the hole. Wood-carved effigies called, *tau-tau*, are human-like statues made to re-semble the deceased person in clothing, body, and appearance. They sit perched on the cliffs near the rocky graves. The Torajan people believe that the *tau-tau* stat-ues protect the village from evil. A single grave can hold between three and five corpses. Once the grave is filled up, the family asks a *pande batu* to carve a new hole near the existing one. The *Erong* grave is when the deceased person is put into a large coffin that holds between two and five corpses. The coffin is then entombed inside of a cave. The *Patane* grave is a modern grave that resembles a house. These graves are used by Christian Torajans, and they are considered to be the second home of the deceased. The coffins are placed inside the house, which can hold up to twenty-five corpses. There is one grave per family, and they are sometimes call *banua tang marambu* or "house that no longer has smoke." A tree grave is reserved for the youngest of deceased Torajans. When babies die before their first tooth is cut, the mother wraps the baby in a blanket or areca bark. Then, she cuts a hole in a "baby tree" and places the child in it. She patches the hole with palm leaves, and the tree eventually grows around the baby's body, absorbing it. The Torajans bury the babies in the trees so that they can continue living.

The *ma 'nene'* ritual is also practiced by Torajans. Once every few years in Au-gust, family members clean the coffins and corpses of their ancestral relatives whom they believe remain important members of their community. They remove the coffins from the caves and rock graves and take them to the place of the cer-emony. They remove the bodies from the coffins and change their clothing. The family members treat the corpse as if it is a living member of the family. For exam-ple, for a few days after death, the families will sometimes even carry the deceased family members around the village. This ritual allows for the family to show com-passion and love to their ancestors. By keeping the spirits happy, the community hopes to ward off crop pests and misfortune to their families. If someone gets sick or if something goes wrong in his or her life, he or she visits the "holy man." Ac-cording to the old beliefs, the holy man will read pieces of bamboo and tells the person which ancestral spirit is angered and what he or she needs to do to stop the misfortune. Sometimes, the family members are instructed to remove the corpse of the ancestor from the village in order to put an end to the family misfortune. The relationship between family members and their deceased relatives is such a strong bond that, if a villager ever moves, they will also exhume the bodies of their ances-tor and take them along.

Stefanie A. Babb

Further Readings

Bigalke, Terance William. *Tana Toraja: A Social History of an Indonesian People.* Singapore: Singapore University Press, 2005.

Coville, Elizabeth. "Remembering Our Dead: The Care of the Ancestors in Tana Toraja." In *The Potent Dead: Ancestors, Saints, and Heroes in Contemporary Indonesia*, edited by Henri Chambert-Loir and Anthony Reid, 69–87. Honolulu: University of Hawai'i Press, 2002.

Crows Nest, Australia: Asian Studies Association of Australia in association with Allen and Unwin; Honolulu: University of Hawai'i Press, 2002.

"Dressing the Dead." http://www.thejakartaglobe.com/eyewitness/dressing-the-dead/540350#Scene_1 (Accessed on October 25, 2012).

Dunham, Chris. "Life and Death in Tana Toraja, Indonesia." http://www.transitionsabroad.com/listings/travel/narrative_travel_writing/life_and_death_in_tana_toraja_indonesia.shtml (Accessed on October 23, 2012).

"Funeral Ceremony in Toraja." http://www.incitoprima.com/details.php?catid=5&aid=5 (Accessed on October 28, 2012).

Volkman, Toby Alice. *Feasts of Honor: Ritual and Change in the Toraja Highlands*. Urbana: University of Illinois Press, 1985.

LOBOLA: **BRIDAL AND FINANCIAL CONTRACT**

Lobola, translated as "bride-price" or "bride-wealth," is a centuries-old South African tradition that is still practiced in many South African communities today—particularly in the rural districts of Zimbabwe and Lesotho. The cultural tradition of *lobola* is also known as *Roora* in Shona, and *Mahadi* in Sesotho, and it is considered a financial and social contract in South African communities. While this tradition is deeply rooted in ancient customs, it is a cultural practice that is very much alive in the twenty-first century in the region of South Africa. Compared to the European custom of *dowry*, *lobola*'s goal is to unite two families together through a gift offering of wealth. Opposite of *dowry*, in which the burden of payment rests on the women's family, *lobola* recognizes the value of the women, and the man pays his fiancé's family an agreed-upon price in order to marry his bride. The custom is meant to cultivate communal respect between the families and to prove that the man is financially able to care for his new wife. Traditionally, *lobola* was calculated using cattle, as cattle were the primary symbol of capital in most African societies. However, modern urban couples usually pay the bride price in cash. The practice of *lobola* is controversial as it has been simultaneously both criticized and supported throughout contemporary African society.

According to the ancient tradition of *lobola*, men must exchange wealth for women and the privilege of marriage. *Lobola* serves multiple purposes in South African society, including but not limited to: the distribution of material sources, the establishment of relationships between and within lineages, the creation of social identity, and the maintenance of social conditions. The complex and formal negotiation process of *lobola* is a practice central to contemporary African society which many modern couples and their families insist on practicing. The process has complicated procedures that must be followed and can certainly cause confusion for modern couples. The negotiation procedures must be completed through formal written agreements and a traditional ceremony as opposed to less formal and more modern communication methods such as telephone conversations or informal meetings. Even if the two families are neighbors or long-time friends, there are formalities in which the process must be adhered. The custom varies in practice from culture to culture in the general region of South Africa.

The custom of *lobola* begins when the two groups in charge of negotiations from both families get together for a meeting. The parents of the prospective groom usually choose other family members, typically uncles of the groom, to act as negotiators while emphasizing the importance of extended family to South African culture, especially in the institution of marriage. Traditionally a bottle of brandy is placed on the meeting table to symbolically break the tension between the families. The bottle of brandy is not opened or consumed, but instead represents relaxation and acceptance. This part of the ceremony is called *mvulamlomo*, which is translated as "mouth-opener." The negotiations can take up to two days or until the negotiators can agree upon an amount of cattle or cash that is to be paid as *lobola*. After negotiations, there are other rules in which the couple must follow. The couple is usually forbidden to meet until the wedding day. These procedures are important to the *lobola* contract because they represent a mutual understanding of trust and community between the two families.

Controversy has always surrounded the practice of *lobola*, especially since the early colonists in Africa interpreted it as the "sale of daughters for cattle" (Ansell 2001). At that time, women were seen as chattels, with marriage being no more than a commercial transaction for obtaining property. At its worst, *lobola* allows for some women to be treated as property and subjected to abuse by both her husband and his relatives. This tradition is more prevalent in the rural districts of South Africa that suffer from high poverty rates, migrant labor, unemployment, and landlessness. There are two types of marriage in the rural districts of South Africa: customary and civil. In a customary marriage, there is no minimum age requirement; it is potentially polygamous, and it requires both fathers of the bride and groom to sign an agreement and pay *lobola*. Civil marriage is monogamous, has a minimum age of sixteen for women and eighteen for men, and is usually performed by a religious leader or district administrator.

THE CONTEMPORARY BURDEN OF *LOBOLA* PAYMENTS

The tradition of *lobola* payments to the bride's family is more prevalent among lower-income groups. Many youngsters trying to get married now believe that it is no longer a token contribution as originally intended to foster respect and trust between two families but rather a greedy attempt by many unscrupulous family members who use it for their own benefit. In addition, the *lobola* payment is actually not a reachable goal for a large percentage of the South African population who barely earns a minimum living wage. In this context, the use of *lobola* payments seems rather extravagant. This potential impediment has created two unintended consequences. One of them is that a young impatient couple simply decides to move in together without getting married. The other consequence is that many women end up waiting a long time for a suitable partner who can afford such a financial commitment, which can place women past their most fertile years for having children and raising a family.

Javier A. Galván

Customary marriage takes precedence in these rural areas, though usually the marriage is a combination of the two different types. Customary marriage promotes discrimination against women, and—in both Zimbabwe and Lesotho—customary laws are exempt from the constitution's laws on discrimination. Zimbabwe, as opposed to Lesotho, has made attempts to end discrimination against women due to the practice of *lobola* and customary marriage. In 1991, the government of Zimbabwe ratified the Convention on the Elimination of the Discrimination against Women. *Lobola* is no longer a legal requirement of customary marriage; though, it is rare that couples over eighteen—who have the right to refuse *lobola*—choose to not include it as part of their marriage. A survey in the 1980s showed that only 5 percent of couples chose not to practice the custom of *lobola*.

As another aspect of customary marriage, the practice of polygamy is closely connected to *lobola*. The same 1991 law that ratified the Convention on the Elimination of the Discrimination against Women allowed polygamy to remain a component of the customary marriage laws. Customary laws allow men to have many wives, but because of *lobola*, usually only the wealthy can afford to do so. Nowadays, fewer and fewer modern South Africans practice polygamy, but it remains constitutional in South African societies. White South Africans disproportionately disparage the practice of polygamy, but the blight of the AIDS epidemic in South Africa has created more opposition to the practice in traditional South African societies. Polygamy promotes gender inequality despite the fact that the constitution requires all customary marriages to be registered in order to ensure that each wife in a polygamous family has equal rights to property. This government policy, however, does not protect women against other problems associated with polygamy, such as abuse, neglect, or the spread of sexually transmitted diseases. In an effort to promote gender equality, the South African constitution states that the Bill of Rights should take precedence over the rights of customary law, even though they are contradictory. Polygamy also has major social ramifications in that it promotes social inequality when a man marries more than one woman, leaving some men with no one to marry.

There are many advocates for customary marriage law and *lobola*, many of whom are part of the educated and more modern communities of women in South Africa. Many of these women argue for the custom of *lobola* because they believe the practice does not hinder them in any significant way, while at the same time provides protection for them. South Africa offers women strong constitutional protection, but customary laws are often given precedence over constitutional rights in most African communities. Women's rights activists were some of the top supporters of a new law enacted in 2001, which helped protect women living in common law unions with their children, by recognizing African customary law. Divorce, however, is not usually granted in most situations because money or goods were exchanged for the bride. Divorce is usually only granted in cases where the family can pay back the *lobola* amount. Because repayment is rarely possible in these situations, women are often forced to remain in sometimes abusive or unhappy marriages. Other negative aspects surrounding *lobola* are closely connected with how the bride-price is spent by the woman's family. Traditionally, the money or cattle received by the bride's family was supposed to be used in helping the new couple set up a household, and it was not intended to be used for the personal gain of individual family members. However, it has become increasingly more common that *lobola* is actually used for paying off the family's debt. The cultural practice of *lobola*'s in South Africa has relatively few negative effects; consequently, it remains as a popular custom in South African societies, and it is intended to promote trust and community between families.

Stefanie A. Babb

Further Readings

Ansell, Nicola. "'Because It's Our Culture!' (Re)Negotiating the Meaning of 'Lobola' in Southern African Secondary Schools." *Journal of Southern African Studies* 27, no. 4 (December 2001): 697–716.

Chigwedere, A. S. *Lobola—the Pros and Cons*. Harare, Zimbabwe: Books for Africa, 1982.

Mufana, Bill. *The Lobola System and a Few Other Topics*. Lusaka, Zambia: Zambia Educational Publishing House, 2006.

Mvududu, Sara C. *Lobola: Its Implications for Women's Reproductive Rights in Botswana, Lesotho, Malawi, Mozambique, Swaziland, Zambia, and Zimbabwe*. Harare, Zimbabwe: Women and Law in Southern Africa Research Trust, 2002.

"South African Traditional Marriage Customes: Lobola and Polygamy." http://www.south africaweb.co.za/article/south-african-traditional-marriage-customs-lobola-and-polygamy (Accessed on October 12, 2012).

"Understanding Lobola." *Health.iafrica.com*. December 13, 2001. http://health.iafrica.com/psychonline/qa/general/124598.html (Accessed on October 12, 2012).

LOG-RIDING ONBASHIRA FESTIVAL

The log-riding Onbashira festival is celebrated only every seven years during the months of April and May. It is held at the picturesque Lake Suwa in the central part of the Nagano Prefecture on the Japanese island of Honshu. The word *Onbashira* in literal translation from Japanese means "the honored pillars," and it refers to sixteen great trees that are felled specifically for this event and then made into massive logs. These logs are ridden down the mountainside by teams of young men. This is an opportunity for participants to show their masculine bravery and prowess despite the potential peril of being crushed under a heavy log.

The Onbashira festival is believed to have been held every year uninterrupted for the last 1,200 years; according to the Chinese calendar, it is usually on the year of the Monkey and the Tiger. The festival is dedicated to Suwa-no-Kami, the major goddess in the pantheon of the traditional Japanese religion of Shinto. The Suwa Taisha is the main temple of the Suwa-no-Kami and also one of the most ancient Shinto shrines. The waters of the Lake Suwa never freeze except for the top, which takes peculiar ice formations because the circulation of the lower water is kept warm by a hot spring running underneath. The ancient local belief that helped in explaining this natural phenomenon was by imagining gods traveling underwater across the lake between the various parts of the Suwa temple. The Onbashira festival is supposed to be as old as the temple itself, and it originated as a ritual of

Shrine parishioners ride a log (Onbashira) down the hill in Shimosuwa, Japan. (AP Photo/ Hiro Komae)

regular renewal of the Suwa Grand Shrine. It was first mentioned in the first Japanese book of writings, the Kojiki, giving account of Shinto mythology, and it dates back to a period about 1,400 years ago.

The log-riding festival consists of three main parts. The first one takes place in April and is called *Yamadashi*, which translates as "coming out of the mountains." Prior to this part, some of the largest trees are felled in a forest covering a nearby mountain. This activity is performed as a part of the ceremony, and only by means of axes specially made for the event. These trees are then adorned in red and white decorations, which are the traditional Shinto colors. The logs are about 17 meters long (52 feet), 1 meter in diameter (3 feet), and may weigh up to 12 tons. The first and most recognizable event of the festival features volunteers riding and occasionally dropping the logs down the steep mountains slopes and fast rivers. This log-riding tradition is called *kiotoshi*, and it is preceded by a spiritual activity in which each participant goes through a special Shinto purification ritual. The second part of the festival is called *Satobiki*; it is celebrated in May, and it includes placing the sixteen logs in each corner of the four parts of the Suwa shrine: the Kamisha (upper shrine), the Shimosha (lower shrine), the Harumiya (spring shrine), and the Akimiya (the autumn shrine). Each log is raised ceremoniously, and its successful lifting is celebrated by a team atop of the log with a song. The third part of the event (and comparatively the less known part) is called "Building of Hoden," and it serves as the mark of ending the festival.

The Onbashira log-riding festival is considered an important part of Japanese cultural heritage, and it is also a spectacular event that has lately been estimated to attract about a million onlookers each year, not counting direct participants. The cultural tradition received international exposure when the raising of the logs ceremony (similar to the *Satobiki* part of the festival) was performed during the opening ceremony of the Eighteenth Winter Olympic Games of 1998, which actually took place in Nagano. As a result, the Onbashira festival was popularized in the West, which in turn attracted more visitors to the area. However, the log-riding during the *Yamadashi* is considered very dangerous, especially for the team member who seats in the very front of a log. Each time the festival takes place, several people are injured, and sometimes even killed. For centuries, these deaths were considered honorable, but now the local authorities have implemented measures designed to prevent further casualties. The potential for injury and death (rather than the religious significance of the ceremony) explains why at the Onbashira events, unlike most other Japanese festivals, outsiders are welcome only as spectators but not as participants. In 2004, for the first time in the long history of the festival, the comprehensive medical care system was provided to deal with cases of emergency, so that serious incidents were prevented. During the next festival, held in 2010, however, two men, aged forty-five and thirty-three, died after crashing from a 10-meter (30 feet) high log that was being raised during the *Satobiki* ceremony. Two other men were injured during the same part of the festival, but they quickly received medical help from the emergency team.

After a long tradition lasting over 1,200 years, the Onbashira log-riding festival continues to retain its dual meaning: it represents a celebration of the masculine side of Japanese culture, suffused with danger and risk of destruction, but it is also related to the renovation of one of the most ancient and honored Shinto temples. In 1998, the Japanese musician Kitaro released an album named *Gaia Onbashira*, featuring two compositions entitled "Satobiki" and "Kiotoshi" and dedicated to the log-riding festival as a symbol of tradition and continuity.

Marharyta Fabrykant

Further Readings

Collins, Sandra. "'Samurai Politics: Japanese Cultural Identity in Global Sport—The Olympic Games as a Representational Strategy." *The International Journal of the History of Sport* 24, no. 3 (2007): 357–74.

Gerbert, Elaine. "The Suwa Pillar Festival Revisited." *Harvard Journal of Asiatic Studies* 56, no. 2 (1996): 319–74.

Imazato, Satoshi. "Semiotic Structure of Traditional Japanese Rural Space: Hagikura Village, Suwa Basin." *The Public Journal of Semiotics* 1, no. 1 (2007): 2–14.

Kitazawa, Masakuni. "The Twilight of a Tradition." *Tulane Drama Review* 39, no. 2 (1995): 106–14.

Macé, François. "Woods and Sanctuaries in Japan." In *Cultural Diversity and Transversal Values: East–West Dialogue on Spiritual and Secular Dynamics,* edited by Samantha Wauchope, 111–18. Kyoto, Japan: International Research Center for Japanese Studies, 2006.

Melton, J. Gordon. *Religious Celebrations: An Encyclopedia of Holidays, Festivals, Solemn Ob-servances, and Spiritual Commemorations.* Santa Barbara, CA: ABC-CLIO, 2011.
Yazawa, Kazuyuki, et al. "Medical Care for a Mass Gathering: The Suwa Onbashira Festi-val." *Prehospital and Disaster Medicine* 22, no. 5 (2007): 431.

LOSING HMONG FEMALE NAMES

Members of the Hmong cultural group are spread out throughout Laos, Vietnam, Cambodia, Thailand, and Burma. According to Hmong traditions, women experi-ence a number of name changes throughout their lives. For major life changes, such as marriage and childbirth, a woman's name is modified to reflect her position within the family. Over a lifespan, a woman's name changes three or more times, reaching a point when the original name is lost and no longer remembered. This naming convention reflects the high value that Hmong place on social structure; changes to a woman's name are a clear indicator of status within her husband's clan and family unit.

The Hmong are a patriarchal, patrilineal, and patrilocal culture. They practice a patriarchal hierarchy, meaning that men maintain the highest social rankings. Due to the male's social standing, the Hmong are a patrilineal society where lineage is traced through the father. It is also a patrilocal culture, requiring women to relo-cate close to the husband's family upon marriage. Daughters are not considered true members of the clan into which they were born; instead, they are educated to be good wives and mothers in their husband's clan, of which they become per-manent family members. Birth, marriage, and childbirth mark the most important changes in a woman's life; because these changes impact the family, they are cel-ebrated with a new name. In certain cases, names can also be changed to reflect traumatic occurrences or to protect a person from the spirits; these types of nam-ing are not exclusive to women. In general, the Hmong's naming practices have the goal of reinforcing traditional social and cultural values.

Name changes in Hmong culture underscore the importance of kinship; all major life events affecting the family are celebrated through this tradition. The nam-ing cycle begins at birth, when a Hmong female receives her father's clan name and a first name. After she marries, the couple moves to the husband's family where her name changes to reflect entrance into the new clan. While she technically retains her clan name, her first name is altered to mirror her husband's name. Some clan members will use kinship terms (such as daughter-in-law or sister-in-law) instead of her name to note her relationship to the family. After the birth of her first child, a woman's identity becomes expressly linked to the child. As a mark of prestige, a woman's name changes again to that of the child, a process known as teknonymy. Female personal names traditionally have little value to the maintenance and ex-pansion of the family unit; replacing a first name with a kinship term or teknonym solidifies a woman's connection and status within the family.

To illustrate these changes, take the example of Fang Mee, a daughter named Mee born into the Fang clan. When Fang Mee marries Tong Xang, she becomes Niam Tong Xang, or Tong Xang's wife. Some family members will call her by a kin-ship term, such as daughter-in-law or sister-in-law, to signify familial relationship.

Niam Tong Xang's name changes again with the birth of the couple's first child. For a child named Tou, Niam Tong Xang receives the teknonym Tou Niam, or Mother of Tou. By the time Tou Niam has grandchildren, several generations will have passed. Her name would have changed multiple times, making it unlikely that family members would remember her original name.

Hmong people originated in southwest China, and they migrated to Laos, Vietnam, Thailand, Cambodia, and Burma in response to brutal oppression experienced under the Qing dynasty. Historical records date the Hmong, also known as the Miao, to 2500 BCA, making them an indigenous Chinese ethnicity. The largest migration south occurred in the early 1800s, when the Hmong were forced to resettle outside their traditional homeland. While in China, the Hmong developed an intricate worldview centered on family and ancestor worship. Loss of female names developed in China to reflect the importance placed on family and spirituality. Name loss does not strip of woman of her birth clan's identity; instead, it reinforces her absorption into her husband's family, ensures the longevity of the clan, and it assures there will be children to support the family in life and the afterlife. The name change reinforces Hmong patriarchies, patrilineal descent, and spiritual beliefs. Hmong traditional customs, including name modification, continue to be practiced in China and Southeast Asia.

A CULTURE IN TRANSITION: THE HMONG IN FRESNO, CALIFORNIA

Between the period of 1975 and 1995, over 110,000 Hmong people migrated to the United States with the status of refugees. Over half of that group settled in California, especially in the cities of Fresno and Merced. Without a country of their own, they immediately felt pressured to adapt to the American culture and social practices. After one or two generations, the Hmong population is in transition regarding its traditional cultural values, and it is deeply divided among generational lines. The older generation tries to preserve important components of Hmong culture, including their language, marriage practices, and funerary customs. The younger generation is often more concerned with being accepted as part of the larger culture to which they belong, which implies speaking English, listening to rock music, and not attending many of the Hmong cultural events organized in their communities. In simple terms, teenagers are concerned with assimilation, which often also includes changing their names to sound more "American." Given the large number of Hmong population in Fresno, California, they have developed a large network of businesses and community organizations that provide services to them, including radio stations, newspapers, supermarkets, churches, and lots of restaurants.

Javier A. Galván

In the 1970s, the Vietnam War greatly impacted the Hmong. Many families fled to Australia, Europe, and North and South America. Integration and acculturation in these new societies placed constraints on aspects of traditional culture, including name loss for women, as these traditions directly conflict with social concepts of equality and individual freedom. Some members of the second generation adopted naming conventions that mirrored standards in the new society: first names written before clan names, decisions to alter names for specific life-changing events, and hyphenation of married women's last names to show both birth and husband's clan names. Reasons for changing traditional naming practices include lessening perceived discrimination, building personal and professional relationships in the non-Hmong community, and avoiding the bureaucratic maneuvering required for multiple legal name changes. Altering the traditional naming convention often creates tensions between first- and second-generation Hmong. In contemporary settings, the first generation perceives movement away from traditional culture as an irreparable loss, while second- and third-generation immigrants seek to bridge traditions from the homeland with the local culture. Naming practices, among other traditions, are becoming more fluid to preserve Hmong identity and the role of family within the context of new nationalities.

Laura Steckman

Further Readings

Burt, Susan M. "Naming, Re-naming and Self-Naming among Hmong-Americans." *Names* 57, no. 4 (2009): 236–45.

Cooper, Robert. *Scarcity and the Hmong Response.* Singapore: Singapore University Press, 1984.

Lee, Gary Yia. "The Religious Presentation of Social Relationships: Hmong World View and Social Structure." *Lao Studies Review* no. 2 (1994–1995): 44–60. http://members .ozemail.com.au/~yeulee/Culture/hmong world view and social structure.html (Accessed on October 25, 2012).

Lee, Gary Yia, and Nicholas Tapp. *Culture and Customs of the Hmong.* Santa Barbara, CA: Greenwood Publishing Group, 2010.

Owens, Christine W. "Hmong Cultural Profile." *Ethnomed.* May 1, 2007. http://ethnomed .org/culture/hmong/hmong-cultural-profile (Accessed on November 3, 2012).

LOTUS BIRTHS

A lotus birth is the practice of childbirth where the baby's umbilical cord is not cut. It is commonly accepted that in a normal birth, the newborn's umbilical cord is immediately clamped and cut. Meanwhile, when delivering a child with the lotus birth method, the umbilical cord is not clamped and cut so that the placenta and the baby remain connected for a few more days. The goal of a lotus birth is to let the placenta perform its final "duty," which is to help release the umbilical cord from the baby's body naturally. The umbilical cord and placenta attached to the baby's navel is left alone to dry, and then it separates naturally within three to four days. This method of childbearing is widely common in Bali, Indonesia.

During a lotus birth, the placenta needs to get the proper treatment until it separates from the baby. For example, when the baby takes a shower, the placenta should also be cleaned and dried gently with a towel. The placenta is stored in a basin or large bowl nearby with salt and aromatic fragrances. The aromatherapy usually consists of selected flowers, herbs, or spices that emit appealing scents such as lavender and goldenseal. The practice is expected to accelerate the drying process of the placenta, to neutralize the smell of decomposition, and to protect against antibacterial properties. After it detaches naturally from the baby, both the umbilical cord and the placenta are buried near the house so that children will always know where their roots are located.

Leaving the placenta attached to the baby after birth provides tangible medical benefits during an infant's early life. Upon birth, this vital organ is actually still channeling blood rich in nutrients and mineral substances (urea, sodium, and iron), oxygen, and antibodies to the baby. The process of cutting the umbilical cord essentially "cuts off" the blood supply and oxygen; consequently, the baby loses the opportunity to get about 30 milliliters of blood from the placenta, which is nutritionally comparable to 600 milliliters of blood of adults. This component is believed to prevent infant iron deficiency and to assist babies in developing a strong immunity system.

Medical research has also demonstrated that lotus births provide additional benefits to babies. In a study conducted in Sweden of 400 infants, it was concluded that babies whose umbilical cord was cut off after a 3-minute delay have higher iron levels at the first four months of their lives compared with infants whose umbilical cord was cut a few seconds immediately after birth. The study, published in *The British Medical Journal* (van Rheenen and Brabin 2006), found that the delayed cutting of the baby's umbilical cord for three minutes is an effective method for preventing anemia. The analysis also found that newborns with the delayed clamps have greater amounts of iron in their blood. The iron levels at birth can affect a baby's health, and it can be particularly risky for babies to suffer anemia in the first months of life. In addition, a related study carried out on primates by primatologist Jane Goodall found that wild chimpanzees also practice this instinctive mammal process of lotus births. Chimpanzees—which have 99 percent of genetic material similar to humans—always let the placenta intact and never damage or cut it. She claimed that such innate predisposition toward a lotus birth among primate could also be applicable to humans.

In addition, lotus births provide a few potential psychological benefits to newborn babies. The delivery process is a transitional phase in the baby's life. At the moment of birth, the baby's environment suddenly changes from the womb to the outside world. The practice of a lotus birth minimizes the trauma during such transitional period. When the newborn baby stays connected with the placenta and umbilical cord, babies are believed to live their early lives in the world with a more familiar, relaxed, and calmed environment without feeling insecure due to sudden "loss" and "separation" from their main connection to the womb. Other attributions observed on babies born as part of a lotus birth include that they sleep better, have a calmer personality, and can be breastfed much better than babies whose umbilical cord was cut immediately after delivery.

However, despite these benefits, another study also found that infants in the delayed-clamping group were more susceptible to jaundice. Many babies get a mild form of jaundice at birth because of an immature liver that cannot process bilirubin, a yellow byproduct of red blood cells. When the liver cannot process bilirubin, it can make the baby look a little yellow. In this case, the umbilical cord should be clamped to prevent jaundice. This happens especially when there are differences in maternal and infant blood type, such as the mother's blood type being O and the babies' blood types being A, B or AB. The longer the umbilical cord is left, the more the mother's incompatible blood is mixed with the baby's blood.

From a global perspective, the practice of lotus births is a relatively new phenomenon, but the delay in cutting the umbilical cord has been practiced for centuries in Balinese culture and the Aboriginal culture of Australia. Spiritual references to lotus births can also be found in the religious traditions of Buddhism, Hinduism, Christianity, and Judaism. In Tibetan and Zen Buddhism, the term "lotus birth" is used for describing the spiritual teachers such as Gautama Buddha and Padmasambhava (Lien Sen-hua), insisting they go into the world as holy children. In Hinduism, for example, the lotus birth appears in the story of the birth of Vishnu.

The island of Bali in Indonesia has multiple traditions and rituals related to the birth process. Every baby-birth brings a new and different story. The birth of a baby is a moment for joy and celebration. Most women sing their own songs to their babies. Balinese Hindu people also recite a mantra prayer (*gayatri*), and they sing to welcome the birth of a baby into the world. Besides singing Hindu mantra prayers, the parents tend to the umbilical cord as an extension of the child for several days after birth. The umbilical cord is part of the baby's organs, and to cut it suddenly will surprise the baby both physically and emotionally. When the placenta naturally gets separated from the infant, it will be immediately taken by the baby's father to be buried in the family yard, so that the children will always be able to find their way back to the family home.

Balinese mothers are typically encouraged to deliver their babies naturally without much intervention. Her husband and family usually need to help convince her with the constant reassurance that she is able to have her baby born normally because she has actually been designed to be able to give birth naturally. Lotus births are also a way for the mother and baby to have an emotional attachment by having a rest together, skin-to-skin contact, and a breastfeeding connection as soon as the baby starts to move. This tradition nurtures the mind, body, and spirit of both the mother and baby. When the tradition of lotus birth is conducted, then it strengthens human affection, which is indispensable for human survival.

When the placenta takes a little long to separate from the baby's body, one technique that is sometimes performed is to slightly burn the umbilical cord. According to Balinese belief, burning the cord transfers all the life-force energy from the placenta onto the baby, allowing the infant to feel complete despite missing the connection to this vital organ. During the combustion process of the umbilical cord, the Balinese Hindu people also sing another *gayatri* mantra prayer until the cord is completely burned and separated.

The tradition of lotus births—as part of a method of gentle birth—is a movement back to nature which attempts to restore the old wisdom of human life. When people find a variety of tools, they want their lives faster, practical, and comfortable. However, technology has also had an impact on the harmony of life, including on newborn babies. When we eliminate the elements of hassles, then unconsciously we have lost the hidden benefits behind natural events.

Patit Paban Mishra and Abubakar Hara

Further Readings

Davies, Leap, McDonald. *Examination of the Newborn & Neonatal Health: A Multidimensional Approach.* Philadelphia: Elsevier Health Sciences, 2008.

Lim, Robin. *After the Baby's Birth: A Complete Guide for Postpartum Women.* New York: Ten Speed Press, 2001.

"Lotus Births." http://www.ayahbunda.co.id/Artikel/Terbaru/Terbaru/lotus.birth/001/006/897/3 (Accessed on November 11, 2012).

"Lotus Births, Indonesia." http://www.cmindonesia.com/1/post/2012/7/kala-dokter-bicara-soal-lotus-birth.html (Accessed on November 11, 2012).

"Urban Mama." http://theurbanmama.com/articles/lotus-birth.html (Accessed on November 11, 2012).

van Rheenen, Patrick F., and Bernard J. Brabin. "A Practical Approach to Timing Cord Clamping in Resource Poor Settings." *British Medical Journal* 333, no. 7575 (2006): 954–58.

World Health Organization (WHO). *Care in Normal Birth: A Practical Guide, Report of a Technical Working Group.* Geneva: World Health Organization, 1997.

MAASAI CIRCUMCISION CEREMONY

The Maasai circumcision ceremony is a maturity rite of passage for the Nilotic (or Nilotes) ethnic group of semi-nomadic people located in Kenya and Tanzania. The Maasai are one of the best-known African ethnics groups. In 2009, the Maasai population in Kenya was 841,622, up from 300,000 in 1979, and they are the eleventh largest of Kenya's forty tribes. They speak Maa, part of the Nilo-Saharan language family, as well as Swahili. Many of Kenya's towns and villages have Maasai names because the entire area used to be Maasai lands.

Since the Maasai had relatively little contact with European colonial governments and missionaries, they have retained much of their traditional culture. Therefore, they have become a contemporary tourist favorite. Because Kenya's economy is dependent upon tourism, the Maasai are important players in a very profitable industry. Nairobi souvenir shops sell picture books, trinkets, carvings of warriors, and lion spears. Critics consider contemporary Maasai not the "real Maasai" because they follow some modern ways, such as working as security guards or hanging out in urban neighborhoods. Traditionalists also criticize the sharing of tourist revenue with the Maasai in areas where Maasai land overlaps other privately held property.

The Maasai were most powerful during the nineteenth century when they controlled about 75,000 square miles of African territory, roughly the size of South Dakota. Their lands ranged from Lake Victoria to the Indian Ocean, from Mount Kenya to south of Kilimanjaro. The first European explorer, Joseph Thomson, arrived in 1883. Subsequently, British and German agreements with the Maasai in 1904 and 1911–1912 guaranteed them lands in two reserves, which eventually were reduced to one large reserve. After that arrangement, the Maasai resisted contact with Europeans, refused military service, fought with government tax collectors, and maintained their traditional ways and customs. After Kenya became independent in 1963, the Maasai who had left returned to their lands.

Modern Maasai continue to resist modern efforts, such as the Tanzanian law requiring bus passengers to wear pants. They are semi-nomadic pastoralists, despite the Tanzanian and Kenyan governments' programmatic efforts to force them to settle into permanent communities. As a result, there are ongoing problems with the Maasai and their lands. Since Kenya outlawed hunting in 1977, and the game areas are so rich, there are multiple complaints that the Maasai are poaching in the wildlife parks. Many of today's Kenyans are not very sympathetic with the Maasai, seeing them as stubborn and arrogant, with "barbaric" customs, and a lifestyle that retards Kenya's development. Because only 15 percent of

Kenyan land is suitable for agriculture, and the population is expanding rapidly, there is significant development pressure on Maasai lands. Tanzania's former president Julius Nyerere (1922–1999) once said that the country could not afford to maintain the Maasai as a "human zoo," meaning that the nation had to pursue a development policy that inherently would stress Maasai autonomy and traditions. Many would like to acquire the Maasai's land for commercial farming, such as the Kikuyu farmers who have bought sizeable land parcels to plant wheat.

Maasai society is strongly patriarchal, and elder men (sometimes joined by retired elders) decide most important issues in the community. The Maasai are monotheistic, worshipping a single deity called Enkai or Engai. Many modern Maasai have become Christian, and to a lesser extent, Muslim. Their calendar includes over thirty different tribal ceremonies throughout the year. Most events include the brewing of honey beer and collection of sacrificial animals, symbolic of blessings and sacrifice. Most ceremonies include special symbolism related to fertility and sexual relationships. For example, cattle are the basis of the Maasai's self-identification and survival: milk is a central part of the diet; cowhides are utilized to make sandals, bed mats, ropes, and ceremonial clothing; their huts have cow dung wall plaster and cattle are an ever-present stylistic accompaniment on sneakers and dresses. This near-fanatic devotion to their cattle is cult-like, and it carries strong religious undertones.

A major rite of passage from boyhood to adulthood is the male circumcision ceremony. In its traditional manner, it is performed in public before scrutinizing witnesses and without anesthetic. The boy must endure the *emorata*—the Maa word for circumcision—in silence and without showing any expression of pain or emotion, which could bring him dishonor and perhaps permanently stain his reputation. Until a boy is circumcised, he must greet his elders with a bowed head instead of a handshake, but it is a myth that he must kill a lion first. The boys prepare for the ceremony by pinching one another to practice tolerating pain. Sometimes a singing contest is held the evening before, between those who have been just circumcised and the ones who face it the next day. The boys sing about lion hunts and cattle raids, beautiful girls, and courageous deeds. At least one song usually encourages the noncircumcised boys.

The *emorata* circumcision ritual is typically performed by the elders, who use a sharpened knife and cattle hide bandages. The boy takes off his turquoise *shuka* (a decorative cotton fabric he wears wrapped around the body), and it is placed on a goat hide. Several elders pin him to the ground, and one supports his back. The boy's face is splashed with milk, and the knife is displayed for all to see. A small bell is rung, and the cutting begins. A 7-inch knife with a curved end is used. The elders carefully watch the boy, searching for any sign of emotion or pain. The cutting takes several minutes, with the foreskin loosened but intact, until the cutter stands. His assistant splashes more milk on the wound, and then the boy is carried to one of his mother's huts. The healing process takes approximately three to four months, if there is no infection or complications. The circumcised boys must wear black clothes for up to eight months, and live in a *manyatta* (camp of simple huts) built by their mothers. More passage rites follow before the young man endures the *eunoto* (final initiation ceremony) allowing him to become a senior warrior.

In recent years, certain aspects of the circumcision tradition have begun to be ignored by a few Maasai members. While it has been usual for members of the Dorobo (a small hunting tribe) to do the actual circumcisions, some Maasai now utilize modern health clinics for the circumcision. It is both cheaper and much more sanitary. Also, the Dorobo were used to be paid in animals, but now it is currency. Boys must confess their sexual transgressions before they begin the circumcision ceremony. In one reckoning, if a boy had not slept with circumcised women, his family pays 100 shillings ($6). If he had, the price is one cow and 600 shillings. The important element is for the boy to confess any transgressions of the traditional rule. If he does not, the circumciser's knife might "slip."

Young Maasai women have excision (female circumcision) in a similarly required rite of passage into adulthood. The young woman is placed on a dirt floor; she is splashed with cold water thought to be a mild anesthetic, and a curved razor begins cutting. Her clitoris and the outer lips of her vagina are sliced away. The women laugh heartily, while the young woman screams with pain. Finally, she is splashed with milk, and she is carried off to sleep. She is given sheep fat to drink to induce vomiting and prevent infection. These circumcisions are usually performed by someone not Maasai, usually Dorobo. The knives and blades utilized in the cutting procedures are made by blacksmiths, usually avoided by the Maasai because they make weapons that are used to kill. Similar to the young men's tradition, the young women who will be circumcised wear dark clothing and paint their faces with various symbolic markings. They also cover their faces when the ceremony is concluded. Updated information reveals that almost all of these circumcisions are done carefully with complications rarely arising.

Circumcision is an important element of Maasai cultural traditions. Maasai men may reject any noncircumcised woman as not marriageable or worth a much-lower bride price. Most family unions follow a tradition of arranged marriages called *emuratare*. In eastern Africa, noncircumcised women are considered not mature enough to be taken seriously. To others outside and inside Africa, the practice of female circumcision is technically known as female genital mutilation and is severely criticized. Partially in response to these criticisms, the circumcision ritual has been occasionally replaced by a "cutting with words" ceremony that substitutes the cutting of the flesh with singing and dancing.

William P. Kladky

Further Readings

Bentsen, Cheryl. *Maasai Days*. New York: Summit Books, 1989.

Maasai Association. "Maasai Ceremonies and Rituals." 2012. http://www.maasai-associa tion.org/ceremonies.html (Accessed on April 5, 2013).

Maathi, Wangari. *The Challenge for Africa*. New York: Pantheon Books, 2009.

Payne, Doris L., and Leonard Ole-Kotikash. "Maa (Maasai) Dictionary." 2005. http://dark
    wing.uoregon.edu/~dlpayne/Maa%20Lexicon/index-english/main.htm (Accessed on
    April 4, 2013).
Spear, Thomas. "Introduction." In *Being Maasai: Ethnicity & Identity in East Africa*,
    edited by Thomas Spear and Richard Waller, 1–24. Oxford, UK: James Currey Ltd,
    1993.

MAN VERSUS HORSE MARATHON

With pint-sized beginnings, the Man versus Horse Marathon has surmounted its
fledgling origins in Wales. Now accepted as a legitimate competition in which
nearly 300 runners annually compete against forty horses for a modest purse, the
success of the Man versus Horse Marathon was not always a certainty. In November 1979, while enjoying beverages in the back bar of the Neuadd Arms Hotel
in Llanwrtyd Wells, Gordon Green (a Welsh pub owner) and Glyn Jones (a local
decorated huntsman) debated whether a man could outrun a horse. Green argued
that over a particular distance, a man could outrun his equine opponent. Jones
vehemently differed. Wishing to settle the dispute, Green organized a race between
fifty runners and fifteen horses. Participants were instructed to cross 22 miles
of creeks, swamps, fields, and uneven terrain in the Welsh town of Llanwrtyd
Wells. Without difficulty, Jones, who had entered the race as a rider, and his
horse, defeated the runners. Recognizing the immediate popularity surrounding
the event, Green organized another competition the following year. As followers speculated whether a man could really outrun a horse, the race caught public
attention.

During the first years of the competition, horses continuously won, despite terrain changes made in 1982 with the intention of delaying the horses' pace. In
1989, four years after the event welcomed cyclists, British mountain biker Tim
Gould finally outpaced a horse. Though Gould defeated his opponents, followers
still questioned when, and if, humans would outrun horses. Fifteen years later, in
2004, Huw Lobb—a British distance runner—thwarted probability and bested
the other runners and horses competing. That year, gamblers had set the odds of
crowning a horse at 16 to 1. Lobb, defying the perceived handicap, took home
roughly £25,000, a collection of winnings that had accumulated annually since
the inception of the race twenty-five years earlier. Scientists explained that Lobb's
victory resulted from sweltering temperatures experienced that day. Citing evolutionary advantages, experts claimed that humans are better suited for greater
heat. Specifically, humans more easily cool their bodies when they sweat, whereas
horses are hampered by their heavy coats of horsehair. The theory was substantiated three years later, when in 2007, during another extremely hot day, Florian
Holzinger (a German runner) defeated all human and equine entrants.

The Man versus Horse Marathon has several rules. Runners begin the race fifteen
minutes before the horses take off. At the conclusion, the horses have fifteen minutes subtracted from their time of finishing. The separated start prevents the horses
from being frightened by the mass of swarming runners. Runners may enter the

race individually or as part of a team. The prize fund is a collection of the participants' entry fees. In addition, beginning in 2012, horses were required to wear metal shoes.

Since its inception, the Man versus Horse Marathon has yielded various unusual related events. The host town, Llanwrtyd Wells in Wales, now features numerous exotic sporting competitions, including bicycle chariot racing, bog snorkeling, and bicycle bog snorkeling. Coinciding with the 2012 London Olympic Games, Llanwrtyd Wells hosted the World Alternative Games. Events included worm charming, downhill mountainboarding, wool sack carrying, finger jousting, hay bale throwing, chariot racing (while dressed in Roman garb), tractor pulling, egg throwing, competitive bathtubbing, and wife-carrying competition. Youth-oriented programs included pooh sticks and rock, paper, scissors competition. Part of the games included a "Twinning Day," where delegates from Llanwrtyd Wells' twin cities of Český Krumlov, Czech Republic, and Mériel, France, participated in regional activities, such as French cockerel throwing, French cheese rolling, croquet, bubble blowing, and the Welsh Crempog Race, where competitors walked 100 yards while flipping a pancake in a skillet. The winner of the unusual Welsh Crempog Race was the first person to cross the finish line, while holding on to the pancake.

Though Llanwrtyd Wells has risen in international fame, it is not without controversy. The British Horse Society refuses to endorse the Man versus Horse Marathon, the town's signature event. Similarly, the Royal Society for the Prevention of Cruelty to Animals expressed concern during the first years of the Man versus Horse Marathon; however, more recently, the Society has withdrawn its complaints, due to the race's staff of professional veterinarians. Apart from organizations, the Man versus Horse Marathon has brought discord to many of its own participants. In 2009, Martin Cox was initially thought to have won the race as a runner; though, after judges' review, a horse called Duke's Touch of Fun was awarded the victory after time was discounted for a veterinarian's midrace checkup. Cox was infuriated by the decision, and he vowed never to return to the event. Other examples of discord include instances of interrace bickering between runners and riders over the divisive economic aspect of the race. Several rivalries have developed between the entrants, as riders are perceived as wealthy competitors without regard for their lowly human running counterparts. In another case, an entrant once brought her horse to compete against her running boyfriend. She and her horse won by twelve minutes.

Gordon Green may have ambitiously created the Man versus Horse Marathon, but a checkered history of competition already existed between the species. In 1940, Arne L. Suominen, a Finnish doctor, stated that he could outrun a horse over 40 miles. Suominen wagered $50 against a group of merchants in support of his claim. Although he led for the first 18 miles, the horse eventually passed him; at mile 35, Suominen withdrew, citing blistered feet. Alternatively, following his four gold medals at the 1936 Berlin Olympic Games, American Jesse Owens returned home without endorsements to a racially bias United States. Employing his notoriety as an Olympic runner, Owens raced against horses for money. Owens later acknowledged the degrading nature of his efforts and remarked that although he won four gold medals in Berlin, he could not eat any of them.

There is a long history of humans racing horses, and such competition has generated the occasional conflicts. In Wales, the Man versus Horse Marathon offers not only a venue for such competition but also a colorful and festive event to be enjoyed by the entire town of Llanwrtyd Wells and its visitors.

Adam Reinherz

Further Readings

"Doctor Finds Race Bet Just Horse on Him." *The Miami Daily News.* June 20, 1940. http://news.google.com/newspapers?nid=2206&dat=19400620&id=rG8uAAAAIBAJ&sjid=W9gFAAAAIBAJ&pg=5799,4744413 (Accessed on October 18, 2012).

Fragala Smith, Karen. "Haiti: A Historical Perspective." *Newsweek.* January 16, 2010. http://www.newsweek.com/2010/01/15/haiti-a-historical-perspective.print.html (Accessed on April 28, 2011).

Leach, Ben. "Equestrian Victory in Man vs Horse Marathon." *The Telegraph.* June 12, 2010. http://www.telegraph.co.uk/news/newstopics/howaboutthat/7823261/Equestrian-victory-in-man-vs-horse-marathon.html (Accessed on October 18, 2012).

Miller, John W. "Bipeds Make a Horse Race Out of Contest of Man vs. Beast." *The Wall Street Journal,* June 13, 2011. http://online.wsj.com/article/SB10001424052702303714704576381593288615606.html (Accessed on October 18, 2012).

Schwartz, Larry. "Owens Pierced A Myth." *ESPN.com.* 2007. http://espn.go.com/classic/biography/s/Owens_Jesse.html (Accessed on October 18, 2012).

MATIS HUNTING TRIALS

The Matis hunting trials are an initiation ceremony by which young male Matis tribe members gain their formal admission to adulthood and after which they are allowed to participate in hunting. As hunting is a very important part of Matis tribal life, all men have to go through these painful hunting trials before their first participation as part of the hunting party. Moreover, in order to have all their senses perform at their peak, all men continue to repeat these rituals during their life again and again to ensure they maintain their hunting abilities.

The Matis are a semi-nomadic tribe living from slash-and-burn agriculture and the hunting of animals such as apes. The tribal people live in the Vale do Javari in Brazil, a type of indigenous park that is 32,000 square miles in area and is situated close to the triple border of Brazil, Peru, and Colombia. The Matis Indians in former times lived in five different villages. Today only two of these villages are left because many Indians died after contact with other civilization and its diseases: Aurelio with around 160 people and Beija Flor with around 130 people. Both villages are located on the banks of the River Itui. The Matis Indians living in this area were not known until their first contact with Brazilians in the late 1970s. However, since the Matis Indians are an exotic and very photogenic tribe, they became a famous image for the Indians living in the Amazonas rainforest. It was Bruce Parry's BBC documentary that made the Matis tribe known all around the world. Due to their facial tattoos and ornamentation, which can give their face the appearance of a jaguar, the Matis became a very fascinating tribe. Furthermore, their rich culture and their different ceremonies—especially the poison frog ceremony—provided fascination for global reporters to cover this peculiar group of Amazonas Indians.

The Matis live in villages without a fixed shape, but there is a longhouse on top of a hill, which serves as the center of the village. This house is decorated by using bones of animals like peccary and tapir, and the Matis men meet there to prepare their deadly blowpipe darts for the next hunt. Most Indians live in family groups in smaller houses, which are located around the longhouse. Even if there exists some kind of family life, marriage is not part of Matis culture. Usually men and women live together, but this way of living does not preclude additional sexual partners, and it is not uncommon for brothers to share their wives for sex. Even if the Matis cultivate some crops to supplement their daily diet, hunting is the primary method to acquire food and all men of the tribe are specialists in blowpipe hunting.

For this method of hunting, Matis men use 3.5 meters long (11 feet) blowpipes, which are an especially good example of Indian craftsmanship. The blowpipe usually consists of a hollow mouthpiece and a main body, which is constructed from palm strips. The advantage of hunting with blowpipes is the fact that the Matis are able to hunt larger groups of monkeys, because the latter ones will not recognize that they are being hunted until they are silently killed like their conspecifics. The poisoned blowpipe darts kill the monkeys, and when they fall down from the trees, the Matis hunters just have to collect the killed animals. The poison used is toxic, which is traditionally extracted from the curare vine, which is boiled and finally reduced in water, during a process which might last up to two weeks.

This poison is known as *Kampo* (frog poison) and is a very important part of the cultural heritage of the Matis. Though it can be deadly, it also has curative properties, which make people stronger and fitter. The poison is extracted from the skin of the monkey frog. During this process, the frog is stretched over a burning fire, and the toxic excretions are taken from its back. The obtained poison is a fundamental part of the hunting trials, which must be initially practiced by the Matis before their first hunt. As hunting is a highly respected part of the male trait (a man can make a large compliment to a woman by bringing her meat), and each young male has to go through the initial hunting trial. This ritual consists of a number of very specific procedures.

First, bitter poison is poured directly into the eyes of the boys who will be recruited into the ranks of the hunters. The aim of this painful experience, which has the effect of temporary blindness, is to enhance all other senses to make the boys stronger and more successful hunters. Hunting in the rainforest is not an easy task, and the hunters will need all their senses to be able to find and hunt animals in the jungle without warning them of the hunter's presence. Particularly for this task, the young men need all their senses in the best possible condition. This is the main justification for having them suffer temporary blindness to strengthen all the remaining senses. Second, the aspiring hunters are beaten and whipped. This part of the rite of passage is not necessarily that painful, but the final trial most certainly is. Because the final trial makes use of the aforementioned frog poison, it is commonly called the poison frog ceremony. Initially, several points of the skin (usually on the arms) are burned, and the layer of burned skin is removed to create an open wound. The frog poison, which has been mixed with the saliva of an Indian to activate the poisonous effect, is placed on the wound from where it is able to directly enter the blood circulation. As a consequence, the effect is very fast. The poison is not a hallucinogenic one, but has enormous impact on the person who has been poisoned. The reaction of the body is usually shown by the need of the poisoned person to vomit. The Matis believe that this procedure is needed to become a better hunter, as the ceremony will make them stronger.

Regarding the fact that the Matis are subsistence hunters, it is no surprise that all men of these Indian communities are expected to become successful hunters. Similar to other indigenous communities all around the globe, the young Matis boys need to prove their strength to become an equal member of the adult community. Even if the Matis had abolished some parts of their religious world view (which is built on the division of the world upon contact with Brazilian settlers), diseases spread and the Indians began to fear the gods. Consequently, the hunting trial never disappeared from their cultural traditions. Other ceremonies were recovered and are practiced again, but in contrast to the hunting trials, they seem not to be important enough to be defended. The hunting ceremony is crucial for their cultural survival as the young Matis Indian will get the experience of an older person due to the saliva which had been mixed with the frog poison. This kind of initiation ritual is a consequence of the livelihood and the needs of Matis society. These communities will be able to survive only if their members are good hunters who are able to provide sufficient meat for all members of the tribe. Despite the fact that there are about 300 Matis people living in a very wide area, it is expected that this ritual will be continued by future generations of Matis Indians as well.

Frank Jacob

Further Readings

Arisi, Barbara Maisonnave. "Amazonian Exchanges: Txema's Lessons with Outboard Engines, Mosquito Nets and Images." *International Review of Social Research* 2, no. 1 (February 2012): 167–84. http://www.academia.edu/1469453/Amazonian_Exchanges_ Txemas_Lessons_With_Outboard_Engines_Mosquito_Nets_And_Images (Accessed on March 23, 2013).

BBC. *Tribe-Matis.* http://www.bbc.co.uk/tribe/tribes/matis/ (Accessed on March 24, 2013).

Chaumeil, Jean-Pierre. "The Blowpipe Indians: Variations on the Theme of Blowpipe and Tube among the Yagua Indians of the Peruvian Amazon." In *Beyond the Visible and the Material. The Amerindianitation of Society in the Work of Peter Rivière*, edited by Laura Rival and Neil Whitehead, 81–100. Oxford: Oxford University Press, 2001.

Erikson, Philippe. "Myth and Material Culture: Matis Blowguns, Palm Trees, and Ancestor Spirits." In *Beyond the Visible and the Material. The Amerindianitation of Society in the Work of Peter Rivière*, edited by Laura Rival and Neil Whitehead, 101–22. Oxford: Oxford University Press, 2001.

Gibbon, Pierce. *Tribe: Endangered Peoples of the World*. London: Castle Illustrated, 2010.

Pantone, Dan James. *Matis Indians: The Jaguar People*. http://www.amazon-indians.org/page01.html (Accessed on March 24, 2013).

Santos-Granero, Fernando. *The Occult Life of Things. Native Amazonian Theories of Materiality and Personhood*. Tucson: University of Arizona Press, 2009.

MENSTRUAL ISOLATION RITUAL

When a Dogon woman from Mali who adheres to her culture's traditional way of life has her menstrual period, she does not react in the way that most Western women do, managing it discretely and with as little disruption as possible to their routines. The Dogon are an agricultural society numbering as many as 800,000 people, most of whom inhabit hundreds of small villages in the dry regions south of the Niger River in the West African country of Mali. When Dogon women menstruate, they isolate themselves from much of the daily life of their families and villages. They continue to spend their days doing agricultural work, but they spend as long as five nights sleeping in a communal menstrual hut, and they stop cooking and washing for their families and spending time with relatives other than their youngest children. They are also prohibited from approaching village altars, where the men of the community make sacrifices and pray in order to protect it. An average Dogon woman will spend many of her reproductive years either being pregnant or nursing a child, which prevents menstruation. Nevertheless, she will most likely use the menstrual hut somewhere around a hundred times during her life.

The Dogon believe menstrual blood to be "bad blood" that is associated with death and the dispersal of spiritual power. In contrast, "good blood" that flows through the body is associated with fertility, pregnancy, and men's semen. Dogon culture isolates menstruating women and prevents them from having contact with men for fear that the impurity associated with bad blood will damage a village's religious life by disrupting its relationship with the spirits who are worshiped at the altars, and who respond to community needs such as healing and the need for water that is necessary to survive in their dry homeland. Furthermore, menstrual blood threatens men's abilities to carry out other social roles. It could damage their ability to perform work such as healing, hunting, and blacksmithing, which depend on spiritual power, and it is thought to decrease their virility.

Menstrual blood is not the only bad blood in the Dogon's world view, and women are not the only ones to produce it. Blood that is shed when a young man is circumcised is also bad, and when men work at making the wooden masks which are an important part of Dogon religious practice, carving them from the wood of a tree whose red flowers are associated with menstruation, and tinting the fiber used to trim them with red dye, they are symbolically described as "menstruating" and considered to be impure. Women are prohibited from having physical contact with men in the same way that men are prohibited from having contact with menstruating women. Because women menstruate, however, the burden of isolation due to bad blood falls much more heavily on them.

The Dogon share their belief in the power of menstruation with societies around the world and in many periods of world history. It is usually understood as a capacity to upset the social order. Menstrual blood and menstruating women are ascribed the ability to disrupt, damage, or destroy things that their cultures consider to be important, both religiously and practically. This often includes an understanding of the menstruating woman herself as polluted or impure. The customs that have emerged to counter these perceived threats by preventing menstruating women from doing harm are known as menstrual taboos. These beliefs are diverse, but they all segregate menstruating women from people or places that are believed to be vulnerable. While some taboos, like those against cooking or sexual activity, can be observed in the privacy of a woman's home, menstrual isolation is public. Everyone can see when a woman begins to use the menstrual hut and when she stops, and use communal pressure to make sure that women do not "cheat" by ignoring the taboos. From a global perspective, isolation emerged as a widespread response to the perceived problem of menstruation in human societies. During the twentieth century, menstrual isolation was known to have been practiced in many parts of Africa, the Pacific, India, the Caucasus, and among native peoples in North and South America.

Anthropologists and other social scientists have long been interested in why menstrual isolation has been so widely practiced. They have begun to consider whether it offers any concrete benefits, apart from those claimed by the belief systems that demand it, that would have caused it to evolve in the first place. The Dogon are beginning to provide an answer. Anthropologist Beverly Strassmann, who has studied them since 1986, found that because women usually follow the rules and visit the huts when they are menstruating, the practice provides Dogon communities with information about when women are fertile and when they are pregnant, which can be used to assign paternity to children. Since inheritance in Dogon society is through the male line, this is crucial information to know. Strassmann and her colleagues have recently received scientific confirmation that menstrual isolation is an accurate way of inferring this information. They completed a genetic study of Dogon fathers and sons which found that among families where mothers used the menstrual huts, the percentage of mismatches—times when a child's biological father was different from his social father—was only 1.3 percent, significantly lower than the 2.9 percent found among those who had converted to Islam or Christianity and stopped using the menstrual huts.

From the Dogon perspective, menstrual isolation is a religious practice. Women do not like doing it, but believe that they will be responsible if something bad happens to their villages when they do not follow the rules. If they or their husbands convert to Christianity or Islam, or if they move from small and interconnected villages to larger and more impersonal towns, women generally stop observing the taboo. From a scientific perspective, however, menstrual isolation rituals provide something else: a higher chance that men will father the children they claim as their own.

Sara C. Jorgensen

Further Readings

Buckley, Thomas, and Alma Gottlieb, eds. *Blood Magic: The Anthropology of Menstruation.* Berkeley: University of California Press, 1988.

"How Religion Promotes Confidence about Paternity." *University of Michigan News Service.* June 5, 2012. http://www.ns.umich.edu/new/releases/20423-religious-patriarchy-pro motes-confidence-about-paternity (Accessed on November 30, 2012).

Price, Sally. "The Curse's Blessing." *Frontiers: A Journal of Women's Studies* 14, no. 2 (1994): 123–42.

Small, Meredith F. "A Woman's Curse?" *The Sciences* (January/February 2009): 24–29. http://www.anthroprof.org/documents/Docs102/102articles.curse24.pdf (Accessed on November 30, 2012).

Van Beck, Walter E.A., and Stephanie Hollyman. *Dogon: Africa's People of the Cliffs.* New York: Harry N. Abrams, 2001.

MIZUKO KUYŌ, MISCARRIED AND ABORTED FETUS CEREMONY

In Japan, the ritual of *mizuko Kuyō* is a religious ceremony performed at Buddhist temples for people who have had a miscarriage, an abortion, or a stillbirth. It also serves to remember children who died as infants within a short period of being born. In English, it is loosely translated as a "Fetus Memorial Service." While this tradition has been practiced for centuries, it became more prevalent and visible during the 1960s and 1970s. The popularity of the ceremony increased tremendously in 1975 when a local television station showed a film highlighting the actual *mizuko kuyō* ceremony as part of a program showcasing unusual events in Japan. In contemporary Japan, however, the women who attend the ritual are not the only ones who had an abortion or miscarried a child, but they also include other relatives who have lost a family member—such as a nephew or a granddaughter—and some people go just to support their friends. What they all share is a sense of spiritual consolation. Overall, *mizuko kuyō* is considered as a ceremony within a larger concept of veneration of ancestors. The ritual is mostly attended by women of varying age groups (but also by men), and it is practiced by Japanese people from all socioeconomic levels. Some of the women who attend the ceremonies have been doing it monthly for years, and they intent to continue doing it for the rest of their lives. This is not a private and secretive event; on the contrary, the ceremonies are public.

People have multiple reasons to attend these rituals, including a mother's grief, desire to offer peace to the fetus's soul, and fear of retaliation from the vengeful spirit of an angry fetus. The word *mizuko* literally means "water child," which is a Japanese term for a dead fetus, or an unborn child. It is also crucial to highlight that the Japanese do not consider a *mizuko* as fully human but rather only as a "potential person." The work *kuyō* means "offering." Thus, *mizuko kuyō* is an offering to an unborn child. In the English language, there is no equivalent word for a miscarried or aborted fetus that conveys the same meaning as its Japanese counterpart.

There are two main religions in Japan: Shinto and Buddhism. Most Japanese follow both religions simultaneously. In practice, most followers are more concerned with daily rites and services than they are with theological differences between the two religions. The ceremony of *mizuko Kuyō* can be traced back to the 1700s in Japan, and the Shinto symbols used in the ritual have been adapted to a contemporary society. While it is disputed whether the ceremony is purely of Buddhist origin, the ritual is nowadays mostly associated with Buddhist temples and traditions. From a historical perspective, Jizō statues have been used in Japan to console the baby victims of infanticide, starvation, or abortion since the early 1700s. Jizō is considered to be a *bodhisattwa*, or divinity who is believed to be the protector of children. Nowadays, Buddhist temples display rows of small statues as offerings to him. These carved figurines are often dressed in baby clothing, such as sweaters, red bibs, and bonnets. It is also common to see small toys and piles of stones surrounding the statues.

Currently, abortion is widely accepted in Japanese society, and it has been legal since 1948. In the period after World War II, it was widely practiced as the main method of birth control. Demographic data reveals that between 1 million and 1.5 million abortions take place in Japan every year. With an increase in the number of abortions, the number of people attending *mizuko kuyō* ceremonies has also grown significantly since the 1980s. The Jizō statues have become perhaps the most recognizable figure in *mizuko kuyō* rituals due to a social need created by the widespread practice of abortion in Japan since the 1980s (Brooks 1981, 131).

There is considerable variation on how the *mizuko kuyō* ritual is actually performed. The ceremony usually takes place during the summer and spring months (especially in April), but numerous temples offer weekly and monthly ceremonies as well. First, the tradition begins with purchasing a small stone statue that resembles a monk, which represents the Jizō deity. Then, the figures are dressed with baby garments and placed on the temple terraces. These areas are not necessarily gloomy but rather joyful locations with childish decorations around a small manicured garden. Various temples also assign a posthumous Buddhist name assigned to the fetus. Women (and sometimes men) passing by the shrines usually stop in front of them for a few minutes of silence. They also pour water on them since they represent "water babies." The ceremony also includes a Buddhist prayer and multiple offerings such as food, candles, flowers, toys, incense, and money. As part of the ritual, women usually light a candle and say a quiet prayer. In addition, women write brief messages of remembrance or apology to their lost children; these are then attached to a wooden tablet next to the figurines.

Since the practice of *mizuko kuyō* has grown so much in contemporary Japan, now there are temples completely dedicated to these ceremonies, such as the Shiun-zan Jizo-ji Temple in Chichibu. It is a large commercial location that shows Buddhist influence in architecture, but it is not actually affiliated to any of the branches of the Buddhist religion. However, most legitimate Buddhist temples also charge for performing these ceremonies, which vary from reasonable prices to exorbitant fees. The largest temples have sparked recent criticism regarding the commercialization of *mizuko kuyō* rituals. The Japanese media has forcefully denounced this tradition as a money-grabbing scheme orchestrated by unscrupulous religious leaders who prey on vulnerable women who might be experiencing feelings of grief, guilt, and remorse for having had an abortion. Even feminist organizations in Japan have declared *mizuko kuyō* as a plot to keep women submissive and controlled by male religious leaders. However, these criticisms are well known in Japan, and the popularity of this religious practice has continued to flourish, which indicates that there is a tangible social and spiritual need for such ceremonies. Moreover, not all the Buddhist temples and priests are negative and opportunistic. All over Japan, there are small neighborhood temples that perform a wide array of ceremonies, including *mizuko kuyō.* These intimate locations are usually not glamorous, but they fulfill the spiritual needs of their followers at a minimal cost. Many women here attend *mizuko kuyō* services every month, and they form a social bond that extends beyond the ritual itself. Regional temples usually organize a tea gathering after the ceremony. However, researchers who interviewed women practicing the ritual found that these small religious gatherings do not necessarily evolve into a support system. Women often socialize after the ceremony, but they never really discuss the reasons why any of them are there. Nevertheless, the group does not make any distinctions between having lost a baby by miscarriage, abortion, or stillbirth. What they do share is a collective sense of child loss, regardless of the actual circumstances. Overall, the people who practice *mizuko kuyō* are likely to find spiritual comfort, sorrow, and a personal sense of closure.

While there is no similar ceremony in the United States to address the social need for grieving parents, the practice of *mizuko kuyō* is already beginning to be offered by a few selected U.S. Buddhist locations. A nun serving in a Buddhist temple in Hawaii introduced the rite to the United States for the first time in 1978. Since then, the meaning and purpose of *mizuko kuyō* has evolved in order to be adapted to the local social needs. In the United States, the ceremonies serve as a vehicle for mothers to mourn the loss of an unborn child, and Buddhist temples offer small gatherings for the attendees, which have evolved into actual support groups. In addition, a few hospitals have become aware of the tradition, and they often accommodate such ceremonies as part of the cultural services they make available for grieving families. The general goal is to provide a sense of comfort to grieving mothers for the loss of an unborn child.

Javier A. Galván

Further Readings

Betty, Stafford. "After the Abortion, Misuko Kuyo." *National Catholic Reporter.* July 25, 2008. http://ncronline.org/node/1462 (Accessed on June 25, 2012).

Brooks, Ann Page. "Mizuko Kuyō and Japanese Buddhism." *Japanese Journal of Religious Studies* 8, no. 3–4 (September–December 1981): 119–47.

Iwao, Sumiko. *The Japanese Woman: Traditional Image and Changing Reality.* Cambridge, MA: Harvard University Press, 1993.

Kamachi, Noriko. *Culture and Customs of Japan.* Westport, CT: Greenwood Press, 1999.

Martin, Elaine. "Rethinking the Practice of Mizuko Kuyo in Contemporary Japan: Interviews with Practitioners at a Buddhist Temple in Tokyo." http://bama.ua.edu/~emartin/publications/mkarticl.htm (Accessed on June 20, 2012).

Norbury, Paul. *The Essential Guide to Customs and Culture of Japan.* London: Kuperard, 2011.

Smith, Bardwell. "Buddhism and Abortion in Contemporary Japan: Mizuko Kuyō and the Confrontation with Death." *Japanese Journal of Religious Studies* 15, no. 1 (December 1988): 3–24.

Wilson, Jeff. *Mourning the Unborn Dead: A Buddhist Ritual Comes to America.* New York: Oxford University Press, 2009.

MOKO: MĀORI MALE FACIAL TATTOOS

For centuries, the Māori tribes of New Zealand have displayed some of the most distinctive and unique tattoos in the world. They are considered part of an ancient tradition of sacred art in the Polynesian world of the South Pacific. In Māori culture, the head was considered to be the most sacred part of the body. While facial tattoos (called *moko*) are the most recognizable, men also tattooed them on their buttocks and thighs. The designs use mostly elegant curvilinear and spiral lines rather than geometrical shapes, lettering, or human figures. For example, a warrior's tattoos on his buttocks usually revealed swirling double spirals on both buttocks (called *raperape*). One of the most important reasons for obtaining facial tattoos was family significance. They also provided distinguishable marks of belonging to a specific tribe, a person's rank among his peers, and a warrior's history of past battles. During the 1700s, Māori adults with no tattoos were viewed as having no status in society at all. Tattooing usually started at puberty to mark successful completion of rites of passage. Getting the first *moko* was an important transition between childhood and becoming an adult, which also involved other rituals. After such initiation, tattoos were used to mark important events in a man's

A Māori warrior with a *moko*, a male facial tattoo. (Patricia Hofmeester/Dreamstime.com)

life. In addition, they had a practical aspect to it: to make warriors more attractive to the opposite sex. While men catch most of the attention for their facial tattoos (*moko*), Māori women also displayed tattoos on their faces but less extensively. Their *moko* were usually concentrated on their lips and chin; occasionally women were also tattooed on the neck and back.

The unique tattooing technique developed by the Māori tribes since the 1500s was done by carving the facial skin with a chisel (*uhi*) and a small hammer rather than puncturing the tissue with needles. As a result, facial skin ended with grooves rather than a smooth texture. Then, the *tahunga-ta-moko* (*moko* specialist or tattoo artist) would pour black color ink onto the open grooves, which was made from burned timber, tree soot, and dead caterpillars. The artists stored their pigment in specially decorated vases called *oko*, which were passed on from generation to generation. The original instruments used for carving tattoos were chisels made from albatross bones. They had extremely sharp straight edges but also serrated blades. Obtaining a *moko* took serious preparation, including the study of a person's occupation and family lineage. The first step was to study the bone structure and facial symmetry of the person. Second, the artist would create a unique design to reflect the person's heritage, tribal affiliation, and personal accomplishments. Third, the *moko* specialist would proceed to cut deep carvings onto the skin. Fourth, the chisel was dipped onto the pigment to be used, which was mostly dark black ink for facial tattoos. Fifth, the artist carefully dropped the dye into the open wounds and wiped away the excess ink. During the session, there was usually soothing music playing on the background. The work was very painful, detailed, and time-consuming. Finally, to help with the healing process, the Māori used leaves from a local Karaka tree, which were placed over the newly carved facial wounds. Men endured the pain because *moko* tattoos were a reflection of self-identity, courage, and strength. Since there was a high risk of infection, the person obtaining the tattoo was prohibited from sexual activity and eating solid food during the healing period. For nutrition, they were fed water and liquid food through a special funnel that would not touch the skin during the recuperation stages. It is important to highlight the distinction between *ta moko* (the process of making the tattoo) and *moko* (the final product). The *ta moko* process could take up to one year in order to reveal the final *moko* in full display. While the Māori tattoo artists have used similar designs for centuries, their use of tattooing instruments and techniques evolved toward the end of the 1800s when *moko* artists started using needles instead of chisels. The transition made the process much faster, the healing period shorter, and the texture of the skin a bit smoother. Despite the elegant representation of Māori tattoos and their strong linkages to cultural pride, there was a loss of interest in facial traditional tattoos during the first few decades of the 1900s, and the art form went into a period of decline.

The history of Māori and the development of facial tattoos as an artistic form are intrinsically related. The islands of New Zealand were settled by Eastern Polynesian groups before 1000 ACE. Over the next centuries, the Māori groups developed an advanced civilization that was constantly at war with multiple tribes. They also developed an artistic tradition with an emphasis on body art. The first encounter with Europeans occurred in 1642 with Dutch explorers. A century later, Captain James Cook arrived on the islands in 1769, which sparked a contentious relationship between Europeans and the different regional tribes in the area. By the early 1800s, several local tribes allied themselves with Europeans in exchange for weapons; such alliance quickly unleashed bloody battles against other tribes. To the Europeans, the *moko* facial tattoos of the powerful Māori warriors were highly valued. In their attempt to collect them, they made an unusual offer to other rival tribal groups: one musket in exchange for four Māori heads, as long as they had intricate *moko* designs. Following the European explorers, the Christian missionaries to New Zealand eventually followed and settled in the area by the 1850s. In their efforts to convert followers to Christianity, they labeled *moko* art as the "art of the devil." As large numbers of Europeans settled in New Zealand, the ancient tradition of body art slowly faded away. The tradition had become less acceptable in the new society of New Zealand that had become increasingly more European, or *Pākehā.* By the early 1930s, most of the men who had full face tattoos had died.

Since the early 1990s, there has been a resurgence of Māori cultural pride, including a renewed interest on Māori tattoos. Cultural centers in New Zealand have created detailed Māori genealogy studies and documented history to enhance cultural traditions. As part of the efforts, multiple museums have gathered ancient original tattoo instruments from centuries ago, and they also offer information on the *moko* designs that are appropriate to reveal family lineage, tribal heritage, and personal identification. As a result, there has been a noticeable increase on young Māoris obtaining *moko* tattoos, but now it is not limited to the face, but rather on the arms, shoulders, and chest area. In addition, more women have become trained as *moko* artists—a field that used to be reserved mostly for male artists.

Cultural exchange happens at a much faster rate during the twenty-first century. Nowadays, the revival of the Māori *moko* has become so popular that it is being imitated worldwide. However, the recent interest on Māori body art in the Western world has generated heated controversy in New Zealand. More specifically, members of the Māori culture have expressed that *moko* tattoos should be used only for personal and tribe identification. They are their cultural signature and a direct link to their Māori ancestors. When outsiders imitate their art, they feel insulted because it resembles a situation where someone steals a personal and cultural identity. In some cases, Māori tattoo artists have tried to rally their peers to discourage the training of outsiders who are increasingly seeking to benefit from the commercialization of Māori traditions. However, Māori leaders also realized that they needed to analyze their art in a larger global context that is no longer under their control. An introspective view also made them aware of how they have adopted modern tattoo techniques themselves, such as the use of sterilizing machines, latex gloves, and electric needles. As a result, contemporary imitations of Māori tattoos in the Western world have forged an artistic compromise. In attempts to find a middle ground, multiple *moko* artists and cultural

CONTROVERSY OVER MĀORI TATTOOS BY FAMOUS CELEBRITIES

The imitation of Māori tattoos has proliferated in the past two decades. However, the controversy emerges when the people sporting such body art are not of Māori heritage. Since these tattoo patterns are very personal and based on family history, Māoris are not flattered when their cultural trademarks are copied and displayed by outsiders. A recent example took place when popular singer Rihanna received a Māori tattoo in October 2013 during her world tour that took her to New Zealand. She decided to go the traditional route, and she obtained a tattoo in her right hand by using the original Māori method of cutting flesh with a chisel, applying local ink pigment instead of regular ink, and the use of a mallet to complete the process. The event was widely published in all the local media. Nevertheless, in the opinion of many Māori people, the appropriation of Māori tattoos by other people simply amounts to identity theft because they are stealing an extremely important cultural trait that has been preserved for centuries.

Javier A. Galván

leaders agreed that it was better to participate in the process of protecting their culture rather than letting someone else modify and define their traditions. The compromise was the development of *Kirituhi*, which is a series of tattoo designs made available to outsiders. *Kirituhi*—which literally means "drawn skin"—became an acceptable form of Māori-style patterns, but it was specifically created to not make references to Māori cultural and historical symbolism. The compromise was created to fulfill the demand for such designs in the Western world but still remain respectful of original Māori traditions.

Javier A. Galván

Further Readings

Brooking, Tom. *The History of New Zealand.* Westport, CT: Greenwood Press, 2004.

Jahnke, Robert, and Huia Tomlins Jahnke. "The Politics of Maori Image and Design." *Pukenga Kokero Journal* 7, no. 1 (Summer 2003): 5–31.

King, Michael. *Moko: Maori Tattooing in the 20th Century.* Auckland, New Zealand: David Bateman, 1992.

Mitchell, Ryan. "Maori Chief on Facial Tattoos and Tribal Pride." *National Geographic News.* October 14, 2003. http://news.nationalgeographic.com/news/pf/84577710.html (Accessed on June 25, 2012).

PBS. "Maori Moko." *Skin Stories: The Art and Culture of Polynesian Tattoo.* http://www.pbs.org/skinstories/culture/role2.html#moko (Accessed on June 21, 2012).

Te, Awekotuku. "More Than Skin Deep." In *Claiming the Stone: Naming the Bones: Cultural Property and the Negotiation of National Ethnic Identity*, edited by Elazar Barkan and Ronald Bush, 243–54. Los Angeles: Getty Press, 2003.

MONKEY BUFFET FESTIVAL

The Monkey Buffet Festival is an annual feast especially organized to thank and recognize wild monkeys that live around the Lopburi Province in Thailand. It is located roughly 150 kilometers (93 miles) northeast of the capital city of Bangkok. Since 1989, every year on the last Sunday of November more than 2,000 city monkeys are brought to the Pra Prang Sam Yod Temple, which was originally a Khmer Hindu shrine to feast on food ranging from fruits, vegetables, cookies, and even Coca-Cola. Over 3,000 kilograms (over 6,600 pounds) of fruits, grilled sausage, vegetables, ice cream, milk, and jelly are offered to the attending guest monkeys. Multiple banquets are arranged at three different locations around the city that are populated by such monkeys: Phra Prang Sam Yod, City Shrine, and Downtown. The organizers use dozens of long buffet tables at all three locations to display colorful dishes and towers of multiple fruits.

The monkeys (which are everywhere near the temples) are a bit shy at the beginning, and they are initially reluctant to come down from the trees due to the hundreds of tourists standing around the tables anxiously waiting to take their picture. However, they eventually come down and show their gratitude to the audience by shrilling, fighting, and fornicating on the surface of the tables. In the monkey buffet, visitors can watch the monkeys enjoy the culinary delight especially prepared for them. Monkeys that are typically naughty and always steal from people can become well mannered at the festival, and they can play around with curious tourists and people who want to take their photos. The monkeys are

Long-tailed macaque monkeys at the Pra Prang Sam Yod Temple for the annual monkey buffet festival in Lopburi. (Koon Hong Kang/Dreamstime.com)

naturally stunned to have so much food offered to them in such a free manner. Normally they have to work for it.

The Monkey Buffet Festival typically starts at around 10:00 A.M. with musical performances and human monkey dances. The event has grown in stature and influence so much that usually the governor of Lopburi gives a speech to commemorate the event. After the official ceremony, the monkeys come down from the trees to eat from the buffet tables. The festival goes on all day with two more rounds in the afternoon starting at 2:00 P.M. and 4:00 P.M.

There are very specific religious and practical reasons why the city of Lopburi was chosen as the place to celebrate these unusual festivities. The official reason involves the history of Hinduism and the belief that the long-tailed macaque monkeys are descendants of soldiers who should be respected. For centuries, monkeys have been crucial to define the identity of the city of Lopburi. In the Hindu story "The Ramayana," people are told that Lopburi was founded by Hanuman, the monkey anthropomorphic hero who helped the legendary King Rama to rescue his wife from Ravana, the ten-head demon. King Rama gave a piece of land known as Lopburi to Hanuman who was also the Monkey King. Consequently, local people believe that monkeys are descendants of Hanuman. In daily life, however, these monkeys are routinely seen stealing items from people. A pair of dangling earrings or swinging shopping bags invites them to rob. Street signs, trees, and telephone poles are places where monkeys like to swing. They can bother people with the horizontal and vertical swings. While the monkey's antics can certainly be a thrill for outsiders, local people considered the loud monkeys as unavoidable noise. In Thailand, Buddhism has long replaced the reference to Hindu, but Hanuman and his offspring will not be evicted anytime from the region of Lopburi. Monkeys are considered the animal that brings good luck to believers of Buddhism—even though monkeys disrupt their heads, pull their hair, and steal their wallets.

However, a much more tangible reason to select the province of Lopburi as the location for the Monkey Buffet Festival is simply because the tourist authorities want visitors to visit Lopburi, which is ranked among the second tier of Thailand tourist destinations. The monkey feast was actually the concept of an astute businessman and hotelier, Yongyuth Kitwattananusont, who was concerned with the low number of tourists coming to Lopburi. The first Lopburi Monkey Buffet Festival took place on Sunday, November 25, 1989. At that time, there were thirty-five Chinese tables set up and covered with an abundance of food. The guest of honor in that first year was the former Thai prime minister M. R. Kukrit Pramoj. Mr. Kitwattananusont has always been an active participant in the festival since the beginning. He once appeared wearing a monkey suit such as many other participants in this festival and landed with a parachute. He also mobilized support to increase the amount of food donated for the festival. Now, with sponsorship from the Tourism Authority of Thailand, the show attracts thousands of tourists. With such support, the popularity of Lopburi does not depend on Mr. Yongyuth anymore. The event is expected to continue "enticing tourists . . . especially the foreigners that show interest year after year."

Patit Paban Mishra and Abubakar Hara

Further Readings

"Monkey Buffet Festival." 25 November 2012. http://www.thaifestivalblogs.com/festivals/monkey-buffet-festival.html (Accessed on November 10, 2012).

"Monkey Buffet Festival 2011 in Thailand Offers Treats to Local Animals (PHOTOS)." http://www.huffingtonpost.com/2011/11/28/monkey-buffet-festival-thailand-2011_n_1116574.html (Accessed on November 10, 2012).

"The Monkey Buffet Festival—Body Paragraph about the Monkeys." http://inglesmonkeybuffetfestival.blogspot.com/ (Accessed on November 10, 2012).

"Monkey Festival in Lopburi." http://www.thai-blogs.com/2011/11/28/monkey-festival-in-lopburi/ (Accessed on November 10, 2012).

"Thailand: Food Orgy in Monkey Town." http://www.globalpost.com/dispatch/thailand/101124/thanksgiving-monkey-buffet-festival-tourism (Accessed on 10 November 10, 2012).

NAG PANCHAMI, FESTIVAL OF SNAKES

Nag Panchami, a Hindu festival in India, is celebrated on the fifth lunar day in the rainy month of Shravan (July and August) of the Hindu calendar. As the name implies (*Nag* meaning snakes; *Panchami* meaning fifth), snakes are worshipped by Indian Hindus with milk, sweets, crystallized sugar, and flowers. Snake charmers wander about with different species of snakes, and people pay them money to worship live snakes. Devotees observe a religious fast, and Hindu priests are fed with lavish food. People believe that if they worship snakes, they and their families would be protected from snakebites. According to religious beliefs, digging ground in the month is forbidden as it may kill a snake accidently. On the day of the festival, many people decorate their houses, walls, and doors with multiple colorful images of snakes. They also display statues of snake deities made out of silver, wood, or stone. These figures are bathed with water and milk and then worshipped with various mantras that are chanted to ward off dangerous snakes.

Nagas (snakes) occupy special places in Hindu mythology. Religious texts such as *Puranas* include detailed descriptions of various snakes. Some of the most prominent snakes are Anant, Vasuki, Shesh, Padma, Kanwal, Karkotak, Kalia, Aswatar, Takshak, Sankhpal, Dhritarashtra, and Pingal. For example, scriptures depict Lord Vishnu reclining on the couch made of Shesh Nag (a giant snake and symbol of eternity), and it is a religious belief that snakes are loved and blessed by Lord Shiva, as he wears a snake around his neck as an ornament. Hindu mythology further explains that earthquakes occur due to shaking of the hood by Shesh Nag, the giant snake which holds the planet on its hood. There are also various legends associated with snakes in Hindu mythology. The most popular is of Lord Krishna who in his childhood saved his people from the giant sea serpent Kalia. Krishna's victory over the serpent is remembered and commemorated during the festival of snakes.

The festival is celebrated in different ways across India. In Varanasi, *dangals* (wrestling matches) are organized along with religious rituals. The *akharas* (stadiums) are cleaned and decorated with images of snakes drinking milk from a bowl. In Bengal, Goddess Manasa (Hindu serpentine deity) is worshipped for an entire month. In Karnataka, the preparation for the festival starts five days earlier before the day of *Nag Panchami*. A day before, fast is observed or a strict salt-less diet is consumed. Girls offer prayers asking god to find a good husband by offering special puja and preparing clay images with white dots on them. In certain other parts of India, the festival is also celebrated by women with a belief that their brothers would be conferred with longevity. Married women who are unable to bear children worship snake deities by installing stone images of snakes at foots of a peepal tree. Overall, the Festival of Snakes serves the purpose of worshipping religious deities while also bringing communities together for regional celebrations.

Haris Qadeer

Further Readings

Jagannathan, Maithly. *South Indian Hindu Festivals and Traditions.* New Delhi: Abhinav Publications, 2005.

Kalman, Bobbie. *India: The Land (Lands, Peoples, and Cultures).* New York: Crabtree Publishing Company, 2009.

Verma, Manish. *Fast and Festivals of India.* New Delhi: DPB (p) Ltd, 2007.

NAIDOC ABORIGINAL WEEK IN AUSTRALIA

NAIDOC Aboriginal Week is an annual Australian period of observance that commemorates and celebrates the history and culture of Aboriginal and Torres Strait Islanders, the first inhabitants of Australia. Lasting from the first Sunday in July until the following Sunday, NAIDOC Aboriginal Week encompasses nationwide celebrations across cities and communities. NAIDOC originally stood for "National Aborigines and Islanders Day Observance Committee," the group responsible for organizing national activities during this special week. Over time, the acronym became the official name of the week. Great emphasis is placed on the participation of all Australians as NAIDOC Aboriginal Week seeks to bridge the gap between the original inhabitants of the continent and Australians of European descent. Despite the positive aspects and the often fun and festive nature of the celebration, the roots of NAIDOC Aboriginal Week are intertwined with the history of the struggle for Aboriginal rights, the often tragic legacy of European colonization, and the ongoing effort to properly acknowledge the role of Aboriginal people in Australian society.

Although the current observation was created in 1957, the events that led to the creation of NAIDOC Aboriginal Week have antecedents stretching back to the colonial history of Australia and the formation of the Australian nation. The arrival of British settlers in 1788 had destructive consequences for the indigenous peoples. The introduction of European diseases, conflicts with settlers, and the eventual loss of traditional lands shattered indigenous communities and relegated most of Australia's first peoples to second-class status often dependent on European settlers for survival. When the six British self-governing colonies of Australia federated to become the Commonwealth of Australia in 1901, Aborigines were not granted the same rights as other citizens. Despite this disparity, the move toward nationhood was seen by most Australians of European descent as a tremendous achievement. To celebrate the new nation, January 26 was declared Australia Day, and yearly commemorations were held on that date.

By the 1920s, Aboriginal rights groups routinely boycotted Australia Day in protest against the often poor treatment of indigenous Australians. However, it became increasingly obvious that passive actions such as boycotts were failing to win the support of the majority of the national population. During Australia Day in 1938, a "Day of Mourning" protest march was held in Sydney by Aboriginal groups to highlight the inequitable and often callous treatment of indigenous people. The name Day of Mourning was chosen to symbolize that Australia Day was not a time of triumph and celebration for all Australians. The actions during January 26 were considered one of the first civil rights protests in the world. The relative success of the march and the associated calls for action resulted in the Day of Mourning becoming an annual event held on the Sunday before Australia Day. From 1940 to 1955, the Day of Mourning was organized under the name of Aborigines Day, and then in 1955, it was decided to shift Aborigines Day to the first Sunday in July.

In the 1950s, NADOC, or the National Aborigines Day Observance Committee, was formed by the joint actions of governmental and community organizations as part of a growing move toward reconciliation. Along with the formation of this group, the second Sunday in July was set aside as a day for the remembrance of the heritage of Aboriginal people. By 1974, it was decided to extend the event to an entire week, connecting the two days and creating the current period of national celebration and observation. By 1991, awareness of the fundamentally distinct identity and culture of Torres Strait Islanders resulted in the expansion of NADOC. The group was renamed as the National Aborigines and Islanders Day Observance Committee (NAIDOC).

In its current form, NAIDOC Aboriginal Week is a national annual event celebrating the history, culture, and achievements of Aboriginal and Torres Strait Islander peoples, while also highlighting the long and continuing indigenous struggle for equal rights. NAIDOC Aboriginal Week follows a different theme each year, commemorating a pivotal moment for aboriginal rights or an inspirational idea or message. For example, the 2013 theme was a celebration of the 1963 Yirrkala Bark Petitions, a request by the Yolngu people of northeast Arnhem Land asking for recognition of their claim to traditional lands on the Grove Peninsula. Each year a new city is selected as the focus for NAIDOC celebrations, and this location becomes the host of the annual NAIDOC Ball, where special awards are presented to noteworthy indigenous Australians after national nominations.

Local celebrations are encouraged and often organized by communities, government agencies, and schools. Events include art exhibitions, screenings of documentaries and films directed and produced by indigenous filmmakers, and concerts by modern indigenous musicians, as well as traditional performances using instruments such as the didgeridoo. Lunches with local Aboriginal or Torres Straits Islanders' elders are a frequent NAIDOC Aboriginal Week event. Stand-up comedy performances, fashion shows, and demonstrations of traditional crafts are also among some of the popular activities that take place during this week.

Other festivities are often geared toward families or specifically designed for children. One major example is the celebration held at Hyde Park in Sydney in 2012. The all-day affair featured hand-weaving demonstrations and multiple workshops on indigenous cooking techniques. Since 2007, a special Australian football match between the teams Claremont and South Fremantle is part of NAIDOC Aboriginal Week with the winner receiving the Jimmy Melbourne Cup. The Jimmy Melbourne Cup is named for a pioneering indigenous Australian football player, while Claremont and South Fremantle are the two teams that have traditionally had the largest number of Aboriginal players.

NAIDOC Aboriginal Week has generally been regarded favorably for its efforts in highlighting the unique culture and the many struggles of indigenous Australians. While many of the events seek to stress the unique perspective and culture of indigenous Australians, others work toward fostering stronger connections between the first Australians and the descendents of the European settlers. However, despite the historical and cultural significance of these events, both NAIDOC Aboriginal Week and Aborigines Day are not official Australian national holidays.

Daniel Fandino

Further Readings

ABC Indigenous Information. "ABC Indigenous South East SA Region. Information Regarding Aboriginal and Torres Strait Peoples." http://www.abc.net.au/indigenous/features/naidoc/ (Accessed on August 19, 2013).

Macintyre, Stuart. *A Concise History of Australia*. Cambridge, UK: Cambridge University Press, 1999.

"NAIDOC History." http://www.naidoc.org.au/about/naidoc-history/ (Accessed on August 16, 2013).

NAIDOC Perth. Official Website for the Celebration of Aboriginal and Torres Strait Islander Peoples, Cultures, and Communities. http://www.naidocperth.org/ (Accessed on August 16, 2013).

NECK STRETCHING IN THAILAND

In the hills of northern Thailand, a tribe of long-neck women has attracted worldwide attention. Since a very young age, Kayan Lahwi women (also called Padaung) wear ornamental brass coils around their neck that seem to have stretched their necks. The practice is based on a general concept of beauty that an elongated neck is attractive and is highly valued in their community. The Kayan custom of body modification by wearing neck rings is centuries old; the Italian explorer Marco Polo was the first outsider to describe the tradition in the 1300s. However, it has only been in the past two decades that the Kayan cultural traditions have been openly accessible to outsiders. In fact, the Thai government has actively promoted villages near the Thai border with Burma (which is now known as Myanmar) in order to attract more tourists to the area. As a result, anthropologists, historians, teachers, journalists, filmmakers, and general tourists have flocked to these hillside villages in the Thai jungle. Such approach, however, has also generated international controversy as to whether Kayan customs are being exploited for financial gain by unscrupulous regional government officials.

The Kayan tribe is a subgroup of the Karen population, which is a minority group from Burma. While the available literature provides multiple names making reference to these specific tribes (Kayan, Karen, and Padaung), they actually call themselves Kayan. During the 1980s and early 1990s, Burma experienced widespread political turmoil propagated by an authoritarian military junta. As a direct result of the social convulsion and the attacks on minority groups, numerous Kayan tribes migrated across the border from Burma to northern Thailand. One of the reasons for Kayan women to continue wearing the neck rings is to preserve their culture while they live in exile from their homeland. While the Thai government still has not provided a definitive solution to the legal status of the Kayan groups, it did allow them to settle into separate

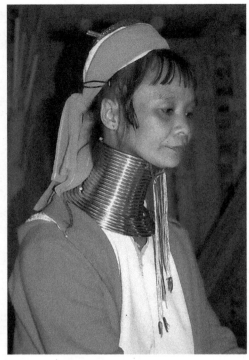

Kayan woman wearing brass neck rings in Chiang Mai, Thailand. (Jjspring/Dreamstime.com)

villages in the hills. For example, Huay Pu Keng is a small village located in the Mae Hong Son area of northern Thailand; it is populated by the Kayan (long-neck women) and the Kayau (people with big ears) tribes. After their initial settlement was accomplished, the Kayan refugee villages were first open to the public and tourism in 1984. While Kayan men work on the nearby rice fields and vegetable gardens, they remain almost invisible during the day. The real attraction to the villages is the women who gracefully (and slowly) stroll around their communities wearing the famous shiny brass coil rings that have earned them the names of long-neck or giraffe women. They also wear colorful hats and long white cotton dresses adorned with colorful designs in hues of vibrant red and blue colors.

Kayan women begin wearing the brass coil rings when they are about five years of age. These rings have a polished shiny golden color, and they are roughly half-an-inch in diameter. As the girls age, the length of the coils is increased in a very gradual fashion to a point where it reaches roughly twenty turns around their neck. The brass coils weigh approximately between 5 and 20 pounds (roughly 2.25 to 10 kilograms), which is a considerable weight to carry on their shoulders twenty-four hours a day. Usually, they wear at least two separate coils: The lower part includes the wider coil placed around the shoulders, and the shorter brass coil is wound around the neck area. When women reach adulthood, the rings around their necks are between 12 and 15 inches in height (30 to 38 centimeters). Once a woman begins wearing such neck rings, she keeps wearing them for life, removing them only once during their wedding night. The removal of the brass coils is a painful and lengthy procedure that also requires the assistance of other women in order to avoid potential suffocation. The removal of a twenty-turn spiral can take up to four hours. It is widely accepted as conventional wisdom that if women remove the brass rings, their muscles alone may no longer have sufficient strength to support the neck, which might even cause them to choke when they try to swallow food. Kayan women have occasionally removed their rings for medical reasons, and they discovered that their necks are usually bruised and discolored because the skin has been hidden behind the brass coils for many years. From a practical point of view, the practice of wearing the neck rings makes routine activities extremely difficult, such as trying to tie shoe laces, sleeping, collecting vegetables from the fields, drinking from a cup, and even looking straight up.

Despite the women's elongated appearance, their necks are actually not stretched. In reality, the heavy weight of the brass coils pushes down on the collar bones and muscles while also placing excessive pressure on the rib cage. The result is that the upper ribs are compressed down at an angle almost 40 degrees lower than ribs on average women. Another gradual consequence is that the shoulders are forced down over a long period of time. The illusion of a longer neck is created because the clavicles become deformed overtime.

The condition of the Kayan women in northern Thailand has generated controversy based on a dilemma that they are being exploited for monetary gain by regional government administrators, and tourism does not necessarily provide tangible benefits to Kayan women themselves. Their custom of wearing neck rings is precisely what has placed them in a cycle of dependency. Their tradition is the main reason for drawing tourists to their remote villages who then take photographs of them (especially the young girls). They also purchase an occasional souvenir, such as woven scarves and textiles. The government does pay Kayan women a stipend a month to be available for tourists, but their salary is roughly half of the money that agricultural workers make in a day. The Thai government needs the women to stay in their villages so that the tourists continue to come and spend money in the region. Consequently, Kayan girls are not allowed to attend school in the nearby towns because Kayan villages have their own schools that are not part of the Thai educational system. Instead, they are funded by donations and charitable organizations that support them. All their teachers are village residents who are extremely knowledgeable regarding their own cultural traditions, but they do not have much formal education. Occasionally, women from the villages have attempted to leave their communities to move somewhere else, even to other countries, but the Thai government denies them permission to do so. Kayan women have reported that they are being forced to remain in the villages because they continue to generate money for the provincial tourism bureau.

In 2008, the United Nations High Commissioner for Refugees (UNHCR) challenged the government of Thailand because it had refused to allow members of a Kayan tribe to relocate to other countries reportedly because such move would

ZEMBER, A COURAGEOUS KAYAN WOMAN WHO CHALLENGED TRIBAL TRADITION

Zember is a former Kayan refugee who lived in the Thai village of Nai Soi up until the time she was twenty-three years old. Her real name is Mu Lo Peh, and she was born in Burma in 1985. Due to constant attacks on her village by Burmese soldiers, she fled with her family when she was four years old; they settled in a refugee camp in neighboring Thailand and eventually in the village where tourists go to visit the long-neck women. Through her early education, she learned English from books. When the UNHCR offered the option for Kayan families to be resettled in other countries, she was very interested to go to New Zealand. She wanted to escape the tourist village, move about without limitations, and live a simple life of freedom. Zember, her sister, and her brother-in-law were accepted to resettle in New Zealand in 2005. However, after all the necessary paperwork was approved and the medical exams were completed, she was told that they could not leave because the Thai government would not approve her permit to leave the country, in order to "protect" her as a minority group. Zember was so enraged that she did the unthinkable: she took her neck rings off in protest. Then, her sister and her niece also took all their rings off. She loved her culture, but she felt that the main marker of her traditions (the neck rings) had also turned her into an exploited prisoner. The result was that many of her own people in the village turned against her because she had brought shame on them. However, her story brought a lot of publicity from local and international networks such as BBC and Al Jazeera. Given all the public controversy, she was allowed to leave Thailand in 2008 to relocate in the town of Nelson, New Zealand, together with her sister, her brother-in-law, and their four children. Zember's parents eventually also joined them in their new home country.

Javier A. Galván

result in a loss of tourism revenues, and it did not take into consideration the potential benefits to the Kayan population. The Refugee Agency argued that these Kayan women are in a situation akin to a "human zoo" where they have been reduced to be a tourist attraction for curious outsiders who want to photograph them. According to the UNHCR, the authorities of New Zealand and Finland had already accepted twenty Kayan women to settle in the country in 2006, but the Thai government refused to process their paperwork because of the money these women generate for the local tourism industry. The Thai administration defended itself by arguing that these women are kept in villages where they receive assistance, a salary, and medical benefits. Consequently, it alleged that the women are not really refugees because the Kayan women are technically not in a refugee camp, which would invalidate the potential jurisdiction of the United Nations Refugee Agency. However, these women are not Thai citizens either; they are lost in a legal and political limbo. Based on extreme frustration, some of the women threatened to simply take off their neck rings to protest the prisoner-like conditions they experienced. Their rationale was that if they stopped practicing their customs, they would no longer be a tourist attraction, and perhaps the Thai government would agree to let them relocate to another country of their own choice. The result was that Thai officials became more lenient regarding their migration policy of hill tribes. In 2008, a small group of twenty Kayan women and their families were allowed to leave Thailand and relocate to New Zealand where they were allowed to either retain their culture or slowly integrate themselves into the regional society.

Javier A. Galván

Further Readings

Eden, Phan Khon. *The Narratives, Beliefs, and Customs of the Kayan People*. Mae Hong Son, Thailand: Kayan Literacy and Cultural Committee, 2004.

George, Lianne. "A 'Human Zoo' for Burma's Giraffe Girls." *Maclean's* 121, no. 7 (February 25, 2008): 36.

Goodman, Jim. *Thailand*. New York: Marshall Cavendish, 2002.

Huay Pu Keng Village Information. http://huaypukeng.com (Accessed on February 11, 2014).

"Karen and Kayan Traditions." http://www.peoplesoftheworld.org/text?people=Karen (Accessed on February 11, 2014).

Kislenko, Arne. *Culture and Customs of Thailand*. Westport, CT: Greenwood Press, 2004.

Rastorfer, Jean-Marc. *On the Development of Kayah and Kayan National Identity*. Bangkok, Thailand: Southeast Asian Publishing House, 1994.

United Nations High Commissioner for Refugees. http://www.unhcr.org (Accessed on February 11, 2014).

NGABEN CREMATION CEREMONY

Ngaben (cremation ceremony) is a purification ceremony of the soul (*atma*) in Balinese Hindu, Indonesia. According to the Balinese people, the human body consists of body, subtle body, and *karma*. The body has five essential elements called *Panca Maha Bhuta*: solid (*pertiwi*), liquid (*apah*), hot substance (*teja*), wind (*angin*), and a vacuum (*akasa*). The five elements are fused to form the human physical body, which is mobilized by the soul (*atma*). When people die, only the body dies, and the soul (*atma*) does not. Ngaben is the process of sanctification of the soul as it leaves the body.

The ngaben cremation ceremony is performed with a series of ceremonies, consisting of various forms of offerings, specific symbols, and other rituals performed by Hindus in Bali. Ngaben ceremonies (sometimes also called *Pelebon*) are considered very important and lively. With this ceremony, the family is able to liberate the deceased from their worldly ties to heaven, and they are transformed back into the world through reincarnation.

The goal of ngaben is to make the body (*ragha sarira*) quickly return to its home, which is called the *Panca Maha Bhuta*; then the soul (*atma*) can also safely join its ancestors *Pitra*. Consequently, the ngaben ceremony should not be delayed; the dead body should be cremated as soon as possible. However, because such ceremonies require effort, cost, and time, it is often done so long after death. To bear the burden of the cost, labor, and other preparations, contemporary Balinese Hindu people often perform ngaben together with other families or villagers. As a temporary measure, the bodies of the dead are often buried underground before the family has enough money to cover the expenses of cremation. For families who can afford cremation, they

A Ngaben Cremation Ceremony in Bali. (Courtesy of Davenbelle)

can do the ceremony immediately. This is particularly true for members of a high caste. It is reasonable for them to perform this ritual within three days after death. However, for members of the lower castes, the bodies are often buried first in the ground, then exhumed at a later time, and eventually the corpses are cremated in a group event for the entire village.

The appropriate days for the ngaben cremation ceremony are always discussed with a Hindu priest in order to select the most auspicious day for the event. While waiting for a good day, the family is usually assisted by the community with the work of arranging the preparations for the traditional cremation. They usually make a coffin and a bull-shaped replica made of bamboo, wood, and colored paper, which will be used to bring the corpse to the crematorium. Early in the day when ceremony is held, the whole family and the community come together for all the preparations. Before the cremation ceremony is held, the corpse is meticulously washed and bathed. The process is always led and supervised by a priest or a *Brahmin*.

Once the bathing process is complete, the corpse is dressed in traditional Balinese clothing. All family members gather to pay their respects and pray for the consecrated souls to find peace at a better place. The corpse that has been washed and dressed in the traditional clothes is then placed in a coffin (*bade*). All members of the family and society walk in the front line after the coffin. In the ceremony, the body of the deceased will be placed, and the family will continue to treat the deceased as sleeping. No tears are shed, because the deceased family members are only temporarily not present, and they will be reincarnated or find their final rest in *moksha* (freeing from the reincarnation and death cycle). On the way to the ceremony, if there is a crossing or junction, the casket will be rotated around three times. By performing such rotation, it is believed that the spirits will be confused, and they do not come back again.

The procession is followed by gamelan music and holy songs. In the front and back of the coffin, there is a white cloth that represents a bridge for the spirit to be able to get to the place of origin. After arriving at the crematorium that has been previously identified, the corpse is put on the bull replica prepared by a priest or someone from the *Brahmin* caste who also recites mantra and prayers before the corpse is cremated. The climax of ngaben is the burning of the whole structure, including the body of the deceased along with the replica. The fire is necessary to free the spirit from the body and enable reincarnation. Ashes from the cremation process are inserted into coconut skin and are then scattered onto the sea or onto rivers that are considered sacred by the local Balinese Hindu population.

The ngaben cremation ceremony is also practiced by followers of Hinduism in India. It has been implemented for a long time in a more modest way than in Bali. The ceremony in India is not complicated; it only needs *Pancaka* (the cremation place) and fragrant fire woods, but the ceremony is performed without mantras or songs. In one Hindu story of Baratayuda, Yudhistira cremated heroes killed during wars in Tegal Kurusetra. A more recent example illustrates this tradition in India: Prime Minister Indira Gandhi was also cremated shortly after her death. In principle, ngaben in Bali follows India's cremation practice. However, the ngaben cremation ceremonies in Bali takes longer than in India because the family provides an alternative to waiting for a while, probably intended for the gathering of relatives, waiting for adults, and choosing an appropriate day to carry out the event. However, the ngaben practice should not take place later than twelve months after death.

Patit Paban Mishra and Abubakar Hara

Further Readings

Agung, I Gusti Ngurah. "Unsur Metafisika dalam Upacara Ngaben" ("Metaphysic Elements in Ngaben Ceremony"). *Jurnal Mahasiswa Filsafat Universitas Gadjah Mada*. http://jurnalmahasiswa.filsafat.ugm.ac.id/nus-10.htm (Accessed on November 3, 2012).

Hutagalung, Lusianna M. E. "Ngaben Upacara Kematian sebagai Salah satu Atraksi Wisata Budaya Bali" ("Ngaben, Cremation Ceremony as Tourist Attraction in Bali"). Medan, Fakultas Sastra Universitas Sumatera Utara. 2009. http://repository.usu.ac.id/bitstream/1234567809/13758/1/09E01088.pdf (Accessed on November 5, 2012).

Kaler, I Gusti Ketut. *Ngaben: Mengapa Mayat Dibakar?* (*Ngaben: Why Corpse Is Burn*). Denpasar, Indonesia: Yayasan Dharma Naradha, 1993.

"Upacara Adat Ngaben Umat Hindu Bali" ("Ngaben Adat Ceremony in Balinese Hindu"). http://dewaarka.wordpress.com/2009/06/15/upacara-adat-ngaben-umat-hindu-bali/ (Accessed on November 5, 2012).

"Upacara Ngaben di Bali" ("Ngaben Ceremony in Bali"). http://baliohbali.blogspot.com/2010/02/upacara-ngaben-di-bali.html (Accessed on November 5, 2012).

Widana, I Gusti Ketut. *Lima Cara Beryajna (Five Ways of Beryajna)*. Denpasar, Indonesia: PT. BP., 2002.

Wikarman, I Nyoman Singgin. *Ngaben, Upacara Dari Tingkat Sederhana Sampai Utama (Ngaben, Ceremony from Simple to Superior Level)*. Surabaya, Indonesia: Paramita, 2002.

NYABINGI RASTAFARIAN SESSIONS

Rastafarian culture and traditions are often severely judged and frequently misunderstood. Jamaica is the third largest island in the Caribbean, and almost 98 percent of its citizens are the descendants of African slaves. The Rastafarian movement emerged in Kingston, Jamaica, during the 1930s; it was a period of economic stagnation and social oppression for disenfranchised blacks. The followers of the spiritual and social movement are commonly known as Rastafarians or simply Rastas. They are usually recognized for styling their hair in dreadlocks, actively participating on reggae music, and smoking *ganja* (weed). Two of their most controversial customs are the "reasoning" sessions and the Nyabingi "grounation" (holy day) ceremonies.

The Rastafarian movement can be best viewed as a combination of religion, social traditions, and a way of life. Its followers consider Haile Selassie I (a former emperor of Ethiopia from 1930 to 1974) as their God and a reincarnation of Jesus Christ. They refer to God simply as *Jah*. It was the 1930s that Ethiopian repatriation became an ideal for Rastas. In addition, Rastafarians follow the writings of Marcus Garvey, a Jamaican activist who proposed an economic philosophy of black empowerment during the same decade. In contrast to mainstream religions, Rastas do not have any religious buildings for their gatherings. They claim that their own bodies are the only temple of God. Yet, they meet regularly to confirm and further reaffirm their beliefs. They usually gather on a weekly basis at a local community center or a leader's home. Small and intimate "reasoning" sessions usually include the ritual of smoking *ganja* and the discussion of contemporary topics, such as government policies affecting the Rasta community. They also do not believe in either heaven or hell; they prefer to concentrate on the present and live well. The way Rastas interpret the Holy Bible has an influence on their way of life. For example, men are not allowed to subject their bodies to cuttings of the flesh. Consequently, they do not shave their face or ever cut their hair. Instead, they let their hair grow in a natural flow without cutting it or brushing it, which they then style as dreadlocks. As part of their lifestyle, Rastafarians are mostly vegetarian: they do not eat pork or shellfish. The Rastas diet (called *Ital*) avoids the consumption of meat because they believe that by eating dead flesh they are turning their bodies into a cemetery. They do eat fish, but it cannot be longer than 12 inches. In addition, they reject the consumption of alcohol because it is viewed as an instrument of Babylonians (the Western world) to control and confuse the masses.

As part of their social message, Rastas have adopted specific symbols to visually represent their movement. By far, the most visible Rastafarian icon is definitely the way they use their hair styled as dreadlocks and grow hair as long as

20 inches. However, most Jamaicans view Rastas with dreadlocks with apprehension and sometimes fear. It has become a visual symbol of rebellion against the larger society. In addition, Rastas use specific colors for clothing and decorations: green, red, and black are the colors that represent Africa; green, red, and yellow are the colors of the Ethiopian flag.

Rastafarians consider Nyabingi sessions as exceptional ceremonies, which are also called "Grounation" communal gatherings. They can be viewed as large group conventions with hundreds of followers that can last anywhere from three to seven days. The first Nyabingi took place in March 1958 near Kingston. These meetings are considered special holy days in Jamaica, and they are celebrated about nine times a year to commemorate significant historical events such as the birthday of Emperor Haile Selassie (July 23), African Liberation Day (May 25), and the Anniversary of Selassie's visit to Jamaica (April 21). These gatherings are usually held in a large compound and always include music, food, dancing, drumming, singing, and collective prayers. Traditionally, there is a large bonfire in the middle of the ceremony, and men in dreadlocks organize themselves around it. These meetings always begin and conclude with a prayer thanking God. Once the meetings start, there are constant drumming rhythms playing nonstop. The group's leader leads discussions of both historical and contemporary relevance to the followers.

One of the most controversial Rastafarian practices at Nyabingi meetings is smoking cannabis as part of their rituals. In Jamaica, however, they do not call it "marihuana" but rather refer to it as the *holy herb*, *Iley*, or *wisdom weed*. The herb has a spiritual significance for the Rastas, and they consume it only after the appropriate prayers have been performed. The holy herb is blessed and then prepared in smoking pipes that are passed among the men attending the ceremony (women are rarely participants in these sessions). Rastafarians view the smoking of weed for recreational purposes as both insulting and disrespectful. The practice of smoking *ganja*, however, continues to be one of the group's biggest struggles with the larger communities in which they live. The main source of conflict is that *ganja* continues to be illegal in Jamaica and most countries around the world. As a consequence, Rastas on the island are often viewed as social deviants who smoke drugs and keep a grungy appearance.

Music has a long tradition associated with Rastafarians rituals. Nyabingi sessions include a mix of African percussion instruments and nineteenth-century church gospel singing. While various musical styles have been used (mostly based on African percussion instruments), reggae became the rhythm most closely associated with Rastas. Perhaps it was due to the international recognition of Rastafarian musicians such as Robert Nesta "Bob" Marley and Peter Tosh. Reggae became the voice of the poor and struggling black population of Trenchtown, a suburban slum near Kingston, Jamaica. The Reggae sound achieved international prominence during the 1970s with Bob Marley's recognizable hits such as "No Woman No Cry," "I Shot the Sheriff," and "Belly Full, But We Hungry." They were full of Rasta symbolism, and his lyrics addressed potent issues pressing the island such as poverty, hunger, political repression, and police brutality. International audiences became enthralled with the image and music of this Rastafarian legend who died in 1981 when he was only thirty-six years old.

Since the 1980s, most Rastafarians have given up on the idea of returning to Ethiopia; it is no longer the promised land. Instead, they have migrated from Jamaica and settled in multiple countries, including England and Canada, and in many African countries. In the United States, New York City has the largest concentration of Rastas followed by California and Texas.

Javier A. Galván

Further Readings

Barrett, Leonard E. *The Rastafarians*. Boston: Beacon Press, 1997.
Daschke, Dereack, and Michael Ashcraft. *New Religious Movements: A Documentary Reader.* New York: New York University Press, 2005.
Edmonds, Ennis Barrington. *Rastafari: From Outcasts to Culture Bearers.* New York: Oxford University Press, 2003.
Lewis, William F. *Soul Rebels: The Rastafari.* Prospect Heights, IL: Waveland Press, 1993.
"Rastafari and Jamaican Culture." http://www.jamaicans.com/culture/rasta/culture.shtml (Accessed on July 28, 2012).
Salewicz, Chris, and Adrian Boot. *Reggae Explosion: The Story of Jamaican Music.* New York: Harry N. Abrams, 2001.

P

PARRANDA DE REMEDIOS CHRISTMAS FESTIVAL

On December 24 of each year, the people of Cuba celebrate Christmas Eve, as do many nations around the world. However, Cuba has a unique holiday tradition that dates back centuries. At the same time as Christmas, another holiday is also celebrated in the town of Remedios. Although technically localized in a small area of the island, the celebration is considered potentially more important to the local population because of its nationalistic rather than religious identity. Cuban authorities promote the celebration of Parranda de Remedios (also known as the Fiesta de Remedios) as an example of honoring the nation's unique cultural heritage. In the province of Villa Clara, in the city of San Juan de los Remedios, which is recognized as one of the oldest Cuban cities having been founded in 1524 by Spanish conquistadors, the celebration is performed with a carnival atmosphere that encompasses the entire city and almost every person within the city itself. People come from miles around to celebrate Parranda de Remedios with their family, friends, and neighbors.

Since the early nineteenth century, the city of San Juan de los Remedios, more familiarly known as Remedios, has enjoyed this unique holiday. The festivities begin with a carnival to celebrate one of only three national holidays recognized by the Cuban government. Despite the precarious economic state of the country of Cuba, no expense is spared in the celebration, and funds are often diverted locally from what are considered essential programs in order to have bigger and more impressive displays and to promote tourism. Several Cuban commentators have protested against the extravagant expenses when there are so many poor people in the nation. However, such objections are usually given little consideration by the majority of the people who travel to Remedios to celebrate and enjoy this special holiday. Parranda de Remedios is marked by elaborate light displays, fireworks, costumes, floats, lanterns, and a large amount of frivolity and revelry, with everyone doing his or her best to forget the hardships of his or her life and instead just embrace the joy of the season.

The city of Remedios is essentially divided into two main neighborhoods called El Carmen and San Salvador, which are separated by a large section of empty land. At approximately 4:00 P.M. on December 24, the inhabitable areas of the city are filled with people who conflagrate at the meeting point of the two neighborhoods of the city. During the day, people dance, sing, and celebrate until the evening when the true festivities begin. At nightfall, Cuban citizens watch as the enormous city square, called Remedios Square, is filled with colorful light displays. Each building is designed with unique aesthetic decorations, including colors and patterns that are both breathtakingly beautiful and intended to tell a story. There are also massive amounts of fireworks that light up the sky long into the night. The festivities continue until well into the following morning. Throughout the night, the people of Remedios drink, dance, and unleash further pyrotechnics all in the name of celebration with little regard for personal safety. In fact, the injuries from ash or sparks are so frequent during this event that many celebrants choose to wear glasses and long sleeve clothing, despite the warmth of the humid Cuban climate. Quite a few people have had to call their evenings short and head to the nearest hospital because of an ill-timed firework or failed landing.

Originally, the Parranda de Remedios had religious connotations. The most accepted story narrates that the tradition began in the year 1820 when a local priest named Francisquito or Francisco Virgil de Quinones sent some of his altar boys out into the streets of San Juan de los Remedios. On that particular Christmas Eve, the priest's church was empty, and he had no worshippers to attend the midnight Advent Mass, called the *Misa de Gallo*. He sent the boys out with pots and pans and ordered them to make as much noise as possible to remind the citizens of their responsibility as Catholics to attend church on Christmas Eve. The two parts of the city supposedly felt a sense of competition over which group had the largest number of worshippers in attendance.

This competitive spirit fed right into an antagonism that was already present between the two main neighborhoods of the city, which have eventually culminated into the Parranda de Remedios festival. In the years that followed, parishioners began to go out on their own on Christmas Eve to duplicate the actions of the young altar boys. They then started bringing colorful paper lanterns with them and lighting fireworks. By 1871, the structure of events as it now exists had been formed. San Juan de los Remedios is a national historic landmark, and only two neighborhoods are available to the general public: El Carmen and San Salvador. These two neighborhoods hold a fraternal and friendly competition to see which faction can put out the most elaborate and colorful decorations. The region of El Carmen (known as Carmelitas) represents itself by the color brown, a globe, and the sparrowhawk. Its counterpart of San Salvador (locally known as Sensaries) uses the colors red and blue, and it is symbolized by a rooster. At 9:00 P.M. on December 24, the bells ring at the Great Parochial Church (Iglesia Parroquial Mayor); this action prompts all the town's residents to reveal their secretive efforts at creating the best decoration for the festival. People come to the center of town dressed in elaborate costumes which have been sown in secret and only revealed on that special occasion.

Both of the neighborhoods light up their buildings and construct floats—also built in secret—which are designed to reflect their neighborhood symbols and also to outdo their opposition. In addition to the floats of Parranda de Remedios, there are many stationary displays in the main city square, known as *trabajos de plaza*. However, arguably the most famous aspect of the celebration is the massive, extraordinary floats which somehow always manage to surpass what was created the year before. In the past, the massive floats have exceeded some

60 feet (2 meters) in height, used miles of lights, and hundreds of fireworks. The floats make their appearance in the square at approximately 3:00 A.M. on December 25. They usually also feature an elaborate theater production with citizens performing a live play right on the top of the float. After both neighborhoods reveal their work and all the performances have finished, the leaders of the city traditionally announce the winner for the year's efforts. The president of the winning neighborhood will be hoisted onto the shoulders of his neighbors and paraded up and down the street in victory until exhaustion overtakes the populous, and they return home for the rest of their Christmas holiday.

The religious aspects of the celebration have more or less fallen out of favor nowadays. However, the bells of the church are still an important component of the festivities. Also, the traditional music of the Parranda de Remedios is reminiscent of the religious origins. This style of music, called *repique*, is played with cowbells, drums, trumpets, and other brass instruments, and it is designed to sound like the pealing of bells that call the parishioners to mass. A more secular origin to the Parrandas celebration is the assumption that it had to do with the end of agricultural work in Cuba for the year. It celebrated that the harvest had finally ended, and it would be several months before the new planting season would begin again. Therefore, this would be the only time of the year where farmers and farm laborers would have to relax and rest before another grueling year in the fields.

The Parranda de Remedios began centuries ago as a Christmas Eve tradition in a small village in Cuba. Today, the celebrations begin weeks before Christmas with preparations and float building begins sometimes months in advance. The residents of Remedios enjoy the event so much that the Parranda festivities have begun to spread to neighboring villages and towns that also create massive lights and firework displays. On the morning of December 25, most of the people in the city come together for another day's worth of celebration, partying, and recovering from the night before. There is an expression that is rampant in Remedios which says, "For 364 days, the villagers save their energy, only to spend it all in one evening."

Rachelanne Smith

Further Readings

Bucuvalas, Tina. "The Patronal Festival of Vueltas." In *The Florida Folklife Reader*, 25–35. Jackson: University Press of Mississippi, 2012.

"Clubbing of Remedios, Cuba's National Holiday." Cuban Institute of Radio and Television. December 24, 2010. http://www.cmhw.cu/mitos-y-leyendas/1208-parranda-de-remedios-fiesta-nacional-cubana&prev=/search%3Fq%3DParranda%2Bde%2BRemedios%26hl%3Den%26biw%3D1173%26bih%3D462%26prmd%3Dimvns&sa=X&ei=E7doUISYI4-o9gTayYGgDQ&ved=0CEcQ7gEwCA (Accessed on September 11, 2012).

DK Publishing. "Remedios." In *DK Eyewitness Travel Guide: Cuba*, 177–80. London: Dorling Kindersley Limited, 2011.

Hughes, Susan, and April Fast. *Cuba: The Culture*. New York: Crabtree, 2004.

McAusian, Fiona, and Matthew Norman. *The Rough Guide to Cuba*. New York: Penguin, Press, 2012.

"The Remedios Sprees." Buenavista V Cuba. July 27, 2006. http://buenavistavcuba
.blogcindario.com/2006/07/00090-las-parrandas-de-remedios.html&prev=/search%3
Fq%3DParranda%2Bde%2BRemedios%26hl%3Den%26biw%3D1173%26bih%3D46
2%26prmd%3Dimvns&sa=X&ei=E7doUISYI4-o9gTayYGgDQ&ved=0CFAQ7gEwCQ.
(Accessed on September 1, 2012).

PENILE SUBINCISION CEREMONY

Many cultures practice ritualized circumcision as part of a ceremony that indicates a transition from adolescence to adulthood; however, only a few cultures engage in a form of genital modification called subincision. The physical process involves slicing open the penis to the urethra all along the underside. The cultures most commonly associated with this practice are the Australian aborigines, although, varying forms of this modification can be found in multiple regions of Africa, Polynesia, and South America. While subincision was widely practiced among the Aboriginal Australians until the early half of the twentieth century, it has been on a significant decline with changes in recent demographics. Today, this tradition is rarely practiced among Aboriginal populations, but it is still practiced by a few traditional communities.

Aboriginal groups make up approximately 2.3 percent of the population of Australia and number around 517,000 individuals. The Aboriginal population's average is twenty-five years of age, which indicates a significant shift in demographics among members of this indigenous group. Aboriginal populations are represented by over 200 distinctive languages that can be further broken down into over 400 unique dialects or communities. While most Aboriginal Australians are now living in urbanized environments, 27 percent still live in rural or outback communities. Traditional aboriginal groups practice various forms of animism or belief in the existence of spirits in nature that are attributed to a religious concept called Dreamtime. Today, whereas 72 percent of the Aboriginal people practice some form of Christianity, 16 percent claim no religious beliefs, and a small minority have converted to Islam. Among those who have converted to Christianity, there is a syncretism with traditional beliefs to a lesser degree.

The practice of subincision among the Australian Aborigines is tied to their traditional cosmological belief in Dreamtime. It references a point during Aboriginal creation when the empty landscape was crossed by totemic beings and imbued with the spirits of plants, animals, and locations from their spiritual existence. In Aboriginal mythology, each Dreamtime animal, place, or event has a myth or story associated with it—which is passed on through oral tradition and ritual celebrations among community members. Through the stories of Dreamtime, the Aboriginal people learn that society is not human centered, but instead needs to be focused on nature. It is this shared worldview that has helped the Aboriginal population to realize that they are part of the land with multiple levels of interconnectedness to all things. Myths associated with Dreamtime define all aspects of Aboriginal culture such as customs, taboos, social norms, and ritualized events such as death, fertility, and marriage.

According to the Aboriginal population, subincision has existed among the native Australians since their creation; although detailed references to its origins in Aboriginal mythology are scarce. While the origins of subincision may be absent from most Aboriginal myths, the processes and rituals surrounding this specific rite of passage are more prevalent in their cosmology. These rites are typically attributed to a number of localized totemic spirits; however, there may be overlap in geographically adjacent groups. For example, among the Aranda Aboriginal community, there are two different groups of ancestral spirits who are responsible for instructing the populations on the rituals associated with circumcision and subincision. The hawk-men spirits from northern Australia called Lakabara brought the ritual of circumcision, while the southern Tjilpa cat-men are said to have brought the rite of subincision and ordeal by fire to the Aranda. In general, subincision is more widely practiced among Aboriginal groups from the central desert regions of Australia, while coastal groups to the north and south tend not to perform the genital alteration. The variation in practice is often attributed to the primary religious themes of those centrally located groups such as rituals focused on life, birth, and fertility. Researchers looking beyond a mythological explanation suggest that this process was originally diffused to Aboriginal populations by way of Polynesian groups who practice a less invasive form of foreskin subincision.

In most Aboriginal groups, the ritual of subincision is tied to rites of passage indicating a transition from adolescences to adulthood, which is often associated with maturity, ability to endure pain, and readiness for communal responsibilities. The ritual usually begins when a group of males from the community arrive decorated as spirits, and they take the young man from his mother's protection for the last time. The initiate is then taken to a sacred area that is for male members only, where he undergoes a series of ordeals (ritualized testing) and a sharing of knowledge that will transform him into an adult member of the community over several weeks. These ordeals vary in time, events, and sequence but often involve a circumcision ritual, a blood drinking and decoration ritual, and finally the subincision ritual. During this period of transition, there are reenactments of mythological stories and specialized sacred language instruction which passes on the knowledge of the Aboriginal people from one generation to the next. Upon return to their communities, they are now seen as men and begin to take part in an arranged marriage ceremony with a partner who has been selected based on kin obligation in adherence to local traditions.

The physiological process of subincision involves cutting open the underside of the penis using a sharpened rock or other instrument. The incision is made by cutting through the corpus spongiosum to the urethra; the cut extends all along the underside of the penis from the urethral opening (the meatus) on the glans of the penis to the beginning of the scrotum. In Western medical practice, this procedure is referred to as urethrotomy, and it is most often therapeutically performed to address issues of urethral constriction due to medical complications or scaring. This process does, however, present a number of problems due to the relocated opening of the urethra. One of the primary challenges related to subincision is the need to crouch while urinating due to the fanning of the urine as it is now expelled through the subincised urethra on the underside of the penis. It also complicates the ability to channel the delivery of semen for reproductive purposes since the urethral opening is now located near the scrotum. This is generally addressed by squeezing the two halves of the penis together during ejaculation in order to increase reproductive success. There is also an increased risk of sexually transmitted infections due to the exposure of the urethra.

There have been many analytical approaches to examining the reasons for subincision among Aboriginal Australians. Since the procedure often precedes marriage and fertility rituals, it has traditionally been concluded that the modification is an acknowledgment of the power of the female to produce life. Much of this is based on the symbolic interpretation that the underside of the subincised penis resembles the mammalian vulva and subsequent blood lettings that occur at the point of subincision resemble menstruation. Other research focuses on the subincision and periodic bloodletting as a process that serves to strengthen kinship bonds and homosocial relations among male members of the community. There are also suggestions that due to the eroticized nature of the Aboriginal populations this type of genital modification is a way to widen the penis when erect, and it is also believed to increase the level of sexual stimulation of their partners. In addition, recent interpretations compare the aesthetic result of the process with the naturally bifurcated penis of the kangaroo, which is notorious for prolonged copulation. Other researchers state that Western interpretations of the process are pointless since the Aboriginal cosmology does not explain why but only how to do it.

Since 1960, there has been a significant decrease in the number of Australians—both Aboriginal and non-Aboriginal—practicing any form of circumcision and the process of subincision. In 2010, the Royal Australasian College of Physicians released a statement that advised parents in Australia and New Zealand to avoid circumcision except under therapeutic conditions. This has had a significant impact on the regularity and willingness of Aboriginals to undergo the rituals of both circumcision and subincision that have traditionally governed their cultural beliefs. With a significant portion of the Aboriginal population being young, urbanized, and removed from their traditional lifestyle, the rite of subincision has all but disappeared except among a select few individuals. In modern society, any Aboriginal who is subincised holds great reverence and social capital among his people.

Mario Robertson

Further Readings

Basedow, H. "Subincision and Kindred Rites of the Australian Aboriginal." *Journal of Royal Anthropology Institute* 57 (1927): 123–56.

Campbell, Joseph. *The Hero with a Thousand Faces.* New York: Meridian Books, 1956.

Cawte, J. E., Djagamara Nary, and M. G. Barrett. "The Meaning of Subincision of the Urethra to Aboriginal Australians." *British Journal of Medical Psychology* 39, no. 3 (September 1966): 245–53.

Morrison, J. "The Origins of the Practices of Circumcision and Subincision among the Australian Aborigines." *Medical Journal of Australia* 199 (January 21, 1967): 125–27.

Pounder, D. J. "Ritual Mutilation: Subincision of the Penis among Australian Aborigines." *American Journal of Forensic Medical Pathology* 4, no. 3 (September, 1983): 227–29.

Roheim, G´esa. "The Symbolism of Subincision." *The American Iago* 6 (1949): 321–28.

Singer, P., and D. E. Desole. "The Australian Subincision Ceremony Reconsidered: Vaginal Envy or Kangaroo Bifid Penis Envy." *American Anthropologist* 69 (1967): 355–58.

PHUKET VEGETARIAN FESTIVAL

The Phuket Vegetarian Festival is a nine-day event held annually in Phuket, an island province in southern Thailand. The festival occurs during the ninth lunar month of the Chinese calendar, and it is marked by sacred rituals from local residents of Chinese ancestry, many of whom strictly observe either a vegetarian or vegan diet with the intent to cleanse the spirit and grant merit. As part of the festivities, people participate in multiple rituals at various Chinese shrines and temples on the island, which are also accompanied with parades and fireworks. The rituals entail performances by entranced devotees, such as walking barefoot on burning coals, climbing a bladed ladder, and cutting and piercing their body with sharp objects without causing injury; all these events are taken as signs of spiritual power under the direct influence of the gods. The festival attracts both the domestic Thai population and tourists from around the world.

Taoist devotees participate in the Phuket Vegetarian Festival in 2012 held in Thailand. (Jaroon Ittiwannapong/Dreamstime.com)

The Vegetarian Festival in Phuket has a history that dates back to 1825 when the regional governor moved the island's principal town from a different district on the island, where there were numerous tin mines covered by jungle. A malaria epidemic gripped the island in the late nineteenth century when a traveling Chinese opera company came to perform for the Chinese immigrants working in the tin mines there. Members of the visiting opera company recalled the religious rites they had known in China, and they decided to perform these rites for nine days and nights, during which they abstained from eating meat. The company had to keep to a strict vegetarian diet during the ninth lunar moon that honored two emperor gods as a remedy. The visiting performers adhered to the strict vegetarian diet and soon recovered from their illnesses.

The annual Vegetarian Festival is also known as the Nine Emperor Gods rite. It begins on the last night of the eighth month, and concludes on the widely observed festival day known as the Double Nine (ninth day of the ninth lunar month). The series of events and practices occurring during the nine days of the festival are strictly regulated by both tradition and divination. The Nine Emperors are invited to come among the worshippers from the direction of their home in South China. Once they arrive, they are welcomed from the sea and dispatched back again at the farewell ritual.

The rules of the vegetarian festival include observing cleanliness of bodies, using clean kitchen utensils, wearing white clothing, behaving physically and mentally, refraining from eating meat, not consuming alcoholic beverages, and abstaining from all sexual activity. Men who intend to participate in the firewalking ceremony must not wear shoes or metal objects, including rings, buckles, or jewelry. In addition, those in mourning should not attend the festival, and pregnant ladies are not allowed to watch any of the rituals being performed. Women are not permitted to walk across the fire since it would be harmful to their yin qualities. Many women take up residence in the temples throughout the period where they meditate, chant, and help prepare the vast quantities of vegetarian food provided to devotees who have made a small donation in advance.

During the Vegetarian Festival, extreme examples of flesh modification are displayed. For example, men and women puncture their cheeks with various items, including knives, skewers, and other household items. It is believed that the Chinese gods will protect such persons from harm, and little blood or scarring results from such mutilation acts. They also believe that good fortune is bestowed upon religious observers. The sacred rituals are widely performed at Chinese shrines and temples on the island. The rites include performances by entranced participants, such as walking barefoot on burning coals, climbing a bladed ladder, and cutting and piercing the body with sharp objects without causing injury, all taken as signs of spiritual power under the direct influence of the gods. Entranced devotees ask the gods to enter their bodies, and they pierce their faces with everything from hooks to large spears with the help of a support team. Multiple followers also lay on beds of knives (very slowly and carefully) without receiving any cuts at all.

Firewalking and many feats of bodily powers, including placing hands and arms in boiling oil, self-flagellation with spike balls and axes, and a variety of other potentially dangerous actions are performed only by senior devotees. They believe that demons living in the area will be attracted to such performances, and that they will flee or be expelled because they will be overwhelmed by the extraordinary powers of the possessing deities. Devotees claim to be possessed by gods when they pierce their tongues, cheeks, and other parts of the body with sharp implements. The most skilled of the devotees claim to feel no pain, and they show little or no sign of real injury. In the festival's piercing procession, the devotee pierces his tongue, nose, and ears with skewers. Followers of this tradition are usually entranced while performing the painful rituals, believing it gives them supernatural powers and the ability to endure such excruciating tortures for the common good. They believe that their suffering draws out the evil from the community around them, and they also believe that this practice will bring positive luck to their friends and village.

The ceremonies of the festival take place in the vicinity of the six Chinese temples scattered throughout Phuket. The preparations begin in the afternoon before the festival begins when a great pole at each temple is raised with which the gods are invited to descend. At midnight, the organizers hang nine lanterns on the pole, which signals the official opening of the festival. The festival ends with merit ceremonies at each temple and the farewell to the gods on the last night, when firework displays are most elaborate.

Dustin Garlitz

Further Readings

Cohen, Erik. *The Chinese Vegetarian Festival in Phuket: Religion, Ethnicity, and Tourism on a Southern Thai Island.* Bangkok, Thailand: White Lotus Press, 2001.
Cohen, Erik. "The Vegetarian Festival and the City Pillar: The Appropriation of a Chinese Religious Custom for a Cult of the Thai Civic Religion." *Journal of Tourism and Cultural Change* 10, no. 1 (2012): 1–21.
Hamilton, Annette. "Performing Identities: Two Chinese Rites in Southern Thailand." *International Journal of Asian Studies* 5, no. 2 (2008): 161–85.
Landon, Kenneth P. *The Chinese in Thailand.* New York: Russell and Russell, 1941.
Maud, Jovan. "The Nine Emperor Gods at the Border: Transitional Culture, Alternate Modes of Practice and the Expansion of the 'Vegetarian Festival' in Hat Yai." In *Dynamic Diversity in Southern Thailand*, edited by Wattana Sugunnasil, 153–78. Prince of Songkla University, Patanni: Silkworm Books, 2005.
McDowall, Siriporn. "The Festival in My Hometown: The Relationships among Performance Quality, Satisfaction, and Behavioral Intentions." *International Journal of Hospitality and Tourism Administration* 12, no. 4 (2011): 269–88.

POLTERABEND

Hosted on the eve of a couple's wedding, the Polterabend party is an established tradition in German culture. Translating roughly to "noisy evening," the exact origins of Polterabend remain unknown; however, the custom seems to date back to ancient Germanic tribes. Due to pagan beliefs in evil spirits, guests involved in the Polterabend broke dishes, knocked pots and pans, and cracked whips in order to banish negative forces that could possibly sabotage a marriage. In addition, the

Polterabend tradition offered an opportunity for family and friends to congratulate the engaged couple on their approaching nuptials.

According to a legend, the bride's family would host a grand feast the night before their daughter's wedding. During the celebration, close female friends of the bride would present her with a myrtle wreath that they had either bought or crafted themselves. This wreath would serve as the bride's crown during the wedding. While the wreath is adorned predominantly in white, when the bride reveals touches of another color, it provides an indication that she would soon don her wedding gown. The bride also bore the responsibility of touching all the wine glasses of every single guest present at the feast. Many guests brought small gifts for the couple, while reserving larger gifts for the actual wedding day. When all the guests had eaten their fill, the evening's amusement commenced as some of the bride's friends performed a play for all the attendees. As servants prepare the stage for the wedding, music and singing provide an ambiance of celebration. Guests also played games and the plays performed were usually comedies. This merrymaking proceeded throughout the evening, with a great deal of noisemaking to follow at midnight.

Earlier that day, prior to the feast, villagers outlined a long list of the couple's attributes and shortcomings. If the couple's virtues prevailed, the villagers indicated their approval of the union by generating a great deal of noise in front of both the bride's and the groom's house. Upon their arrival at the stroke of midnight, members of the community would throw old crockery, pots, and pans at the front door of the house. By morning, broken shards and other debris scattered by the townspeople lined the path. As the custom continued to evolve, friends and community members began smashing kitchenware during the party against the sides of the house, as well as dropping it out of windows. However, it is important to highlight that most of the dishware and cookware broken as part of this tradition is usually made of ceramic and clay; glass—a big taboo for this event—is simply never used, as it was perceived to bring misfortune and bad luck upon the marriage. Families also began leaving the door ajar, hoping to ensure the swift departure of evil spirits. Furthermore, some families even saturated the walls of the home with holy water, intending to terrorize residual ghosts living in the walls.

Overall, this ritual of smashing dishes and making noise became a way to wish young brides and grooms of the community a happy marriage, as well as purify the couple of any destructive forces. The party in general marks the bride's and groom's shift from childhood to adulthood, as they venture into a new life joined together. While the wedding represents the present and the future, the Polterabend is intended to venerate the past. Friends and neighbors who partake in the ritual are often childhood friends of the bride and groom, who have walked with them on the path to maturity. Additionally, the bride and groom clean up the broken dishes together the next morning. This shared action alludes to the cooperation that a thriving marriage requires, as well as cements the couple's promises to remain together, especially in the face of adversity.

The practice of Polterabend endures today in many parts of Germany, as many families wish to honor the superstitions of their ancestors. Because German weddings have been first and foremost civil ceremonies enacted by a registrar since the nineteenth century, many choose to supplement the wedding with a religious service. Thus, the civil marriage often takes place one day, and it is then followed by a religious ceremony the subsequent day. Many modern Polterabend parties occur on the evening of the first day, after the civil ceremony; yet, still some couples choose to celebrate their Polterabend a few days before the civil wedding. Although the ceremony historically ended around midnight, nowadays many modern Polterabends persist into the early morning hours. As a result, many members of the wedding party prefer to have the Polterabend earlier in the week. As far as the guest list is concerned, many of the bride's and groom's friends at the Polterabend are sometimes not invited to the wedding. Therefore, Polterabend parties offer an opportunity to include those who will not be attending any of the wedding ceremonies but still wish to congratulate the young couple in person.

In the afternoon before the party begins, many friends and neighbors decorate the entrance of the bride's house with flowers. Tradition forbids the couple from seeing the decorations until the party begins. Upon their arrival, party guests bring already chipped or cracked dishes, china, and ceramics that they have set aside throughout the year in anticipation of future Polterabends. The bride and groom serve their guests a variety of food and drink, often including a cake, beer, and other alcoholic beverages. While many Polterabends are also catered, most guests actually dress quite casually for the affair in order to complement the party's informal atmosphere. While socializing, friends and family members share memories and stories about the pair, often comical and personal in nature. After the cake has been served, the energy begins to soar as guests start shattering dishes, crockery, and earthenware, cracking whips, and producing as much celebratory noise as possible. The party continues late into the evening, as guests drink, dance, and shower the marrying couple with good luck and blessings.

While Polterabend parties have traditionally been hosted by heterosexual couples, many homosexual couples have now begun adopting the custom as well, as Germany extended legal recognition to same-sex couples in 2001. Couples who cohabitate before marriage may also choose to host the party at their own home. Furthermore, the parties have become increasingly commercialized, as many businesses offer venues and hired planners to help the bride and groom with all the preparations. The businesses not only advertise their venues as capable of maintaining the rustic features of traditional Polterabends but also emphasize the little work is required by the couple and the bride's family. In addition to convenience, renting a venue affords party guests a space in which they can be as loud as they deem appropriate, without disturbing any of their neighbors. Many venues used for the celebration (including hostels and hotels) also offer overnight accommodations for guests to retire after the festivities end, as well as playgrounds to entertain any children present. Generally, these party locations can hold approximately 100 people.

Overall, wedding customs belonging to other cultures may be connected to Germany's tradition of Polterabends, particularly in the area of noise-making. For example, weddings in Finland incorporate an evening of festive racket; however, rather than remaining at the bride's house, friends of the bride parade her around the city, often in costume, on the eve of the wedding. The bridal party draws attention to the bride by making a great deal of noise and collects money from generous passersby. In addition to Finland, many customs from various countries seek to draw attention to the wedding party, such as the bachelor and bachelorette parties characteristic of the United States. These customs likely originated from similar rituals, yet have transformed and evolved into their current form due to commercialization. Ultimately, Polterabend has undergone several changes since members of Germanic tribes first observed it; however, the fundamental integrity has been preserved, and the custom survives as an important component of marriage celebration in Germany, as well as other European countries.

Kellie Money

Further Readings

"Der Polterabend." http://www.der-polterabend.de (Accessed on September 1, 2012).

Kienitz, Doris. *East Germany and the Escape: Kitchen Table Memoirs*. Victoria, Canada: Friesen Press, 2011.

Leriton, Richard. *Weddings by Design: A Guide to Non-Traditional Ceremonies*. New York: Harper Collins, 1993.

Monger, George. *Marriage Customs of the World: From Henna to Honeymoons*. Santa Barbara, CA: ABC-CLIO, Inc., 2004.

Polterabend-Hamburg. "Auβergewöhnliche Location für Ihren Polterabend in Hamburg?" http://www.polterabend-hamburg.de (Accessed on September 1, 2012).

"Polterabend in Germany: Ancient Ceremonies Kept Up at Weddings in Some Quarters." *The New York Times*. September 20, 1894. http://query.nytimes.com/gst/abstract.html?res=9E00E4D91730E033A25753C2A96F9C94659ED7CF (Accessed on February 11, 2014).

Siegel, Robert. "Analysis: German Law Permits Gay Couples to Wed." *National Public Radio All Things Considered*. August 1, 2001.

POLYANDRY MARRIAGE

Polyandry is derived from the Greek *polys* meaning many and *aner* meaning man. It refers to the practice of a woman taking two or more husbands simultaneously. This tradition is still actively practiced in the Himachal Pradesh area of India and small regions of Tibet. Polygamy is having more than one mate at the same time and colloquially refers to a man having more than one wife (the proper term for this practice is polygyny). However, monogamy (the union of one man to one woman) is the most common practice in most societies, and it is generally the rule of law in most Western countries.

When defining polyandry within the context of marriage (a woman must be married to two or more men simultaneously), the occurrence of polyandry is very low in human societies. However, there are cases of stable long-term polyandrous relationships (some of them in the Western world). An instance where a woman lives with both her husband and her boyfriend could be, more broadly, defined as a polyandrous relationship.

Part of the reason why contemporary polyandrous relationships are rare is because they are usually illegal. The world's religions have held varying views on polyandry (and in some cases, these views have changed through the ages). The Abrahamic religions (Christianity, Judaism, and Islam) prohibit polyandry, although some interpretations tolerate polygyny. While an ancient instance of polyandry can be found in the Hindu epic Mahabharata (where Draupadi marries five Pandava brothers), most expressions of Hinduism disapprove of polyandry as do most other Eastern religions. Even in the most tolerant living religions, the occurrence of polyandry is rare, and in cultures where it is practiced, it is on the decline.

The most common type of such relationship is fraternal polyandry in which a woman marries two or more brothers. Fraternal polyandry is practiced in isolated communities in the Himachal Pradesh area in India and in Tibet. It is also the most studied type of polyandry. When the eldest brother marries, all his younger brothers automatically become co-husbands to his wife. All the brothers live in the same house and share the wife equally (typically starting with the eldest and going down in birth order); no one in the group has exclusive privilege to her. Younger brothers do have the option to "opt-out." Some of them find another bride; others migrate in search of other economic opportunities, and still others may become monks and commit themselves to a life of celibacy. Generally in India, the eldest brother is socially considered the father of all the children (regardless of which brother is the biological father). All the children refer to the eldest brother as "father" and the younger brothers as "uncle." In Tibet, all the brothers are socially recognized as fathers to all the children. In fraternal polyandry, a marriage creates ties between just two households. If it is paired with sororal polygyny (where the wife's sister is taken as another wife), the ties between the two families deepens.

Associated polyandry is open to men who are not necessarily related (although in most cases, they are). The most studied form of associated polyandry is practiced in Sri Lanka. The union starts out monogamously, and a second husband (generally the husband's younger brother) is brought into the union later. The first husband is the principal husband in terms of authority, and he generally has significant say in the major family decisions. A woman and her husbands live and work together in the same household, and both husbands are considered fathers of any children the woman bears.

This polyandry system allows for many variations. For instance, the two husbands and wife may elect to bring in another woman (generally the wife's sister) into the marriage. Hence the household becomes polygyandrous (simultaneously polygynous and polyandrous). In some instances, associated polyandry is only a temporary relationship serving to fill the role of "the man of the house" when the principal husband is disabled or away for an extended period. In this case, the secondary husband is expected to fulfill all the duties of the principal husband, including satisfying the wife's sexual needs. It is expected that when the principal husband returns (or has regained full health), the household and the relationship will return to their former state.

The main economic advantage of polyandry is that it brings several providers into the family—especially in cultures where men are the primary economic providers. This practice creates stability of the family unit, especially in regions where women have very limited economic opportunities. In cases where there is a large sex ratio disparity (due to female infanticide or systematic neglect of female children, or systematic female migration), polyandry may serve to reduce competition among males when attracting a mate. Fraternal polyandry has the added advantage of ensuring that there is always a father figure in the family. As the children are from the same bloodline, establishing paternity may not be relevant as they will be cared for regardless of who the biological father is. Polyandry helps keep inheritance (land or herds) intact when passing from one generation to the next. If one generation of brothers lives together with one wife, the next generation of children would do the same. Hence there is no need to divide the inheritance among the children (as they all still live in the same house and share the same resources). In instances of small herds or scarcity of arable land, polyandry confers significant economic advantages. A few anthropologists have argued that polyandry keeps birthrates low as a woman can get pregnant only so many times. However, other studies have cast doubt on such conclusion.

Polyandry does have its challenges. As authority customarily rests with the oldest brother (or primary husband in nonfraternal polyandry), the other husbands have to subordinate themselves typically with little hope of changing their status if they are to continue as part of the family unit. When younger brothers are individualistic, the relationship within the family may be strained. Another challenge is asymmetry in relationships between the wife and her husbands. While the ideal may be symmetrical treatment in terms of affection and sexual access, the reality may be different—potentially straining the family and sometimes causing outright conflict. In some cases, there could be a large age difference between the oldest and youngest brother. As the younger brothers become part of the marriage union initiated by the oldest brother, it is very likely that the youngest brother may be a decade younger than his wife. This age disparity could result in a poor relationship with his wife in terms of companionship or sexual relations.

Recent research on why polyandry occurs and what happens to the "surplus" women has provided interesting results. Rather than highly skewed sex ratios or female-dominated societies, economic considerations seem to be the major driver for polyandrous unions. The land (or herd) is too small to divide into economically viable units, and the economy tends to be male-dominated. In most cases, females are still subservient to males. In cases of skewed sex ratios, a significant contributor seems to be systematic migration of women to areas where they can be more economically productive rather than female infanticide. Polyandry flourishes when economic opportunities are scarce, and younger brothers feel that they cannot economically sustain themselves if they go it alone. Hence individual freedom is traded for economic security. In contemporary societies—even remote ones—polyandry is declining as globalization has brought in its wake notions of family planning, anti-polyandrous religions, and visions of romance between just two people.

Muhammed Hassanali

Further Readings

Berreman, Gerald D. "Ecology, Demography and Domestic Strategies in the Western Himalayas." *Journal of Anthropological Research* 34, no. 3 (Autumn 1978): 326–68.

Goldstein, Melvyn C. "When Brothers Share a Wife." *Natural History* 96, no. 3 (1987): 109–12.

Ingoldsby, Bron B. and Suzanna D. Smith. *Families in Global and Multicultural Perspective.* Thousand Oaks, CA: Sage Publications, Inc., 2005.

Kaur, Ravinder. "Dispensable Daughters and Bachelor Sons: Sex Discrimination in North India." *Economic and Political Weekly* 43, no. 30 (July 26–August 1, 2008): 109–14.

Levine, Nancy E., and Joan Silk. "Why Polyandry Fails: Sources of Instability in Polyandrous Marriages." *Current Anthropology* 38, no. 3 (June 1997): 375–98.

Opler, Marvin K. "Woman's Social Status and the Forms of Marriage." *The American Journal of Sociology* 49, no. 2 (September, 1943): 125–48.

Peters, John F. "Polyandry among the Yanomama Shirishana Revisited." *Journal of Comparative Family Studies* 13 (1982): 89–96.

Raha, Manis Kumar and Palash Chandra Coomar. *Polyandry in India.* New Delhi: Gian Publishing House, 1987.

Singh, Sarva Daman. *Polyandry in Ancient India.* New Delhi: Motilal Banarsidass Publications, 1988.

Starkweather, Katherine E., and Raymond Hames. "A Survey of Non-classical Polyandry." *Human Nature* 23, no. 2 (2012): 149–72.

Stephens, M. E. "Half a Wife Is Better Than None: A Practical Approach to Nonadelphic Polyandry." *Current Anthropology* 29, no. 2 (April 1988): 354–56.

Zeitzen, Miriam Koktvedgaard. *Polygamy: A Cross-Cultural Analysis.* New York: Berg Publishers, 2008.

PUCK FAIR

Puck Fair, or *Aonach an Phuic*, is one of Ireland's oldest fairs in which a wild billy goat is crowned King Puck by a local girl known as the Queen of the Puck Fair. The fair is held over three consecutive days in August each year (usually the 10th, 11th, and 12th) in the town of Killorglin in County Kerry. Though no written record exists which states when the fair began, the first written mention of the Puck Fair can be found in a charter dated 1613 in which King James I granted legal status to a fair already occurring in the Killorglin region. Another record from the seventeenth century states that a local landlord was given the right to collect a sum of money for every animal sold at the August Fair, thus suggesting that a fair was an already well-established August event in the town.

The origins of the Puck Fair are unknown, but several theories have been proposed to explain the existence of the festival. For instance, since the highlight of the Puck Fair is the crowning of a he-goat by a young girl, it has been suggested that the festival began as a pre-Christian celebration for a bountiful harvest and that the figure of Puck, as a male goat, is a pagan fertility symbol. It has also been suggested that the fair began as a form of worship of the Celtic God Lugh whose sacred month is August. However, the most famous story relating to the origins of King Puck associates the king with Oliver Cromwell (1599–1658), the controversial English political and military leader proclaimed Lord Protector of the Commonwealth of England, Scotland, and Ireland and whose actions in Ireland have been strongly criticized by some historians. Legend tells that while Cromwell's men were sacking the Irish countryside around Shanara and Kilgobnet at the foot of the McGillycuddy Reeks, the highest mountains in Ireland, they came across a herd of goats grazing on a hillside. The goats were scared of the men and all but one of the goats ran away together. The goat which broke away from the herd and fled by himself was the he-goat, or Puck. The Puck lost contact with his herd, for while they ran up the mountains, he fled toward Cill Orglain, now known as Killorglin, on the banks of the river Laune. The Puck arrived in the village in such a distressed state that the villagers realized that danger must be near, and they immediately began to protect themselves and their livestock. In order to thank the he-goat for warning of the approaching danger, the villagers decided to begin a special festival of thanksgiving in his honor and the Puck Fair has been held ever since. Another legend associates the Puck with Daniel O'Connell—the nineteenth-century Irish political leader who campaigned for Catholic emancipation. Before 1808, the Killorglin Fair had been a toll fair but an Act of the British Parliament allowed the viceroy or lord lieutenant of Dublin decide whether a toll could be levied at sheep, cattle, and horse fairs. The toll collector of Killorglin was at this time a local landlord who had fallen out of favor with the authorities at Dublin Castle, and so the viceroy chose to deny the landlord the right to charge a toll at the fair. The landlord enlisted O'Connell to help get the decision reversed. O'Connell successfully argued that goats were not covered by the viceroy's document and declared that the landlord would be legally entitled to host a goat fair and levy a toll as per usual. Thus, the fair was advertised as a goat fair, and it was hastily arranged to take place on August 10, 1808, and—in order to prove to all those attending that the fair was indeed a goat fair—the organizers hoisted a male goat on to a stage.

On the first day of the fair, known as Gathering Day, a traditional horse fair is held early in the morning. Then in the evening, King Puck, his horns decorated with ribbons, is paraded through the streets of Killorglin to the town's main square where he is introduced to the Queen of Puck Fair who is embodied by a local schoolgirl who has won an essay competition judged by the fair's organizing committee. The queen reads aloud the Puck Fair Proclamation in Irish, English, French, and German and the gathered public hail the goat as the new King Puck. The king is placed on a platform in the Market Square, and it remains there for the remaining two days of the festival. King Puck is pampered and presides over both the livestock markets which are a feature of the fair and the visiting crowds. The second day of the festival, known as Fair Day, sees a variety of events taking place, including storytelling workshops, puppet shows, dances, bands, beautiful baby competitions, and the chance to meet King Puck himself.

On the third day, known as Scattering Day, King Puck is relieved of his duties. In the evening, crowds gather once more in the town's main square to salute the king and queen as they are paraded back through the streets of Killorglin. The goat who acted as King Puck is released back into the mountains and local shops and businesses stay open long into the night with much drinking taking place. The fair finishes at midnight with a fireworks display.

Puck Fair earns around £6 million in income for the local community, and it brings in tourists from as far afield as Zimbabwe and Dubai while many former inhabitants of the town return especially for the Puck Fair festivities.

Victoria Williams

Further Readings

Day, Catharina. *Cadogan Guides: Southwest Ireland.* London: New Holland Publishers, 2007.

Langan, Sheila. "Puck Fair: Ireland's Oldest Festival." *Irish America Magazine.* http://www.irishcentral.com/IrishAmerica/Puck-Fair-Irelands-Oldest-Festival-130660028.html (Accessed on December 2, 2012).

MacConnell, Mickey. "Merry in Kerry under King Puck's Long Reign." *The Irish Times.* August 13, 2012. http://www.irishtimes.com/newspaper/features/2012/0813/1224322099426.html (Accessed on December 2, 2012).

"Puck Fair." http://www.puckfair.ie/history.php (Accessed on December 2, 2012).

PUFFIN HEARTS, A RAW DELICACY

Puffins are small seabirds (10 inches tall or 18 centimeters) mostly known for their colorful beaks, which have earned them popular nicknames such as "sea parrots" and "clowns of the ocean." These little birds are not very agile but rather clumsy—a feature that makes them more adorable in the eyes of bird lovers. They live mostly on the North Atlantic Ocean. In North America, they nest near the northeastern areas of the United States. In Europe, they are spread throughout Iceland, Greenland, and northern Russia. Iceland, however, has the largest colonies of puffins where over 60 percent of the worldwide population is located. Throughout most of the world, these colorful seabirds are not usually associated with something that would appear listed on the menu of the restaurant. However, in Iceland, the Atlantic Puffin has been part of the national diet for centuries. The Icelandic shores provide a vast area for "sky fishing," which consists of fishermen using large nets to catch these low-flying birds as they are sitting on top of the water waiting to feed on fish. The government of Iceland is keenly aware of the importance of sustainable puffin populations, and it runs a harvesting program to sustain the numbers of puffin birds at appropriate levels to avoid extinction while still providing fishing licenses for both personal and commercial consumption.

The preparation of puffins for human consumption is very controversial, and animal rights activist organizations constantly voice their objections in Reykjavik, the capital of Iceland. First of all, puffins are killed by swiftly breaking their necks. Then, they are skinned and quickly cut open so that people can eat their tiny heart raw, preferably while it is still warm. The meat is usually prepared grilled, smoked, or fried on a pan. Since puffins eat mostly ocean fish, consumers of puffin meat have described it as having a consistency somewhere between a chicken and a duck but with a fishy taste—mostly due to its diet.

While animal defenders decry the methods of killing these small birds, their outrage seems to be targeted at the way puffin hearts are consumed by humans.

A salient example of a recent controversy occurred when television celebrity chef Gordon Ramsay ate a raw puffin heart during his cooking show aired on European television. After multiple complaints reached the entertainment network, the chef and show producers explained that they had obtained all the necessary government licenses for capturing the birds, and that raw puffin hearts are traditional delicacies in Iceland. The birds are nowhere near extinction. In addition, they explained that eating puffing meat (including raw hearts) might not be for everyone's taste, but it is quite common in Icelandic culinary culture, and their cooking show routinely covers the experiences of local tastes and regional traditions throughout the world.

Javier A. Galván

Further Readings

Audubon Society. "26 Questions about Puffins." *Project Puffin*. National Audubon Society. 2013. http://projectpuffin.audubon.org/puffin-faqs (Accessed on January 14, 2013).
Pegg, David. "Puffin Heart." *25 of the Strangest Foods from around the World*. http://list25 .com/25-of-the-strangest-foods-from-around-the world/5/ (Accessed on January 14, 2013).

Q

QINGMING FESTIVAL, TOMB-SWEEPING DAY

Qingming, or "Tomb-Sweeping Day," is a traditional festival to honor dead ancestors in China. Qingming Festival falls on the fifteenth day after the spring equinox, and it is considered an important family obligation among many Chinese populations throughout the world today. The ancient celebration originated in the "Spring and Autumn Period" of China, around 770 BCE–476 BCE, where important government officials would ritualistically honor ancestors to celebrate the arrival of spring. Falling on the first day of the fifth solar term (called Qingming), the name entails a time when people should traditionally enjoy the greenery of the spring season. The festivities are also called by an alternative name as the Clear Bright Festival, and it is attributed to the Tang emperor Xuanzong in 732 ACE, who tried to curb continued extravagant celebrations to honor ancestors and proclaimed that formal respects should be paid only once a year. While such rule is mostly followed in mainland China, Hong Kong is one major exception since it has another celebration: the Double Ninth Festival (following on the ninth day of the ninth month in the Chinese calendar) to honor ancestors.

The Tomb-Sweeping Day has traditionally been an important holiday among the ethnically Han Chinese. However, it was suppressed during the Cultural Revolution, where many religious, historic, and cultural institutions were attacked by the government. Although the festival was continuously celebrated in Taiwan, Hong Kong, and Macau, the festival was only recently reinstated as a nationwide holiday in mainland China in 2008.

In ancient times, the Qingming festival was a time for families to take walks and play traditional games like *cuju*, a game similar to soccer involving the kicking of a leather ball. Today, the festival has incorporated additional customs. Nowadays, during the festival, tombs of ancestors are visited. Family members clean the tomb, and they prepare offerings of food, flowers, joss sticks (long and thin incense sticks), wine, and tea to be placed at the cemetery. In addition, they traditionally burn incense, fly kites, and set off firecrackers to mark the occasion. As part of the Qingming festivities in urban areas, people have also attached special significance to willow trees, as it is believed that branches ward off evil spirits. As a result, willow branches are carried and adorned on doors and gates. In the countryside, this is the approximate time when farmers begin plowing their fields. In addition, during the past two decades, thousands of young Chinese have moved from the countryside to the larger cities for better job opportunities. During the time of the Tomb-Sweeping holiday, a large number of migrants take the time to travel back home to reconnect and visit with family.

Women participating in the Qingming Festival in China remember their ancestors through ceremony. (Hupeng/Dreamstime.com)

Recently, new noticeable trends have become popular in the type of offerings that people leave at their ancestor's tombs. In Hong Kong, for example, Qingming has seen more unusual offerings of paper goods. In addition to joss sticks and paper money, everything from shirts and shoes to imitation jewelry, handbags, and cigarettes are now commonplace. There are even high-end versions of paper decorations available, such as paper yachts, villas, helicopters, cars, and watches. Replicas of fake electronics, including iPads, iPhones, and computers, with connection cables and plugs, are also now common figures for offerings used during Tomb-Sweeping Day.

The Qingming festival is so embedded in Chinese culture that overseas Chinese communities continue to celebrate this family-oriented event. In countries and cities with sizeable Chinese populations, such as New York City, Indonesia, Singapore, and Malaysia, phone calls and letters are used as a means to connect to relatives in mainland China during this special day. In return, people in China arrange visits to the graves of dead relatives who migrated overseas. Chinese communities may also commemorate the holiday by placing advertisements in local newspapers to show respect for their ancestors.

At a national level, the Tomb-Sweeping holiday also marks a patriotic duty by showing respect toward deceased historical figures, especially leaders who played a significant role in Chinese heritage. In some cases these traditions have resulted in events important to Chinese history. For example, when Premier Zhou Enlai died in 1976, thousands visited to show their respects during Qinming. When displays of mourning were ordered to be removed, the populace loudly voiced their protest and disapproval. When the area was ordered to be cleared, it resulted in a protest that is now known as the Tiananmen Square Incident (separate from the Tiananmen Square Massacre).

There is another important celebration that is intrinsically linked to Qingming Tomb-Sweeping Day. Hanshi (or the Cold Food Festival) serves as a precursor to Qingming. It is celebrated in China, Vietnam, and Korea. In China, however, it is celebrated three days before Qingming, which is intended to symbolize and celebrate the change of seasons. The name of "Cold Food Festival" is directly related to a historical period of struggle. It is believed that it is connected to an ancient period when the type of wood available changed, and the fires needed to be relit using a different form of starter. Before the new fires were lit, food had to be eaten cold, and this tradition continues today, but it has evolved into a social celebration. Nowadays, people celebrate the event with cock fighting, playing on swings, cleaning the house, and playing games like tug-of-war.

Another unusual aspect of Qingming is *minghun*, or ghost marriages, practiced in rural areas in the northern provinces of China. Ghost marriage is a ceremony that blends weddings and funerals together. As part of this tradition, dead family members who were unmarried are given "ghost spouses" to give them happiness in the afterlife. This practice has led to a market of corpse matchmaking, with sums of money exchanging hands to procure a partner for the afterlife. After a suitable match has been made, the two corpses are buried together, with food offerings such as dumplings laid upon their newly joint graves.

Biju Sukumaran

Further Readings

Fang, Liu. "Travel Peaks Ahead of Tomb Sweeping Day." *CCTV.com*. March 26, 2012. http://english.cntv.cn/program/china24/20120326/109627.shtml (Accessed on September 19, 2012).

Krishnan, Ananth. "World Space—iPad for Ancestors." *The Hindu*. April 14, 2012. http://www.thehindu.com/arts/magazine/article3314452.ece?css=print (Accessed on September 19, 2012).

Staff. "Traditional Chinese Qingming Festival." *The Epoch Times*. April 5, 2010. http://www.theepochtimes.com/n2/china-news/qingming-festival-chinese-culture-chinse-tradition-ancient-china-32715.html (Accessed on September 19, 2012).

"Tomb-Sweeping and Bodysnatching." *The Economist*. April 2, 2012. http://www.economist.com/blogs/analects/2012/04/chinas-qingming-festival (Accessed on September 19, 2012).

Wassener, Bettina. "For the Dearest Departed, Nothing Is Too Good." *International Herald Tribune*. April 5, 2012. http://rendezvous.blogs.nytimes.com/2012/04/05/nothing-is-too-good-for-the-dearly-departed-in-hong-kong/ (Accessed on September 19, 2012).

QUEMA DEL DIABLO, BURNING THE DEVIL

On December 7, Guatemalan households participate in an activity that dates back over 300 years: *Quema del Diablo*, the traditional Burning of the Devil festival. *La Quema del Diablo* has been practiced since the sixteenth century, and it marks the beginning of Guatemalan Christmas festivities. During this traditional festival, large wooden devils, papier-mâché piñata devils, and garbage cleaned from peoples' homes are all burned in a large community celebration. This is not a regional tradition; instead, people from all over Guatemala participate. They clean out the areas of their houses where they believe the devil lurks: under the beds, in closets, and in most of the corners of the house. People collect their garbage, set it in a bonfire pile outside, and place a papier-mâché devil on top. In an effort to completely clean the house of unwanted clutter, items like old brooms and old newspapers are littered with fireworks. Guatemalans of all ages and incomes participate, though at different levels. Children collect sticks, and each family makes its own fire. In the larger festivals, it is not uncommon to see a child holding a match to the bottom of a bonfire that contains a devil figure 50 or 60 feet high. The general motivation for cleaning the house of garbage to burn is the belief that the devil inhabits the garbage and it brings misfortune to the home. When the trash is burned, people believe that the devil is remanded back to hell. Once a family has achieved the task of completely cleaning and sweeping their living areas, it is quite common to invite a Catholic priest to sprinkle with holy water throughout the house. As a result, the house is then cleansed of evil spirits, and it is considered to be ready in preparation for the Christmas holiday.

The *Quema del Diablo* festival is the first in a series of celebrations associated with Christmas. According to many historians, the practice originated during the Spanish colonial era (1520s to 1820s). During this historical period, people placed lanterns on the street to light the path for an important religious procession—the Feast of the Immaculate Conception. This was a tradition imported from Spain and brought to the Americas by Catholic priests. At the time, people who were too poor to afford lanterns would build *fogatas* (small bonfires). At some point, the meaning of the fires began to represent the victory over the devil by the Immaculate Conception. The purification and brightness of the fire are attributed to the power of the Holy Virgin Mary of the Catholic Church. While this tradition is common throughout Guatemala, the largest celebration held in the town of Antigua attracts thousands of local and international spectators every year. At this event, markets sell devil piñatas of all sizes, fireworks, candles, and sparklers. In a playful manner, men dressed as devils chase and scare the children in the street. Charges against the devil are announced by a costumed figure as the six o'clock hour approaches. The giant effigy of Lucifer is stuffed with flammable materials and is covered in fireworks, wood chips, and sawdust. The devil is then doused in gasoline and ignited.

The celebration is widely popular with Guatemalan families, and the details of how each family celebrates the event serve as a cultural reference point for each generation. Some of the traditional foods that accompany the celebration are *chuchitos* and *buñelos*. There is often a sense of nostalgia—as older Guatemalans share memories of earlier celebrations, such as joining friends for gathering sticks and papers to burn, and spending time with family. Another aspect of the celebration is a performance by costumed dancers who dance to the traditional song "Son de la Quema del Diablo" played on marimba and flute. As the celebration has become more commercialized, businesses have sponsored devil effigies in order to promote their products to the local population. At most events, vendors set up stalls to sell *atole* (a hot beverage made with masa, cinnamon, and sugar), coffee, chocolate, and fried bananas. Across the largest celebrations and the smallest, there always seems to be an abundance of firecrackers. In addition to the religious aspect, the burning tradition at the end of the year is also seen as a way to liberate people from the problems that plagued them during the previous year. Much more than a simple house cleaning, the fire is seen as a means of house purification that brings peace and serenity to Guatemalan families.

The celebration of *Quema del Diablo* owes its genesis to a blending of Maya and Spanish cultures, and it has been continuously celebrated since the sixteenth century when Guatemala was under Spanish colonial rule. The Spanish conquistadors considered the Maya indigenous population as "heathens" who were doomed to hell, and who therefore required subjugation and conversion. The exploitation of indigenous people took many forms, and the forced conversions of Mayas to Catholicism resulted in a new hybrid form of religious syncretism. This blending is responsible for the unique cultural forms and the contemporary festivals celebrated with unique traditions in Guatemala.

Guatemala achieved its independence from Spain in 1821. For the decades that followed, Guatemala was ruled by a series of military leaders. Then, in 1954, the democratically elected president of Guatemala, Colonel Jacobo Arbenz Guzmán, was overthrown in a military operation that was both funded and armed by the United States. The country suffered enormously, as hundreds of thousands of Guatemalans fell victim to death squads during a thirty-six-year civil war. During this period of military oppression and social convulsion, religious festivals such as *Quema del Diablo* took on an added significance, and they became a cornerstone of national identity for the masses of people of Guatemala, especially the indigenous and peasant populations. Their influence was so strong that, in 1954, most religious festivals became officially recognized as national holidays. As a result, festival celebration became more elaborate and more inclusive of the general population. Faced with the incredibly violent and brutal reality of life during the civil war, active participation in the ceremonial ridding of evil spirits actually gave oppressed people a sense of empowerment, even if it was ephemeral. Subsequently, such social cohesion added a new dimension to the cultural and religious significance of this traditional event.

The most significant changes in the way *Quema del Diablo* is celebrated nowadays have come as a result of increased environmental concerns. People are increasingly encouraged to burn piñatas at home instead of burning their garbage. Although this cultural and religious festival continues to receive government support, the National Environmental Commission of Guatemala—La Comisión Nacional del Medio Ambiente—has asked people to avoid burning items that release toxic smoke, such as rubber, plastics, mattresses, tires, paints, and batteries. Nevertheless, environmentalists continue to criticize the high level of pollution caused by the event.

A large number of contemporary Guatemalans fear that *Quema del Diablo* celebrations are diminishing and will eventually come to an end. Some of the main reasons they feel this historical tradition will disappear are increased ecological awareness, population growth, and degradation of the traditional spirit. As more Guatemalans become aware of the ecological impact of this cultural celebration, they are choosing either not to burn anything, to burn only a small piñata or at least to abide by the government burning recommendations. In addition, as the population of Guatemala surges in the twenty-first century, the number of fires is growing. This has led to increased incidences of accidental property damage and bodily injuries. Consequently, many older Guatemalans, especially those with cherished childhood memories of the event, feel that the tradition has devolved from a spiritual celebration into little more than trash burning. Lastly, some religious groups in Guatemala have condemned the event as a form of devil worship and a departure from a truly spiritual experience.

For many Guatemalans, however, *Quema del Diablo* is the perfect time to incinerate the newspapers full of bad news, overdue bills, and other reminders of unhappy times. Although the civil war officially ended in 1996, the people of Guatemala still suffer greatly. A wide disparity between living conditions for the rich and the poor is becoming increasingly more evident, with the indigenous people suffering the worst standards of living conditions. As a result, when the time of year for *Quema del Diablo* comes around again to burn away the evil—and especially considering the high rate of violent crime in Guatemala—a few community leaders have expressed that perhaps the fire needs to be bigger as a symbol to express the frustrations of the large majority of Guatemalans.

Michelle E. Houle

Further Readings

Armstrong, Luke Maguire. "The Burning of the Devil in Guatemala." *Perceptive Travel.* http://www.perceptivetravel.com/issues/0210/guatemala.html (Accessed on October 2, 2012).

Grandin, Greg, Deborah T. Levinson, and Elizabeth Oglesby, eds. *The Guatemala Reader: History, Culture, Politics.* Durham, NC: Duke University Press, 2011.

Ordóñez, Juan Carlos. "The Devil Gets His Due." *Revue Magazine.* June 28, 2006. http://old.revuemag.com/article201.html (Accessed on October 13, 2012).

Shea, Maureen E. *Culture and Customs of Guatemala.* Westport, CT: Greenwood Press, 2000.

Vaughn, Lisa. *Guatemala—Culture Smart: The Essential Guide to Customs and Culture.* London: Kuperard Publishers, 2007.

RAMADAN: FASTING, PRAYER, AND CHARITY

Ramadan is the ninth month of the Islamic calendar. During this month, Muslims are required to abstain from taking food and drink during all daylight hours. The requirement of fasting during Ramadan is one of the Five Pillars of Islam. These Five Pillars are the basic requirements of belief and practice for Muslims. The first pillar is the confession of faith whereby Muslims express their belief in Allah and their belief that Muhammad is their prophet. The second pillar is prayer whereby Muslims are expected to pray five times a day bowing toward Mecca. The third pillar is almsgiving or giving finances to help the Muslim community and the poor. The fourth pillar is fasting during the month of Ramadan. The fifth pillar is the Hajj in which Muslims who have the health and financial means are expected to travel on a spiritual pilgrimage to Mecca in Saudi Arabia once during their lifetime. In addition to fasting during Ramadan, Muslims are expected to be involved more intently in almsgiving or charity. Prayer is another focus of Ramadan. Muslims use Ramadan as an opportunity to draw nearer to God. They see the gates of heaven as open and approachable during Ramadan. They believe that they can make real spiritual progress during the month. At the same time, the gates of hell are thought of as being especially closed during this month.

The origin of Ramadan is believed to come from the Prophet Muhammad's having received Allah's teachings on the Night of Power, and on other nights that occurred during the month of Ramadan. Portions of what became the Koran (the holy book of Islam) were given during this time. Due to the significance of this event for Muslims, the entire month is set aside for a celebration. The portions of the Koran calling for fasting provide the spiritual foundation for fasting during the month.

Ramadan is determined to begin when the new crescent moon is first visible, signifying the beginning of the ninth month. There are sometimes controversies between different Islamic leaders over exactly when the moon is first visible due to their different locations on the globe. In addition, the day marking the beginning or end of the month may differ among some Muslim groups. The dates of Ramadan are based on the Islamic lunar calendar, which is 350 days long. Ramadan begins on different dates on the Western calendar since it is not based on the phases of the moon but on the orbit of the earth around the sun.

Fasting is the most important aspect of Ramadan. It is expected that Muslims abstain from taking food and all liquids during all the daylight hours. Exceptions are made for young children, nursing mothers, pregnant women, and those whose health could be in danger if they took part in the fast. Those who are unable to fast are expected to donate their time to working with the poor or to donate money in lieu of fasting. There can also be exceptions for athletes who are competing during Ramadan and for others who have special circumstances. However, these athletes are expected to make up the missed days of fasting. Families will begin their day especially early during the days of Ramadan in order to have a meal together, maybe getting up as early as 3:00 A.M. or 4:00 A.M. People try to finish their food and drink, their last liquid of the day, before dawn. Brushing of the teeth is also prohibited after dawn since it would involve putting liquid in the mouth. The family would then partake in their morning prayers. Sometimes individuals try to get a little more sleep after eating. At the end of the day after dusk, Muslims break their fast with a large and joyous meal called the *iftar*. Care is taken that the fast is not broken a second too early. Various means of technology or even announcements in the television signal the moment when the fast is over. The meal is often begun with people eating one or more dates following the tradition that the Prophet Muhammad broke his fast by eating such fruit this way. People may also drink water at the initial breaking of the fast. A time of prayer often follows the eating of the first food. The prayers of fasting people are thought to be powerful. This is one of the reasons that prayer is emphasized so much during Ramadan. The full meal can be a sumptuous feast made up of many delicacies. This is a special time for Muslims.

Muslims may invite non-Muslim friends to join them for the *iftar* meal. The meal may be held in homes, in mosques, or in other public places, or people may choose to eat in a restaurant. In areas where many Muslims live, restaurants may offer special deals for *iftar* meals. Restaurants often give away meals during the evenings of Ramadan as a way of carrying out the obligation of giving to the poor during this time. If the meal is not observed at a mosque, individuals will often visit a mosque after *iftar* for a time of prayers and recitations from the Koran.

The month of Ramadan is likely to alter Muslim's routine and activities. After the evening meal and prayers, many people will go shopping and have a long night. In many Muslim countries, during the month of Ramadan, the pace is different for Muslims. Lack of sleep may mean that people will take naps during the day. Hunger may also contribute to the need for sleep. Businesses may run on a different schedule during the month because of the unique patterns of life during the month. In addition, Muslims are expected to abstain from sexual activity during the day and to avoid tobacco products throughout the day as well. They are expected to refrain from harsh language, immoral activity, and impure thoughts during the month of Ramadan.

Sometimes Muslims will try to read through the entire Koran during Ramadan. This charity goes along with the increased emphasis on prayer. All of Ramadan is seen as an opportunity for Muslims to focus on God instead of focusing on fulfilling normal desires. Muslims are expected to pray five times a day every day. During Ramadan, these prayers are especially important. People who may be lax in their prayers during the rest of the year may renew their prayer lives during Ramadan. Mosques may have lengthy prayer services throughout the month. Quite often, the Koran may be read in the mosque during the thirty nights of Ramadan.

A large group of Muslims believes that their acts of kindness and gifts are twice as valuable during the month of Ramadan. Often people will organize free meals for the poor during this month, carrying out the obligation to be generous to the poor. Almsgiving (or charity) is one of the Five Pillars, and Muslims may focus much of their giving during the year by helping to pay for the meals of the poor.

The Night of Power is celebrated during each Ramadan to remember the night when parts of the Quran were first given to the Prophet Muhammad. Therefore, this is a celebration of the holy book for Muslims. Worship and prayer on this night are said to be better than 1,000 months of worship otherwise. It is believed that angels are very active on the Night of Power, and that they will grant requests. For this reason, Muslims will often stay up all night on this special night. Muslims appear to be especially open to dreams and visions on this night, which they interpret as guidance for their future.

The festival of *Eid-ul-Fitr*, Breaking of the Fast, comes at the end of Ramadan, on the first day of the following month. It is a celebration after an entire month of fasting. In Muslim countries, this is a recognized national holiday. It is celebrated in the morning with a time of group prayers. This is followed by a time of feasting, and then with the joining of friends and families for enjoying each other's company. It is a time for wearing new clothes and also a time for providing additional assistance to the poor.

Muslims look forward to Ramadan despite the strict rules followed during this special month. They see it as a time of refreshing and reconnecting with their faith. Followers of Islam believe that the tradition of fasting increases discipline to the life of the person fasting.

Ken Taylor

Further Readings

Barakat, Noorhan. "The History, Significance of Ramadan around the World." *Gulf News .com.* July 19, 2012. http://gulfnews.com/news/gulf/uae/heritage-culture/the-history-significance-of-ramadan-around-the-world-1.1051436 (Accessed on April 8, 2013).

Budak, Ali. *Fasting in Islam and the Month of Ramadan: A Comprehensive Guide.* Translated by Suleyman Basaran. Somerset, NJ: The Light, 2006.

Haq Islam. "Ramadan." Website. http://www.haqislam.org/articles/ramadan/ (Accessed on April 8, 2013).

Islam 101. "Ramadan—Month of Fasting." Website. http://www.islam101.com/ramadan/ (Accessed on April 8, 2013).

Otterman, Sharon. "Summer Nights: Times of Celebration, before and after a Daily Fast." *The New York Times.* July 27, 2012. http://www.nytimes.com/2012/07/28/nyregion/celebrating-ramadan-in-new-york-between-fasts.html?_r=0 (Accessed on April 8, 2013).

The Royal Embassy of Saudi Arabia, Washington, DC. "The Five Pillars of Islam." http://www.saudiembassy.net/about/country-information/Islam/five_pillars_of_Islam.aspx (Accessed on April 8, 2013).

REDNECK GAMES

The Redneck Games (also called Redneck Olympics or Redneck Festival) is a multiday festival held in a rural park or field featuring competitive events and games, live country rock music, food and drink vendors, and fireworks. Some events might include copious consumption of alcohol and adult-themed games. Attendees usually camp or stay in motorhomes or recreational vehicles. There are regularly occurring games in at least six U.S. states, all independently produced, though they take their inspiration and format from the original event held in Georgia in 1996. These games began as a reaction to the 1996 International Olympic Games in Atlanta, and the original intention of the Redneck Games was satiric. Over time, however, they have evolved into an ironic celebration of rural and southern stereotypes, as well as related aspects of Americana.

In general, the "redneck" was stereotyped in twentieth-century media and popular culture as a poor, dirty, uneducated, and racist southern white man. Since the 1960s, however, a small number of working-class southerners began proudly calling themselves rednecks, meaning an honest, working man who respects traditional southern values. Increasingly, more people identified with the label of a redneck because it connotes a confrontational attitude based on a marginalized southern identity. The redneck's popularity in recent American popular culture is indicated (and strengthened) by comedian Jeff Foxworthy, whose book and CD *You Might Be a Redneck, If . . .* sold millions of copies.

According to general popular versions, the Redneck Games started with jokes about a "bunch of rednecks" hosting the Olympics that were held in 1996 in Atlanta, Georgia. In East Dublin—a Laurens County city of 2,484 people about 120 miles southeast of Atlanta—a few friends concocted a farcical schedule of "Redneck Games" in which locals could compete. A promoter and a charity got interested, and they quickly involved the town. The local radio station promoted it as an Olympic spoof for charity. They expected 500 people to attend, but over 5,000 actually came. Suddenly, a small town had a popular event that drew thousands of people and generated mostly positive publicity and substantial economic benefit.

The Redneck Games were immediately attacked by the U.S. Olympic Committee, which held that the games did not have the legal right to use the word "Olympic" in its title because it was the committee's property. Numerous others also have not been amused by such redneck games, which have garnered unflattering national media attention with a conspicuous display of Confederate flags, as well as racially divisive slogans. To its fans, however, the Redneck Games convert what once was an insult to southerners into a humorous, enjoyable source of pride, humor, and innocuous outdoor recreation. While individual games vary considerably, they seem to be basically either family-oriented or adult-oriented.

The family-oriented redneck games are typified by the original Summer Redneck Games in East Dublin, now an annual major July event, with about 10,000 people attending. Events include the hubcap hurl, the bobbin' for pig's feet fest, the big hair contest, and the dumpster diving contest. In redneck horseshoes, toilet seats are thrown. Each event has its own drove of fans, popular competitors, and tradition-loaded history. The lighting of the ceremonial grill begins the festivities. To the organizers, "All in all, the Redneck Games are just a silly good time. The yearly tradition is still as wholesome and pure as it was back in 1996. Everyone and their butt crack is welcome—even Yankees" (Summerredneckgames.com 2010). The games are dependent upon sponsors and many volunteers, with vendors selling arts, crafts, and food. Annually, roughly $11,000 to $15,000 are raised for charities, and about $200,000 is generated in business for local merchants and motels. To one attendee, "it's like a grandiose bake sale, only with butt cracks and hubcaps instead of brownies and pie" (Summerredneckgames.com 2010).

The Redneck Olympics held in Clinton, Arkansas, also aims at a family audience, with its four-wheeler rodeo, lawn mower races, wheelbarrow races, watermelon or pumpkin seed spitting, big Bubba belly art contest, and a barbeque competition. No beer is allowed. In 2012, the games added a chicken nugget speed eating, a dead lawnmower race, round bale hay roll, three-man sling shot, redneck bowling (rolling a tire into trash cans), shorty-shorts contest, and a four-wheeler rodeo. It also included several events for children: spare tire roll, cow chip toss, and "get daddy/momma a cold one."

The Redneck Olympics in Hebron, Maine, attracts a family crowd, but it also has some adult-oriented activities later in the evening. It features tire-popping, a greased watermelon haul, a wife-carrying race over sand berms and mud, a tire beer trot, a tug-of-war, and bobbing for pig's feet. In the mud-runs, drivers go speeding through many feet of muck. The Redneck Blank Games and Redneck Rodeo, whose promoter is praised by many benefiting charities (including the Maine Veterans' Home, Boy Scouts, and the Carousel Horse Farm Scholarship Fund), are held in a 2,000-seat amphitheater. Adult-oriented events include a "very" wet T-shirt contest with $300 in prize and "plenty of ice cold beer in the Red Solo Cup Saloon." The Redneck Rodeo—advertised as "The First PRCA (Professional Rodeo Cowboys Association) Sanctioned Rodeo in Over Ten Years In Maine!"—has wild horses, bucking bulls, 100 cowboys and cowgirls, horse-pulled wagon rides, country-sing-a-yokky contest, a lil' buckaroos rodeo, and a greased pig scramble. Donations go to the Jimmy Fund, to fight cancer in children. After the first of these games was held, one newspaper commented: "A quaint little festival. Don't ask me why this event happened in Maine" (Zaretsky 2011).

Adult-oriented Redneck Games have many similar events, but also feature alcoholic beverage consumption, wet T-shirt contests, and other adult-themed (i.e., raunchy and off-color activities) events. The best prototype is probably the 2012 Ninth Annual Texas Redneck Games in an Easton park with several lakes and creeks in the beautiful Piney Woods. Competitions included the starter toss, mattress chunk (two-man teams throw a mattress from the back of a pickup truck), Spam eating, mud pit belly flop, as well as "Mudchicks Gone Wild." The Ugliest Butt-Crack Contest has men and women lowering their drawers and waving their hindquarters for the crowd. The "Girls Gone Wild" draws crowds because "women will come to see if they can appear on camera, and men will come because there are so many women there" (MacCormack 2007). The "mud chicks" wet T-shirt contest awarded a $1,500 first prize and an appearance on a "Girls Gone Wild" DVD. In the Spam-and-jalapeno-eating contest, ten males tried to eat the meat and many hot peppers while Steppenwolf's *Born To Be Wild* played on the background. Redneck Fear Factor's contestants bobbed in a large container of tomato-paste soup for raw chunks of cow tongue, chicken feet, and sheep kidneys. Roughly 8,000 people attended in 2012, and it recently had 377,345 Facebook friends, which reveals its popular appeal. According to one participant, "It's the freedom. A lot of these people work 60 hours a week, and all they have off is the weekend. There's no fighting. There's no litter. There's just a bunch of people having a good time" (MacCormack 2007). However, Henderson County public officials called these games a "bloated bacchanal of disorder, drunkenness and debauchery" (MacCormack 2007). They highlighted the negative aspects of the event, such as lots of nudity, rowdiness, intoxication, people running wild on their four-wheelers, underage drinking, fights and assaults, and several serious injuries. Almost 100 people were either arrested or cited for offenses that included speeding, driving while intoxicated, and marijuana possession.

The Weissport Redneck Festival in Pennsylvania's Poconos region, is a twelve-year-old adult festival with some activities that are family-friendly, and yet somewhat raunchy. There is an ugliest versus jacked-up pickup truck contest, a junkman's match, Mr. redneck competition, a Miss Daisy Duke contest, a watermelon-eating challenge, a big wheel contest, chariot races, tractor races, I luv my mummy contest, and the "best rack" competition. For the Daisy Duke challenge, young women wearing shorty-short shorts and shirts tied at their midriff saunter across the stage to applause and catcalls; the winner is chosen by the loudest audience reaction. According to the promoters, the games are "[a] mud covered celebration of your redneckism combined with the study of aerodynamics and nutrition, or AKA Runnin' trucks in the mud with occasional

THE ORIGINAL REDNECK GAMES IN GEORGIA CANCELLED FOR 2013

After seventeen years of fun based on mud pit belly flaps, armpit sounds, and toilet seat toss, the directors of the original Redneck Games in East Dublin, Georgia, have decided to cancel the games for the summer of 2013. The main reason was a declining attendance pattern that had seen a height of almost 5,000 people in 2006 but was reduced to barely 1,500 attendees in 2012. A major shift took place when the directors of the games decided to move the competition from July to May, which seemed to really hurt attendance. However, the games coordinators are hoping to revive the festivities once again in 2014 after they regroup and agree on a better time to hold the games again, perhaps after the July 4 weekend.

Javier A. Galván

breaks for beer-pong and food!" (Redneckfest.net 2009). Such is Americana in the new century.

William P. Kladky

Further Readings

"About the Summer Redneck Games." *Summerredneckgames.com*. 2010. http://summerred neckgames.com/about/ (Accessed on April 4, 2013).

Huber, Patrick. "A Short History of 'Redneck': The Fashioning of a Southern White Masculine Identity." *Southern Cultures* 1 (1995): 145–66.

MacCormack, John. "Authorities Not Amused by Texas Redneck Games; The Promoter May Be Charged after Rowdy Event." *San Antonio Express-News*. August 9, 2007. http://www.chron.com/news/houston-texas/article/Authorities-not-amused-by-Texas-Redneck-Games-1803597.php (Accessed on February 13, 2014).

Maholick, Gail. "Weissport Redneck Festival This Weekend." *Times News LLC*. September 1, 2011. http://www.tnonline.com/2011/sep/01/weissport-redneck-festival-weekend (Accessed on April 4, 2013).

McCoy, Randy. "Redneck Olympics under Fire." *B98.5—Central Maine's Country*. 2012. http://b985.fm/redneck-olympics-under-fire/ (Accessed on April 4, 2013).

"Redneckfest FAQ?" *Redneckfest.net*. 2009. http://redneckfest.net/ (Accessed on April 4, 2013).

Tracey, Brian. "Olympics Beware, Rednecks Going for Gold." *NBCNews.com*. 2007. http://www.nbcnews.com/id/20198627/#.UVYqvxzvsS4 (Accessed on April 4, 2013).

Tucker, Kathryn Hayes. "Playing Redneck Games." *Georgia Trend* 20 (2005): 75.

Zaretsky, Staci. "The 'Redneck Olympics' Try to Jump the Hurdle of Law." 2011. http://abovethelaw.com/2011/08/the-redneck-olympics-try-to-jump-the-hurdle-of-law Abovethelaw.com (Accessed on April 4, 2013).

REED DANCE CHASTITY CEREMONY

Every year in August or September, thousands of Zulu maidens gather at their King's royal palace for the Reed Dance Chastity Ceremony or *umhlanga*. It is a vibrant eight-day cultural ceremony that is practiced in Swaziland by the Zulu people to promote respect for young women and to preserve the custom of maintaining the girls' virginity until marriage. Historically, the main purpose of the Reed Dance Chastity Ceremony was for the king to find a new wife. The royal family appoints an *induna* (or captain of the girls) chosen from the commoner maidens of the community, who then announces the dates of the ceremony over the radio. The *induna* is familiar with royal protocol, and she is typically an expert dancer. One of the king's daughters is also chosen to be the *induna's* royal counterpart. Childless unmarried girls take part in the ceremony by first cutting reeds, then by presenting the reeds to the Queen Mother or *Indlovukazi*, and finally by performing a dance.

The Kingdom of Swaziland is a landlocked country in the area of Southern Africa, and its area is roughly the size of New Jersey. The Reed Dance Chastity Ceremony was developed in this isolated country with rich cultural traditions. It comes from the old *umcwasho* custom developed in the early 1940s to the mid-1950s. In *umcwasho*, all young girls were placed in a female age-regiment to help protect their virginity. The girls wore a large tassel that signified their virginity, and they could remove it only when they reached an age that was appropriate for marriage. If a girl became pregnant outside of marriage, her family was required to pay a fine of one cow to the local chief. After a number of years, when the girls had reached a marriageable age, they would perform labor service for the Queen Mother. After they performed their labor for the queen, the girls danced and feasted. The *umcwasho* or *umhlanga* was preceded by less-organized forms of maiden dancing first recorded by colonial Europeans in the late seventeenth century in Mbekelweni. There are three main objectives of the Reed Dance Chastity Ceremony. The first is to preserve the girls' chastity; the second is to provide tribute labor to the Queen Mother; and the third is to demonstrate solidarity by working and dancing together.

The Reed Dance Chastity Ceremony is an eight-day custom. On the first day, the young maidens meet at the Queen Mother's royal village. Currently, the royal village is located at Ludzidzini. The girls arrive in groups from the over 200 Zulu chiefdoms, and they are immediately registered for security purposes. The girls are supervised by men who their respective chiefs appointed for protection. Huts of relatives in the royal village or classrooms from the nearby schools serve as sleeping quarters for the girls. On the second day the girls are separated into two groups. The younger group is made up of girls aged between around eight and thirteen years old, while the older group consists of fourteen- to twenty-two-year-olds. In the afternoon the girls march in their local groups, accompanied by their supervisors to the reed beds. The younger girls travel to the closest reed beds from the current royal village, which is about 10 kilometers (6.3 miles) away in Bhamsakhe near Malkerns. The older maidens go to Ntondozi, about 30 kilometers (18 miles) away. Sometimes the girls are sent to Mphisi Farm for the reeds; because of the distance, the girls are provided lorries for transport, as opposed to having to march the entire distance. Usually arriving in the evening when it is getting dark, the girls stay overnight in government-provided tents before cutting their reeds. In the past, local villagers accommodated the girls in their homes.

The third day marks the cutting of the reeds. Using long knives, the girls will usually cut between ten and twenty reeds. The more traditional girls will cut grass, and then they usually weave it into rope to tie her reeds into bundles. Nowadays, the girls mostly use strips of plastic bags for the tying. The girls then spend another night in the government-provided tents. During the afternoon of the fourth day, the girls start their journey back to the Queen Mother's royal village, each carrying her own bundle of reeds; this is a long process, and the girls usually reach the village at night. Arriving in the dark signifies that they traveled a great distance. Day five is a day of final preparations to the girls' hair and dance costumes, which typically consist of a bead necklace, sash, anklets made from cocoons, and a skirt. They also carry the long knife that they used to cut the reeds as a symbol of their virginity. The king's daughters are allowed to participate and distinguish themselves by wearing a crown made from red feather. The fifth day also marks a day of rest from all the hard labor.

The first day of dancing is on the sixth day, and it lasts for about two hours—from about 3:00 P.M. to 5:00 P.M. While dancing, the girls deposit their bundles of reeds outside the personal quarters of the Queen Mother, after which they continue dancing to the main arena. Each group, according to chiefdom, dances and sings together—each group simultaneously singing different songs. The seventh day is the final day of dancing in which the girls perform for a large group of spectators, including villagers, foreign dignitaries, and tourists alike. The king is present on the second day of this ceremonious dancing. On the final day of the ceremony, the king orders the sacrifice of a number of cattle in honor of the girls. After collecting their pieces of meat, they return home, and the ceremony ends.

Stefanie A. Babb

Further Readings

Gianturco, Paola. "Virgins: Umhlanga, Swaziland." In *Celebrating Women*, 16–33. New York: PowerHouse Books, 2004.

Kuper, Hilda. *The Swazi, a South African Kingdom: Case Studies in Cultural Anthropology.* Orlando: Holt Rinehart and Winston, 1985.

Patricks, Richard. *Umhlanga Reed Dance: Incwala Kingship Ceremony.* Lobamba, Swaziland: Swaziland National Trust Commission, 2000.

Swaziland Digital Archives. http://www.sntc.org.sz/sdphotos/photos.asp?pg=8&decade=189 (Accessed on October 23, 2012).

Swaziland National Trust Commission. "Swazi Culture: The Umhlanga or Reed Dance." http://www.sntc.org.sz/cultural/umhlanga.asp (Accessed on October 23, 2012).

ROGAINING INTERNATIONAL COMPETITIONS

The term "rogaining" refers to the team sport of long-distance, cross-country navigation involving timed journeys conducted on foot. Walking, climbing, and hiking have long been worldwide avocations for those who enjoy outdoor activity. Rogaining had its beginnings among just such enthusiasts. As early as the 1940s, races conducted by the Melbourne University Mountaineering Club in Australia incorporated elements that anticipated rogaining as a sport.

There are two explanations for the origins of the activity's name. The first pays tribute to pioneers of the sport, suggesting that rogaining derives its name from a composite of the names of three avid rogainers—Rod Phillips, Gail Davis, and Neil Phillips (RoGaiNe). Representing the Surrey-Thomas Rover Crew, this trio took part in the world's first rogaine competition. The second account of the sport's name suggests a descriptive acronym: "Rugged Outdoor Group Activity Involving Navigation and Endurance." Both explanations may be accurate, particularly if the second is in fact a "backronym," a name devised to fit an existing abbreviation.

During a rogaine competition, participating teams, generally with two to five members each, use a magnetic compass and topographical maps to earn points over a specified duration of time. Such maps not only signal directions and distances but also present contour lines to locate landforms and demarcate where the terrain is flat or steep. Course maps are made available at a specified interval prior to the rogaine, typically two hours before the race begins. The team garnering the most points during the time allotted, usually ranging from six to twenty-four hours in length, wins the competition. Points are deducted from a team's score according to every minute they arrive late to the administrative station representing the race's conclusion. Any given team arriving at the designated final checkpoint thirty or more minutes late may be disqualified or categorized as "did not finish." In many instances, the starting and finishing locations are the same. This central station, sometimes dubbed the "Hash House," hosts participants for hot meals, strategy sessions, and other purposes related to the race.

A twenty-four-hour competition usually involves mapping and traversing 100 square miles of terrain. Rogaines of this length customarily begin midday on a Saturday and conclude at midday on the following day (Sunday). Especially in long rogaines, route planning represents an important team activity at the outset of the race. In this context, competitors often work to collect flags or other tokens of their progress, such as stamps or punches on a card. In this way, they document the team's journey and achievements. In most rogaines, competitors determine how many checkpoints they wish to visit and in what order they will attempt them. In instances where flags or other markers appearing on the competition map carry different values, teams may form strategies in order to optimize their performance. For example, if the rogaine does not involve a set pathway, teams may chart a course that conserves their resources while still yielding high rewards. Depending upon the demands of a given race, rogaining can be enjoyed by participants of all ages, with teams setting their own pace.

Rogaine competitions may be held at any time of year. It is customary to schedule races during weekends, particularly those closest on the calendar to a full moon. This timing preference likely reckons the enhanced night vision possible when the moon is full. Those electing to utilize darkness for travel still do well to bring flashlights and compasses that can be used without daylight. Since rogaines are not canceled for inclement weather, it is imperative that participants anticipate needs related to temperature, wind, or precipitation.

Most rogaines specify required items for participants to carry with them, such as whistles, pencils, first-aid kits, and compasses. The whistle is used when racers experience difficulty or require assistance. Teams are advised of the help signal to be used (e.g., three sharp blasts in succession on the whistle). Anyone within earshot, including competitors, is required to lend aid when they hear the help signal. This provision ensures timely help to the lost, injured, sick, or separated team members. Racers typically arrive with a variety of other supplies, including camping equipment, food rations, hydration, and seasonally appropriate clothing. Additional gear may accompany them on the expedition, ranging from map covers to waterproofing items.

Although policies vary among rogaine competitions, there are often numerous restrictions in place regarding the allowable instruments of navigation. Recent advances in technology might tempt racers to employ smartphones, portable computers, and global positioning systems (GPS) receivers in events where their use is authorized, but most rogaines forbid them. Even the use of simpler apparatus, including pedometers and altimeters, may be prohibited in a given rogaine. In noncompetitive events, however, these devices may play some part. For instance, geocaching, the use of such innovations as GPS to locate objects and reach a destination, is a popular activity with scouts and other youth, recasting the childhood tradition of the scavenger hunt.

Rogaining is more or less synonymous with "orienteering" or "marathon orienteering," as the sport is known in regions where an aerobic component is considered integral in the sport. Participants combine their abilities as map readers and navigators with demonstrations of cardiovascular fitness. Rogaining is also known as "bushwalking" or "competition bushwalking" in Australia. This term attends to the special relationship Australians feel to the bush country. Some scholars consider this enthusiasm for the regional landscape constitutive of national identity. Bushwalking clubs are prevalent in Australia, affording urban dwellers the opportunity to venture into wilderness. A standard day bushwalk lasts between six and twelve hours. Such excursions may be undertaken for recreation, exercise, or competition. Some adventures of this kind are destination-oriented. Rogaine races, now quite popular in Australia, often have no preset route.

In the World Rogaining Championships, held at a different location every two years, a twenty-four-hour race is typical. The first such championship took place in Beechworth, Australia, in 1992. Subsequent championships have been held in Canada, New Zealand, and the Czech Republic. The sites of world-level rogaines generally coincide with areas where rogaining enjoys the greatest popularity. In some instances, extended rogaines, known as "endurogaines," offer extreme tests of participant endurance, lasting as long as fifty hours. Rogaine races may feature flat courses but may also involve combinations of elevations and terrain to challenge participants.

Rogainers are held to a set of rules and standards while races are underway. While some of these conduct stipulations involve practices fundamental to maintaining an atmosphere of fair play, there may also be other imperatives in place for rogaine participants. Typically, these expectations involve prohibitions and compulsory behaviors related to participant demonstrations of respect for land, property, flora, and fauna.

Adventure races, whether true or modified rogaines, can now be found at locations around the world. Some of these variations on the sport incorporate other forms of equipment for physical activities as conveyance, such as canoes, bicycles, snowshoes, or skis. Some rogaines of this sort, such as the Oyster Racing Series, focus on urban locations. Oyster Race teams assembled at locations primarily in the western United States use alternate modes of transportation (on foot or on cycle) for different legs of the course. Contestants compete for prizes and the race itself sometimes doubles as a benefit for a charity or cause, such as the Arthritis Foundation.

A well-known contemporary U.S. reality television series, *The Amazing Race*, features a modified version of a rogaine. Contestant teams on this program combine travel on foot with other modes of transportation to perform required tasks and reach checkpoints before their competitors. Each season, participants in *The Amazing Race* travel the globe in hopes of prevailing over the other contestants. The winning team receives a large monetary sum as their reward.

Observers liken today's rogaine competition to other popular pastimes, such as a car rally conducted on foot or an adult's equivalent of an Easter egg hunt. No matter how light-hearted they might appear, however, successful rogaines also rely upon substantial talents of planning, navigation, and teamwork. Wherever they may be held, rogaine competitions combine athleticism and chance, strategy and luck, wisdom and whimsy, as participants encounter nature and strive toward personal best performances.

Linda S. Watts

Further Readings

Harper, Melissa. "Sensuality in Sandshoes: Representations of the Bush in the Walking and Writing of John Le Gay Brereton and Percy Granger." *Australian Historical Studies* 115 (2000): 287–302.

International Rogaining Federation. *Rogaining, 2010 & Beyond: Strategic Plan for the Sport of Rogaining.* Victoria, Australia: International Rogaining Federation, 2007.

Lo, Burt. *GPS and Geocaching in Education.* Eugene, OR: International Society for Technology in Education, 2010.

Regenold, Stephen. "Having Fun Getting Lost in the Woods." *The New York Times.* October 13, 2006. http://www.nytimes/com (Accessed on February 12, 2013)

Victorian Rogaining Association. *Rogaining: The Cross Country Navigation Sport; Which Way's North?: An Introduction to Rogaining.* Victoria, Australia: Victorian Rogaining Association, 2002.

ROOSTER COMB SOUP

Las crestas de gallo (Rooster Combs) are considered a culinary delicacy in parts of Spain, especially in the regions of Cuenca, Zamora, and Salamanca. This is the red skin located on the top of a rooster's head; it often resembles a Mohawk cut. Once cooked in a soup or stew, the pieces of meat have a chewy and collagenous texture. People who enjoy eating them often compare the gelatin-like consistency of rooster combs with a similar experience of eating the flat skin located on the web of duck's feet. Others compare its rubbery feel as being somewhat similar to eating chicken feet. While *las crestas de gallo* can be prepared in a multitude of ways, the most popular cooking method is as a soup.

Recipes for rooster comb soup are quite common and easily available in Spain's recipe books and culinary websites. A typical recipe can be found in www .mis-recetas.org:

Ingredients to Prepare *Crestas de Gallo Soup:*

1 kilogram of rooster combs (2.3 pounds)
2 basil leaves
2 ñoras (small dry spicy peppers)
8 almonds
1 can of fried tomatoes
Water
Salt

1 teaspoon of flour
3 garlic cloves
1 spoonful of sweet peppers flavor

Cooking Instructions:

Using a pressure cooker, place the rooster combs completely covered in water. Add salt and two basil leaves. Cook for one hour. On a separate skillet, use hot oil to roast the garlic cloves and the small spicy peppers (without seeds) and the can of fried tomatoes. Then, add one spoonful of sweet pepper flavor and one spoonful of flour so that the fried tomatoes do not burn. Then, mix everything on a blender, including the eight almonds. Once the rooster combs are cooked, transfer them to a larger skillet where they will be mixed with the contents of the blender. Cook for thirty minutes. Then, add at least two cups of water from the pressure cooker. Add salt and more water as needed to obtain the desired flavor. This delicious soup should serve four people.

While most Western palates might not be used to the idea of seeing rooster comb dishes prominently displayed on a menu, most countries in Europe have become aware of its medicinal properties. Recent biological studies have found hyaluronic acid in rooster combs, and they have applied it as lubricant between human joints. As a consequence, orthopedic doctors often recommend rooster comb injections for patients suffering from arthritis. More specifically, injections are applied to the knees to lubricate the bones in order for them to move smoothly rather than the grinding sensation produced when having lost the cartilage covering the knee joints. Recently, however, a false rumor has evolved into a common misconception in Spain with the idea that eating rooster comb soup will alleviate and lessen the pain suffered from arthritis. Then again, some people also believe that rooster comb soup is supposed to provide virility and strong stamina, none of which has been scientifically proven.

Javier A. Galván

Further Readings

Boardman, Rebecca. "Chicken Comb for Knee Pain." *Healthy Living.* http://www.ehow .com/about_5369657_chicken-comb-knee-pain.html (Accessed on January 24, 2013).
Conte, Kim. "Is Eating Rooster Comb a Big Cock-a-Doodle Don't?" *Café Mom, The Stir.* February 25, 2011. http://thestir.cafemom.com/food_party/116769/is_eating_rooster_comb_a (Accessed on January 22, 2013).
Mis Recetas Website. "Crestas de Gallo." *Mis Recetas.* http://www.mis-recetas.org/recetas/show/25288-crestas-de-gallo (Accessed on January 28, 2013).

RUMSPRINGA AMISH RUN

The Amish are a Protestant sect who migrated from Switzerland, Austria, and southern Germany to North America in the eighteenth century to escape persecution for their religious practices. Today almost 300,000 Amish live in thirty states in the United States and the Canadian province of Ontario. One of the largest concentrations of Amish populations is found in the area of Lancaster, Pennsylvania.

In any location where the Amish have settled, they usually live in their own distinct rural communities, and they typically concentrate on farming and agricultural activities where the entire family has tasks and responsibilities. They also believe that technology, as well as "English" fashions and other influences from the modern world, will divert them from the plain, simple life path that God has intended for them, known as the *Ordnung*. For this reason, the Amish do not own cars, television sets, radios, or computers. They wear distinct clothing without buttons, snaps, or zippers, travel in horse-drawn buggies, and depending on their sect might not smoke or drink alcohol. They have received permission from the federal government on religious grounds to teach their children in one or two-room school houses in their communities and remove their children from school at the age of fourteen.

The Amish do not believe in baptism at birth; they believe that it is the individual's voluntary decision to become a member of the church. A baptismal vow symbolizes commitment to following the *Ordnung* for life. At some point, between eighteen and twenty-two years of age, Amish youth must promise, before God and all other members of their community, that they will be accountable to the church for the rest of their lives. If they stray from the church after this vow, they risk excommunication and shunning from their community. The time in an Amish person's life between childhood and the moment he or she takes the baptismal vow is called *Rumspringa*. Roughly translated as "running around," for most Amish *Rumspringa* simply refers to adolescence, a time in the human lifespan where people at a certain age are expected to question, resist, or defy parental authority and societal norms. Some Amish, however, view *Rumspringa* as the one time in their lives where they can experience the "English" world, and perhaps choose it over the Amish one.

Because they have not yet been baptized, Amish youth have not yet taken vows to submit to their church. While many Amish youth conform to the expectations of their community, others will test cultural boundaries. They will go out into the "English" world, wear non-Amish clothing, go to movies, and learn how to drive. They may buy their own car or purchase a television, DVD player, portable stereo, a cell phone, or mobile computing device. They also might make non-Amish friends and socialize outside of their usual circles. Amish youth are allowed to take on part-time jobs to make extra money for themselves. These experiences allow them to meet non-Amish people and to interact with them at a social level. Consequently, Amish parents often worry about the type of peers with which their children will socialize, as the choice of friends often influences adolescent behavior. Nowadays, however, Amish communities are increasingly interacting more with the "English," as individuals switch from farming to carpentry, furniture building, or factory work.

Amish teenagers are not subject to their parents' authority during weekends. While typical Amish youth group activities include picnics, swimming, volleyball, baseball, ice skating, hiking, singing, and dinner parties, Amish teens engaged in *Rumspringa* will leave their communities to engage in these activities or go to bars or nightclubs. They will rent buildings for parties or go to a non-Amish friend's house to have them. During *Rumspringa*, it is common for Amish youth to experiment with tobacco, alcohol, and recreational drugs. Recently, this new-found freedom has resulted in some Amish youth occasionally becoming drug dealers in their communities. Rural law enforcement agencies have had to educate Amish elders about marijuana, cocaine, and methamphetamine so that they could teach their own communities about meth labs, pot farms, the dangers of drug abuse, and criminal consequences of owning, using, producing, or selling illegal drugs. A more serious problem for Amish youth during *Rumspringa*, however, is alcohol abuse and drunk driving. Police have arrested Amish teenagers for driving buggies or cars while intoxicated and in the possession of alcohol. Amish elders show no sympathy for such behavior, and they encourage authorities to punish drinking teens with the most severe penalty that the law will allow—especially if their actions harmed other people.

Amish children do not usually receive sex education in their schools. Their activities before and after adolescence are gender-segregated. Amish teenagers might engage in unprotected sexual activity during *Rumspringa*, particularly under the influence of drugs or alcohol. Such lack of general sexual information may result in unwanted pregnancies or catching a sexually transmitted disease. Unfortunately, risky sexual behavior places Amish girls at risk for punishment (and even shunning) regardless of whether their sexual partners were Amish or "English." It is also possible for Amish teens to discover their true sexual orientation during *Rumspringa*; gay, lesbian, bisexual, and transgender Amish teens with this knowledge must make a difficult decision—leave the Amish community in order to be "out," or return to the Amish world and live in the closet while conforming to all adult expectations, including getting married, bearing children, and following the strict social norms of the Amish religion.

Between 80 and 90 percent of Amish youth return to their communities after *Rumspringa*, and they take their baptismal vows. A significant percentage of Amish youngsters report a considerable "emptiness" in the "English" world. Those who leave the community do so to seek higher education or escape abuse at home. Most "ex-Amish" remain religious, however, and struggle to balance the strengths of Amish culture with modern Christian practices and culture.

Rachel Wexelbaum

Further Readings

"The Future of the Amish." *Chronicle of Higher Education* 53, no. 46 (June 2007): B4–B4.
Schactman, Tom. *Rumspringa: To Be or Not to Be Amish*. New York: North Point Press, 2006.
Stevick, Richard A. *Growing Up Amish: The Teenage Years*. Baltimore: Johns Hopkins University Press, 2007.

RUNNING OF THE BULLS

The running of the bulls (*encierro* in Spanish) is a traditional practice during which people participate in a run ahead of several bulls, normally on a route through the streets of a town. The birth of this peculiar practice is related to the necessity of transporting bulls from a corral to the bullring, where they will engage in a bull fight (*corrida*). The most famous *encierros* worldwide are those

Runners lead the pack of bulls through the streets of Pamplona, Spain, during the yearly running of the bulls event. (AP Photo)

in the Spanish town of Pamplona, which take place during the festivities of *Sanfermines* (the Fiesta of San Fermín, the patron saint of Navarra), and it is celebrated every year from July 6 to 14. Although the running of the bulls (*encierro*) is only one of the many events of the larger festivities, for many people it is one of the most exciting. The run is broadcast live on national Spanish television, and then it appears in the news of other stations. It can also be seen on the Internet.

The roots of the *Sanfermines* celebrations date back as far as the Middle Ages; however, it grew in popularity in the twentieth century largely thanks to Ernest Hemingway's novel *The Sun Also Rises* (1926). Every year the fiesta draws thousands of people from all around the world, traditionally dressed in white with a red sash and neckerchief. The event transforms the entire town into a feast of joy, music, drinking, and dancing. The celebration starts at noon on July 6 with the *chupinazo* (the inaugural rocket), and it officially ends at midnight on July 14 with the farewell song ¡*Pobre de mí!* ("Poor Me"). The fiesta includes a range of events such as: the parade of the image of San Fermín on the Saint's Day (July 7); the *Comparsa de los Gigantes y Cabezudos* (parade of ceremonial giants and carnival figures); various taurine fiestas, as well as spectacles, dances, concerts, a funfair (known as *Las Barracas*), and fireworks. Another popular event on July 6 has been the *Riau-Riau*—traditionally a procession of city council members to the church of San Lorenzo, both accompanied and obstructed by the crowds. In 1990, it was suspended from the official program due to serious incidents on the course. Typical of the fiesta are also social clubs called *peñas*, which provide a special atmosphere at the bullring and later on into the night with regional music (*la música de charanga*).

The running of the bulls (*encierros*) and the *corridas* are the most important taurine activities during *Sanfermines*. However, there are also other rituals, some of which do not appear in the official program, for example, a silent *encierrillo* not accompanied by runners (when the bulls run from the *corral del gas* located outside the old city gates) to the corral from which they will be released the next morning during an *encierro* and *apartado* (when the bulls are allocated to the bull fighters who will fight them in a *corrida* and then separated from each other). In the process, the local form of *los toros* (*encierrillo* and *encierro*) gives way to the rituals of national identity (*apartado* and *corrida*), while participants of the *encierro* turn into the spectators of the bull fight.

The emergence of the running-of-the-bulls tradition in its present form (with the runners ahead of the bulls) is dated as late as the second half of the nineteenth century. In earlier periods, the bulls were preceded by horseback riders who cleared the way for the animals. Today, the running of the bulls takes place from July 7 to 14 from the corral in Calle Santo Domingo to the bullring. The fighting bulls—some of which have come down to history as particularly dangerous—come from various top-quality breeding ranches (*ganaderías*), for example, Miura, Cebada Gago, Jandilla, Domecq, Guardiola Fantoni, and Antonio Urquijo.

During the *encierro*, the runners not only try to run in front of the bulls but also alongside one particular bull for as long as they can. The best runners, admired for their bravery, are called *los divinos* (the divine ones). Since taking part in the *encierro* is risky, the participants must be aware of the possible dangers and safety measures to participate in the run safely. Some of the "must nots" of the *encierro* are participation of people under eighteen years; running while under the influence of alcohol or drugs; wearing clothes or shoes that are inappropriate for the run; running backward in the direction of the bulls; inciting or harassing the bulls; taking photographs while participating in the run; and crossing safety barriers. The route of the run is protected with a double fence to prevent the bulls from leaving the course, as well as to protect the spectators from injury.

The *encierro* starts promptly at 8:00 A.M. Before the gate of the corral is opened, the runners chant three times (at 5, 3, and 1 minutes to go) to the image of San Fermín placed in a niche in a wall: "*A San Fermín pedimos, por ser nuestro patrón, nos guíe en el encierro dándonos su bendición*" (We ask San Fermín, being our patron saint, to guide us in the bull run and give us his blessing), and they finish up shouting "*Viva San Fermín! Gora San Fermín!*" The run begins with launching of two rockets (the first one signaling the release, the other one that the last bull has left the corral). At the end, another two rockets are fired from the bullring to signal, respectively, that all the bulls have reached the arena and that they have been contained in the corral. The fourth rocket thus signals the end of the run. The route of 825 meters (2,706 feet or 902 yards) is usually completed rather quickly in approximately three minutes.

To help the run go smoothly, the six fighting bulls are released with *mansos* (non-fighting bulls acting as steers), which guide them to the bullring. After two minutes, three more *mansos* (the so-called sweep-up group) are sent to run down the route in case any bull gets separated or stops along the way. The run is also looked over by two groups of people. The task of the *pastores*—wearing green shirts and equipped with long poles—is to make sure the bulls do not run backward, and they are not stopped or separated from the other bulls. The other group is the *dobladores* equipped with capes who await the bulls in the bullring to guide them into the *corral*.

Participation in the running-of-the-bulls events is a dangerous and sometimes deadly activity. While no information on fatalities before 1910 is available, as of

---

THE GREAT BULL RUN COMES TO THE UNITED STATES

From December 2013 until October 2014, several Great Bull Run events will take place across multiple locations in the United States, including Houston, Texas; Dallas, Texas; Chicago, Illinois; Twin Cities, Minnesota; Central Florida, Philadelphia, Pennsylvania; and Lake Elsinore, California. The company organizing the coordinated events has brought together multiple Spanish traditions into one event, including the adrenaline of the running-of-the-bulls experience and the messy Tomato Royale (replicating the famous tomato fight of La Tomatina). The running-of-the-bulls events take place in much safer locations, such as horse-race tracks, rather than on city streets as they are traditionally done in Spain. In addition, the food fight takes place three times a day to give more people the opportunity to participate. While the events are based on ancient Spanish traditions, the participants have to sign up in a more modern manner by registering e-mail and obtaining their tickets online. Thousands of people have already signed up for this moveable celebration.

Javier A. Galván

2012, fifteen people have died of the injuries suffered during the run. The first victim was twenty-two-year-old Esteban Domeño Laborra in 1924; the most recent casualty was twenty-seven-year-old Daniel Jimeno Romero, who was gored by the bull named *Capuchino* in 2009. However, some sources also recall Francisco García Gurrea, who died in January 1911 apparently as a consequence of the injuries suffered in the *encierro* of 1910. The most tragic celebrations were the *encierros* of 1947 and 1980, when two bulls, respectively, *Semillero* and *Antioquio*, each caused the deaths of two runners. The number of the injured people can also be considerable—usually up to thirty people are transported to the hospital after each run. However, if a pile-up (*el montón*) occurs, the number of wounded runners may be much higher.

Both the running of the bulls and bullfights are increasingly criticized by animal rights activists. Organizations such as People for the Ethical Treatment of Animals (PETA) and AnimaNaturalis, for example, protest against both events each year right before the *Sanfermines*. In 2002, the PETA activists initiated the annual "running of the nudes" as an alternative activity during the San Fermín festivities. The first event was attended by twenty-five people; however, the subsequent years gathered many more, reaching hundreds in 2007. In the following years, the PETA and Anima Naturalis protests took the form of half-naked activists laying on the ground "bloodied" and with the *banderillas* (bright harpoon-ended sticks used during a bullfight) on their backs, and in the shape of a giant bleeding bull. In 2012 (the eleventh consecutive year of their protest against the maltreatment of animals in traditional feasts), the activists used their half-naked bodies painted with red and black paint to display the inscription "Stop bull fights."

While the most famous running-of-the-bulls event takes place in Pamplona, other *encierros* are also held in other towns in Segovia (Spain), Huamantla and Tlaxcala (Mexico), and Ayacucho (Peru). In the United States, a local version of running of the bulls was introduced in Crave Creek, Arizona; this event, however, takes place in a fenced desert track, not along the town streets. Pamplona's *encierro* is also replicated in New Orleans during the annual Festival de San Fermin Nueva Orleans, with members of the Big Easy Roller Girls and other U.S. Roller Derby leagues playing the part of the bulls.

Anna Kaganiec-Kamieňska

Further Readings

"Arizona Town Hosts Own 'Running of the Bulls.'" *Foxnews.* October 16, 2011. http://www.foxnews.com/us/2011/10/16/arizona-town-hosts-own-running-bulls/ (Accessed on December 30, 2012).

Diario de Navarra. "El colectivo PETA pedirá el fin de los toros antes de San Fermín." *diariodenavarra.es.* July 03, 2012. http://www.diariodenavarra.es/noticias/san_fermin/2012/07/03/el_colectivo_peta_pedira_fin_los_toros_antes_san_fermin_85526_2101.html (Accessed on December 30, 2012).

Douglass, Carrie B. *Bulls, Bullfighting and Spanish Identities.* Tucson: University of Arizona Press, 1997.

"Kingdom of Navarra." Land of Diversity Website. http://www.turismo.navarra.es (Accessed on December 15, 2012).

Running of the Nudes Website. http://www.runningofthenudes.com/ (Accessed on December 30, 2012).

"San Fermin in Nueva Orleans." 2012. http://www.nolabulls.com/index.asp?id=0 (Accessed on December 30, 2012).

San Fermin Website. www.sanfermin.com (Accessed on December 20, 2012).

RUSSEFEIRING

Every May, graduating high school students in Norway experience a one-of-a-kind event: Russefeiring. The etymology of Russefeiring consists of two root words: *russ* (the graduating student) and *feiring* (celebration). Russefeiring is an annual three-week-long celebration lasting from April 26 to May 17, which coincides with the national Norwegian Constitution Day. During these three weeks, students continue the traditions of the forbearers by wearing color-coordinated overalls, decorating their cars, and participating in parades. However, the tradition has taken a different turn with the addition of new extracurricular activities, much to the chagrin of older generations.

Norway is located in the western portion of Scandinavia with the majority of its coastline dominated by large fjords and small islands. According to a 2011 census, 5 million people live within an area of 125,182 square miles (roughly larger than New Mexico) that is long and narrow. In a length comparison, Norway is almost as long as the U.S. eastern coast. The Russefeiring tradition dates back to the 1700s when Norwegian students wanting to attend Copenhagen University in Denmark had to pass an exit exam. After passing the exhausting test, students officially graduated from high school. The present-day version of Russefeiring began in 1905 when red caps were given to graduating students in order to signify the change from adolescence to adulthood. Each school has its own *Russ* board, which is made of elected students in order to help organize the festivities. Examples of these positions are the *russ* president, journalists, and party organizers. The president is responsible for creating, printing, and running a newspaper to spread the word regarding the festivities going on during the following three weeks. Some of the information published includes an official *knot* list (daring activities to accomplish) and the creation of a spoof Facebook where participants make humorous statements about the life and future of those graduating

One of the most iconic traditions involved in the celebration is the use of wearing overalls for the three weeks and the issuance of the caps at the end of the celebration. One particular oddity about the overalls is that students wearing them are supposed to never take them off during Russefeiring except for when they go to sleep. Students who participate in this tradition are required to wear the color overalls that signify their particular studies. Red is by far the most prominent overall color; it signifies the completion of general studies such as history, math, and English. Blue identifies the students who majored in business administration and economics. Black is for those who are in the vocational studies such as carpentry or information technology. Green reveals the students who focused on the study of agriculture, and white is for those who are going into the medical field.

Another related tradition observed during the Russefeiring period is the creation of faux business cards by the graduating students. They create their own cards, but rather than having actual data, they have crazy information just for the fun of it. Students usually label each card by the nickname they are given during Russefeiring. They then go about handing the cards to strangers all over town. These cards are quite popular among the young children in Norway. In fact, children themselves get involved in the festivities of Russfeiring by trying to collect as many cards as possible from the graduating students. Those who collect the most cards are deemed the luckiest by their peers.

Another relevant tradition tied to Russefeiring is the purchase and decoration of vehicles. The tradition of *russ* cars began in the 1950s when students painted the cars either red or blue and used them in the processional parade for Norwegian Constitution Day. As time went on, cars fell out of favor with students as the availability of vans and buses became more prevalent. In order to offset the cost, contemporary students have decided to pool their money together to purchase a van. Subsequently, they paint the van to match the color of their *russ* and create intricate decals on the sides to differentiate their van from others. For those who purchase a bus, the decorating routine is taken to another level. First, each bus centers itself around a particular theme. Then, large speaker and entertainment systems are usually installed as well as special lighting systems. However, the decoration and augmentation of vans and vehicles can become quite expensive. Students often spend almost US$6,000 apiece just to make the best *russ* vehicle. On the extremely high end of the *russ* vehicle spectrum, one bus cost the students around 2 million kroner (almost US$400,000). To offset the high cost, students approach certain companies to become sponsors of their vehicle. By gaining corporate sponsorship, the *russ* vehicle then becomes a mobile advertisement for those businesses. At the end of the Russefeiring celebration, awards are given out to specific *russ* vehicle owners. "Most Creative Russebuss" and "Most Creative Russebuss Name" are just two of the categories that students have a chance to win. With all of the augmentations, the vans and buses become mobile party stations, which lead to some of the controversial aspects of Russefeiring.

The main controversy that stems from modern Russefeiring is the use of the celebration as a way for students to drink large quantities of alcohol. In Norway, students usually graduate from high school when they are nineteen years old. The legal drinking age in Norway is eighteen. Consequently, many participants often drink excessively and cause many motor vehicle accidents due to their levels of intoxication. In addition, a high number of students develop alcohol poisoning. These accidents have been assuaged in recent years with the passing of certain restrictions. One of those regulations is that now each van or bus is required to have a designated driver who is not going to partake in the consumption of alcohol.

Another controversial aspect is the issuance of *knots* on the string hanging at the back of the *russ* cap. In this specific context, the word *knots* means the completion of a series of pranks. The *Russ* board is responsible for creating the list with the pranks and tasks. The problem with these challenges is that the acts can push the boundary of morality and legality. There are some very tame tasks to get *knots*. For example, if students spend the night in a tree, they earn a stick as a token. By crawling around on all fours for the day, a student gains a toy shoe for their token. If they go to a McDonald's restaurant and eat a Big Mac hamburger in two bites, they earn a piece of the wrapper as the token.

Each one of the previous acts is very tame compared to more daring events that make it on the *knot* list. Students earn a wine cork if they drink an entire bottle of wine in twenty minutes. Also, students can gain a beer bottle cap when they complete the task of drinking twenty-four beers in twelve hours. The *knot* list has been critiqued heavily by the news media in Norway because of the involvement of students performing illegal actions (such as streaking naked down the street and fighting with the local police authority) and the dangers of consuming large amounts of alcohol in such a short period of time. Due to the negative publicity that such events generate, most of the dangerous tasks have now been removed from the official list. However, several dangerous tasks are still being performed.

The three-week celebration ends when the students receive their *russ* cap on the morning of May 17. In the afternoon, the graduating students proceed to join the parade celebrating the creation of the Norwegian Constitution. When all of the fanfare is over, students return home to study for their final exams. Amazingly, students party very hard just days before they have to take the exams in order to graduate. However, students who fail the national exams do get to repeat Russefeiring again the following year.

Even though the celebration of Russefeiring has garnered negative attention in previous years, the tradition is still an important part of the culture of Norway. Besides the fact that Russefeiring celebrates the culmination of the end of one's mandatory schooling, it also signifies the beginning of the next phase in the student's life. No longer is the student just a child within Norway, but they are now official members of Norwegian adult society. It might just be an excuse for some people to drink excessively and commit dangerous acts, but for others, it is the culmination of hard work.

Mark Layne

Further Readings

Bråthen, Turid R. "Norwegian Russ Celebration." *FMR*. November 23, 2003. http://www.fmr.no/om-meningen-med-rusgiftbruk-sett-gjennom-russefeiring-som-et-rituale.107144–17800.html (Accessed on September 18, 2012).

Brown, Berit I. *Nordic Experiences: Exploration of Scandinavian Cultures*. Westport, CT: Greenwood Press, 1997.

Derry, T. K. *A History of Scandinavia: Norway, Sweden, Denmark, Finland, and Iceland*. Minneapolis: University of Minnesota, 1979.

Hubbard, William H. *Making a Historical Culture: Historiography in Norway*. Oslo: Scandinavian UP, 1995.

March, Linda. *Norway-Culture Smart!: The Essential Guide to Customs & Culture*. London: Kuperard Press, 2006.

O'Leary, Margaret Hayford. *Culture and Customs of Norway*. Santa Barbara, CA: Greenwood Press, 2010.

Sande, Allan. *Russ Parties: The Meaning of Substance Seen Through the Russian Celebrations as a Ritual*. Bodø, Norway: Bodø University Press, 1999.

SANNAKJI, EATING LIVE OCTOPUS

Sannakji, or sannakji hoe, is a culinary delicacy served in Korea. The dish is unusual in that its main component—raw octopus—is still moving. Sannakji can be prepared either whole or in pieces. To make such a delicate dish, a small octopus (Nakji) is used. Most of the time, the octopus is prepared whole. However, when it is prepared in smaller pieces, the tentacles are sheared off into bite-sized pieces while the octopus is still alive. In both forms of preparation, the octopus is still moving and wiggling around, and the tentacles continue to squirm while they are severed from the main body of the octopus. For presentation and flavor, the octopus is usually dressed with sesame seeds or sesame oil, and it may be occasionally served with a spicy dipping sauce.

Sannakji is difficult to eat, and in some cases it can be considered a choking hazard. In South Korea, the dish causes an average of six deaths per year. In both preparations the tentacles stick to the plate, to chopsticks, and to the insides of the mouth. When the octopus is prepared whole, it is simply wrapped around chopsticks and placed in the mouth, where the octopus's head is chewed first in order to kill it right away. Despite being dead, the suction of its tentacles continues to be active.

When the delicacy is served whole (and not chopped into smaller pieces), the entire octopus must be placed into the mouth at one time. This type of sannakji preparation is more difficult to eat, and it can cause more of a health hazard. In either case, the sesame oil serves a dual purpose to add flavor and to prevent the tentacles from suctioning too much to surfaces. Sannakji is mild-tasting, though some people describe it as meaty. The tentacles are always served fresh even if chopped into pieces, as they will eventually stop moving. Moreover, customers order the main body of the octopus to be served raw, but restaurants will often cook the remaining tentacles at the request of the customer. This way, they enjoy part of the octopus raw and have a comparison to taste it already cooked. Sannakji is normally served in restaurants or markets that specialize in raw preparations, and a place that is famous precisely for this type of service is the Seoul's Noryangjin Fish Market. Restaurants around such markets will prepare what customers have bought fresh, and they include side dishes such as lettuce, hot sauce, garlic, and kimchi (a pickled cabbage). Sannakji is also often served along with alcoholic beverages such as soju, which is a clear rice wine that is considered Korea's national drink. However, the consumption of alcohol is often said

A vendor selling live octopus in South Korea. (Minyun Zhou/Dreamstime.com)

to increase the chances of choking for those daring palates willing to try sannakji for the very first time.

Biju Sukumaran

Further Readings

Gross, Matt. "A Quest into the Gustatory Heart of Seoul." *The New York Times.* July 18, 2008. http://www.nytimes.com/2008/07/22/travel/22ihttrseoul.1.14610796.html?pagewanted= all (Accessed on August 1, 2012).

Hunt, Katrina Brown. "World's Most Dangerous Foods." *Travel + Leisure.* October 2009. http://www.travelandleisure.com/articles/worlds-most-dangerous-foods (Accessed on August 1, 2012).

SANTERÍA CLEANSING RITUALS

The practice of cleansing rituals has an ancient history throughout the world. Overall, people believe that spiritual cleansings could bring happiness, economic prosperity, love, and family harmony. The santería religion—which is mostly practiced in Cuba, Puerto Rico, the Dominican Republic, and parts of the United States— includes multiple rituals with cleansing ceremonies intended to help its followers. Traditionally, santería practitioners seek the advice of a *santero* or *santera* (priest or priestess) regarding a difficult situation, such as health complications, negative energy, troubled relationships, infidelity issues, financial problems, and family squabbles. Santería teaches that priests have a direct connection to Yoruba gods (*Orishas*), who provide the appropriate direction to keep a person's life in balance. Priests perform a divination ritual that determines the offerings required by the *Orishas*, such as fruit, herbal baths, flowers, and animal sacrifices. Most of the materials used in multiple santería rituals involve a combination of medicinal plants, candles, Florida water (a scent perfume used in santería rituals), cigar smoke, and the blood of sacrificed animals. All *santeros* are expert herbalists; consequently, spiritual cleansings use lots of plants and herbs. The preparation for such rituals usually involves a trip to a *botánica*; these are stores that sell materials for santería rituals, such as candles, plants, powders, incense, and in some cases even chickens to be sacrificed. In the United States, these *botánicas* are quite common in Hispanic neighborhoods with a potential santería following.

Most santería ceremonies and rituals take place in secrecy. However, they should be studied within a larger religious context. For example, santería does not have a central religious book to guide its followers, such as the Bible or the Koran. Instead, knowledge is shared orally, and it has a strong emphasis on active participation in religious rituals. In addition, santería believers aim to achieve spiritual balance while still alive, and they do not seek potential rewards in the afterlife. Most religious gatherings do not take place at an official church, cathedral, or parish. Instead, the houses of *santero* priests (called *ilés*) include simple shrines that serve as common gathering places. These priests are considered godfathers or godmothers to their followers.

Santería has its roots on the African religious practices of the Yoruba people from modern-day Nigeria. During the Spanish colonial period (1500s to 1800s), African slaves were forcefully transported to the Caribbean to work at sugar plantations mostly located in Cuba and Puerto Rico. Once there, they were forced to convert to Christianity and venerate a new God and other saints in the Catholic Churches. Out of necessity to fool their Spanish oppressors, African slaves assigned their traditional Yoruba deities to statues representing Catholic saints. For example, Santa Bárbara was paired with Changó, one of the most powerful Yoruba gods. This parallel representation of deities allowed the slaves to worship their own gods right in front of the Catholic priests who believed that the slaves were actually enthralled with Catholic saints. In fact, the name *santería* originated within this context; it literally means "worshipping of saints." Overtime, santería became a fusion of Catholic elements together with Yoruba polytheistic beliefs and traditions. The new syncretic religion continued to thrive during the 1900s after independence. Despite the fact that Cuba was already independent, most santería followers continued to be baptized as Catholics, even though they no longer had to pretend to believe in Christianity. To complicate matters even more, in contemporary Cuba, most santero priests are also fervent Catholic followers.

There are four important types of cleansings performed in santería. The first one is done to cleanse bad spirits from physical spaces, such buildings, houses, or businesses. During this ceremony, all the santería followers wear white clothing. The *santero* spreads burned sage and incense throughout the building with special emphasis on windows and entryways. They might also kill a chicken and sprinkle some drops of blood on the floor. The other three ceremonies are actually performed on people—not building structures. The second type of cleansing is called a Spiritual Bath (*Limpieza*), which is simply intended to remove negative and undesirable conditions from a person's energy. Devotees can perform this cleansing alone in the privacy of their own home with the guidance of a *santero*, who will recommend the elements to use, such as fresh flowers, plants, and herbs. This type of ritual is rather mundane. The general idea is that by performing a ritual on a person's body, it would have the intended effect on his or her spirit as well. However, the controversy begins with the third type of cleansing when a *santero* has to perform a *parado* (a ritual with the person standing up). This cleansing ritual is usually carried out in the *santero's* home with the help of an assistant. *Santeros* begin by preparing a special mixture of selective herbs, plants, flowers, and water. In the process, they cannot use scissors or knives to cut the materials; they all have to be crushed by hand. Sometimes, they also add oils. The mixed water is intended to provide a feeling of tranquility and is used in two specific ways. The *santero* puts water on his mouth and then sprays it repeatedly and forcefully all over the person's head, chest, shoulders, and back areas. Then, he uses a few branches of wormwood tied together to dip them into the water, which is then shaken and sprinkled all around the person, beginning with the head and heading down toward the feet. Finally, the *santero* smokes a cigar and softly blows the smoke all over the person's head and torso. The goal of this ritual is to expel all the evil spirits, negative energy, and bad luck that surround a person. Once the ritual is over, the mixture of water, plants, and herbs must be discarded since it is believed that it absorbed the negative energy present in the room during the ritual.

The fourth and most controversial type of cleansing is a healing ceremony that involves animal sacrifice and can be performed only by a *babalawo*—the highest-ranking santería priest. Followers request this ritual because the severity of their problem is enormous, or because someone's life may be in danger, either through illness or wrongdoing. Animal sacrifice is considered a gift to the *Orishas* in return for requesting assistance in solving a serious problem. The ceremony also includes other offerings to the gods, such as fruit, candles, and flowers. This type of ritual often takes place by the ocean or a river (never a lake). Usually, the person kneels down; then, the santero says a few prayers and blows cigar smoke around a person's head and torso. Then, he decapitates one or two chickens to pour the blood over the person's head. The offer to the *Orishas* is the blood and not the body of the animal itself. In most santería rituals that involve animal sacrifice, the meat is eaten by the congregation participating in the ritual; however, when the ritual involves the topic of death of malevolent spirits, the animal cannot be consumed. It is important to highlight, however, that regardless of how animals are killed and used in religious rituals, the idea of animal sacrifices is not widely accepted outside of santería circles, especially in the United States.

Santería arrived in the United States with the migration of Puerto Ricans and Cubans. First, when the U.S. Congress granted U.S. citizenship to Puerto Ricans in 1917, they migrated to New York and Florida. While many of them practiced santería, they were rather secretive about it due to fear of oppression or of being ostracized. Then, the Cuban Revolution of 1959 sparked two Cuban waves of migration during the 1960s and 1980s that brought thousands of Cubans who settled mostly in southern Florida. Many of them practiced santería, but they were much more open about it, especially in comparison to their Puerto Rican counterparts.

Since santería priests and priestesses are extremely secretive about rituals that require animal sacrifice, the larger society around them usually does not understand them and their practices. In the United States, this tradition has generated conflict with law enforcement authorities and health agencies. However, *santeros* claim that animal sacrifice is essential for their traditions and an important covenant with their gods. Moreover, the practice is required for the ceremony to ordain all santería priests. Nevertheless, the religious right to perform animal sacrifices was actually challenged in U.S. federal courts. However, the U.S. Supreme Court declared on June 12, 1993, that santería is an established religion, and its practitioners have the constitutional right to practice animal sacrifice as part of their ceremonies and rituals.

At the beginning of the twenty-first century, it is now commonplace to see *botánica* stores in many cities with a Spanish-speaking population throughout the United States. At first glance, unsuspecting customers will notice that these esoteric stores sell incense, candles, and statues of patron saints. They have a nice aroma, too. However, there is much more beneath the surface since most *botánica* owners are also *santero* priests.

Javier A. Galván

Further Readings

Clark, Mary Ann. *Santería: Correcting the Myths and Uncovering the Realities of a Growing Religion.* Westport, CT: Praeger, 2007.

De la Torre, Miguel A. *Santería: The Beliefs and Rituals of a Growing Religion in America.* Grand Rapids, MI: William B. Eerdmans Publishing Company, 2004.

Mason, Michael Atwood. *Living Santería: Rituals and Experiences in an Afro-Cuban Religion.* Washington, DC: Smithsonian Institution Press, 2002.

Rivera, Elliott P. *Healing in Santeria.* Botanica Madre de Agua: Santeria Spiritual Healing and Cleansing. http://botanicamadredeagua.com/healings/healing-in-santeria/ (Accessed on July 1, 2012).

"Text of 1993 U.S. Supreme Court Decision in the Hialeah Case: Church of the Lukumi Babalu Aye, Inc. et al. versus the City of Hialeah, FL." *Journal of Church and State* 35, no. 3 (Summer 1993): 668.

Walsh, Bryan. "How the World Heals." *TIME* 173, no. 7 (February 23, 2009): 80–83.

SAPPORO SNOW FESTIVAL, *YUKI MATSURI*

The captivating country of Japan stretches 1,800 miles from the north tip to its most southern point, and it is home of many exotic landscapes and traditions. Located next to Korea and Russia, Japan is divided into four main islands: Honshu,

A large ice-and-snow sculpture displaying a replica of the Kabuki-za theater in Tokyo as part of the Sapporo Snow Festival in 2013. (Khor Seik Soon/Dreamstime.com)

Hokkaido, Shikoku, and Kyushsu. Religion, geography, climate, food, and historical events lead the Japanese population to conduct many festivals, celebrations, and other cultural events throughout the year. One of the most popular and unique celebrations held in Japan is the Sapporo Snow Festival.

The island of Hokkaido is surrounded by mountains that cover most of its landmass, and the majority of the population lives in Sapporo, the capital of Hokkaido. The regional geography contributes to a unique climate that is better known for its cold, dry winters and its very-short sunny weather. Because of its location, heavy cold winds blow from Siberia onto Hokkaido. From December to March, these cold winds bring a lot of precipitation that ultimately transforms into white and powdery soft snow. As a result, Hokkaido's snowy mountains provide a sign for the locals to prepare for heavy tourism as many skiers and snowboarders travel to Hokkaido to experience its death-defying slopes. However, while the snow is welcome, it also brings with it harsh living conditions. Therefore, the locals have adapted themselves to enjoy the snow, and there is no better way than to conduct an annual festival.

Ever since 1950, the Sapporo Snow Festival (or *Yuki Matsuri*) flourished when several high school students built a snow sculpture of grand size. Within the next five years, the Japanese Ground Self-Defense Force (the national army) began to participate in the event, and subsequently the tradition to build snow sculptures evolved over time. It was not until the Winter Olympics of 1972 were held in Sapporo, Japan, that the grand-size sculptures received worldwide recognition. As a result, the *Yuki Matsuri* event evolved into its current form, and it now welcomes international competitors from around the world to build enormous snow and ice sculptures.

Over the years, *Yuki Matsuri* has increased the numbers in both snow and ice sculptures, which then created additional challenges. For example, in recent years, the festival has included over 220 snow statues and 120 ice sculptures, and the number is expected to increase in future celebrations. To keep up with the demand for materials to build the sculptures, the Japanese Ground Self-Defense Force has contributed by shipping tons and tons of snow from the nearby and not-so-close mountains to Sapporo. Most of the mammoth-size sculptures are located in three sites, but the Odori Koen Promenade Park is the venue where most of the statues are displayed. Most of the curious and surprised visitors are attracted to this location first. This is also the home of the Summer Festival and the Sapporo White Illumination Event. Odori Park is a long strip measuring roughly 1 mile in length, which gives the 2 million spectators plenty of room to view every single sculpture. The other two sites used for displaying snow and ice sculptures for the event are Susukino and Tsu Dome. Held in February every year, the Tsu Dome ice exhibition lasts a week and may overlap with the Sapporo White Illumination festivities in which they adorn the entire park with white lights. The combination of both events makes the Sapporo Snow Festival a must-see celebration for both locals and international visitors. The best view has been recommended to go at night as the lights have been strategically placed toward the sculpture to provide an elegant touch to the already detailed masterpieces.

Cindi Aguilar

Further Readings

Benson, John. *Eyewitness Travel Guide: Japan.* New York: DK Publishing, 2000.
Peppas, Lynn. *Cultural Traditions in Japan.* New York: Crabtree Publishing Co., 2011.
Reiber, Beth, and Janie Spencer. *Frommer's Japan.* 8th ed. Hoboken, NJ: Wiley Publishing, 2006.
Snow Festival. "64th Sapporo Snow Festival. The History." http://www.snowfes.com/english/useinfo/history_e.html (Accessed on February 2, 2013).
Vilhar, Gorazd, and Charlotte Anderson. *Matsuri: World of Japanese Festivals.* Boston: Weatherhill Publishers, 2004.

SCARIFICATION OF CHILDREN'S FACES

The deliberate creation of scars is a form of body art that can carry multiple messages in addition to its beauty. For members of cultural groups that practice scarification, its complex patterns can show whether the wearers have completed the necessary rituals to become an adult or whether they are ready to marry. They can show whether the people are under the protection of a god or gods, or whether they are strong, brave, and capable of enduring the suffering of adult life. They can show whether a man has killed an enemy or whether a woman has borne children. They can communicate the family or tribe to which a person belongs. In many cases, scarification begins in adolescence, as part of the rites that mark a boy's or girl's passage to full social adulthood. Among some groups, however, such as the Bétamarribé people of the West African country of Benin, the creation of these messages begins early in life with childhood scarification. As children grow, they will also receive scars on their face, abdomen, back, legs, chest, and shoulders that reveal their status in society.

When Bétamarribé children stop breastfeeding, usually around two or three years of age, they are given the first of several sets of scars that they will receive during their lifetimes, a delicate pattern of fine lines that covers the entire face. When a traveling scarmaster (*odouti*) visits a village with children who are ready to undergo the procedure, he or she will determine the appropriate pattern to use for a child by casting small shells called *cowries* into a pail of water. The pattern they form shows the *odouti* which of the scarification patterns in his or her repertoire to use. The process itself takes place outside, on flat ground under a tree where the recipient lies on a bed of soft green leaves. The *odouti* uses a small, sharp tool called a *teponte* to make rows of small cuts into the skin and create the intricate designs. The scarification of a child usually takes around half an hour, less time than the similar patterns made by *odouti* on adolescents and adults. When it is over, the cuts are washed and treated with a healing shea butter salve. The scarmaster spits charcoal onto the cuts, a practice which, along with the shea butter, is thought to keep away evil spirits that might have been attracted by the blood of the operation. Finally, the cuts are left to heal into scars.

Scarification is a painful and bloody process. While adolescents and adults receiving scars are supposed to bear the pain stoically in order to prove their toughness, young children cry, scream, and sometimes curse the *odouti* and their community. It can be difficult for parents to watch, and some modern Bétamarribé people are beginning to decide not to scarify their children. However, parents also have many reasons to proceed with the ritual, because the scars have several important functions in Bétamarribé culture. Most basically, they differentiate Bétamarribé from all other people. Wearing them honors the children's ancestors and offers them protection. It is also the way that a child becomes a full member of the society; if children die before receiving the markings, they are considered not to be Bétamarribé in the eyes of the community's ancestral spirits, and they cannot be buried in the village cemetery. For the Bétamarribé and some other cultures with a tradition of scarification (e.g., the Baule and Senufo peoples of Cote d'Ivoire and the Bafia of Cameroon) scars symbolically make a person "human." They add beauty by separating a human being's intentionally decorated skin from the naked, natural skin of other species. From a more practical point of view, someone without scars might have a difficult time finding a wife or husband after reaching adulthood.

Bétamarribé scarification is part of an ancient human tradition, and body scars represent specific events in life (marriage, child delivery, adulthood, etc.). In Africa, the first evidence of the practice from rock paintings in the Sahara Desert is 7,000 to 10,000 years old. Many examples of visual art made in West Africa in centuries past also include human figures with scar-like markings. Scarification is also practiced in Papua New Guinea, where it is a part of young men's initiation rituals, and it was once common among Australian Aborigines, although it has mostly died out in Australia. Throughout its long history, scarification has acquired a wide range of meanings. Scars serve as identification marks, showing the ancestry or tribal or ethnic affiliation of the wearer. In many cases, they also indicate that the wearer has reached a specific stage of his or her life. For the Bétamarribé people, the scars given in childhood mark the children as part of the group. At adolescence, boys go through an initiation ceremony that marks their transition to adulthood, during which they are scarred on their chests and abdomens. Adolescent girls receive scars on their abdomens, lower backs, and buttocks, after which they are considered adults and ready to marry. When women marry, they receive scars on their shoulder blades, with additional marks added when they become pregnant for the first time. Other African peoples also blend social status and identification in the scars they wear, like young Dinka men from South Sudan who receive a series of horizontal scars across the forehead that both mark them as Dinka and initiate them into manhood.

Scarification can offer evidence of a group's values and way of seeing the world. Bétamarribé scars, including those given to children, serve a protective function by pleasing the ancestors and warding off bad fortune. In Nigeria, Yoruba people used scars called *abiku* marks to protect children seen as particularly vulnerable to being pulled into the spirit world through death; if a twin child died, the surviving twin would be scarred in this way. Scars also reveal other things that the people who give them consider to be important to pass on to the next generation. Among the Ga'anda people of northeastern Nigeria, girls once underwent a process of scarification that, like that of the Bétamarribé, began in childhood. This series of rituals, called *hleeta*, began when a girl was five or six. Over six stages carried out in two-year increments, scars would be made on her abdomen, buttocks, back, chest, legs, arms, and forehead. They took place as part of the process of cementing an arranged marriage, which could take place once the scars were completed. They also sent the message that adult status was earned with pain. While the Ga'anda did not scarify their boys, young men received a similar message through a three-month initiation ordeal called *sapta*, during which they were whipped and subjected to other physical and psychological ordeals.

Scarification practices also reflect a group's dramatic and painful history. Overall, childhood scarification is much less common than that carried out during adolescence or adulthood, but it occurs relatively frequently among ethnic groups in West African countries like Benin and Nigeria. This tendency reflects the terrible impact that the Atlantic Slave Trade had on this region during the eighteenth and nineteenth centuries, when millions of people were captured and shipped to the Americas as slaves. The demand for slaves at the coastal trading ports and the heavy flow of weapons that was introduced to the region by traders led to political instability, warfare, and slave raiding that separated families and destroyed communities. Marking children's faces with scars indicated what tribe, clan, or family they belonged to, and it made it possible for parents and communities to identify their lost children if they later had the opportunity to do so. Nineteenth-century warfare and political disorder in what is now southwestern Nigeria also encouraged many separate groups speaking closely related Yoruba dialects to come together as a larger Yoruba ethnic group. Their scars were usually done during childhood, and the scars were a declaration of Yoruba citizenship as well as potential insurance against kidnapping.

People's changing environments and expectations continue to affect scarification traditions today. In some cases, governments oppose its continued practice. Ga'anda scarification was outlawed in 1978. The Bétamarribé are able to carry on their traditions only in the countryside and not in Benin's cities and towns. Some elements of scarification have also fallen victim to changes in other customs. The Bétamarribé traditionally wore very little clothing, leaving their elaborate body scars clearly visible to all. Now that much of the body is usually concealed by their clothes, some people are choosing to wear only their facial scars. Parents continue to have their children scarred, honoring tradition and marking boys and girls as members of their culture and community.

Sara C. Jorgensen

Further Readings

Blier, Suzanne. *The Anatomy of Architecture: Ontology and Metaphor in Batammaliba Architectural Expression.* Cambridge: Cambridge University Press, 1987.

Krutak, Lars. "Scarification and Tattooing in Benin: The Bétamarribé Tribe of the Atakora Mountains." *Lars Krutak: Tattoo Anthropologist.* 2008. http://www.larskrutak.com/articles/Benin/index.html (Accessed on November 30, 2012).

Rubin, Arnold, ed. *Marks of Civilization: Artistic Transformations of the Human Body.* Los Angeles: UCLA Museum of Cultural History, 1988.

"Scarification." *Body Arts.* Oxford: Pitt Rivers Museum. 2011. http://web.prm.ox.ac.uk/bodyarts/index.php/permanent-body-arts/scarification.html (Accessed on November 30, 2012).

"Scarification." *National Geographic Channel.* December 20, 2007. http://www.youtube.com/watch?v=Lfhot7tQcWs (Accessed on November 30, 2012).

SCORPIONS ON A SKEWER

The Chinese capital of Beijing offers a unique mixture of new technology, old architecture, historical sites, and delicious food. Beijing's highlights include the Forbidden City, the Olympic Village, Tiananmen Square, and open street markets. In addition, the city is known for its culinary delicacies, and most restaurants satisfy the palates of both locals and international visitors. For eaters with a daring appetite, the Night Street Market provides a popular venue into an exotic dining experience.

The Beijing Night Market is frequented by both locals and tourists who want to arouse their taste buds to items not easily cooked or served at home. This open-air market is on Wangfujing Street, and it is easily accessible by public transportation.

A vendor selling fried scorpions, sea horses, and sea stars at the night market in Beijing, China. (Chrispyphoto/Dreamstime.com)

It is technically an alley with hundreds of vendors where unusual delicacies are sold on a skewer, including seahorses, grasshoppers, and large black scorpions. Right after entering the alley, it becomes apparent that the food being sold there is decidedly different, and all the five senses are enhanced during this outdoor experience. Visitors first hear the sizzling frying sound of oil. Next, the familiar smells of garlic, onion, cumin, and sugar fill the air. However, other unrecognizable smells begin to emerge. As curious customers approach vendors to see what is being fried, reality hits, and their mouths drop in disbelief. In the glass displays, there are live and dead scorpions (small and big), tarantulas, eels, grasshoppers, snakes, and other strange critters awaiting hungry and curious customers. The vendors try to lure the potential customers to their stand by offering small samples of food. Most vendors only speak Mandarin, but both parties somehow negotiate the number of items ordered and the monetary value for the delicacy about to be prepared. The clever vendors also have numeric signs posted to facilitate the transaction.

Most daring customers seem as if they want to flee, but curiosity gets the best of them. First, they approach the vendors to take a picture of their snack about to be eaten. In the meantime, there are other visitors haggling over the price. The situation is kind of comical because both parties do not understand each other but somehow they come to an agreement. Then, daring clients select the scorpions they want; the scorpions are placed on a skewer; they are then prepared and seasoned, and finally dropped into hot oil to be fried. It only takes a few minutes

BIG CRITTERS FOR INFORMAL DINNER AT THE NIGHT MARKET IN BEIJING

At the Night Market in Beijing, China, tourists can experience a unique regional culinary delight: scorpions on a stick. They are usually fried in sizzling oil and then sold on a skewer. A common concern among intrepid eaters is whether the scorpions are poisonous or carry any diseases. As a result, it is quite common to have a general sense of apprehension about eating the creepy crawlers. Most foreigners simply close their eyes and then take a big bite of the fried critter. The texture of fried scorpions is crunchy, and the taste is generally not all that bad. It really does taste like chicken. While many tourists eat these large scorpions on a dare combined with a moment of insanity, the experience is often described as quite memorable.

Peter Luévano

to cook them. The moment of truth arrives, and daredevils must prove that they are actually adventurous and crazy enough to eat their scorpion snacks.

Peter Luévano

Further Readings

Hopkins, Jerry. *Extreme Cuisine: The Weird and Wonderful Foods That People Eat.* Berkeley, CA: Periplus, 2004.
Lonely Planet. *Extreme Cuisine: Exotic Tastes from around the World.* Oakland, CA: Lonely Planet, 2009.

SETSUBUN, BEAN-THROWING CHILDREN'S FESTIVAL

Japanese people have celebrated the arrival of spring for thousands of years. For centuries, they have also practiced multiple rituals aimed at expelling and chasing away the presence of wondering evil spirits. In contemporary Japan, a festival called *setsubun* is celebrated throughout the nation on either February 3 or 4 to mark the start of the spring season (*risshun*). The word *setsubun* literally means "seasonal division." In relation to the Japanese Lunar Year, the spring *setsubun* tradition can be viewed as a type of New Year's Eve celebration, which usually includes rituals to get rid of negative spirits in order to begin the New Year surrounded by health, prosperity, and happiness. This day used to be symbolic of rebirth traditions and the farming preparations for the planting upcoming season.

However, the modern *setsubun* rituals performed to get rid of evil spirits are not obscure and full of mysticism but rather happy, celebratory, and even comical—especially for young Japanese children. They certainly look forward to this day because the activity of throwing beans at people while yelling loudly can be a lot of fun. Like most celebrations, there are traditional food and drinks associated with this custom. Roasted soy beans (called fortune beans or *fuku mame*) are an essential part of the festivities since the bean-throwing (*mame maki*) practice is an essential element of *setsubun*. In addition, ginger sake (*shōgazake*) is a rice liquor often associated with this festival; it is a holiday tradition similar to the way eggnog is consumed during the Christmas season in the United States. As part of the *setsubun* celebration, families also decorate their homes with colorful paper designs in the shape of sardine

Participants dressed as devils during the *Setsubun* Festival in Japan. (Kingyo/Dreamstime.com)

heads to keep wondering evil spirits from entering the home.

Setsubun celebrations take place essentially at two levels: at family homes and at religious centers. At home, Japanese people perform bean-throwing events in a more intimate manner with the goal of driving away bad spirits and invite happiness into the household. To celebrate this tradition, someone has to be the bad guy. Traditionally, the oldest male member of the family (usually the father) takes on the role of the demon or ogre (*Oni*) by wearing scary masks, which are traditionally blue or red. From inside the house, the rest of the family members (both adults and children) throw beans at this person dressed as a demon while shouting "*Oni wa soto, fuku wa uchi*," which means "Get out demons, good luck and happiness is within." Children continue to repeatedly throw beans at the demon figure and yell at him until they chase him out of the house and slam the door behind him. After throwing beans at the ogre, people eat the same number of beans as their age (a thirty-year-old person would eat thirty beans); this practice is believed to bring good personal luck and health for the year to come. However, many families no longer celebrate this tradition at home; instead, they attend a religious center for a larger event that includes music, food, neighbors, and games in a carnival environment.

Throughout Japan, people also visit Buddhist temples and Shinto shrines for community *setsubun* celebrations and to pick up beans for good luck. At prominent

CHILDREN, DEMONS, AND THROWING THINGS

The Bean-Throwing Festival is loved by children all over Japan. An illustrative example reveals the imagination and creativity of young Japanese children. There was a five-year-old boy, who was very excited to learn that his father was to be dressed as the *Ao-Oni* (the blue demon) for the festival. However, what was surprising was the ferocity in which he pelted his father with beans. He had completely ignored driving away the red demon (the *Aka-Oni*) and focused on his father. The boy's mother encouraged him to throw more gently and divided his attention between the two demons, but immediately he would return to firing beans at his father. When asked about his behavior after the festival, the boy said that he had heard his father complain about being bothered by demons at the office, and he wanted to help drive them away.

Raymond Hicks

temples, the festivities are large regional affairs that often include local celebrities such as actors and sumo wrestlers in events that receive national television coverage. Priests and other community leaders hand out roasted beans, candy, red envelopes with money, and special prizes to all the attendees. However, large crowds can sometimes turn wild and unpredictable. As a result, celebrations at large temples can be overwhelming for small children, and families often chose to attend a fun but simpler ceremony at a neighborhood temple or shrine.

The contemporary *setsubun* celebration has certainly changed since it first appeared in Japan during the Muromachi period (1337–1573) when it quickly reached imperial status. While the tradition has always included the need to chase away wondering evil spirits, it used to be mainly accomplished with other practices that have slowly disappeared, such as fasting, religious dances, and solemn spiritual prayers. Nowadays, the festivities are more inclusive of adults, families, teenagers, and especially young children. In addition, the use of roasted soy beans for the bean-throwing aspect of this cultural custom has evolved toward commercialism as it was influenced by grocery and candy stores. Since soy beans could be expensive, now the tradition is to use cheaper peanuts (usually cooked and covered in a crunchy batter with a sugary flavor).

Javier A. Galván

Further Readings

Craig, Timothy. *Japan Pop!: Inside the World of Japanese Popular Culture*. Armonk, NY: M. E. Sharpe Publishers, 2000.

Mishima, Shizuko. "Setsubun—Bean Throwing Festival." *Japan Travel*. http://gojapan.about .com/cs/japanesefestivals/a/setsubun.htm (Accessed on January 10, 2013).

Renshaw, Steve, and Saori Ihara. *Get Out Ogre! Come in Happiness! Setsubun in Japan; A Lunar "New Year's Eve."* http://www2gol.com/users/stever/setsubun.htm February 2000. (Accessed on January 11, 2013).

Sosnoski, Daniel. *Introduction to Japanese Culture.* North Clarendon, VT: Tuttle Publishing, 2006.

Thacker, Brian. *The Naked Man Festival: And Other Excuses to Travel around the World.* Sydney, Australia: Allen and Unwin, 2005.

SHABKA: EGYPTIAN WEDDING JEWELRY

Family is central to the lives of people in Egypt. It is treated with great respect by Egyptians, who often regard the family as the main channel for social cohesion, social security of the elderly, and because families represent a major tool to endorse sick and disabled individuals. Families are also perceived as a central socioeconomic basis for raising children and youth and for supporting unemployed members and other dependents. In the Egyptian culture, parents carry the responsibility of raising children, and children, in return, are expected to take care of their aging parents. Therefore, the institution of marriage is usually sanctified since it represents the only legitimate mechanism for the formation of families. Among Egyptians, marriage is also a cornerstone associated with prestige, recognition, and societal approval. While young men and women generally have the chance to choose their own spouses, marriage in Egypt remains a socioeconomic contract between two families. It is also a rite of passage that transforms individuals into socially, culturally, and legally accepted social roles through marital relationships.

Despite variations in income or geographical backgrounds (rural, urban, or Bedouin), the average cost of marriage in Egypt has lately been increasing significantly. This is mainly due to the rising expenses of marriage items and requirements and because of the complex procedures associated with marriage. Various customary steps are usually imposed on brides, grooms, and their families. Marriage typically takes place in stages that involve special and often costly marital ceremonies. A man is expected to pay a *dowry* (a sum of money transferred to the wife's family) in order to help her buy the *gihaz* (trousseau composed of home furnishing and electric appliances). Other marriage costs often include housing for the couple. The groom and his family carry almost two-thirds of the cost of marriage. Although the increasing expenses of marriage and the increasing participation of young women in the labor force have resulted in some brides and their families contributing to marriage expenses than traditionally proclaimed, grooms and their families still carry the greatest burden in securing a marriage. *Gihaz* and other goods purchased to set up the new family are expected to be new and not used items, regardless of the economic conditions of marrying couples and their families. The groom's side of the family customarily provides the couple's housing (the major wedding expense) as well as any other equipment for the household, such as the television or refrigerator. The rising cost of marriage is in part attributed to the rising expectations and consumerism that have accompanied the open-door economic policy adopted by Egypt since the 1970s. The country's high cost of housing and furnishings have had a number of unintended consequences for marriage patterns, such as youth entering into *urfi* marriage (customary marriages that are unregistered and generally concealed) as well as men marrying women who are older and financially more secure than younger ones.

Marriage protocol entails that the groom should provide his bride with a *shabka* at wedding. The term *shabka* in Egypt has two meanings in common usage. It can directly refer to the gold or diamond gift the groom presents to his bride and her family at wedding, but it can also refer to the engagement party and official commitment (or tying as commonly used) of both the bride and the groom to the wedding. *Shabka*, as a wedding gift, relates to both the value of the wife to the husband (as a reflection of his affection) and an indicator of the socioeconomic status of the families of both the bride and the groom. It is also treated as a proof of the seriousness of the groom to the wedding. Accordingly, the value of *shabka* varies considerably among Egyptians. For low-income and middle-class families, people usually buy a *shabka* made of gold, whereas among upper-class families, a diamond is usually utilized. When in gold, the average value of an acceptable *shabka* ranges between 700 and 2,000 Egyptian pounds (US$120–US$350), and typically consists of one or two 21-carat gold bracelets and a gold wedding band. The formal signature of the marriage contract and religious ceremony, *katb il kitab*, sometimes takes place at the same time as the *shabka*, the formal engagement party, and sometimes at the time of the consummation of the wedding.

Financial arrangements of marriage are usually similar among Muslims and Copts (Christians) in Egypt. The *shabka* is also an essential constituent of Coptic engagements, and the value of the *shabka*, however, is written into the engagement contract. For Egyptian families, *shabka* is usually connected to status and prestige. It plays a significant role, especially to the wife, in establishing social status among relatives and friends. Therefore, as a common ritual in wedding ceremonies, the bride's family usually displays *shabka* to the wedding attendees in order to reveal the bride's value to the groom. The ritual usually entails that the bride's mother or sister carry *shabka* on a silver plate filled with flowers (or any other form of plates) and move with it among all the wedding attendees. The procedure is meant to help people take a closer look at the components of the *shabka* (bracelets, rings, necklace, etc.). Wedding attendees are not supposed to touch the *shabka*, and typically the mother or sister ensures its safety. The ritual ends when the groom receives the *shabka* from the bride's mother or sister and begins to give it to his bride in front of the attending public. He is supposed to help the bride wear the *shabka* in the wedding ceremony, while women declare the wedding.

Shabka plays many roles among low- and middle-class families in Egypt. It is usually treated as a form of money saving to be used when needed in the future. Married couples and their families usually comprehend that marriage is for life. Therefore, people often expect economic hardships that married partners may encounter in the future or in cases when extra money is required to cover growing extra-familial expenses. Understanding that the value of gold is sharply increasing, buying and storing gold for future needs have become a form of saving against future financial difficulties. Future hardships may include the setting up of the house, children's educational and marital needs, or other unexpected household expenses. A wife is required to keep her *shabka* at home under her supervision and protection. *Shabka* is usually worn by married women when invited to other weddings. In most cases, this procedure is meant to reveal their social statuses and to declare that they still keep the *shabka* and have not sold it due to any form of economic hardships.

In cases of economic difficulties, selling *shabka* may be perceived as one of the options available for the family. This procedure is typically perceived as a major sacrifice from the side of the wife to help her husband or the main breadwinner in sustaining the family. Husbands, in most cases, usually consider this procedure as a last resort when they become unable to secure funds for supporting the family, and they usually appreciate their wives' moral and psychological sacrifice. Women who sell the *shabka* are usually appreciated by their families, neighbors, and friends, who generally perceive the act as a form of utmost sacrifice of the wife to her husband. Many families, on the other hand, support the idea and consider the procedure as an obligation of the wife to help in sustaining her family. When selling their *shabka*, men usually promise their wives to buy them better *shabka* when things get better.

Nashaat H. Hussein

Further Readings

El-Kady, Heba. *Defiance and Compliance: Negotiating Gender in Low-Income Cairo*. New York: Berghahn Books, 2002.

Hamon, Raeann, and Bron Ingoldsby, eds. *Mate Selection across Cultures*. Thousand Oaks, CA: Sage Publications, 2003.

Hasso, Frances. *Consuming Desires: Family Crisis and the State in the Middle East*. Stanford: Stanford University Press, 2011.

Hopkins, Nicholas. "The New Arab Family." *Cairo Papers in Social Science* Vol. 24, no. 1–2. Cairo: The American University in Cairo Press, 2003.

Jensen, Robert, and Rebecca Thornton. "Early Female Marriage in the Developing World." In *Gender, Development, and Marriage*, edited by Caroline Sweetman, Vol. 11, no. 2, 9–19. Oxford, UK: Oxfam Publications, July 2003.

Joseph, Suad, ed. *Encyclopedia of Women and Islamic Cultures: Family, Body, and Sexuality*. Vol. 3. Leiden, The Netherlands: Brill Academic Publishing, 2006.

Monger, George. *Marriage Customs of the World: From Henna to Honeymoons*. Santa Barbara, CA: ABC-CLIO, 2004.

Shaham, Ron. *Family and the Courts in Modern Egypt: A Study Based on Decisions by the Sharia Courts, 1900–1955*. Leiden, The Netherlands: Brill publisher, 1997.

Welchman, Lynn. *Women's Rights and Islamic Family Law: Perspectives on Reform*. London: Zed Books Led, 2004.

SHARO: PUBLIC FLOGGING AND BRAVERY

Among the Fulani (also called by the names Fula or Fulbe), a nomadic people of northern Nigeria, institutions and customs are of great importance in providing continuity and a sense of culture and community. They have been practicing initiation rituals for centuries. As a result, ceremonial rituals serve as a foundation for the Fulani civilization of West Africa. One of the most pivotal and famous ceremony among the Fulani tribes is the *sharo*, which serves as both a test of manhood and a coming-of-age ritual for young men. At its basic function, *sharo* is a public flogging rite of passage intended to be a test of bravery and manhood for adolescent members in the tribe. Some Fulani groupings require a young man to successfully complete the *sharo* ritual before he is considered worthy of marriage, but for other Fulani communities, it is considered a form of sport that can be held as a competition between groups, during a marriage, in honor of a chief, or as part of another large community gathering. The *sharo* ritual is usually held twice a year: once during the corn harvest time in the dry season and again during the Muslim festival of Id-el-kabir. It is also sometimes celebrated during the festivities of Sallah at the end of the Muslim Ramadan tradition (called the Babban Sallah), or even on weekly market days. Whatever its purpose, *sharo* is a serious and necessary prerequisite activity in order for young Fulani boys to be accepted into manhood. The most fervent practitioners of *sharo* are the Jafun Fulani tribes, which are a subgroup of the larger Fulani people. In the *sharo*, a young man (usually about fifteen years of age) undergoes painful flogging in a public display of endurance and bravery. The beating is to be endured without flinching or crying out in order to prove the recipient's strength and resolve.

When the *sharo* ritual is about to begin, community members (both men and women) assemble in the market place. They all wear their best clothes for the special occasion. Before the main event starts, there is a festive ambience of general music, dancing, and roving tricksters around the market area. Then, the women begin to dance a well-choreographed performance, and the young male participants appear, attended by their assistants (who would be flogged in place of the participants if necessary, to save face), and surrounded by friends and family as well as the young single girls of the village who wish to see which available men will have the endurance to complete the *sharo* proceedings and thus prove themselves able to protect a family. The young men who succeed in completing the painful event will be eligible to marry girls in the community. Right before the competition begins, the ground is cleared by fierce men with weapons. The first young man to be flogged appears, striking a defiant pose by posing bear-chested and standing firm. At this time, percussion music increases in both sound and tempo creating more anticipation for the main event. The participant then crosses one leg over the other and raises his arms while holding a staff—a mirror is sometimes used, to maintain a gaze look unaffected by the pain. Another young man (also bear-chested) then enters the public area set aside for the ceremony brandishing a cane roughly half-an-inch thick, and he takes aim at the victim. The challenger delivers blows heavily, drawing blood as the victim calls for yet more and more powerful hits. The striker is observed intently to ensure that he does not pull away, flinch as he hits the other person, or reveal any attempts to soften the blows. The victim must not attempt to avoid the blows, call out in pain, or flinch in any way because such demonstrations of emotion will cause him to be branded as a coward among his community. Complete indifference to pain must be demonstrated, perseverance must be maintained throughout the event, and the victim should sneer at and even taunt the attacker (charms, spells, or pain-reducing drugs may be used by the victim in order to endure the ordeal). It is expected that the adolescents are completely able to withstand the pain until the end of the ceremony. As the ritual comes to an end, the wounds are treated quickly with herbal medicines; once the wounds heal, they leave a prideful set of scars that the owner can display as proof of his manhood and worthiness for marriage. The initiate is then congratulated by family, friends, and potential brides within his clan.

After centuries of practicing this cultural tradition, the custom of *sharo* has recently given rise to a revenge culture in which the victim often exacted later revenge upon the attacker in the form of fighting with urine-soaked sticks (very painful and infectious) or by demanding retribution payment in the form of livestock. As a result, legal authorities in the region of northern Nigeria have attempted to ban *sharo*, but the Fulani consider it as an integral part of their culture and would not dream of ending it. Even as the Fulani customs have been heavily influenced by Muslim traditions, this nomadic tribe from West Africa has managed to retain the *sharo* rituals as an indelible part of their historical and cultural struggle.

Kevin Wozniak

Further Readings

Currey, James. *UNESCO General History of Africa, Volume III: Africa from the Seventh to the Eleventh Century*, edited by Ivan Hrbek. Berkeley: University of California Press, 1992.

Falola, Toyin, and Mathew Heaton. *A History of Nigeria*. New York: Cambridge University Press, 2008.

Heilpern, J. *The Conference of the Birds: The Story of Peter Brook in Africa*. New York: Routledge, 1989.

McDonald Shaw, Thomas. *The Fulani Matrix of Beauty and Art in the Djolof Region of Senegal (African Studies)*. Lewiston, NY: Edwin Mellen Press, 1993.

Ndukwe, Pat I. *The Fulani: Heritage Library of African Peoples*. New York: Rosen Publishing Group, 1996.

SKY BURIALS

Burial practices, and associated methods of corpse disposal, tend to make people uncomfortable—perhaps none more so than the Tibetan Sky Burial. The majority of people who die on "the Roof of the Earth," the Qinghai-Tibetan Plateau of Central Asia, are carried beyond the mountains by massive vultures that arrive in droves to readily and completely consume the flesh and bones of those who have died. Sky Burial is rooted predominantly in Buddhist and ancient Bon religious practices that are observed in Tibet. It is thought that participation in these ritual ceremonies prior to exposure free the soul of the deceased for rebirth, while the Sky Burial itself is a final act of generosity—providing nourishment to other living creatures on the Himalayan Plateau. Although a Sky Burial can be extremely hard to watch, it functions like all manner of burial practice in that spiritual preparation and ritual observance help the living make peace with the realities of appropriate and practical disposal of the recently deceased.

The Qinghai-Tibetan Plateau is the largest and highest plateau on Earth. Surrounded on all sides by massive mountain ranges, the plateau spans over 2.5 million square kilometers (1.5 million square miles) and covers most of the Tibet Autonomous Region and Qinghai Province in western China. Average elevation on the plateau is over 4,500 meters (14,000 feet) and includes fourteen of the world's peaks that exceed 8,000 meters (26,000 + feet), where winter temperatures can fall to –40°C (–40°F). Permafrost exists over much of the plateau, and frost penetrates all land for at least six months annually. Distribution of plant and animal species in this vast region are extremely uneven due to drastic ranges in topography and climate. Habitation is isolated in this inhospitable region, and it exists well above the tree line. The natural obstacles of daily life in this region remain obstacles in death as well.

Sky Burial is a particular type of funeral practice that makes use of excarnation, or the deliberate exposure of a human corpse to scavengers, for corpse disposal. No one is certain when the practice of Sky Burial originated in Tibet as there is little archaeological evidence to support this practice, and the historical record only dates back to approximately 640 ACE. Other types of burial—ground burial (inhumation or internment), fire burial (cremation), and water burial—also occur in Tibet, but air burial (Sky Burial) is the most common. Arable land is in short supply, comprising just over 10 percent of the plateau. The rest is extremely rocky and frozen for most of the year, making ground burial unilaterally hard to accomplish. Cremation demands fuel for burning and most of the plateau exists above the tree line where trees are hard to come by, difficult to transport, and arguably more necessary for building projects. Ground burial and fire burial are generally, and historically, reserved for religious personnel, political figures, and some other community personnel (soldiers, teachers, some tradesmen, and the wealthy).

Sky Burial is less costly than other burial options: it reduces instances of predation by carnivorous mammals, it decreases the spread of unwanted disease, and it falls in line culturally with the wide range of religious ideas and concepts that are held in Tibet. Ceremonial aspects engaged in prior to the exposure elements of Sky Burial are familiar to Buddhists of various sects. The ceremonial components generally seek to reconcile the twin trajectories of benefitting the deceased and protecting the survivors. The funeral practice of Sky Burial encompasses a complex range of activities and rites, some of which are handled by religious professionals and others by laymen. There is a certain amount of regional, community, and individual variation in practice.

Excarnation is not unique to the Tibetan Plateau; it was once practiced through the Middle East and Asia, as well as numerous other parts of the world. Several religious and ethnic groups in this part of the world continue to make use of excarnation in their burial practices, most notably Zoroastrians in Persia and two Parsi groups in India. It is uncertain as to whether the practice of Sky Burial in Tibet arose from the interaction and coexistence of these groups long ago in Central Asia or out of the need to adapt to the plateau's unique environment. All groups follow a similar general pattern where the deceased goes through a series of rituals and ceremonies to ready the corpse for exposure. The major difference between Sky Burial and other types of excarnation comes once the scavengers and the elements have done their work. Most groups collect the sun-bleached bones and intern them in an ossuary for safekeeping—except that in the case of Sky Burial, the bones cannot be collected because nothing remains of them once the scavengers are finished.

Large populations of carrion-eating birds enable Sky Burials in Tibet. Predatory vultures such as the Bearded Vulture (*Gypaetus barbatus*) and Himalayan Griffon (*Gyps himalayensis*) are prominent on the plateau. These Old World vulture species are massive and highly efficient scavengers with a wingspan exceeding 2 meters (7–9 feet). Rarely seen below 2,000 meters (6,600 feet), the vultures of the Tibetan Plateau, occupy enormous territories year-round in search of food. Old World vultures are physiologically designed to break down the high-fat content found in bone marrow, which makes up as much as 85 percent of their diet. Vultures are known by several terms dependent on their behavior; in flight vultures are referred to as a *kettle*, a terrestrial or arboreal gathering is a *committee*, and vultures engaged in feeding are a *wake*. Vultures in Tibet have learned that certain human tendencies present opportunities for feeding, a prominent example being Sky Burial.

The series of rituals that culminate in Sky Burial can take up to several days to complete. Initially, the deceased is bound in fetal position and wrapped in bolts of cloth. The human bundle is transported to an appropriate sacred space and elevated from the ground on stones. Adjacent to the time of dying, all aspects of ceremony are presided over by a *lama* (priest or village ritual specialist). Guidance of the deceased through *bardo*, an uncertain intermediate state that exists between death and rebirth, is the foremost task of the *lama*. The journey through *bardo* is facilitated by the *lama* in various ways: engaging in *powa* (or "transfer of consciousness"), reciting orations, and sounding ceremonial instruments (drums, cymbals, and thigh-bone trumpets). Sometimes death horoscopes or name placards are also prepared by the *lama* for the deceased to aid in their journey or to display in a place of prominence after all exposure rituals are complete, somewhat like a tombstone in a cemetery. Once *bardo* has been navigated, purification rites or ritualized dancing may ensue prior to setting out on the ceremonial procession, away from the community to the designated exposure and burial site.

From time of death to final exposure, professional religious personnel rarely handle the corpse directly—they engage with the deceased through ceremony and the direction of rites, including leading the procession and overseeing excarnation. *Ragypapas* or *topden* are the corpse handlers, or the laymen specialists, of the Sky Burial. The corpse is released from its shroud and bindings while committees of vultures wait eagerly for the feast to come. Then the corpse is ritually sliced and partially dissected using sharp knives and hooks. Upon completion of dissection, wakes of vultures quickly clean the corpse of all flesh and organs. At this juncture, the massive birds are forced back while the corpse handlers use mallets to smash the larger bones into smaller pieces. The bones may be mixed with grain or other offerings, but the result is the same regardless. The vultures leave nothing of what was a human corpse only a couple of hours prior.

The most controversial aspects of Tibetan Sky Burial are related to the "otherness" that permeates the Western mind concerning the grisly nature of corpse dismemberment and its consumption by carnivorous birds. Death, and the various burial customs that accompany it, make many people sad and uncomfortable. Human populations do not always realize what they are actually doing for themselves and the deceased by engaging in ceremonial funeral practices. Sky Burial is generally thought of as *gcod* (*cho*), which is identified as a key concept in all four schools of Tibetan Buddhism as well as the pre-Buddhist Tibetan religion known as Bon. The idea being that Sky Burial, as a type of "body donation," is intended to promote the tenants of generosity and compassion. In death, the last act of a religious person becomes a life-sustaining resource for their avian neighbors on the plateau. As a result, the people of Tibet do not generally eat birds.

Stephanie L. Hamilton

Further Readings

Fleming, Robert, Dorje Tsering, and Liu Wulin. *Across the Tibetan Plateau.* New York: WW Norton, 2007.

Gouin, Margaret. *Tibetan Rituals of Death: Buddhist Funerary Practices.* New York: Routledge, 2010.

Martin, Dan. "On the Cultural Ecology of Sky Burial on the Himalayan Plateau." *East and West* 46, no. 3/4 (December 1996): 353–70.

Metcalf, Richard, and Richard Huntington. *Celebrations of Death: Anthropology of Mortuary Ritual.* 2nd ed. New York: Cambridge University Press, 1999.

Serjeanston, Dale. *Cambridge Manuals in Archaeology: Birds.* New York: Cambridge University Press, 2009.

Shellgrove, David L., and Hugh Richardson. *The Cultural History of Tibet.* Bangkok, Thailand: Orchid Press, 2006.

"Tibetan Sky Burial." http://www.youtube.com/watch?v=b6hSK8CluxQ (Accessed on November 15, 2012).

Xin Lu, Dianhua Ke, Xianhai Zeng, Guohong Gong, and Ren Ci. "Status, Ecology, and Conservation of the Himalayan Griffon *Gyps himalayensis* (Aves, Accipitridae) in the Tibetan Plateau." *AMBIO: A Journal of the Human Environment* 38, no. 3 (2009): 166–73.

SNAKE HANDLERS IN CHRISTIAN APPALACHIA

An old man's arm, from his elbow to his wrist, and from his wrist to his fingertips, hangs distorted, twisted, abnormally bent. It is not a repulsive site to his peers, but a badge of honor and testimony to the strength of his faith. He believes that his God has rescued him from the death bite of the venomous snakes of the Appalachia region of the Eastern United States. Most often it is the deadly Eastern Timber Rattlesnake, but it can include the Cottonmouth also known as the Water

Members of the Pentecostal Church of God handling snakes as part of their religious gatherings in Kentucky. (AP Photo)

Moccasin, as well as the brightly ringed Copperhead. These snakes not only represent death, but they are also deadly. To take hold of them in a worship service is to grasp death in faith of living beyond death's grasp.

Most cultures have some form of a death ritual. After all, it is the final experience of this life that engulfs all people, rich or poor, East or West, secular or religious. Most people do not think that a modern and technological society such as the United States would still have subcultures that practice regular death rituals. Instead, this country perpetuates the myth of eternal youth with a flourishing industry of cosmetic surgery. Yet, there remain those who take hold of death ritually and literally; they are the distinctly Christian snake handlers of the Appalachian mountain chain that runs from as far north as Pennsylvania to as far south as central Alabama. It is a practice that prevails in the face of laws that prohibit it in almost every state in the region.

The handling of snakes as part of a Christian religious service had its beginnings from a reference in some but not all of the ancient manuscripts of the Gospel of Mark. The specific Christian scripture is found in Mark, chapter 16, verse 18:

they will pick up serpents with their hands; and if they drink any deadly poison, it will not hurt them. (The Gospel of Mark, New International Version)

Although these scriptures do not require or promote the ritual of snake han-dling, the practice has evolved and has taken hold in many mountain Christian groups whose history has been filled with hardship and a harsh environment. The practice of snake handling sets these believers apart from other fellow Christians around the world who reenact the Last Supper of Christ as their death ritual. Jesus himself prescribed and modeled partaking of the bread and the cup representing his physical death in payment of mankind's offenses against God.

Believers from West Virginia to Tennessee go a deadly step further than the em-blems of Jesus broken body and shed blood. Even though pictures of the Lord's Supper hang on the walls of their small mountain churches, they also partake of the living image of Satan: the ancient serpent and author of death in the earliest Jewish scriptures of Genesis 3. Members bring their Bibles, their offerings, baskets of food to share in a common meal, and they also bring snakes. There are usually several vipers present in any one worship service hidden away in an inconspicu-ous box, although everyone present knows what is inside.

The religious service includes singing, preaching, and ecstatic dancing "in the Spirit." The serpents are brought out only when the believers sense that they are under the protection of the Holy Spirit, or in the "fullness of the Spirit." First, the one who brought the snake takes it into his hands, all the while praying in Jesus name and proclaiming Christ's authority over death. Typically, a circle is formed as others join in, and the serpent is passed around until it is replaced in the box. The big timber rattlers can be as large as 5 feet long. They are heavy and powerful, but they are not handled harshly or defensively. Their sweeping heads are free to roam, and their thick bodies naturally writhe and glide over the hands and arms of those who have faith. Even though a sudden strike may maim or even kill one of the han-dlers, the snake is never harmed but shown respect and always returned to the for-est. The same creature is not knowingly used again in the serpentine sacrament. As a precaution, children are not permitted to handle the poisonous snakes, and they are kept out of the range of snake's ability to strike. After the serpent is safely put away, there is much rejoicing, praise, and even a dance of thanks for the Lord's protection.

Not too often, but occasionally and regularly enough to be expected, someone is bitten. Fellow congregants immediately pray for them, and they quickly lay their hands upon the wounded brother or sister. However, no medical attention is of-fered; it would only be rejected. The stricken people grow ill, swell, vomit blood, and become terribly sick for days, but they will have faith to be healed. When the swelling subsides, the extremity may be deformed—fingers and hands have been known to be lost. Almost all the believers will recover and return again to their dangerous form of worship. Their faith has been tested, and the healing power of Christ has prevailed. As a result, every other trial of life seems inconsequential and can be faced with fearless confidence.

On rare occasions, there are some people who die from the snake's bite. Their faith is never questioned nor is the ritual itself. In fact, often the mourners bring a snake to the funeral, which is then passed around in honor of the deceased and the faithful manner in which they died. The old men and women who have been bitten many times are the most revered in these mountainous communities.

There will eventually come a time when they and all the other mountain saints will someday walk through death's door, but in the meantime, they trust in Jesus' promise of resurrection from the dead.

Christ's greatest requirement of his disciples in this lifetime is a deeper and more difficult death to self. For now, however, the people of the Appalachian Mountains demonstrate a more literal reality: they will continue to grasp death and refuse to live in fear of it.

Steven A. Baeder

Further Readings

Burton, Thomas. *Serpent Handling Believers.* Knoxville: University of Tennessee Press, 1993.
Daugherty, Mary Lee. "Serpent Handling as Sacrament." *Theology Today* 33, no. 3 (October 1976): 232–43.
The Holy Bible New International Version. Grand Rapids, MI: Zondervan Publishers, 1985.
Lane, William L. *The Gospel According to Mark: The New International Commentary of the New Testament.* Grand Rapids, MI: Eerdmans Publishing Company, 1974, 601–05.

SNAKE WINE

The ancient Greeks brewed snake wine, and they included it in the Hippocratic Corpus of medicinal elixirs as "viper's broth." The enchanters of Europe's medieval forests prescribed it as a cure for common ailments. In Brazil, the preferred vintage is *Pinga de Cobra* for which venom is mixed with *cachaca*, a fermented sugarcane juice. The newest connoisseurs and pharmacologists of the serpentine drink are in the United States where Texans have steeped ripening rattlesnakes in vodka to make an illegal intoxicant that shook regional cultural sensibilities. In India, a predominantly vegetarian country, "snake wine" has seeped into major cities, but pure venom is the holy grail of a promised euphoria. However, East and Southeast Asia are currently the cultural cores of this vinous tradition.

Three thousand years ago during the Western Zhou dynasty of China, snake wine (or *Shéjiǔ*) became traditional Chinese medicine in which different breeds of snakes were used to stabilize multiple sections of the body. Since then, use of the tonic has spread to other East Asian countries such as Japan and Korea. However, today it is mainland Southeast Asia—and Vietnam in particular—that has the most developed snake wine industry in the world. The region's comparative advantage is its bubbling geographic biodiversity resulting from the merging of tropical climates with rich alluvial lowlands, and the Eurasian landmass with the sprawling Mekong Delta. The number of endemic snake species is substantial, and so is the number of snakes. As a result, the people of the Delta prefer ophidian meat which is harvested with nets, or dip lines baited with frog or fish. Snake bones are fried crisply, and they are considered a local culinary delicacy. The versatile reptile can certainly make unusual pets, but snakes can also be grounded into powder to be used in cosmetics, perfumes, moisturizing oils and creams, and religious artifacts. Still, it is the snake wine industry that has turned the use of snakes into a commercial bonanza in Southeast Asia.

Vietnam is the leading exporter of snakes and wines to East Asia, but the Vietnamese consume most of the wine, which is made from around twenty species of typically small and prolific, but sometimes also venomous snakes. The regional generic name for the most common wines is *ru'o'u thuốc*. The less common wines (and hence most sought after and expensive) are called *ru'o'u rắn* or cobra wine. Both types of wine can be bought on sidewalk cafes, restaurants, markets, and even in homes throughout the country. The most visible containers of snake wine (and perhaps the most visibly appetizing) are the bottles containing actual snakes inside clearly steeping in rice wine or grain alcohol, and sharing space with herbs, turtles, insects, and birds. In Vietnam, Laos, and Cambodia, the display of liquor bottles can be both impressive and frightening since the drama of tasting such wine sometimes seems to end with an actual snake bite. In Singapore and China, small snakes and other ingredients simply assemble at the bottom of the bottle, with snakes not necessarily poised to strike.

Snake blood wine is part street performance. The process involves slicing a snake from head to tail, scraping the insides with a thumb in the same direction and over a sieve, mixing visceral fluids with wine or alcohol, and then pouring it all into a highball glass. In addition, bar tenders often squeeze the contents of the snake's gallbladder into the glass to make snake bile wine. Venomous snakes are believed to offer masculinity to the male consumer, but the alcohol actually inactivates the proteins of venom making it safe for all to drink—though it is not necessarily recommended for women. The brand names of bottled venomous liqueurs such as Luckymen, Dragon, and Phoenix suggest that they offer some type of masculine virility.

The increase of tourism in mainland Southeast Asia along with the rise of e-commerce has spurred the sale of bottled snake wine. Consequently, it has led to regional concerns over depletion and sustainability of a variety of snakes. The Convention on International Trade of Endangered Species of Wild Fauna and Flora includes three kinds of cobra in its lists; this means that consumption should be closely monitored. Moreover, it specifically lists the python as an endangered species. In addition, at the local level, Vietnam's Red Book has stricter standards and cautions against the use of certain types of snakes. Just recently, the country banned the export of several species to East Asia because of an unexpected jump in the population of rats. As a result, those hankering for a sip of Dragon-Fights-with-Tiger Soup will have to wait until these legendary creatures first binge on rats.

Kenneth Whalen

Further Readings

Samson Katz, Niel. "Vietnam Culture by the Glass." *New York Times.* March 9, 2008. http://query.nytimes.com/gst/fullpage.html?res=9D01E2D6123CF93AA35750C0A96E9C8B63&pagewanted=all (Accessed on August 12, 2012).
Somaweera, Ruchira, and Nilusha Somaweera. "Serpent Jars: The Snake Wine Industry in Vietnam." *Journal of Threatened Taxa* 2, no. 11 (October 2003): 1251–260.

SPITTING AS GREETING TRADITION

The Maasai (sometimes also spelled Masai) tribe is an indigenous population of African pastoralists in modern-day Kenya and Tanzania with a population close to 800,000. To many people, the Maasai remain as a symbol of African tribal life who continue to reject the ways of the Western world, even as governments continually pressure them to abandon their practices for a more sedentary lifestyle. One of the more interesting traditions of Maasai culture is that they use spitting as a form of social greeting, which in the Western world is often seen as a sign of disgust and disrespect. To the Maasai, however, it is a long-held belief that imparts good luck and good spirits during greetings. Part of this belief stems from the tradition of water as holy, and water that is from inside a person is even more holy since it is placed there by the god of the Maasai. To spit on another person then is seen as giving them part of your water—an act of reverence and generosity.

Prior to shaking hands upon greeting one another, the Maasai must spit on their hands as a sign of respect, especially when dealing with older members of the community. By doing so, the individuals honor one another through the swapping of spit on each other's hand. The practice of spitting in the society, however, is a custom that occurs much more often than just as a simple handshake; it is also used by the natives to conduct official acts of business. When a deal is agreed upon, it becomes official after the respective parties perform the ritual of spitting and seal the transaction with a handshake.

Another frequent social context in which Maasai often spit with reverence is upon meeting an infant for the first time. When the individuals meet the infant, the Maasai will spit on its head, as a way to bless the child. However, they also tell the child that spitting on people's head is bad, and they tell children that they must grow up to be strong. It is the action of spitting that shows respect for the child, even while the elder claims it is bad. It seems to be contradictory, but it is intended to build stronger character among children as they become older. Overall, the act of scolding young infants is thought to make the children humbler. However, the spitting action does continue while the elder Maasai then whispers under his breath that this child is, in all reality, a good child.

Marc Sanko

Further Readings

Hollis, Sir Alfred Claud. *The Maasai: Their Language and Folklore.* Oxford, UK: Clarendon Press, 1905.

Lekuton, Joseph Lemasolai. *Facing the Lion: Growing Up Maasai on the African Savanna.* Des Moins, IA: National Geographic Books, 2005.

Merker, M. *The Maasai: Ethnographic Monograph of an East African Semite People.* Berlin: Dietrich Reimer, 1910.

Thomson, Joseph. *Through Maasai Land: A Journey of Exploration Among the Snowclad Volcanic Mountains and Strange Tribes of Eastern Equatorial Africa.* London: Sampson Low, Marston, Searle and Rivington, 1895.

Wiszowaty, Robin. *The Maasai Life: From Suburbia to Savannah.* Toronto, Canada: Me to We Publishers, 2010.

SPRINKLING CAKE ON A CHILD'S HEAD

Almost universally, a high level of importance is placed on the concepts of love, marriage, and fertility. However, in the Republic of Ireland, a unique custom has evolved from a combination of cultural and religious practices in the country. The custom of eating wedding cake on a wedding day is ubiquitous across much of the Western world, and it is enjoyed by guests and parents alike as they often discuss the arrival and characteristics of the future children of the couple. Part of the wedding cake—usually the top tier—is often saved and kept for a special occasion, such as the one year anniversary or the birth of the first child. The Irish have a unique twist to this concept, which has been passed down through generations as the custom of sprinkling cake on the head of a child—typically the first born.

At the marriage ceremony of a couple, an Irish tradition is to present the couple with a more specific type of wedding cake—a whisky cake, which, in Ireland, is symbolic of fertility. Many people in Ireland are (whether practicing or not) also from the Roman Catholic faith, and this serves as something of a cultural marker for Irish identity. In the Catholic religion, there are several rites that a person must go through in life, one of which is baptism. When a child's parents are Catholic, baptism is often done early in life wherein a priest sprinkles holy water on the head of a child.

The custom of sprinkling of cake on a child's head is therefore a mesh of Roman Catholic religious practice and Irish cultural traditions. The aforementioned top layer of a wedding cake saved by the parents from their wedding is preserved and then eaten when their first child is born. As a celebration, Irish couples often sprinkle some crumbs from the whiskey wedding cake on top of their newborn child's head as a symbol of good luck, prosperity, and long life. Multiple sources also mention examples of other Irish traditions involving sprinkling something on the head. One example is that recently married couples often save a bottle of champagne from the wedding celebration, and they similarly "wet" the head of the infant. Another example is that a future mother-in-law similarly sprinkles cake on the head of the bride as she enters the couple's house after the ceremony—this, according to tradition, means that the mother-in-law and the daughter-in-law will be friends for life.

The custom of sprinkling cake on the head of a child is by no means universal in Ireland, but it is a practice that is utilized by people as an expression of culture. Members of the Irish diaspora in North America and the United Kingdom are also encouraged to participate as an expression of Irish custom, which, in some respects, serves as a form of Irish identity, whether people find themselves in Ireland or abroad.

Glen M. E. Duerr

Further Readings

Evans, E. Estyn. *Irish Folk Ways*. Mineola, NY: Dover Publications, 2000 (reprint of 1957 edition).

Haggerty, Bridget. *The Traditional Irish Wedding*. Minneapolis: Irish Books and Media, 2001.

TARANTULAS AS FRIED DELICACY

People all over the world enjoy culinary delicacies that sound strange to some people's ears, but the consumption of arthropods, including spiders, is extremely common and practiced worldwide. This particular culinary custom is practiced in Skuon, Cambodia, where scores of people frequent open-air markets daily to eat deep-fried tarantulas the size of a grown man's hand. This delicacy can be found in several Cambodian towns, but the availability of fried spiders for roadside and in-house consumption is mostly limited to the city of Skuon—the definite center of their regional popularity. The daily, and largely commercial, custom of eating deep-fried tarantulas has created its own infrastructure and supply chain local to Skuon. These furry critters provide a reliable daily income to both those who gather the spiders themselves and to the vendors who prepare and sell the delicacy to both foreign and local clientele.

Situated on the Indochinese Peninsula, Cambodia is bordered by Thailand and Laos on the north, the Gulf of Thailand to the west, and Vietnam to the east and south. Occupying an area roughly the size of Missouri, Cambodia has a population of 14.7 million (2010 estimate), not including the nearly 3 million tourists who visited Cambodia in 2011. A high proportion of tourists pass through Skuon as they make their way to or from international airports in Phnom Pehn or Siem Reap. Known for its roadside markets—and its large spiders—Skuon is the district capital of Cheung Prey, Kampong Cham Province. It is located at the junction of two national highways, about 32 miles (50 kilometers) northwest of Cambodia's capital, Phnom Penh.

Cambodia is currently a multiparty liberal democracy under a constitutional monarchy, but it has not always been this way. The culinary custom of eating fried tarantulas is less than fifty years old, and it likely originates from the national food shortages that characterized the 1970s in Cambodia under the repressive communist regime known as Kymer Rouge (1975–1979). The authoritarian regime is now largely remembered for their reactionary experiments in social engineering and agricultural reform that resulted in nationwide genocide and massive instances of famine. Skuon, strategically located where two major transport routes intersect, was vital to prolonged control of Cambodia—and the daily custom of consuming large and readily available arachnids, seasoned and fried in oil, developed out of the desperate situation that surrounded Skuon and the rest of Cambodia under Kymer Rouge. During this period of social convulsion, tarantulas provided the general population with a food source in the face of starvation, and these arachnids now continue to live plentifully in the forestlands near Skuon.

Tarantulas were not just a source of protein, but they turned out to be rather tasty, and today fried tarantulas are one of the hottest wares to be peddled at the daily roadside markets and street stalls of Skuon. The general popularity of the delicacy has increased since the 1990s—coupled with a triple-fold increase in tourism since 2007—and it has evolved from a culinary custom that developed out of desperation into one that now serves a prominent commercial and economic function in this region of Cambodia.

A-ping, the Thai Zebra tarantula (*Haplopelma albostriatum*), has long been known by its common name as the "edible spider," and they are collected by the hundreds from the forestlands surrounding Skuon. In fact, the demand has become so high for this specialized delicacy that the tarantulas are now deliberately being bred outside of town solely for human consumption. Measuring roughly 6 inches (15 centimeters) in diameter, large *a-ping* make their burrows in the forest floor and they are gathered using large sticks to coax them from hiding. The tarantula's substantial fangs may or may not be removed by gatherers prior to their sale to a vendor. Known to be somewhat aggressive, the spiders are calmed when gentle pressure is applied to its thorax between a thumb and forefinger. The vendor washes the large tarantulas before they are prepared, usually twice, to remove any debris and some of their hair. Subsequently, the *a-ping* are then seasoned in large steel bowls. Recipes vary but usually consist of combinations of spices, garlic, salt, and sugar. The hairy critters are stirred in the seasoning until the sugars start to breakdown; they are then ready to be cooked. The cook places six or more spiders at a time into hot oil, usually with the legs up and their face down. The tarantulas whistle and pop as they are cooked in the oil, which takes about three minutes. Once a large platter has been prepared, it is transported to the market for sale. Fried tarantulas fetch twice the price they were originally bought for, meaning vendors can make roughly $25 per day by selling deep-fried tarantulas to curious tourists and hungry locals alike.

The only controversial aspect of this custom seems to stem from the idea of actually eating palm-sized, fully intact, deep-fried, creepy-crawly spiders. Numerous videos on the Internet, predominantly posted by Western tourists, document the process of psyching themselves up with anticipation to actually eat *a-ping*. Reactions to consuming this delicacy vary from unrestrained excitement to complete disgust, and some people are adamant that *a-ping* should not be eaten at all; but for the most part, the general response to the taste and texture of this Cambodian delicacy is favorable. Expertly fried head, thorax, and legs have been compared in taste to the sweet and nutty meat of a soft-shelled crab—which should not come as much of a surprise since terrestrial *chelicerates* (i.e., spiders and scorpions) and aquatic *crustaceans* (i.e., lobster and crab) are related subphyla under the order Arthropoda. Some specimens of tarantulas, however, are said to taste more like potato chips, and they can be overly crunchy or even hard to chew. In addition, there is always the potential risk that the abdomen of an adult tarantula could be filled with 50 to 200 somewhat flavorless undeveloped spiderlings. Nevertheless, connoisseurs maintain that there is nothing especially "spidery" about the unique experience of eating deep-fried tarantulas.

Stephanie L. Hamilton

Further Readings

Chandler, David P. *A History of Cambodia.* Boulder, CO: Westview Press, 1992.

DuFord, Darrin. "How to Eat Tarantulas in Cambodia." *Worldhum: The Best Travel Stories on the Internet.* December 18, 2009. http://www.worldhum.com/features/how-to/how-to-eat-fried-tarantulas-in-cambodia-20091201/ (Accessed on August 18, 2012).

Goldish, Meish. *Spider-Tizers and Other Creepy Treats.* New York: Bearport Publications, 2009.

Ministry of Tourism of Cambodia. "Ministry of Tourism Annual Report for 2011." http://www.tourismcambodia.org/images/mot/statistic_reports/tourism_statistics_annual_report_2011.pdf (Accessed on August 18, 2012).

Schanberg, Sydney. *Beyond the Killing Fields.* Dulles, VA: Potomac Books, 2010.

Travel Channel. "Eating Tarantula (Deep Fried) in Cambodia." *Bizarre Foods with Andrew Zimmerman.* http://www.youtube.com/watch?v=vkTJWoUMbGk (Accessed on August 16, 2012).

TẾT, VIETNAMESE LUNAR YEAR

Vietnamese Lunar Year includes two major events that are central to Vietnam's cultural identity: the Spring Festival known as *Tết Nguyên đán* meaning "First morning of the first day" and the Harvest Moon Festival or *Tết Trung Thu*. The customs and rituals associated with each event are different as is the intensity of revelry. The more cultivated, festive, and engaging is *Tết Nguyên đán* which not only ushers in the New Year, but it is also the official birthday of each

Musicians playing drums during the *Tết* Lunar New Year celebrations in Ho Chi Minh City, Vietnam. (Salajean/Dreamstime.com)

and every Vietnamese person. So the customary greetings *Chúc Mừng năm Mới* and *Cung Chúc Tân Xuân* mean both a healthy, happy year and (by association though not in translation) happy birthday. According to the solar calendar, this event falls between January 21 and February 19. According to the lunar calendar, which has 355 days per year, each new month begins with a new moon, as does every new year (and therefore birthday). Yet, the number of moons one has lived through pales in significance to the year in which a person is born. In the cosmological animal race set off by the Chinese Jade Emperor, a demigod who was the founder of Chinese civilization and lord of the cosmos and underworld, the first twelve animals to finish would each represent a year in the cycle of the Zodiac. Although the Vietnamese replaced the ox with water buffalo and the rabbit with the cat (either because cats were pets in Vietnam but not in ancient China, or the rat tricked the cat into missing the finale, thus the endless chase), the symbolic-animal year nevertheless shapes an individual's character and portends life events. Such links between human beings, the natural, and spiritual world can also be seen in the myriad of time-honored ways the Vietnamese people observe *Tết*—a tradition that owes much to Chinese culture but has been remade to fit into an animistic and agricultural way of life in tropical Southeast Asia.

Tết Nguyên đán can be divided into three phases, unlike *Tết Trung Thu* which occurs on the fifteenth day of the eighth month when the largest of full moons appears in the sky. *Tết Niên* is a seven-day celebration that takes places before *Giao Thừa* or New Year's Eve, and the final phase *Tân Niên* which is the first days of the new year celebrated for seven days in some regions of Vietnam or to the fifteenth day of the month when the first full moon of the year arrives. Overall, festivities go on for two to three weeks, four days of which are public holidays. With Vietnam's recent entry into the globalized economy, commercial concerns have reduced what was once a month-long marking of the occasion.

SOUTHERN CALIFORNIA HOSTS THE LARGEST *TẾT* FESTIVAL IN THE UNITED STATES

The small city of Garden Grove, California, hosts the largest *Tết* Festival outside of Vietnam. It is organized by the Union of the Vietnamese Student Associations of Southern California, and it donates most of its proceeds to local cultural organizations. The family event lasts three days, and it is estimated that it attracted over 100,000 people in 2012. The main goal is the preservation of Vietnamese culture, which is represented in the festival in the form of live musical performances, carnival-type of games, traditional dances, the *Tết* parade, and lots of food.

Javier A. Galván

Tết Niên

During the period of *Tết Niên*, Vietnamese join in several rituals that clear the way for the midnight moment when they exit the old year and enter the new. For this to happen, the elements of bad luck must be expunged. This takes some time so people take leave from work, or at least shorten their work day, and students take break from school. Time is spent shopping for new clothes, paying off debts, returning things borrowed, and buying and cooking food for continuous savoring and upcoming feasting.

It is said that Vietnamese eat *Tết* and what is eaten most often is the traditional dish of *bánh chung* which is a blend of glutinous rice, bean paste, and pork that is wrapped in bamboo leaves then tied with bamboo string. The cake is square and symbolizes the people's gratitude for the cornucopia of food on earth. For *Tết*, *Trung Thu* (moon cakes) are true delicacies sometimes showcased with an egg-yolk moon right in the middle of them. The preferred sweet for the New Year is called *mứt Tết*, a candied fruit made with ginger root, pumpkin, and banana or even flower blossoms. When families visit the graves of ancestors for the annual cleaning, they leave trays of fruit that will nourish the reawakened spirits of the dead. They lay out sweets for *Ông Táo*—the spirits of the hearth—who travel to heaven to brief the Jade Emperor on family affairs who in turn foresees the future of households.

The absence of *Ông Táo* exposes homes to wayward spirits. To keep them at bay, some families, particularly those in the north, raise a bamboo tree. Stripped of its leaves except for a top-tip wisp, and adorned with bows, arrows, bells and gongs, the *cây nêu* offers security. In other regions of Vietnam, families bring in peach trees with plenty of blossoms which repulse evil. They may also nurture a new Kumquat tree to encourage an abundance of buds, flowers, and fruits each representing a generation of the family lineage, and to shape its symmetry so that the tree's crown reflects the strength of family bonds. Once the trees are in place, the red banners hung, dwellings cleaned, and other preparations taken care of, the way is clear for the transition from old to new.

Giao Thếa

On New Year's Eve, people dress in their most auspicious finery and set about to enjoy an evening of entertainment and camaraderie. Traditional music and sweet incense enlivens the landscape and home. The good luck of red infuses the scene. Here and there, performers dance like dragons and lions, while gamblers wage bets on the coming year; those who win will continue to win, those who lose will prevail in the coming year but not at the gambling table. This expresses the deep optimism of *Tết*, as does the distinctive poetry of the season recited by all. Flower markets and dinner banquets attract crowds, as do the art shows where Vietnam's famous miniature landscape art (*Hòn Non Bộ*) are on display. Then at the stroke of midnight, the ensemble of drums, gongs, and firecrackers warmly greets

Ông Táo who have returned to earth after meeting with the Jade Emperor. By this time, families have moved their ancestral altar to the front of the house to welcome the spirits of the dead. They surround the altar with photographs of the deceased and adorn them with betel nuts, flowers, and a bowl of five fruits. Family members keep the joss sticks lit throughout the holidays.

For *Tết Trung Thu*, one notable ritual is the making of rice paper lanterns in the shape of stars, fish, and other figures. These figurines are hung on long bamboo poles that children hold up in the hope of guiding back to earth the unfortunate legendary character who has been abandoned on the moon for urinating against a sacred tree which then grew to place her there.

Tân Niên

The customary events and proceedings of the first three days of the New Year are the essence of *Tết*. To begin with, all must enter the year with a frame of mind that promotes peace, forgiveness, mutual respect, and good cheer. On the first day, homes open for the most special of guests who are usually the husband's closest relatives. There is a desire, however, to attract into the home a special person who the family respects and whose early presence on this day would bring good luck throughout the year. During the day, there is an exchange of moral tales, worldly experiences, personal advice, and *Li Xi*, which is a moderate amount of lucky money put into red envelopes and given to children. Many older women of Ho Chi Minh City spend the day en route on the pagoda pilgrimage which can take them miles from their homes. On the second day, the wife's extended family and other valued guests visit the home.

On the third day of *Tết*, families play host to teachers, colleagues, supervisors, and the like. The watermelon becomes the prized refreshment—the redder the better for luck. It is on this day that the spirits of ancestors return to heaven. Families visit graves, decorate them with flowers and candles, and purify them with incense. The otherworldly travelers receive cars and clothing, but these figurines are made of paper, which are burned so that they too may transcend. Many Buddhists will pray in a temple and have their fortunes told.

After the third day of *Tết*, the festivities begin to whine down. In most parts of the country, save for Ho Chi Ming City and its surroundings, *cây nêu* is taken down thus signifying the end of the celebration of the first new moon of the year. In the urban areas, the holiday may last until the first full moon of the year that moves over Vietnam. The counting of these moons began in 2637 BCE in China, and they continue to be a significant component of Lunar Year celebrations in Vietnam.

Kenneth Whalen

Further Readings

McAllister, Patrick. "Connecting Places, Constructing Tết: Home, City and the Making of the Lunar New Year in Urban Vietnam." *Journal of Southeast Asian Studies* 43, no. 1 (February 2012): 111–32.

McLeod, Mark W., and Thi Dieu Nguyen. *Culture and Customs of Vietnam.* Westport, CT: Greenwood Press, 2001.

Queens Botanical Garden. "Tet Nguyen Dan: The Vietnamese New Year." http://www.queensbotanical.org/education/56902/57016/vietnam (Accessed on September 22, 2012).

Sullivan, James. *National Geographic Traveler: Vietnam.* 2nd ed. Des Moines, IA: National Geographic, 2010.

THAIPUSAM, EXTREME FLESH MODIFICATION

On the eve of a full moon in January or February each year, practitioners of the Hindu religion with ethnic origins in the Indian state of Tamil Nadu celebrate their most important god, Lord Muruga, with painful acts of extreme penitence. After fasting for at least one month, Tamil men pierce their lips and tongues with small spears. In addition, they affix small hooks all over their backs and chests, which carry small pots of milk, limes, wheeled shrines called *rathan*, or heavy planks called *kavadi*. Each year, over 1 million individuals, including men undergoing flesh piercing, their families, and tourists, participate in the largest *Thaipusam* festival in the world, which takes place in Kuala Lumpur, Malaysia, and culminates in the Batu Caves, one of the main shrines for Lord Muruga outside of India. Even though participants endure extreme flesh modification such as cheek and tongue piercing, or bodily hooks with weighted objects attached, they rarely incur scars from the experience due to the application of a traditional healing balm.

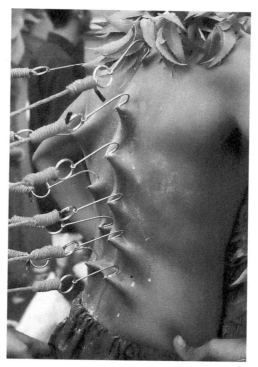

A Hindu devotee participating in the painful ritual of *Thaipusam* in Kuala Lumpur, Malaysia, in order to demonstrate his faith and penance. (iStockPhoto.com)

Thaipusam draws its name from the time of year when the festival takes place. *Thai* is the tenth month in the Hindu calendar, extending from the end of January through the end of February, and *pusam* is the name of a star that passes through the night sky during this period. *Thaipusam* honors Lord Muruga, the younger son of Shiva, the god of the destroyer in the holy trinity of the Hindu religion. According to Hindu mythology, on the day of *Thaipusam* Lord Muruga received a lance (*vel* in Tamil) from his mother, Shiva's consort, Goddess Parvathi. This lance was blessed to bestow wisdom on the bearer and fend off evil. He then slayed the demon

Soorapadman, who is considered to be an immortal evil who torments the good souls in the world by using his lance. Though Lord Muruga is revered by all Hindus as part of their pantheon of thirty-three gods and goddesses, he has special significance for Hindus from the southeastern state Tamil Nadu. In other parts of India, he is often referred to as "God of the Tamils." The many names Muruga is known by (primarily Kartikeya, Subramanian, and Swaminathan) are also common first and last names for Tamil people.

Lord Muruga is the Hindu god of spirituality, discipline, austerity, and final liberation from the trappings of physical incarnation. *Thaipusam* is the time of year when Tamil Hindus perform these acts of penance to request that the god reverse negative karma or help them achieve nirvana or full self-actualization. The spiritual trance (induced by drumming, gongs, and ritual fasting) employed by devotees during their piercing is based on a period of deprivation endured by Lord Muruga after he was defeated by his brother Ganesh, the Hindu half-elephant, half-man god. While the act of temporary body piercing is a show of discipline, the instruments of these flesh modifications are the symbols of Lord Muruga's warrior side. Though Muruga is primarily invoked as a calm god, he also symbolizes a warrior who defends the devoted by vanquishing evil spirits. The spear that devotees use to pierce their cheeks and tongue symbolizes Lord Muruga's lance.

The *Thaipusam* festival is celebrated around three days, but the preparations begin one to two months in advance. Those who will bear the skin hooks and carry heavy weights on the shoulders (the *kavadi* carriers) are primarily men who are eighteen years old and above, whose nutrition is limited to only one meal per day consisting milk, fruit, and vegetables. Beginning at least two days before the *Thaipusam* festival, they must also abstain from sexual contact, alcohol, and tobacco. Prayers, chants, and dancing are also often practiced during the fasting period to prepare the body and mind for the trance state employed during the procession. Typically, the entire household fasts in solidarity with the *kavadi* carrier, and their support continues throughout the festival days, as the family accompanies the relatives on the procession route, chanting, cheering, and encouraging them when they falter. Devotees who choose to carry the *kavadi* do so intending to achieve a specific goal through their act of penance, ranging from thanksgiving for something that has already happened to difficult prayers for the future, such as healing a sick family member. In order to achieve their aim, devotees pledge to carry the *kavadi* for a certain number of years, typically one to five. The size of the *kavadi* is related to the gravity of the individual devotee's prayer, and each devotee designs his or her own *kavadi* from wood or metal and decorates it with flowers, colored paper, and peacock feathers, as Lord Muruga rode a peacock.

On the day of the festival, the image or statue of Lord Muruga is carried on an ostentatiously decorated chariot at the head of a procession composed of *kavadi* carriers, their families and supporters, and other devotees carrying smaller offerings of milk pots in their hands or on their heads. Early in the morning at the origin of the temple, priests prepare the devotees for the piercing experience. Ecstatic drumming and chanting allows the kavadi carriers to enter a trance state, which medical studies have shown is the result of a heightened state of endorphins that mitigates the pain responses to the extreme piercings. Piercing does not begin until an individual has reached a sufficient trance state, for safety reasons. Before a section of the body is pierced, priests apply a balm called *vibhuti* (or holy ash) to the area to be pierced. *Vibhuti* is primarily composed of cow dung, as cows are sacred in the Hindu religion, mixed with a wide variety of ingredients, including ash, milk, butter, and spices with healing properties. Small lances (or large pins) are then pushed through both cheeks, piercing the tongue in between and holding it in place. In the meantime, trained priests also pierce through the outer layer of skin on devotees' torsos with small hooks and attach the *kavadi* heavy planks to the hooks. Once devotees have been pierced with spears, they begin a trance dance, noted for its whirling and its heaving-like falling and rising motions. Along the procession route, stalls serve meals, cold drinks, and snacks to those participating in the procession and other attendees. If a *kavadi* carrier falls during the route or his or her *kavadi* comes off of its hooks, the devotee's family or other participants help him or her regain the path. A communal energy of encouragement aids the processors in finishing their path, which can be as long as 4 kilometers traversed at a crawling pace due to traffic jams. At the end of the procession, priests tend to the *kavadi* carriers. When they reach the last temple in the procession, these individuals typically fall into a deeper trance or sleep-like state, during which time priests remove the devotees' piercings and again rub holy ash on the pierced areas. The devotees then carry their *kavadi* offerings up the temple steps and present them to the image of Lord Muruga.

The celebration of *Thaipusam* with flesh modification is no longer practiced in India, as it has been legally banned, but the festival has become a cultural rallying point for Tamil Diasporas in other parts of Southeast Asia, notably Malaysia, Singapore, and Sri Lanka, and certain other immigrant settlements primarily in Fiji, Mauritius, Trinidad and Tobago, South Africa, and Toronto, Canada. In Malaysia, where *Thaipusam* is a holiday in six states, the celebrations in Penang draw around 300,000 participants each year, while the procession to the Batu Caves outside Kuala Lumpur draws nearly 1.3 million devotees. Though Indians comprise less than 10 percent of Malaysia's population, *Thaipusam* is one of the largest religious festivals celebrated in the country, particularly for Hindus, regardless of which region in India they originate from. In Singapore, where Tamil Hindus are joined by Chinese, Singhalese, and Sikh Singaporeans for both the *kavadi*-carrying and procession, local laws regulating the scope and scale of minority holiday celebrations have diminished many aspects of the traditional *Thaipusam* festivities. The lengthy festival route passes every Tamil temple in the city and includes around 10,000 devotees each year. The Periyanayaki Amman Temple in Palani, India, hosts the primary *Thaipusam* celebration in India, though it does not include any flesh piercing.

The central controversy of the *Thaipusam* ceremony is the same element that draws so many tourists and local bystanders each year—the audacious acts of flesh modification. After *Thaipusam* became more popular in the 1970s and 1980s, these methods became more dangerous, including shoes made of nails or machete-like blades worn by devotees who walked by leaning on the shoulders of two helpers. Some devotees also began threading daggers up their arms or carrying their *kavadis* with large hooks. Seeing the festival becoming a rational for dangerous acts based more on daring acts than religious significance, the Indian government officially banned all flesh piercing during *Thaipusam*.

While *Thaipusam* has been regulated in India due to the severity of the flesh modification practices, in Singapore, comprehensive legislation has addressed other aspects of the celebration. In 2011, in Singapore, the government released a comprehensive guide for the celebration of *Thaipusam* that strictly regulates the permissible locations for both amplified and live music and the maximum size of *kavadis*. The new law also requires the prayers and procession to take place after midnight. While these regulations have ostensibly been put in place to reduce the noise and traffic issues and police force strain arising from the festival, the Indian community in Singapore has perceived these regulations to be a racist act on the part of the People's Action Party government and protested these changes to their traditional festivities.

Gabi Logan

Further Readings

Eng, Ah Lai. *Religious Diversity in Singapore*. Singapore: Institute of Southeast Asian Studies, 2008.

Lee, Raymond L. M., and Susan E. Ackerman. *Sacred Tensions: Modernity and Religious Transformation in Malaysia*. Columbia: University of South Carolina Press, 1997.

Mani, A., P. Ramasamy, and K. Kesavapany. *Rising India and Indian Communities in East Asia*. Singapore: Institute of Southeast Asian Studies, 2008.

Melton, J. Gordon. *The Encyclopedia of Religious Phenomena*. Canton, MI: Visible Ink Press, 2008.

Simons, Ronald C., Frank R. Ervin, and Raymond H. Prince. "The Psychobiology of Trance I: Training for Thaipusam." *Transcultural Psychiatry* 25, no. 4 (December 1988): 249–66.

Ward, Colleen. "Thaipusam in Malaysia: A Psycho-Anthropological Analysis of Ritual Trance, Ceremonial Possession and Self-Mortification Practices." *Ethos* 12 (1984): 307–34.

LA TOMATINA, TOMATO FOOD FIGHT

Once a year, the streets of the Spanish city of Buñol run red with the juice of hundreds of thousands of tomatoes as locals and visitors alike participate in the biggest food fight on the planet. Held on the last Wednesday in August as the centerpiece of a week of festivities, *La Tomatina* is an event where thousands of participants from all over the world battle in the streets using tomatoes as their only weapons.

Although Spain has dozens of cultural traditions that are centuries old, the celebration of *La Tomatina* is a fairly recent celebration dating back only to the 1940s. However, the exact origins of *La Tomatina* tradition are rather obscure. Most accounts point to a food fight during an annual parade in 1945 between groups of young people from different parts of town who took tomatoes off a

People throwing tomatoes at each other in the biggest food fight in the world (*La Tomatina*) in Buñol, Spain. (Iakov Filimonov/Dreamstime.com)

nearby food truck and began pelting each other. Another version has an angry parade performer attacking teenagers who had knocked him over. The young people, or rival groups of juvenile delinquents depending on yet another variation of the story, were either arrested or chased off by local police. The next year on the same day, the teenagers came back already armed with tomatoes to continue the fight, and local law enforcement again attempted to break up the melee and arrest the perpetrators. While the food fight between youths is the most popular of the origin theories, other possibilities include a scuffle between street vendors and customers, a protest by disgruntled citizens upon city councilmen, and an attack upon an untalented and unfortunate musician. A newer theory postulates that the tomato-throwing was an act of protest against the Spanish military dictator Francisco Franco who ruled Spain with an iron fist from 1936 to 1975.

Whatever the true beginnings of *La Tomatina* may have been, it seems that the people of Buñol enjoyed the chaos and fun that erupted during the messy street battle, and subsequently a tomato fight would continue to break out each year. Considering the event disruptive and a social nuisance, the town council attempted to block the tomato fights for over a decade. Despite their efforts, the popularity of the tomato battle grew until 1957 when a large number of people demonstrated for the festival in an event called the *Entierro del tomate*, or the Burial of the Tomato. As a result of public pressure, the Buñol town council decided to allow the celebration of the event without any government restrictions or impediments. Now, the social and cultural tradition is conducted with the financial support and backing of city leaders; *La Tomatina* is the main event in a week-long festival that has served to make the town a major tourist attraction.

The modern version of *La Tomatina* follows several established traditions and practices, along with a handful of general rules to ensure the safety of the town and the participants. This is a social and cultural celebration that not only attracts local people from all age groups, but it also draws thousands of visitors from abroad and other regions of Spain. In the week leading up to *La Tomatina*, the town of Buñol hosts parades, fireworks, and a paella-cooking contest. Since the town is relatively small, it does not have enough hotels to host the large number of people who come into town for the event held once a year in the late summertime. Therefore, most tourists and visitors have to stay in the nearby city of Valencia; then, they simply commute to Buñol. On the morning of *La Tomatina*, tens of thousands of people flood the streets in anticipation of the food fight. Most of them come prepared for the occasion wearing disposable clothing and goggles for eye protection. Crowds gather around the *palo jabón*, or the ham pole, a two-story tall greased pole atop which a ham is placed. At around 10:00 A.M., a signal is given and daring individuals attempt to climb the pole and reach the ham, as the festival will not begin until someone has managed the feat. Attempts to climb the pole are far from orderly, as dozens of people will climb over each other and fight for every inch for the right to be the one to begin *La Tomatina*. Once the ham has been reached, trucks enter the town loaded with tomatoes. As the ham can be notoriously difficult to reach, it can take hours for a person to accomplish the task. In practice, *La Tomatina* begins regardless of whether or not the ham has been claimed. A government official will fire a signal rocket to let festival goers know that the world's largest food fight has begun.

For the next hour, the enormous tomato food fight engulfs the street. In 2012, it was estimated that nearly 50,000 people took part in the event, and over 40 metric tons of tomatoes were used for the festivities. In a nod toward avoiding potential criticism for wasting food, the fruits are specially grown for the festival in nearby Extremadura, and they are generally inferior to tomatoes meant for a dinner plate. During the fight, it is generally too chaotic to maintain reasonable order, so only a few rules are enforced. For the safety of the participants, the tomatoes must be softened and squeezed before being thrown and no other objects may be used or thrown during the tomato fight. For the most part, the crowds generally obey the rules and conduct the food fight in the spirit of friendly fun. In all the years that the tomato fight has taken place, there have been no cases of injuries at all. The tomato fight itself lasts for one hour after which a second signal rocket marks the end of *La Tomatina*. Fire trucks emerge to begin hosing down the city streets, while revelers march down to the nearby river to clean up where the town usually sets up a few showers for rinsing. Reportedly, the acidity of the tomatoes does an excellent job of cleaning the city streets. At the end, participants of *La Tomatina* change into a set of extra clothes that they brought with them, as public transportation will not allow passengers to board buses or trains when their clothes are dirty from participating in the *Tomatina* celebrations.

The impact of *La Tomatina* festival has been massive for Buñol. It is normally a small industrial town of approximately 9,000 people located within the Autonomous Community of Valencia (similar to states or provinces), and Buñol has played host to an ever-increasing number of visitors as the popularity of *La Tomatina* grows. The notoriety has put Buñol on the cultural map, and it has certainly contributed greatly to the town's economy. Aside from the early reluctance of the town council to endorse *La Tomatina*, the only other major criticism leveled at the festival was by the fascist government of dictator Francisco Franco who put an end to the revelry on the basis that it had no real religious or historical significance. *La Tomatina* was quickly reinstated after the dictator's death in 1975, and it has been celebrated annually ever since without any cancellations. After 1975, a group called the Clavarios de San Luis Bertrán (which is the Catholic patron saint of Buñol) organized the event until 1980 when the city council became the official body to coordinate all the preparations and logistics of the *Tomatina* festival.

Due to the success of the festival in attracting tourists and bringing fame to Buñol, other towns and cities have attempted to replicate the food fight with varying degrees of success. In Colombia, the small town of Sutamarchán has organized in multiple occasions an event that resembles *La Tomatina* since 2004. However, the town holds the celebration only during times of an abundant harvest of tomatoes that would not affect the food supply. In the United States, the American Cancer Society also organizes an event called *La Tomatina* to raise funds for the organization. It has been coordinating the carnival-like event in Reno, Nevada, since 2009, and they always give credit to the original *Tomatina* festival from Buñol, Spain. However, India has placed multiple barriers to host similar events in Delhi and Bangalore where local government officials have cancelled and banned such events because they consider them to be a huge waste of food, which is badly needed in other towns with poor populations.

Daniel Fandino

Further Readings

García Rodero, Cristina, and J. M. Caballero Bonald. *Festivals and Ritual of Spain*. New York: Harry N Abrams Publishers, 1994.

Lawrence, Chris. "Painting the Town Tomatina: Doing Battle with 150,000 Rotten Reds in Spain's Buñol." *Mail Online*. September 18, 2012. http://www.dailymail.co.uk/travel/article-2204597/La-Tomatina-Bu-ol-worlds-famous-food-fight—makes-fun.html (Accessed on March 2, 2013).

McKay, Susan. *Spain: Festivals of the World*. New York: Gareth Stevens Publishing, 1999.

Riess, Jeanie. "Today Was the World's Biggest Food Fight, Welcome to La Tomatina." *Smithsonian Magazine*. August 29, 2012. http://blogs.smithsonianmag.com/food/2012/08/today-was-the-worlds-biggest-food-fight-welcome-to-la-tomatina (Accessed on March 2, 2013).

"Tomatina Festival." http://latomatinafestival.com/downloads/La-Tomatina-Survival-Guide.pdf (Accessed on March 4, 2013).

Tomatina Official Website. http://www.latomatina.org (Accessed on April 4, 2013).

"Tomato-Throwing Fiesta in Spain." *BBC News*. September 3, 1998. http://news.bbc.co.uk/2/hi/programmes/from_our_own_correspondent/163900.stm (Accessed on March 2, 2013).

TOOTH-FILING CEREMONY

The island of Bali (in Indonesia) celebrates multiple holiday celebrations almost every week of the calendar. Its rich cultural traditions commemorate every stage of human life beginning from pregnancy and continuing even beyond death. Since most of the Balinese population follows Hinduism, the island's version of the religion has been adapted to the local traditions by being more interwoven with social rituals and art, and less concerned with traditional tenants of Hinduism, such as reincarnation. Locally, it is known as Agama Hindu Dharma. The island's religious beliefs highlight important spiritual events in life. More specifically, Balinese Hindus observe thirteen "human-life" ceremonies (called *manusayadnya*) that collectively aim to protect followers and offer spiritual purification. From that group of customs, one of the most unique Hindu rituals in Bali is the tooth-filing ceremony. The religious and social tradition is intended to be a rite of passage for young boys whose voice begins to change and for girls who had their first menstrual cycle. This is an important tradition for the entire family, for parents would never think of allowing their children to reach adulthood without filing their teeth. At the very latest, they are expected to do it before getting married. The ritual is celebrated both in rural communities and in urban centers such as the capital city of Denpasar. These are elaborate religious events, and the entire family wears traditional clothing in white and yellow colors to represent the symbolism of holiness. While the boys wear ornamental clothes, the girls wear much more intricate clothing with decorative fabrics, jewelry, and even golden headpieces resembling a tiara.

During the months of July and August, Hindu families in Bali celebrate the tooth-filing ceremonies for their pre-pubescent sons and daughters. The festivities are locally known as *mapandes* (in the High Balinese language) and *matatah* (in Common Balinese). Archeological evidence has revealed artifacts indicating that this tradition has been locally observed since the Buleleng Regency, which dates back at least 2,000 years. However, the arrival of the first Hindu population groups in Bali dates from the fourth century. Consequently, the tradition of tooth-filing was not originally part of Hinduism, but it has now been almost exclusively associated with such religion on the island. The general goal of the ceremony is to file down six canine pointed teeth to make them flat (similar to molar teeth). At a superficial level, such practice might appear to be only for aesthetic purposes, especially because Balinese consider pointy teeth to be unattractive. However, this cultural tradition is deeply rooted in Hindu beliefs that canine teeth are the hallmark of demons, animal passions, arrogance, and savage tendencies. Therefore, the goal is to grind and flatten the six upper canine teeth to help in the spiritual process of removing six specific destructive forces of evil: greed (*loba*), confusion (*moha*), lust (*kama*), jealousy (*matzarya*), drunkenness (*mada*), and anger (*krodha*). The lower canine teeth are usually left intact. However, it is often believed that— after death—people might not be allowed to enter heaven if their teeth are not filed down properly because they might be mistaken for wild creatures and not necessarily viewed as humans.

The preparations for the tooth-filing ceremony actually begin the day prior to the event. Parents decorate the location (usually with lots of local flowers and fruit), and they place colorful banners with signs written in Sanskrit to announce the event. Then, the family engages in all the necessary preparations to offer a festive meal for their guests. Meanwhile, the priest blesses the instruments. The day prior to the ceremony, the young man or woman cannot go outside the house in order to meditate about the process about to take place. People also believe that youth at this stage are vulnerable to evil influences. The night before the event, the family must also select the exact number of people who will actually be surrounding the young boy or girl during the event because it can only be held with combinations of two, four, or six people in order to be propitious for good luck; groups of three, five, or seven people will bring bad luck and potentially ruin the youngster's chances of marriage.

The ceremony is usually performed early in the morning before sunrise by a priest (*Brahim*) of the higher castes who has been trained as a "dentist" (*Sangging*) to perform these religious rituals. They use three tools that are simple and rudimentary: a file, a carver, and a small hammer; these tools have not changed for hundreds of years. In addition, the family supplies small coconuts, a mirror, and small pieces of sugarcane for the ritual. The ceremony begins with the frightened youngsters laying down flat on a bamboo platform especially built for the occasion. Since they are usually nervous, music is performed on the background to calm them down. Then, family members surround the platform to offer support by standing near their beloved son or daughter. The first step is for the priest to place a small piece of sugarcane between the upper and lower teeth in order to keep the mouth open. When he begins grinding and filing (without any anesthesia), the room is supposed to be completely quiet. The only person allowed to speak is the priest who usually tries to talk to the youngsters to make the time pass by quickly and keep them quiet. The expected result is that the upper canine teeth are filed flat to become even with the other teeth. When the priest reaches an almost even line among all the upper teeth, he lets the initiates use a mirror (specially purchased for the event) to see the result of his work; they occasionally suggest a few minor adjustments. Sometimes, even the family members check if all the upper teeth have been filed correctly, and they ask for further filing, if needed. The entire tooth-filing ceremony takes about ten minutes per person, and the youths are supposed to endure the pain without complaining; it is part of the expectation regarding this coming-of-age ritual. After the priest is finished, the young boys and girls, feeling spiritually strengthened, perform an individual prayer in an isolated location and give thanks for the priest's blessings. They know that now the entire society will view them as adults and incorporate them into a stronger social network. Then, the family invites friends and family members to a festive meal, usually in a buffet style that includes rice, spicy meat, fruit salad, and cakes.

Tooth-filing ceremonies can be elaborate and expensive. Consequently, they have begun to reflect the disparity of income among Balinese families and the sharp divisions that exist on the island based on strict social class status. As a result, adaptations had to be made in order to maintain the traditions alive, but still save money on the events. Wealthy families often use their social affluence to offer extravagant feasts that include expensive catering services, live music, and newspaper announcements on the society pages. On the other end of the spectrum, families of more humble means use the tradition of tooth-filing ceremonies to bring the family closer together and to guide their sons and daughters before marriage but without excessive fanfare; their focus is more on the religious significance rather than on an exaggerated feast. Since some families cannot afford money for such expensive celebrations, they frequently pool their resources together to have a group celebration and offer a shared event. Another strategy used to save money is to combine the tooth-filing tradition with another important celebration in the family, such as a wedding or a cremation ceremony. To accommodate the necessities of all followers, the Hindu religion of Bali provides three different levels of the tooth-filing custom: the minimalist ritual (called *nista*), the medium-scale affair (*madya*), and the most elaborate celebration of them all (*utama*). All the three ceremonies are considered appropriate to fulfill the religious requirements of Balinese Hinduism.

Javier A. Galván

Further Readings

"Bali Ceremonies." http://www.baliholidayisland.com/balinese_ceremony.htm (Accessed on June 30, 2012).

Covarrubias, Miguel, and Adrián Vickers. *Island of Bali*. Jakarta, Indonesia: Periplus Editions, 2008.

"Hinduism in Indonesia." http://www.hindu-indonesia.com (Accessed on July 1, 2012).

Hobart, Angela. *People of Bali*. Oxford, UK: Blackwell Publishers, 2001.

Pindong, J. "Dental Mutilations among Villagers in Central Java and Bali." *Community Dentistry and Oral Epidemiology* 3, no. 4 (August 1975): 190–93.

Pringle, Robert. *A Short History of Bali: Indonesia's Hindu Realm*. Sydney, Australia: Allen and Unwin Publishers, 2004.

TUNA-THROWING COMPETITION

Australia is a country with several unique traditions which the population celebrates to honor their predecessors and universal heritage. Arguably the most interesting among these is the annual tuna-throwing championship which is held during Australia's Tunarama festival in Port Lincoln, South Australia. Port Lincoln, which is known as "The Tuna Capital of the World," is a fishing town with a large number of self-made millionaires, all of whom owe their livelihood to the tuna market and the lucrative contracts they have to sell the fish in other countries, such as Japan. To celebrate and honor their most profitable fish, the town of Port Lincoln holds a festival to celebrate the tuna fish, the occupation of fishing, and the sea which allows the fisherman to thrive.

It is believed that the celebration actually started as an extension of the traditional blessing of the fleet. Every year when the fishing boats left harbor for the first time in a season, they would be blessed by the community in order that they would have a successful and fruitful harvest. Without the blessing, the fishermen believed the harvest would be nonexistent and their financial return sparse. Over the years, more activities were added to the blessing ceremony, culminating in what would become the annual Tunarama festival. Since 1962, Port Lincoln has invited people from all over Australia to participate in fish-themed activities. Although most people who participate are Australian, people now come from all over the world to take part in the fun of Tunarama in Port Lincoln.

Each year at the end of January, during the Australia Day long weekend holiday, when Australia is the middle of its summer season, people flock from all over the world to compete in several categories of fish hurling. There are different tuna-tossing competitions based on weight of fish and the age of the competitor. The winners of each round will then compete against each other on the final day of Tunarama. Winners receive AUS$1,000 for their victory and the ultimate winner will take home the title of tuna-throwing champion for the year. Approximately 25,000 people attend Tunarama each year. The population of the town is only one-half that number, which means that more than 10,000 people make the trip to Port Lincoln, South Australia, each year in order to take part in the event, either as a competitor or merely to enjoy the free festivities, which always includes live music. There are actually quite a few competitions that take place during Tunarama, but none have received as much attention as the tuna-hurling contest, which officially became part of the festival in 1980.

In the tuna-throwing competition, the contestants line up to twirl the fish around their heads and then release them when they have reached the ultimate speed and height, hoping to hurl them as far away from the starting point as possible. The fish are tied with a rope by the tail and swung with the competitor holding on to the end of the rope. The thrower twirls the rope and then releases the fish with as much force as possible. It is a process similar to the more traditional sport of hammer throw, except that the object being thrown is actually a fish rather than a weight. The person who throws his or her fish the furthest will win the round. The record for tuna-throwing is a nearly 40-meter throw which was performed by Australian Olympic hammer thrower Sean Carlin. Several Olympian hammer throwers have taken part in the competition, each breaking the previously established record. Although this is a silly event, the actual tuna hurling is considered very serious, and the winners of the competition are highly respected by the community.

In the past, frozen tuna fish have been used in the Tunarama event. The reason for this is that the frozen fish are considered easier to grip and also travel further distances. Fish up to 22 pounds were traditionally used in the competition. However, in an attempt to go green and be more environmentally friendly, the tuna-throwing contest has taken to using fake fish rather than actual animals. The reason for concern is that the fish that are used in the competition are no longer edible. During the swinging and then in the landing, fins come off as do tails and even eyes. High-quality tuna, as can be found in the fishing waters of Port Lincoln, can be sold for thousands of dollars, and it can feed hundreds of people. The competition has been under public pressure for some time for wasting the animals. As a result, the event organizers rectified the objections by using the new polyurethane fish in the competition. These pretend fish have the same feel, size, and weight of real fish, but they can be used over and over again, making them environmentally friendly. Since 2007, the competition leaders have chosen to use the fake fish rather than waste valuable materials which could feed other people.

Among the other events that occur during Tunarama, the Ambassador Quest and Keg Roll are some of the most popular. There are also tossing contests for throwing wheat and tug-of-wars, as well as the "slippery pole contest" which very few people are able to finish. For those who must throw fish, but are too small to tackle the tuna, Tunarama features a prawn toss. In this event, even the smallest of celebrants can pick up a shrimp and throw it a few feet.

Rachelanne Smith

Further Readings

Connolly, Paul. "Tuna Tossing." In *The World's Weirdest Sports*. London: Murdoch, 2007.

Pedler, Emma. "We Like to Toss Tuna in Lincoln." *Open ABC*. https://open.abc.net.au/posts/tossing-tuna-50gf6sj (Accessed on September 12, 2012).

Squires, Nick. "Australian Tuna Tossing Festival to Use Fake Fish." *The Telegraph*. December 14, 2007. Sydney, Australia: Telegraph Media Group.

Vaisutis, Justine. "Port Lincoln." In *Australia*, 789–90. Oakland, CA: Lonely Planet, 2011.

TURKS AND CAICOS CONCH FESTIVAL

During the weekend of American Thanksgiving in late November, tourists and inhabitants flock to Turks and Caicos for the annual Conch Festival. This annual event takes places in the Blue Hills area of Providenciales, which is the largest island out of the forty that comprise the entire archipelago of Turks and Caicos in the Caribbean. The weekend of festivities includes several competitions for casual entrants, such as conch-blowing, conch-knocking, and a conch hunt in the sea. Bartenders compete to create the perfect mojito cocktail, and the island's most renowned chefs take part in a competition to create the best conch dish. Categories include Best Conch Salad, Best Conch Chowder, Best Specialty Conch, Best Presentation, and Best in Show. Around two dozen restaurants compete annually in the cooking event.

Turks and Caicos are two island groups in the West Indies, and only eight of the forty islands are inhabited. The history of the archipelago reveals that, for centuries, it has been controlled and ruled by multiple nations. The islands were discovered in 1512 by the Spaniard explorer Ponce de León, and they were subsequently raided as a source of slave labor. Over 130 years later, British colonists from Bermuda set up a salt industry in the seventeenth century, but the islands were not actually colonized until the eighteenth century. After disputes with the French, the islands came under British control, but the islands were still a source of strife—especially between the Bermuda and Bahamas colonial administrations. Both governments wanted to levy taxes in the region and profit from the lucrative salt trade. However, it was precisely during this period that the war of 1812 occurred between Britain and the United States, and it completely destroyed the regional salt industry. Over a century later, Jamaica took over the archipelago's administration in 1873. When Jamaica became independent in 1962, Turks and Caicos become a Crown Colony of Britain. In the 1980s, independence from Britain was considered and subsequently rejected. Despite the constant international influence, Turks and Caicos has developed its own identity in the Caribbean, and the Conch Festival has become a recognizable (and marketable) event in the region.

Conchs (pronounced *konk*) are gastropod mollusks or large marine snails. The "queen" or "pink-lipped" conch eaten in the Caribbean is of the species *Strombus gigas*, which can reach lengths of 12 to 13 inches. Conchs are plant eaters, and they can live as long as twenty-five years. They can be found inhabiting warm waters of the Atlantic as far south as Brazil. After the escargot, conch is the world's most popular snail, and it has been eaten in the region since pre-Columbian times. The meat of the conch is mild, with a flavor similar to that of clam. The most common preparations for this Caribbean delicacy are to use the conch in fritters, chowder, salads, and as steaks. The pink and pearly surface of large conch shells is used to make handicrafts and souvenirs, as well as to carve artistic objects.

The Turks and Caicos Conch Festival serves to highlight the creative culinary options based on this iconic Caribbean food. Because conch meat is tough, it must be cooked in a method that tenderizes it, or it must be pounded with a meat mallet for ten to fifteen minutes prior to cooking. One of the most traditional conch recipes is conch fritters, which do not require any tenderizing. The following recipe (from Brown Eyed Baker) is used in Turks and Caicos throughout the year.

Caribbean Conch Fritters

Note: This recipe will yield one dozen large or two dozen small fritters. If conch is not available, it may be substituted by any other bivalve or shellfish, such as shrimp, clams, or lobster.

Ingredients:

1 cup all-purpose flour
1 teaspoon sugar
1 teaspoon baking powder
1 egg, beaten
½ cup buttermilk
8 ounces finely minced or ground conch meat
1 small jalapeño or other hot pepper, minced
¼ cup minced onion
¼ cup minced red bell pepper
¼ cup minced carrot
1 clove garlic, minced
1 teaspoon Creole or Caribbean seasoning
Vegetable oil to fry

Directions

1. Heat the oil in a pot or skillet to a depth of 1–2 inches, to at least 350°C.
2. Combine the first four ingredients in a large bowl and stir to combine; stir in buttermilk to create a thick batter.
3. Add remaining ingredients and combine, making sure everything is well incorporated.
4. Using a spoon or scoop, drop rounded table spoonfuls of the batter into the hot oil. Small fritters will need about two minutes per side; large fritters will need four minutes. Watch them carefully to make sure they do not burn.
5. When the fritters are golden brown on all sides, transfer them to paper towels or a wire rack to drain. Serve immediately with dipping sauce.

Turks and Caicos is the only place on earth where conch is commercially farmed for food, which attests to its popularity in the region. It is particularly favored across the Caribbean as well as with export markets in Florida. Conch farming and export is one of the few viable industries in the islands, whose other main sources of income are offshore banking and tourism—especially from the cruising industry. Currently, unemployment is widespread, and there is very little agriculture. Because of such economic conditions, the conch has assumed iconic status as the most well-known and profitable symbol of the islands.

Erin Pappas

Further Readings

Brown Eyed Baker. "Caribbean Conch Fritters Recipe." *Brown Eyed Baker.* http://www.browneyedbaker.com/2012/03/30/conch-fritters-recipe/ (Accessed on November 16, 2012).
"The Conch Farm Tour in Turks." *Myturksandcaicos.com.* (n.d.) http://www.myturksandcaicos.com/turksandCaicosConchFarm.php (Accessed on August 15, 2012).
"Conch Festival Draws Big, Hungry Crowd." *TCfreepress.com.* December 1, 2011. http://www.tcfreepress.com/index.php?option=com_content&view=article&id=3083:conch-festival-draws-big-hungry-crowd&catid=27:community&Itemid=71 (Accessed on August 24, 2012).
Mills, Carlton. *A History of the Turks and Caicos.* New York: Macmillan Publishing, 2009.
Morgan, Jinx, and Jefferson Morgan. *The Sugar Mill Caribbean Cookbook: Casual and Elegant Recipes Inspired by the Islands.* Boston: Harvard Common Press, 1996.

UMBILICAL CORD AS FAMILY TREASURE

In Japanese culture, a traditional birth custom calls for the family of an infant to preserve the stem or stub of the umbilical cord as a memento. Pregnancy and childbirth are associated with knowledge in most societies, particularly in terms of desired practices and taboos. Japanese customs regarding the handling of the umbilical cord form an integral and ongoing part of traditional birth lore. The dried stem of the cord is collected and kept when it falls from the newborn's navel. Sometimes, the family also retains the band used to tie off the umbilical cord. In part, this practice represents a celebration of the new life. Many consider the cord a charm for the child's luck and longevity. The preserved cord is believed to hold misfortune at bay and death at the greatest possible distance.

The umbilical cord and band are usually enfolded in some form of wrapper for protection, sometimes one as simple as paper. Frequently, the cord is saved in a box. It may also be a device constructed especially for the purpose. In Japanese culture, the box fashioned to hold an umbilical cord as souvenir is known as a *Kotobuki Bako*. The crafted container carries with it wishes for health and renewal. In a ceremony called a *hesono-o*, the mother wraps the cord and places it in this special box. Within the *Kotobuki Bako*, it is traditional for the mother to place a small sleeping doll dressed in a kimono. It is customary to store the saved umbilical cord within the doll's garments. Participants in this practice consider the keepsake to confer good fortune and continued intimacy on the relationship between the mother and child. In addition, the umbilical cord symbolizes the growth of the family and the crucial bond between its generations. Both the box and its contents are accorded honor and their continued care becomes a matter of family duty.

As the child matures, the preserved umbilical cord can play a part in marking turning points in the individual's life. A mother may show her son or daughter the cord on a special occasion such as a birthday. In some cases, Japanese mothers may mark a momentous event in her offspring's development by bestowing the cord upon her son or daughter. This gift ritual typically takes place at a major turning point in the person's life, such as moving out of the familial home or getting married. There is also an occasion in which the preserved umbilical cord represents a tribute to an ancestor in the form of an heirloom held beyond that individual's lifespan, in which case the cord serves as an object of veneration.

This Japanese folk tradition persists over time, even among many immigrants, such as the *Nisei* (second generation) and *Sansei* (third generation) in the United States. With time's passage and the increase in hospital births, however, the tendency has been for parents of Japanese origin to emphasize the guidance of the obstetrician over the midwife as authority during the birthing process. Where this is the case, traditional Japanese birth customs, including preservation of a baby's umbilical cord, may recede.

While distinctive in some respects, traditional Japanese beliefs regarding the significance of a baby's umbilical cord as a family treasure are not entirely unique. Customs in India, Mexico, Turkey, and Native America all provide for the careful handling of the umbilical cord as a symbolic object.

Linda S. Watts

Further Readings

Cavnar, Cynthia. "Harmonious Cord." *Smithsonian* 32, no. 7 (October 2001): 140.

Fiedler, Deborah Cordero. "Authoritative Knowledge and Birth Territories in Contemporary Japan." *Medical Anthropology Quarterly, New Series* 10, no. 2 (June 1996): 195–212.

Kawamoto, Fumi. "Folk Beliefs among Japanese in the Los Angeles Area." *Western Folklore* 21, no. 2 (January 1962): 13–26.

Opler, Marvin K. "Japanese Folk Beliefs and Practices, Tule Lake, California." *Journal of American Folklore* 63, no. 250 (October–December 1950): 385–97.

Smith, Susan L. *Japanese American Midwives: Culture, Community, and Health Politics, 1880–1950.* Urbana: University of Illinois Press, 2005.

UP HELLY-AA, FIRE FESTIVAL

Occurring annually on the last Tuesday in January in Shetland, Scotland, *Up Helly-Aa* affirms itself as Europe's largest fire festival. Marking the end of the Yule season, fire festivals occur in approximately twelve locations in Shetland; however, Lerwick, the capital, boasts the largest number of participants. While *Up Helly-Aa* day acts as a celebration of Scotland's Norse heritage, the holiday is largely contemporary in origin and has undergone numerous changes since its inception. Loosely established in the early nineteenth century, *Up Helly-Aa* originated as nights of rowdy howling, drinking, fighting, and general merry-making among young working-class men during the New Year and Yule season. It now also reflects a strong sense of Viking traditions in Scotland.

As the carousing escalated over the years, participants introduced the practice of burning tar barrels in the 1840s. Because the streets of Lerwick were exceedingly narrow during this time, rival groups of tar-barrelers often quarreled in the middle, as they battled for a particular turf. Due to these outbreaks of violence, the middle class voiced its discontent, and tar-barreling was eventually abolished in the early 1870s. Simultaneously, a group of local young men decided that the Yuletide celebrations needed some fresh ideas.

First, the reformers invented the name *Up Helly-Aa*, establishing the day as a legitimate holiday. Second, the young men shifted the festival to the end of January, in order to correlate with the concept of Old Yule—the date of Christmas according to the Julian calendar. Finally, the men introduced the now signature component of "guizing" into the festivities, with each member of the squad donning an intricate disguise. Within the next decade, guizers adopted Viking disguises, and

Participants at the *Up Helly-Aa* Fire Festival in Lerwick, Scotland, wearing Viking costumes. (AP Photo/Christine Nesbitt)

launched the first Viking long ship, called the Galley in 1889; however, the annual procession of a Viking Squad was not cemented until after World War I. As participants continued to explore Viking lore, they recognized the importance of electing a leader, and in 1882, elected *Up Helly-Aa's* first leader whom they christened Worthy Chief Guizer. The position of Worthy Chief Guizer swelled in consequence, prompting fellow guizers to purchase him a suit of armor, helmet, and other articles of battle gear, as well as refer to him as Guizer Jarl.

In 1931, the *Up Helly-Aa* committee extensively upgraded the Jarl's costume with a new helmet, shield, axe, and dagger, as well as engraved the symbol of a black and red raven into the shield. Although pieces of the costume have been damaged and thus replaced over the years, the committee has retained the same design since the 1930s. Each year the former Jarl bestows the suit of armor, which includes the helmet, breastplate, shield, axe, dagger, and belt, upon the next Jarl, who will customize the design of his kirtle and cloak. The Guizer Jarl also possesses a squad comprising approximately fifty to seventy men who wear matching armor. Each year the suit's design is different, and up to two years of advanced planning determines the unique outfits of the Jarl and his squad. Being selected for the Jarl's personal squad is considered a great honor. Over forty-five squads, composed of roughly twenty-five guizers, partake in the colorful procession and follow behind the Jarl and his squad.

While making changes in the 1870s, the young men also inducted the annual torchlight procession through the streets of Lerwick, the activity by which *Up*

Helly-Aa is now most widely distinguished. During the winter, the Torch Boys—junior members involved in the ceremonies—gather twice a week to construct over 1,000 torches made from hessian sacks and concrete. On the Monday prior to *Up Helly-Aa*, the Torch Boys soak all torches in fuel. The procession usually consists of approximately 1,000 guizers who carry their torches around Lerwick while following the Galley. Over 5,000 spectators line the roads to applaud the guizers as they process. During the march, all street lights are turned off in order to highlight the true magnitude of the torches. The procession culminates at a site called Valhalla, where the men light the Galley ablaze.

Up Helly-Aa's earliest Galley ships were mostly made of light timber frames covered by canvas or were sometimes simply old boats no longer used for sailing. After World War I, however, reputable carpenters began assembling vessels of greater complexity for the festival. The present-day Galley's design has endured since 1949, when a local boat builder and twenty-year committee veteran devised the dimensions for that year's Galley. Today, a group of local tradesmen and volunteers build and paint the Galley under the supervision of an appointed committee foreman, ensuring the preservation of original architectural dimensions. Construction of the Galley begins every October and continues two nights a week until the project is complete. Each year, the Jarl decides the color and name of the Galley, which will ultimately complement the design of his kirtle and cloak. The color choice remains a strictly protected secret until it is revealed on *Up Helly-Aa*.

On the last Tuesday in January, the day's preparations for the large celebration begin in the early morning, when the Jarl and his squad march through Lerwick at 8:30 A.M. As the guizers march, they sing songs detailing the struggles and victories of their Scandinavian ancestors, commemorating their way of life. While following a predetermined course, the squad stops at the Market Cross in order to view the Bill, which has been posted since 6:00 A.M. The Bill, a secret document generated by the committee in advance, originated in 1899 in order to convey the day's instructions to the guizers. Gradually, the Bill assumed the local color of Lerwick, featuring jokes and satire. The Jarl selects a local artist each year to craft the Bill head: a painted scene chronicling the Jarl's history. The public gathers in anticipation each year to behold the Bill, receiving all jests in good humor.

Following the disclosure of the Bill, the Jarl and his squad march down Commercial Street, and they stop at the Bressay Ferry Terminal to take official photographs. Crowds of people, including many school children, gather to meet the men. The squad then marches through Fort Charlotte, receiving a private reception at the Town Hall. During the reception, the city awards the Jarl sovereignty of the town for twenty-four hours. Historically, guizers in the nineteenth century went house to house on *Up Helly-Aa* night to visit the neighbors. Now, the committee secures large halls throughout Lerwick in which to accommodate the squads.

After a reception at the Town Hall, the Jarl and his guizers visit the two primary schools, the hospital, nursing homes, and finally the Shetland Museum. The squad will then ready itself for the processions, which commence at 5:30 P.M.

and 7:30 P.M. The junior procession, beginning at 5:30 P.M., comprises junior guizers who simulate the actions of the older members. Established in 1956 for fostering an interest in *Up Helly-Aa* among Lerwick's youth, the junior guizers attend Anderson High School where second-year boys vote for their Jarl after summer vacation. During the winter, parents of the junior guizers engineer suits of armor for the boys to wear. Gathering on the Hillhead, the junior guizers and the junior Jarl follow their Galley, also built by volunteers, to the burning site in the Junior Torchlight Procession.

At 7:15 P.M., the Jarl and his squad pass through the ranks of their fellow guizers from the back of the procession, in order to assume their position as the leaders of the convoy. At 7:30 P.M. 1,000 guizers begin their march toward Valhalla with torches alit. The Jarl leads the procession at the helm of his Galley (Viking ship), until finally arriving at the King George V playing field where the guizers light the Galley on fire. Members of the public watch from a distance, as they may not enter the burning site. While the Galley descends in a blazing inferno, the crowd sings "The Norseman's Home," which often generates much emotion and patriotism. High spirits then develop among the guizers as they travel to twelve halls in which each squad will perform a choreographed act or dance routine. The revelry carries on until 8:00 A.M. Wednesday morning, which consequently remains a public holiday.

The actual day and evening activities of *Up Helly-Aa* are vigilantly planned and timed by the committee. An organization of seventeen elected volunteers, potential committee members must advocate their capabilities to veteran guizers who will then vote by secret ballot. Ultimately, fifteen individuals will be elected, while the Jarl and the Marshal—an individual who oversees the entire operation—encompass the other two vacancies.

Overall, the residents of Lerwick, Shetland (in Scotland), exude an utmost sense of integrity and commitment toward keeping the tradition of *Up Helly-Aa* alive, having only cancelled the ceremonies for the death of Queen Victoria and the years during World War I and World War II. A fervent loyalty to the Norse ancestry of Shetland undoubtedly fuels the survival of this cherished festival for which its participants remain so proud.

Kellie Money

Further Readings

Brown, Callum G. *Up-Helly-Aa: Customs, Culture and Community in Shetland.* New York: St. Martin's Press, Inc., 1998.

Shetland Tourism. "Up Helly-Aa." http://visit.shetland.org/up-helly-aa (Accessed on August 3, 2012).

Up Helly-Aa Committee. "Welcome to Up Helly-Aa: Europe's Largest Fire Festival." http://www.uphellyaa.org (Accessed on July 29, 2012).

Whyte, David J. *Scotland: Landmark Visitors Guide.* Derbyshire, UK: Landmark Publishing, Ltd, 1998.

V

VARZESH-E BASTANI IRANIAN WRESTLING

The ancient wrestling sport of Varzesh-e Bastani combines aspects of pre-Islamic Iranian culture with elements of moral rectitude, physical strength, martial arts, knowledge, modesty, and spiritual purity. However, there are considerable differences with the concept of wrestling practiced in the Western world. Varzesh-e Bastani (called "Ancient Sport" in Persian) is not intended for show or entertainment. Instead, it is highly ritualized and focused on spiritual aspects of Sufism (a mystical dimension of Islam that believes that prayer and purity of heart can bring followers closer to God). In addition, Varzesh-e wrestlers do not literally wrestle an opponent. Instead, they compete over exercises of strength and flexibility following specific spiritual traditions and ethical guidelines; the events also include the recital of poetry and ceremonial drum music.

Modern-day Varzesh-e had its genesis in the nineteenth century during the ruling period of the Qajar king Nassar al-Din Shah (1848–1896). The sporting competitions were inspired on ideas of Iranian mythology, and they were typically held to celebrate the Persian New Year (March 21). However, the sport declined steadily in popularity from the 1920s until the 1960s when Iran embarked on modernization programs, and Varzesh-e was viewed as a relic of the long-gone Qajar kingdom. Furthermore, the Iranian Revolution of 1979 distanced itself from such sporting competitions and public gatherings. It was not until the late twentieth century that Varzesh-e Bastani wrestling matches emerged again as a proud Persian cultural tradition, and it expanded beyond its borders to neighboring Iraq and Afghanistan. Nowadays, the sport of Varzesh-e is associated mostly with nationalistic pride.

Most Varzesh-e Bastani competitions take place at a covered gymnasium (*Zurkhaneh*) or "house of strength." The structures are designed with a sunken circular or octagonal pit (*gaud*) located right in the center of the building where the athletes compete. There are three major sections for the public: male spectators (women are not admitted) sit around the pit, but they are separated from a section of musicians with drums and a group of Sufi followers who recite stories of Iranian mythology. A wrestling session typically begins with the sounds of a drum played by a highly respected *morshed* who sits in a prominent and highly visible position. The competition includes mostly a combination of calisthenics or acrobatic moves often based on the use of instruments that resemble combat materials such as metal shields (*sang*), iron weights in the shape of a bow (*kaman*), and several rigid wooden clubs or sticks (*mil*).

The athletes can achieve three separate levels of membership into a Varzash-e gymnasium: the lowest rank is that of a novice (*nocheh*) being trained by a designated champion; the next level consists of advanced students (*nokhasteh*) who have obtained substantial training by a champion; and finally there are the champions (*pahlevan*). Then, there are multiple champion grades. There are now two variations of the sport: Varzesh-e Bastani (Sport of Ancients) and Varzesh-e Pahlevani (Sport of Warriors), and some of the champions compete as mainstream wrestlers in the national Iranian team at the International Olympic Games.

Javier A. Galván

Further Readings

Abassi, Mehdi. *Tarikh-e Koshtigari dar Iran (The History of Wrestling in Iran).* Theran, Iran: Beizai, 1984.

Circle of Ancient Iranian Studies. "Iran's Neighbours to Revive Iran's Varzesh-e Pahlevani." *Cultural Heritage News Agency CHN.* November 25, 2005. http://www.cais-soas.com/News/2005/November2005/24-11-iran.htm (Accessed on January 6, 2013).

Luijendijk, D.H. *History and Techniques of the Ancient Martial Art of Iran.* Boulder, CO: Paladin Press, 2006.

"Traditional Iranian Martial Arts (Varzesh-e Pahlavani)." http://www.pahlavani.com (Accessed on January 5, 2013).

VIRGEN DEL CARMEN, FIESTAS DE CUSCO

The Virgen del Carmen celebration is an annual five-day festival held in multiple towns in Europe and throughout the Americas beginning on July 16. It combines religious observance with extremely colorful parades, elegant pageantry, elaborate costumes, regional music, and well-choreographed dances.

It is the liturgical feast day of Our Lady of Mount Carmel, or Virgen del Carmen, which is one of several religious invocations of the Virgin Mary. Its name comes from Mount Carmel in Israel, which is derived from *Karmel* or *Al-Karem*, usually translated as "garden." Devotion to this religious icon began on July 16, 1251, when the Virgin Mary is believed to have appeared to St. Simon Stock, and she gave him the brown scapular necklace (which subsequently became part of the Carmelite habit and a symbol of the order), promising that whoever died wearing it would be saved. The Carmelites see the Virgin Mary as a model of the aspired interior life of prayer and contemplation, a model of virtue, and the person closest to Jesus Christ. The Carmelite Order was subsequently founded and introduced to Europe. Today, the Roman Catholic Carmelite Order has thousands of male and female members in monasteries, congregations, and institutes in all continents. It is widely accepted that the feast of the Virgen del Carmen was probably first celebrated in England during the fourteenth century. It was to thank Mary, the patroness of the Carmelite Order, for her many benefits to the Order during its early years. The beginning of the feast may have been when

Women wearing traditional dresses for the Virgen del Carmen celebration in Cusco, Peru. (Jacek Kadaj/Dreamstime.com)

their title "Brothers of the Blessed Virgin Mary" was instituted in Cambridge, England, in 1374.

Today, the festival varies considerably, depending upon the regional patron saint who is being honored and celebrated. In Spain, the Virgen is the patron saint of the sea. In Chile, it is considered Queen and Patroness of the armed forces and Carabineros police officers. Colombians consider her as the patron of all transportation drivers. Peru honors the "Patroness of Criollismo." In Bolivia, she is regarded as the patron of the nation and its armed forces. In Venezuela, she is venerated as the patron of the Army.

Spain

During the eighteenth century, an admiral of the Spanish Royal Armada named Antonio Barceló Pont de la Terra (1716–1797) became famous for his anti-Algerian privateer raids, bombardments of Algiers, and the use of floating batteries during the famous 1782 siege of Gibraltar from the British. He was responsible for promoting the festival celebrations among his crew. After that, the Spanish navy replaced the patronage of San Telmo for the Virgin of Carmen.

The festival of the Virgen del Carmen is today celebrated in over thirty-nine Spanish cities and towns, including Madrid, Murcia, Malaga, Toledo, and Valencia. As it commemorates the patron saint of sailors, the festivities are mostly held in fishing communities. Homage is paid to the Virgin, whom mariners count on for protection and safety during their voyages. Most festivals have carnival groups, street parties, concerts, giant papiér mâché heads, and fireworks in a week-long celebration. Usually, there is also a maritime procession, where the Virgin's image is carried in a flower-decorated boat accompanied by thousands of devotees. The festival is organized by a coalition of community groups: the local fishermen's association, the association of the Virgen del Carmen, and the local government.

In Malaga, the largest festival is in the La Carihuela district of Torremolinos located about 8 miles (13 kilometers) from the city. The Virgin is both the patron saint of mariners and the entire district. The procession featuring the image of the Virgin begins at the Catholic Church in La Carihuela in the evening, and then proceeds through the streets of the village. When the procession reaches the beach, a solemn mass illuminated with thousands of candles is celebrated. Then, the Virgin's image is taken out to sea, accompanied by a large flotilla, and it passes coastline beaches in a decorated boat. When the Virgin returns to La Carihuela, her followers enjoy an elaborate fireworks display. What follows is a three-day Feria (a "free day"), when no one is obligated to work. There are colorful parades with dance troupes and musical bands, masked dancers, and alcoholic refreshments. The celebration also features local talent and skill, and most of the decorations (e.g., the masks) are handmade by local artisans. The festival also includes memories of the deceased. On July 17, it is common to see the town's residents (and many tourists) go to the cemetery to visit their dead relatives and friends. They carry food and drinks to celebrate beside the graves. Even the dancers go to the cemetery to visit dead former dancers of the troupes.

Mexico and Central America

The festival is also celebrated in Guatemala, Mexico, Nicaragua, Panama, and Puerto Rico. For example, la Virgen del Carmen is venerated as a patron in the city and port of San Juan del Sur, Nicaragua, where she is honored on July 16 as the Queen of the Sea (Stella Maris) and as Protector of Fishermen. The celebrations begin on July 15, with a vigil on the beach of the bay, the singing of songs in honor of the Virgin, accompanied by philharmonic bands, marimbas, and organs. In Mexico, the Virgin is the patron saint of the Yucatan Peninsula and empress of the Mexican southeast region of the country. The fishermen from the Campeche region have a long history of paying tribute to the Virgin. It is well documented that they provided a gold crown to their spiritual protector way back in 1900.

South America

Additional festivals honoring the Virgen del Carmen are held in Argentina, Bolivia, Chile, Colombia, Peru, and Venezuela. Buenos Aires, Argentina, celebrates the Virgin as the local patron. In Bolivia, the Virgin of Carmen was proclaimed "General and Patron of the Armed Forces of the Nation," and all the branches of the military participate in the devout celebration of the feast in multiple towns and cities. Colombian transportation workers (e.g., bus, truck, and taxi drivers) revere the Virgin as their patron for protection in dangerous situations. As a sign of their devotion, many Colombian roads have shrines erected in honor of the Virgin with many candles set by drivers passing by who have stopped to pray. Scapulars (simple necklaces made from brown yarn) and images of their beloved Virgin often hang in cars as a shield or protector.

In Peru, the festival of the Virgen del Carmen has taken special social and historical significance both at the sea-level capital city of Lima and the high-altitude city of Cusco. The festival is held to honor the patron saint of the mestizo population (half-white and half-Indian). The Virgen del Carmen is the most widely venerated image in Peru after the Lord of Miracles. Its worship began when friars from the Carmelite Order arrived when Peru was a Spanish colony. Today, the festival blends pre-Columbian traditions and Catholic rituals that attract thousands of tourists.

The Peruvian festivals are both a religious incantation of the Virgin and a celebration of local talents in a workers' holiday. Historically, the festivities demonstrated the "splendor and supremacy of the Crown and Church." In the New World, this reorientation of the festival's original religious meaning has been explained as an explicit affirmation of Creole patriotism and spirited defense against European accusations of Creole intellectual inferiority. The elaborate dances, music, pageantry, and religious devotion are the New World's assertion of its own cultural prowess (Voigt 2005, 159–160).

The nation's most famous festival is held in Paucartambo, in the Andes, roughly 71 miles (115 kilometers) from the high-altitude city of Cusco. Known locally as "mamacha Carmen" or "mamita del Carmen," the festival sprawls over the main square of the city and features regional dance groups accompanied by musicians who portray historical events and folklore. As a sign of her influence in Peru, the image of the Virgen del Carmen in Sacsayhuamán was crowned by the Catholic Pope John Paul II during his visit to Peru in 1985. During this four-day celebration, over sixteen *comparsas* (a musical band with dancers) play continually. Historically, a *comparsa* derives from traditional African processions of devotees following a saint or deity during a religious celebration. The center of the festival is a somber, reverential procession of the Virgin, who represents both the Quechua goddess Pachamama and the Christian faith.

Peruvians hold a parade with a sacred image of the Virgin carried aloft through the streets accompanied by Inca and magically costumed dancers whose carefully choreographed gestures and movements symbolize the eternal battle between the forces of good and evil. The purpose is to bless those present as well as scare away potential demons. The choreography includes both semi-mythical and Peruvian historical characters. Examples are the Auca Chilenos (the Chilean soldiers who occupied Peru in the nineteenth century) and the Capac Negros, or freed slaves. Others include malaria victims, very ugly gringos, Ukukus (a mythical figure that is half-man, half-bear), and warlike Indians. Finally, a symbolic battle is held between the devoted dancers and the demons, with the faithful winning. Throughout these events, elaborately dressed choirs sing in the Quechua language.

In other Peruvian coastal communities—such as El Guayabo in Chincha (124 miles or 200 kilometers south of Lima)—where most of Peru's Afro-Peruvian population lives, the festival is held on December 27. In this particular region, the Virgin is called La Peoncita ("the little peon"), teenagers dancers are known as *los negritos* and young female performers as *las pallitas* to honor the Virgin. In the Cajamarca region of Peru's northern sierra, Celendín celebrates the Virgin with music, dancing, and bullfights.

Overall, the celebrations attributed to the Virgen del Carmen have become community events that incorporate both traditional and contemporary aspects of

Spanish heritage, Catholic religious foundations, and regional customs in countries throughout the world.

William P. Kladky

Further Readings

"Cultural Traditions of Andean Communities in Peru." http://www.myperu.org/fiestas_paucartambo_virgen_de_carmen_peru.html (Accessed on May 23, 2013).
"History of Nuestra Señora del Carmen." http://www.corazones.org/maria/carmen_virgen/a_carmen.htm (Accessed on May 23, 2013).
International Carmelites Website. http://locarm.org/en (Accessed on May 22, 2013).
Jotischky, Andrew. The Carmelites and Antiquity: Mendicants and Their Pasts in the Middle Ages. New York: Oxford University Press, 2002.
"Prayers for Nuestra Señora Virgen del Carmen." http://www.devocionario.com/maria/carmen_1.html (Accessed on May 23, 2013).
Voigt, Lisa. "Creole Patriotism in Festival Accounts of Lima and Potosí." *Romance Notes* 45 (2005): 159–69.

VISITING-GIRLS COURTING TRADITION

China is a large nation of more than 1 billion people. The country has fifty-six distinct ethnic groups, with the Hans comprising more than 90 percent of the population. The other fifty-five groups make up the remaining 10 percent of the inhabitants. The Dai are a minority group who make up approximately 8 percent of the Chinese population in the Yunnan Province in southwest China. There are actually three different groups that comprise the Dai: Han Dai, the Flower Belt Dai, and the Jinuo Dai. These three factions are very similar, but they honor the customs and traditions of their Dai heritage to varying degrees. While the Han Dai and the Flower belt Dai have incorporated contemporary Chinese and Western traditions into their cultures, the Jinuo Dai group tends to practice customs and rituals very close to the way that their ancestors did. However, one cultural trait that all three Dai groups have in common is a specific type of courting ritual, which has come to be known as the "visiting-girls" tradition (or *gantuozong* in phonetic Chinese), wherein eligible young men and women come together to decide if they have any romantic interest in one another. The ritual begins with a communal meeting, usually held in the middle of the village and continues in the homes of the young girls who still live with their parents. The newly acquainted pairs are constantly chaperoned, and the courtship occurs under the watchful gaze of both the parents of the young lady and the rest of the community as well.

The visiting-girls tradition has its origins in ancient China, and it takes place following the harvest season when the largely agricultural community is at rest. The ritual starts with the young eligible women (usually fifteen or sixteen years of age) in the community sitting together around a bonfire. Each young woman sits turning her individual spinning wheel. From behind the girls, men approach them while covered in red blankets. Each man examines the girls and decides which one is the most attractive to him. As they come near the girls, they play instruments, and each man chooses a girl to individual serenade with his music. They do not speak at all to one another during the initial attraction stage. If the woman chooses the man as well, she will take a small stool out from beneath her skirts and invite her suitor to take a seat beside her. This is the only part of the ritual where the girl has a direct choice in the matter. She cannot ever initiate a courtship with a man because it would be interpreted as being too forward. He must come to her. If a girl is interested in a man who does not choose her, then she has no option but to reject her current suitor and hope the man to whom she is attracted decides to interact with her in a later ritual. However, if the selected suitor accepts to sit down next to the girl, then he will wrap her up in the blanket with him, and they will speak of love to one another and make promises for the future.

The visiting-girls tradition by itself does not constitute a marriage contract. After the conversation under the red blanket, the man and woman may decide that they are incompatible, and their courtship ends. If, however, they are genuinely interested in one another, the young man will visit the woman in her home and continue getting to know one another. The visits continue so long as the young man wishes to see the girl. It is very rare that a woman will reject a suitor outright. Only after several visits is it believed that the couple has enough information about one another to determine their compatibility. Meanwhile, there are very stringent limitations about what the young man and woman may actually do before marriage. They can rarely be alone together, let alone express their affection physically. The visiting-girls tradition demands that no sex is allowed before the marriage, and interaction is to be limited until a marriage ceremony is performed. As long as he continues visiting, the young man will bring the girl gifts, such as hair combs. The courtship is presumed to continue until the girl returns the gifts from her suitor.

So long as the courtship progresses positively, the young man will eventually ask the woman's parents for permission to become engaged, and preparations for marriage will then be made. In certain communities, the young man must not approach the parents directly. Instead, he must make arrangements with a formal matchmaker to work as an intermediary to propose marriage on his behalf. However, a young man can also declare his intention for marriage by removing the girl's scarf or hair adornments. Even if the girl wishes to accept, it will be expected that she put up a resistance and shout loudly at the man. In such a scenario, if the girl does not demand her accessories back, then she has tacitly accepted his proposal. By asking for her items back, she officially rejects the young man and the process begins anew.

In communities which carry out the visiting-girls ritual, it is very rare for males and females to interact socially or romantically before the ceremony. Indeed, formal courting before the ritual is outright forbidden in certain Dai villages. If the meeting at the visiting-girl ceremony does not result in an engagement, then the young women may be forced to participate in another ritual, or they may have the chance to be courted by men outside the ritual, so long as she has participated in at least one ceremony which did not bear fruit.

Rachelanne Smith

Further Readings

An, C., and Liu, B. *Where the Dai People Live*. Beijing: Foreign Languages, 1985.

Curriculum Corporation. *Access Asia: Secondary Teaching and Learning Units*. Melbourne, Australia: University of Melbourne, 1998.

Friedrich, Paul, and Levinson, David. *Encyclopedia of World Cultures: Russia and Eurasia*. New York: Macmillan, 1994.

"The Jingpo Ethnic Group." http://www.msdchina.org/userfiles/file/pdf/Jingpo.pdf (Accessed on August 19, 2012).

Wolchover, Natalie. "Five Strange Courting Rituals from around the World." In *Life's Little Mysteries*. Livescience.com New York: Tech Media Network, 2012. http://www.livescience.com/33020-strange-courting-rituals-from-around-world.html (Accessed on March 9, 2014).

WASHING HANDS WITH COW'S URINE

In a village in western Ethiopia, a Nuer man in an early morning preparing for the day stopped beside a urinating calf and washed his hands in the stream. In the cattle camps of South Sudan, a Dinka youth, who would spend the dry season living close to his herd, washed his hands and face using cow's urine. Young men and women living in the camps also used cow's urine to beautify themselves by dusting their heads with the ashes from a cow-dung fire, then washing hands and faces with urine to create striking white skullcaps against their dark brown skin. Further south, in Tanzania, a Parakuyu woman washed her hands in cow's urine as she prepared to work with milk. None of these men and women thought that using cattle urine to wash was unclean. They are all pastoralists, people whose way of life centers around their livestock and particularly their cattle. East African pastoral groups (including the Nuer of South Sudan and Ethiopia, the Dinka of South Sudan, the Dassanetch of Ethiopia, the Maasai of Kenya and Tanzania, and the Parakuyu of Tanzania) have traditionally used cattle urine in multiple practical ways. In addition to washing with it, they use it as a disinfectant for cleaning wounds and to wash containers used for cooking and storing food. When they use fresh milk to make butter and cheese, urine disinfects the utensils and helps with the curdling process. Nuer and Dinka men bleach their black hair blond using a combination of cow's urine and ashes.

All of these practices reflect the practical and cultural importance of cattle for traditional East African pastoral societies. Cattle are the only animals whose urine they use in these ways, even though they also raise sheep and goats, and they rely on all of their animals for meat, hides, and milk. Their all-encompassing use of the resources provided by cattle reflects a deep relationship between East African pastoralists and their cows, bulls, and oxen. In Nuer, Dinka, and Maasai belief systems, cattle are seen as gifts from the gods; for all pastoral groups, the animals have spiritual, aesthetic, and social value as well as economic importance. Pastoralists use cattle sacrifice as a way of communicating with gods and spirits. They consider their animals to be beautiful as well as valuable. Herdsmen have favorite cows or bulls, and Nuer and Dinka men will adopt names shared with a favorite ox. Dinka men and women use scarification to make permanent designs on their skin inspired by the curves of their cattle's horns. Herders compose and sing songs to and about their beasts.

Traditionally, cattle also bound pastoralists' extended families and communities together through inheritance and complicated patterns of ownership in family herds, although pastoral people's integration into cash economies has undermined these systems by allowing young men to work for wages and buy cattle of their own instead of depending on their extended families for access to this important resource. However, cows still remain an important ingredient in social order. Many pastoral societies use them to formalize marriages through *bridewealth*, a practice in which a groom and his family present cattle to the family of his bride.

However, a competing tradition continues to contribute to social disorder through the practice of cattle-raiding. This is an ancient custom, sometimes sanctioned by religious belief. The Maasai, for example, believe that their god N'gai gave them all the cattle in the world at the beginning of time, which means that taking other people's cows is simply a reclaiming of their own. The influx of guns into the region, particularly in areas like South Sudan which has undergone prolonged periods of warfare, has made cattle-raiding a deadly activity for entire societies, not just the raiders. It continues because cattle provide pastoralists with social status. Even their smell can be important; among the Dassanetch, smelling like a cow traditionally meant fertility and high status, since people without cattle had to practice the less prestigious occupation of fishing. Men washed themselves with cattle urine specifically to attain this odor that signaled their wealth and desirability to women.

The practice of washing with urine is still widespread in the East Africa's pastoral regions. Some groups have adopted ways of life in which livestock is less important. Others stopped in response to European colonial officials or missionaries from Europe and America, who did not think that urine was an appropriate medium for washing. Yet, members of ethnic groups like the Nuer, Dinka, Dassanetch, Maasai, and Parakuyu have continued the practice into the recent past or up to the present. The environments many of these groups inhabit are difficult places to make a living because of their climate. Some areas are prone to drought, making the ability of livestock to move from place to place an important asset. Much of South Sudan, where the Nuer and Dinka live, is dry for four months of the year and swampy for the remainder. By using all parts of their beasts—even urine and dung (solid waste) from their beloved cattle—pastoral people were able to meet their material needs despite difficult conditions.

As these ethnic groups have become more integrated into the national societies to which they belong, many people move back and forth among places with different sets of behavioral expectations. However, in home villages and cattle camps, traditions such as using cow's urine for cleansing are still practiced as part of the long-standing relationship between cows and people. Poverty, political disorder, and the remoteness of some pastoralists' homes also make it difficult for governments and nongovernmental organizations to provide them with reliable supplies of clean water. This means that the need to reserve water for drinking and cooking (which may have originally led people to begin to wash with cow's urine) is still an important concern. As places like the young country of South Sudan push to modernize through increased access to infrastructure and education, this custom may eventually disappear. For the present, it continues to be an expression of the closeness of East African pastoralists to their cattle.

Sara C. Jorgensen

Further Readings

"Dinka Cattle Camp: Southern Sudan." *National Geographic Live!* September 6, 2011. http://www.youtube.com/watch?v=lt-tTVoj_D8 (Accessed on November 30, 2012).

Evans-Prichard, E. E. *The Nuer: A Description of the Modes of Livelihood and Political Institutions of a Nilotic People.* Oxford, UK: Clarendon Press, 1940.

Thibodeaux, Raymond. "Southern Sudan's Rush to Modernize Threatens Traditions." *VOA News.* October 28, 2009. http://www.voanews.com/content/a-13-2005-08-16-voa35-66934932/377375.html (Accessed on November 30, 2012).

WHUPPITY SCOORIE CHILDREN'S CELEBRATION

Spring in Scotland brings flowers and rain showers. It also brings the celebration of the ancient custom of Whuppity Scoorie, a tradition that commemorates the approach of spring. Specifically, the event celebrates the increasing number of daylight hours which usually come with the spring season. Whuppity Scoorie is supposed to date back to at least the mid-eighteenth century. The earliest recorded instance of the celebration was in the nineteenth century, when it was still referred to as the Wee Bell Ceremony. In the town of Lanark in the Scottish lowlands, Whuppity Scoorie is celebrated in early March mostly by children, but the adults of the town participate as well.

On the first of March, the children of Lanark line up at Lanark Cross near St. Nicholas Kirk Church. At 6:00 P.M., the town's "wee bells" ring. These are different from the traditional church bells, and they do not ring for the six-month period before Whuppity Scoorie. When the bells actually ring, the children run about in circles while swinging paper balls over their heads and making as much noise as possible. After they have run three laps around the church, the adults around them throw coins into the air which the children scramble to collect as soon as possible. There used to be prizes given out to the first boy and girl who were able to run the three circles first, but that practice has largely been discontinued because of potential injuries to the younger children participating. Following this event, there usually is a further week of activities for the entire community.

Another part of the Whuppity Scoorie tradition, which is celebrated less nowadays because of potential violence, has the young boys from Lanark meeting up with the boys from New Lanark and the two groups engage in a fight. They were only allowed to fight with their caps tied to the ends of pieces of string, but this often descended into fisticuffs. As a result, this portion of the celebration is slowly being phased out.

Little is known about the celebration's origins or the festival's symbolic purpose. However, there are many theories about the potential reasons for Whuppity Scoorie, including a symbolic cleansing such as the ones taking place in other parts of the British Isles where the dark days of winter were erased via this ritual. From an etymological point of view, "Scooring" is another term for cleaning that is frequently used in Scotland. Some believe the tradition goes back to the pagan period, where people believed that making as much noise as possible would ward off evil spirits and allow them an easier life. There is yet another historical theory that goes back to the late thirteenth and early fourteenth centuries when an English soldier went to the church in Lanark to escape William Wallace and the Scottish forces. Supposedly he had to circle the church three times, all the while shouting, "Sanctuary" before he was allowed inside. His pursuers were simultaneously shouting "Up at ye!" The combination of the two pieces of dialogue became blurred over time and thus formed the contemporary name of the celebration.

Rachelanne Smith

Further Readings

Buchanan, Josephine. *Insight Guide Scotland.* New York: Discovery, 2005.

Griffiths, Jay. *A Sideways Look at Time.* New York: Tarcher Penguin Group USA, 2004.

Hazlitt, W. Carew, and John Brand. *Faiths and Folklore: A Dictionary of National Beliefs, Superstitions and Popular Customs, Past and Prsent, Current with Their Classical Foreign Analogues, Described and Illustrated, Volume I.* London: Reeves and Turned Publishers, 1905 and digitized in 2006.

"Whuppity Scoorie." *Traditional Sports of the British Isles.* March 30, 2010. http://misterda vid.typepad.com/traditional_sports/whuppity-scoorie/ (Accessed on September 1, 2012).

WIFE-CARRYING COMPETITION

The unusual wife-carrying competition, which is held on the first Saturday of July in Sonkajarvi, Finland, has been an annual event since 1992. During the event, males carry females through an obstacle course, attempting to achieve a finishing time of less than one minute. The contest is referred to as *eukonkanto* in Finnish, which officially means "wife-carrying race" but more accurately translates to "old hag-carrying race."

The race course in its original form included rocky terrain, fences that had to be scaled, brooks, and other obstacles, but the course has been adapted for the modern era. Today, sand is used instead of rocks, a pool has been substituted for the original brook, and the fences remain. The 831-foot-long course (253 meters), which is surfaced with sand, gravel, and grass, includes a 3.2-foot deep and 30-foot-long (roughly 1 meter by 9.14 meters) water obstacle that must be waded through, a pit of sawdust, and two fences. Men carry their female partners, who may or may not be their wives, through the obstacle course in heats of two. The female participant is required to weigh at least 108 pounds (48 kilograms). If she does not, her partner carries a backpack filled with weights so that he is lugging at least the equivalent weight of 108 pounds while competing. The woman wears a helmet to protect herself if dropped; if this occurs, the team incurs a fifteen-second penalty. The man is allowed to wear a belt as the sole piece of equipment that the woman can hang onto. The victors of the contest win the woman's weight in beer and competition-related memorabilia. Runners-up are awarded prizes for the most entertaining couple, the best costume, and the strongest carrier.

The contest is held in Sonkajarvi, Finland, which boasts 4,800 residents and is located approximately six hours north of Helsinki, Finland's capital city.

Aleksander Pihlainen and Siiri Salli from Finland compete during the Wife-Carrying World Championship competition in Sonkajarvi, Finland, in 2013. (AP Photo/Roni Rekomaa, Lehtikuva)

The competition was originally created to draw interest to the community, and it has been followed by the creation of other unique summer festivals, including sauna sitting, swamp football, and cell phone throwing.

The number of couples participating in the event has grown steadily over the years. Contestants hail from different nations, including Australia, Estonia, Germany, Great Britain, Ireland, Israel, South Korea, and the United States. As the contest has grown in popularity, it has inspired knock-off contests in the United States, Australia, Ireland, China, and India, among other nations. In fact, former basketball star Dennis Rodman from the United States competed in the 2005 wife-carrying competition, but he could not complete the course due to its high level of difficulty.

The contest's origins are disputed and multiple legends exist. One story claims that in the 1800s a Finnish bandit named Rosvo-Ronkainen and his gang of followers went to nearby villages and robbed the inhabitants of their food while also stealing their women; the thieves would carry the women away on their backs. A second historical tale claims that Rosvo-Ronkainen, in training to be an outlaw, accepted soldiers into his troop only after they proved their worth by racing through a challenging course carrying heavy sacks filled with live pigs or grain. Finally, a third legend states that young men would travel to surrounding areas, steal other men's wives, carry them away on their backs, and later marry the women.

During the actual competition, the contestants have developed several popular strategies for carrying the woman that have been perfected over the years

WIFE-CARRYING COMPETITION, HONG KONG STYLE

Apparently, Finland's tradition of the unusual wife-carrying competition has been adopted in other parts of the globe. Since 2008, a similar competition takes place in Hong Kong during February for the celebration of Valentine's Day. The adapted form of this competition takes place inside a shopping mall, and the contestants often wear superhero costumes and even Chinese wedding outfits. In a similar fashion as the Finnish tradition, the man carries his wife on his back and tries to go over a series of obstacles. However, in the Hong Kong version, the couple is also required to reach down to pick up roses hidden among pools filled with red and pink balloons. The winners routinely receive prizes offered by the event's sponsors, which often are stores in the shopping center.

Javier A. Galván

especially for this type of competition. Estonians have created what is known as the Estonian Carry, which is quite popular as it creates good balance and even weight distribution. This style involves the woman hanging upside-down with the front of her body pressed against her partner's back; her legs are locked at the front of his neck and her arms wrap around his waist for security. Her face often falls at the same level as his rear end. Other common carrying styles include the woman lying around her partner's shoulders like a boa constrictor, an over-the-shoulder carry, the fireman's carry, and the traditional piggyback style.

In 2012, thirty-eight couples competed in front of 8,000 attendees. For the fourth year in a row, Taisto Miettinen and his wife Kristiina Haapanen of Finland won with a time of 1.00.22 minutes. From 2000 to 2001 and again from 2003 to 2007, Estonians won the competition; two brothers, the Uusorgs, dominated the event by winning four of the seven years. The Estonians frequent victories have been attributed to their creation of the Estonian carry, which they created specifically for this event. Prior to the invention of that technique, most competitors carried their wives piggyback style, which is not as streamlined of a method. The world record—which was set in 2000—is 55.5 seconds and is held by Margo Uusorg and Birgit Ulricht of Estonia. Jouni and Tiina Jussila hold the Finnish record of 56.7 seconds.

In addition to the wife-carrying competition, on the same weekend a 100 meter (383 feet) wife-carrying sprint and wife-carrying team competitions occur. The former event occurs on a gravel and sand track and has a 1-meter-deep water obstacle (3 feet). Couples run the qualifying round with approximately five to ten other couples, and the first three finalists of each heat advance to the next round until only three couples remain. The wife-carrying team competition follows the same rules as the wife-carrying world championship competition except that there are three men on each team who carry the "wife" in turns. At the exchange point, the carrier has to drink the official "wife-carrying drink," which is beer, before continuing with the race.

Overall, the spirit of the competition is fun and whimsical. The official rules state that competitors must have fun and that becoming a master wife-carrier is 50 percent fun and 50 percent hard work. The competition has been described as benefitting the participants' relationships as becoming one with one's partner during the race improves performance. A potential critique of the contest is that it reinforces stereotypical gender roles, as the men are active agents who move freely through the course while the women are passively carried. Most see it is a fun form of exercise that has health benefits, such as building strength and endurance, while also helping to foster social relationships.

Sharla A. Blank

Further Readings

Caple, Jim. "Get Off My Back, Honey." *ESPN.com.* July 5, 2005. http://sports.espn.go.com/espn/pring?id=2100658&type=story (Accessed on July 24, 2012).
Finland Tips & Articles. "Wife-Carrying World Championships: A Guide to Finland's Festival of Marital Trust." *Lonely Planet.* 2013. http://www.lonelyplanet.com/finland/travel-tips-and-articles/77266 (Accessed on February 14, 2014).
Sonkajarvi: Official Website for the Wife Carrying World Championships. http://www.eukonkanto.fi/en/. (Accessed on February 14, 2014).
"2012 World Wife Carrying Contest." *CBS Newspath.* 2012. http://www.wtsp.com/news/article/263056/58/2012-World-Wife-Carrying-Contest (Accessed on August 15, 2012).

WODAABE COURTSHIP DANCE AND FESTIVAL

The Wodaabe tribe of Nigeria became famous for its flirtation festival and courtship dance, where in contrast to other cultures of the world, male dancers try to impress women and win their attention and hearts. The flirtation dance and the festival are both named Gerewol, which in Wodaabe language means "to line up." After dancing, young men usually line up in order to be chosen by a group of women acting as judges. Anthropologists working among the Wodaabe people in Northern Nigeria frequently likened this event to beauty contests in Western cultures. However, in Wodaabe traditions, young men are the contestants and young women are the judges. Young women select the most handsome dancer either for a couple of nights or for a prospective marriage. The Wodaabe tribe is known for their unusual marriage system—both men and women can be married to two people at the same time. Members of the clan usually arrange the first marriage, known as *koogal*, in early childhood. The second marriage (called *teegal*) is considered a love marriage, and women choose their future potential partners at the time of the Gerewol festival. The Wodaabe people are also known for their wife-stealing practices, which also take place at this festival.

The Wodaabe is a small pastoralist tribe, which belongs to the Fulani ethnic group. A greater proportion of Wodaabe people live in northern Nigeria. They are known as trans-Saharan pastoralists and traders who also move across Niger and

Wodaabe men dance at the Courtship Dance and Festival in Nigeria. (Iconotec/Stockphoto Pro.com)

northern Cameroon. The flirtation festival takes place once a year, and it usually coincides with the end of fasting for Ramadan and the end of the rainy season. It usually takes place in one of the regional markets, where the tribal meetings and other social gatherings are held. The festival location is kept a secret, and it is released to people only a few days before the event. In-Gall, a town located in northwest Niger, is the most famous place for the Gerewol. Festivals held there usually attract many people of the Wodaabe and other nomadic tribes in the region. Over 50,000 people may gather together to celebrate these festivals.

The Gerewol festival requires a lot of preparations during the year, including practicing popular tribal dances and songs, purchasing clothes, and preparing jewelry and makeup. Wodaabe boys are taught to take care of their body and to dance from a young age. They spend incomparably more time on their beautification than the Wodaabe girls. Body care is considered as important as cattle-herding and trading. According to the Wodaabe beauty ideal, a man should be slim and tall, have a long face, wide eyes with white sclera, thin lips, white teeth, a long and straight nose, and light skin tone. The endurance of the Wodaabe men, their ability to present themselves, and their pleasant manners—which are attractive to the women—are all equally valued. In preparation for the festival, young men paint their face either in red or in pale yellow tones; then, they apply a symmetrical tribal design. In addition, they shave their hairline high, to make their face visibly longer. The Wodaabe men never cut their hair; instead, they braid it in a unique hairstyle. On the day of the festivities, men wear indigo skirts, which are especially handwoven and hand-dyed for the occasion. Male dancers decorate themselves with cowry shell necklaces, which are inserted in their turban's ostrich feathers. These attributes in Wodaabe culture are considered highly erotic because cowry shells symbolize female genitals, and an ostrich feather inserted upright in the turban symbolizes a penis.

The Gerewol festival traditionally comprises a large number of various activities, such as repetitive choral performances, a hypnotic character, opera, line dancing, war dances, and competitions that include a beauty contest and camel races. The most important dances during the Gerewol festival are the Gerewol and the Yaake dances. The Gerewol dance is considered a physical beauty contest, with dancers painting their face in red. The Yaake dance is a contest of charm. The Yaake dancers paint their face in a light yellow color, and young men dance in line in front of the women eligible for marriage. To draw the women's attention, the Yaake dancers may straighten themselves, standing on their tip-toes, and imitate a flying bird. They open their eyes wide and then roll them, fixating their glance for a moment prior to direction change. At the same time, they try to vibrate their throat and lips, mimicking a large graceful bird. The Gerewol festival lasts seven days. At the end of the seventh day, male dancers line up in order to be chosen by the jury. The best performer of the year is chosen by the three beautiful girls, who are traditionally selected by the elders for this purpose. These girls are usually of high social status. They could be the daughters of the past winners. To indicate their preference, they walk toward the winner and perform a gentle hand gesture. The status of the Gerewol winner is highly prestigious in Wodaabe society.

During the festival, the participants eat as little as they can and drink performance-enhancing concoctions made of brewed tree bark, which have a hallucinogenic effect. Consequently, some performers fall into a trance when dancing. The Gerewol dance is considered dangerous by some members of the tribe because it includes elements of magic. The Wodaabe people, as well as other surrounding tribes, describe Gerewol as a festival led by evil forces. Although most Wodaabe people are followers of Islam, men traditionally use magic spells, potions, and some elements of sorcery to make their body beautiful and strong, improve performance, attract women, and harm other competitors. While acknowledging their belief in god, they say that the Gerewol is not a time for prayer.

The dancers' objective is to attract young women from a different clan and to proceed with the love marriage. Flirting among men and women usually occurs at the time of dancing. The attracted young woman usually follows her preferred dancer to the bush. The chosen man is required to be polite and use poetic language to further seduce his partner. If a man is too fast and aggressive, the girl may choose to run away from him. The newly formed couples may spend a couple of nights together, sleeping on the young men's mat in the bush. If they find themselves compatible, they go one step further and proceed with the marriage. Subsequently, the girl takes the chosen partner to her parents. At this first family meeting, the groom negotiates with the parents the price to be paid to them in exchange for marrying their daughter. The bridal price is usually paid in the form of livestock from the herd of the girl's future husband. The young boy then introduces the girl to his clan. Women who are already in a *teegal* (second) marital relationship may also become attracted to a dancer and can be taken by him to his clan. Various life-threatening conflicts may arise between the new and the former husbands, who often claim their wife back. For a man in Wodaabe culture, wife attracting and stealing is considered a positive practice, and wife-losing is considered a disgrace within their cultural traditions.

The Wodaabe culture is not static. An increasing frequency of droughts with their associated lack of grazing and water resources for animals has led many young people to abandon their pastoralist activities and move to cities. Once they migrate to urban areas, the Wodaabe people may celebrate the Gerewol festival twice a year. Since 1970, the Gerewol activities have become even more popular, with new messages promoted throughout the festivities warning against the marginalization of the nomadic groups and urbanization-related sedentary lifestyles. Nowadays, many dances are performed by Wodaabe people as part of the tourism and entertainment industry at any time of the year. However, such performances are no longer directly related to the Wodaabe cultural traditions linking dances with sex and marriage.

Victoria Team

Further Readings

Anthropology and the Human Condition. "Wodaabe Courtship and Marriage." National University of Singapore. http://sc2218.wetpaint.com/page/WoDaaBe+Courtship+and+Marriage (Accessed on October 24, 2012).

Beckwith, Carol. "Niger's Wodaabe: People of the Taboo." *National Geographic* (1983): 483–509, http://iws.collin.edu/mbailey/wodaabe.pdf (Accessed on October 24, 2012).

Bocquené, Henri. "The Dance and the Wodaabe." In *Memoirs of a Mbororo: The Life of Ndudi Umaru: Fulani. Nomad of Cameroon*, edited by Henri Bocquené, *Cameroon Studies*, 151–60. New York: Berghahn Books, 2002.

Bovin, Mette. "Nomadic Performance—Peculiar Culture? 'Exotic' Ethnic Performances of the Wodaabe Nomads of Niger." In *Recasting Ritual: Performance, Media, Identity*, edited by Felicia Hughes-Freeland and Mary M. Crain, 95–114. New York: Routledge, 2005.

GeneExpression. "Wodabout the Wodaabe?" http://www.gnxp.com/MT2/archives/002034.html (Accessed on October 24, 2012).

"Gereewol (Wodaabe)." In *Traditional Festivals. A Multicaltural Encyclopedia*, edited by Christian Roy, 180–83. Santa Barbara, CA: ABC-CLIO, Inc., 2005.

McAllister, Peter. *Manthropology: The Science of the Inadequate Modern Male.* Sydney, Australia: Hachette Australia Pty Ltd, 2009.

Stenning, Derrick J. *Savannah Nomads: A Study of the Wodaabe Pastoral Fulani of Western Bornu Province Northern Region, Nigeria.* Munster and Hamburg, Germany: International African Institute, 1994.

WORLD BEARD AND MOUSTACHE CHAMPIONSHIPS

Since the beginning of time, men around the world have considered facial hair a sign of masculinity, virility, and strength. In ancient Egypt, both male and female rulers wore false beards, sometimes made of gold, to demonstrate their power. In

One of the competitors at the World Beard and Moustache Competition twirls his moustache to prepare for the event. (AP Photo/Al Grillo)

the Old Testament, God had forbidden male Hebrews to cut or shave their facial hair. Not only was facial hair a symbol of man's freedom, but the act of shaving would mutilate the body created in His image. Male Muslims, Sikhs, and Rastafarians also wear full beards based on this original religious instruction. Pre-Christian pagans wore elaborate moustaches and beards; Viking, Anglo-Saxon, Celtic, and Slavic pagan carvings exist of men with full facial hair, sometimes braided, and decorated with jewels. Viking men often had special combs just for their beard. Turkic, Persian, and Hindu warriors are also depicted in paintings with moustaches, beards, or both; male descendants of these warriors maintained their tradition of wearing luxurious moustaches for centuries. The more wealth and power a man had, the fuller he should wear his moustache.

In Europe and North America, the male fashion of full facial hair began to die as razors became sharper and more affordable. Early razors, made of bronze, were expensive and difficult to keep sharp. Alternatives to such a razor were fish scales, sharpened clam shells, and shark teeth. Once steel replaced bronze for swords, it also became the metal of choice for scissors and razors. By the sixteenth century, several beard styles emerged: the Spanish spade beard, the English square cut beard, the Van Dyke, the forked beard, and the stiletto beard. In 1740, English inventor Benjamin Huntsman produced the first superior hard steel grade in Sheffield for the first modern straight razor. As the British and German steel industries expanded, the price of straight razors became affordable for more men so they could shave themselves if they wished, although shaving with a straight razor remained a dangerous practice. In 1901, Gillette invented an inexpensive safety razor that made it possible for working men to shave daily. With the invention of chemical warfare, soldiers had to wear gas masks that would fit properly only on a clean-shaven face. Starting in World War I (1914–1918), all American soldiers were required to shave every day. Visions of these American heroes in the first newsreels and in homecoming parades inspired young men to follow the fashion. A man's value was no longer determined by the fullness of his beard, but the service he could give to his country, his level of education, and the amount of work that he could do. Working men in the United States began to equate beards with laziness, ignorance, poverty, and old age. Moustaches became associated with movie villains, immigrants, and the eccentric Spanish painter Salvador Dali who would use his sharply waxed moustache to catch flies. If an American man wanted to apply for a job, he was expected to have a clean-shaven face, short hair, a buttoned down shirt, and a tie.

During the civil rights movement in the 1960s and the Vietnam War (1955–1975), men in the United States began to question the clean-shaven male authority figures in government, military, and police uniforms. To demonstrate their rejection of "the establishment," they let their hair and beards grow. The 1960s and 1970s saw a Renaissance of male facial hair styles—sideburns, mutton chop whiskers, goatees, and handlebar moustaches—among all classes of men, popularized by musicians and movie stars. Europeans copied the American fashion, in the process rediscovering the facial hair styles of their ancestors. While facial hair once again fell out of mainstream fashion in the 1980s, European men who wished to preserve their facial hair as a statement of ethnic pride or simple vanity formed beard and moustache "fraternities." Such beard and moustache clubs first became popular in Germany.

While the Italians insist that the first beard and moustache competition took place in their country during the 1970s, the German First Höfener Beard Club sponsored the first World Beard and Moustache Competition in Höfen-Enz, Germany in 1990. Representatives from one dozen German beard and moustache fraternities, as well as Swedish, Norwegian, and Italian groups, participated in the event. A world championship did not take place again until 1995. Since then, the championship takes place every two years; so far it has occurred in Germany, Norway, Sweden, the United Kingdom, and the United States.

Beard and moustache clubs and "teams" formed in the United States after people heard about the European competition. The first World Beard and Moustache Championships in the United States took place in Carson City, Nevada, in 2003. While only seven Americans entered that competition, five won gold medals. Today, American teams have local, state, and national competitions in order to prepare; they also have a national team, Beard Team USA. In 2009, the United States established itself as the leader of the sport that Americans call "bearding." At the most recent world championship in Trondheim, Norway, in 2011, the United States sent the largest delegation, but they were beaten by the Germans.

BEARD TEAM USA WINS BIG AT THE 2013 WORLD BEARD COMPETITION IN GERMANY

In November 2013, the World Beard and Moustache Competition was held in Leinfelden-Echterdingen, Germany. This time, Beard Team USA brought home some of the top awards, including: Sean Raiger for his Fu Manchu style, Jeff Langum for Full Beard Natural, Burke Kenny for the Style Moustache category, Patrick Fette for first place in the English Moustache category, Aarne Bielefeldt for Free Beard Freestyle, and Dan Lawlor for Freestyle Moustache. This year's delegation included a large number of contestants from California, many of whom also won second place awards in this internationally recognized competition.

Javier A. Galván

World Beard and Moustache Championships participants must select a category in which to compete—moustache, partial beard, or full beard. From there, they must cultivate their facial hair to meet at least one of six possible standards: moustache, partial beard, or full beard classes. Accepted styles range from "natural" (no styling involved) to "freestyle" (unrestrictive, creative styling). Wax, hair spray, and other hair cosmetics are allowed for styled facial hair classes; unnatural hair color, false facial hair, hair extensions or hair pins are strictly prohibited from competition. While unstated in the rules, most competitors also dress in a costume that would appropriately complement their facial hair. Judges (called "jury members") must give a score between five and ten points to each entrant, with the highest scores of 10, 9.5, and 9 given only once by each judge in each class. These scores are submitted anonymously, and points are counted by the head of the judging panel. The panel selects a first-, second-, and third-place winner based on point totals; each winner receives a prize, and all participants receive a diploma.

Rachel Wexelbaum

Further Readings

Ames, Michael, and F. Stone Roberts. *The World Beard and Moustache Championships: The First Official Book.* New York: Bloomsbury USA, 2005.

Reighley, Kurt B. "Chapter 4: Shave and a Haircut: Grooming: Barbershops, Straight Razors, Championship Facial Hair." In *United States of Americana: Backyard Chickens, Burlesque Beauties & Handmade Bitters: A Field Guide to the New American Roots Movement.* New York: HarperCollins Publishers, 2010, 67–86.

"World Beard & Moustache Championships." 2011. http://www.worldbeardchampion ships.com/ (Accessed on June 29, 2012).

Y

YAMS, SEX, AND MARRIAGE IN TROBRIAND TRADITIONS

The Trobriand Islands are currently known as the Kiriwina Islands, which belong to Papua New Guinea. They became known as the "Islands of Love" after famous anthropological writings, describing culturally approved seductive behavior, early initiation of sexual activity, absence of a traditional marriage ceremony, and sexual rituals accompanying annual yam festivals. This two-month long festivity included harvest distribution, dancing, and sexual activity in public. For example, with the permission of the village chief as part of the celebration, groups of girls were allowed to attack and rape men. They usually hid in bushes and attacked men from other villages. If the man was incapable of getting an erection, he was subjected to physical violence and humiliation. The girls would bite off his eyebrows, or defecate and urinate on him. Most men were cautious of these practices and usually walked in groups during the time of yam festivals.

Yam is a common name for species in the genus *Dioscorea*. These are perennial plants that produce starchy tubers, which can be cooked in a variety of ways, including roasting, grilling, baking, and mashing. Compared with sweet potatoes, yams are hardier and starchier. Men are the predominant growers of yam; they plant and cultivate yams, build the fences around the yam gardens, and collect the harvest. To store the harvest, villagers build special yam houses, which are linked with the prestige of the gardener. Yam distribution is closely linked to kinship. Men usually grow yams for their sisters, nieces, and daughters, but the harvested yams are usually given to their husbands. A special portion of the harvest also goes to the man's father, uncles, and the village chief. Most Trobrianders are subsistence growers. In addition to yams, they plant a variety of staples, including taro, tapioca, and sweet potatoes. In Trobriand culture, yam is a respected vegetable that has traditional meanings. It symbolizes wealth, power, and prosperity. For example, a village chief has the largest and best decorated yam house, which is usually full of yams. When the harvest is poor, people tend to destroy their yam houses. To increase their harvest, Trobrianders commonly use magic spells and rituals surrounding planting, cultivation, harvesting, and weather control. The planting, growing, harvesting, and storing of yams is frequently compared to human life stages—childhood, adulthood, older age, and existence in the form of a spirit after death. Yam contains several natural steroid-like substances, and yam consumption, as some researchers believe, may contribute to early sexual maturation.

Malinowski and Ellis were two famous anthropologists who worked in the Trobriand Islands in the early nineteenth century. In their book *The Sexual Life of*

Savages in North-Western Melanesia, they described that children from an early age were involved in sexual games and imitated adult sexual behaviors. First sexual experiences were usually encountered during early adolescence. Premarital sex was acceptable in the Trobriand culture. Seductive behaviors were encouraged among both men and women. Parents of the girls were responsible for teaching their daughters to exhibit this behavior, using specific movements, dances, charms, and persuasion skills. Banana-leaf skirts, bracelets, and shell decorations were used to make the body of the girl more attractive and adorable. Magic spells promoting attractiveness, persuasion skills, and acceptance by a sexual partner, as believed by Trobrianders, were passed from generation to generation. Each girl was encouraged to learn these spells and practice specific rituals and body image-related practices. Rejecting advances and changing sexual partners, by both men and women, were socially acceptable and frequently encouraged practices.

On the Trobriand Islands there was no traditional marriage ceremony. With time, young people, experiencing sexual pleasures, tended to see their preferred partner more frequently and to reject the advances of other young people of the opposite sex. To announce their intention to marry, the couple declares their plans in their parent's garden, usually in the morning. The new couple lived either in the young man's father's house, or in his maternal uncle's house. The young woman's father, brothers, and her uncles were responsible for provision of yams to the young couple.

Trobrianders traditionally believed that conception occurred when the child's spirit came unto a woman, usually when she is bathing, and they did not link it with sexual intercourse. According to their belief, sexual intercourse may have merely opened the way for the spirit of the child. Some researchers have suggested that yams have natural contraceptive substances, and that its consumption among the islanders might have masked the link between sexual intercourse and pregnancy. Trobriand fathers, lacking the understanding of conception, did not see the biological link that they shared with their children, viewing them as the offspring of the women to whom they were sexually attracted. Their sense of fatherhood was not well developed. Children were treated as property by Trobrianders, which belonged to a wife and her brothers. Having children prior to marriage was considered acceptable, and young girls with and without children had equal chances of being married. Divorce was considered acceptable, and husbands or wives could initiate it equally. Remarriage occurred frequently for both spouses.

The Trobriand Islands were part of British New Guinea, and they came under the rule of Australia in 1906. Subsequently, there were a lot of European Christian missionaries and other foreigners who resided on the Islands. Although Christian missionaries were promoting abstinence, monogamy, and controlled sexual behaviors, other colonial settlers were establishing and maintaining brothels. Sexually transmissible infections, which were introduced to the country by the foreigners in the late 1980s and early 1990s, had increased in prevalence. Native people were blamed for spreading them because of their perceivably immoral and uncontrolled sexual behaviors.

Published ethnographic works by Malinowski and Ellis describing Trobriand sex and marriage-related behaviors received interest beyond academia. Co-published fiction novels were mistakenly interpreted as facts and led to increased public curiosity about the islands. Later, public interest relating to these behaviors, boosted by tourism advertisements, gave rise to sexual tourism, including sexual experiences with children. Islanders' social values of sex and traditional practices were misinterpreted as promiscuity. Some writers openly accused Trobriand women of attracting sexual tourism because of their wearing of banana-leaf skirts, leaving their breasts naked and having open attitudes toward sexuality. They also blamed native women for having sex with tourists in exchange for money, neglecting the fact that foreign men had established prostitution on the island and promoted it, facilitating tourism. Child sex tourists believed that they had a lower risk of contracting sexually transmissible infections, including HIV/AIDS from the children. Supporters of human rights raised voices, and they took action against this type of "civilization." Many countries in the world extended their laws prohibiting sexual tourism extraterritorially.

Since the publication of the first ethnographic works during the late 1920s, the anthropologists working on the Trobriand Islands have not observed these extremely exotic traditional practices. Nowadays, these behaviors are equally exotic to Trobrianders themselves. Some authors, usually tourists or short-term visitors, have reported anecdotal evidence of men being raped by girls at the time of yam festivals in isolated villages. These stories were usually told and retold by someone else, and they were not directly observed by the authors. There are some views that yam festival-related male rape, if it occurs, should be promoted as a gang rape and not as exotic behavior. Contemporary Trobriand community approves and values adolescent sex as part of the transition to adulthood. Trobriand youth are now educated on safer sex practices, particularly since the early 1990s, when Papua New Guinea became an epicenter of the AIDS epidemic in the Pacific, and the "Islands of Love" became known also as the "Islands of Risk." Sexual freedom at the yam festivals nowadays is granted only for unmarried people.

Victoria Team

Further Readings

Lepani, Katherine. "Fitting Condoms on Culture: Rethinking Approaches to HIV Prevention in the Trobriand Islands of Papua New Guinea." In *Making Sense of AIDS: Culture, Sexuality, and Power in Melanesia*, edited by Leslie Butt and Richard Eves, 246–66. Honolulu: University of Hawaii Press, 2008.

Malinowski, Bronislaw, and Havelock Ellis. *The Sexual Life of Savages in North-Western Melanesia*. London: George Routledge and Sons, 1929.

Mosko, Mark S. "The Fractal Yam: Botanical Imagery and Human Agency in the Trobriands." *Journal of the Royal Anthropological Institute* 15, no. 4 (2009): 679–700.

Reed, Adam. "Contested Images and Common Strategies: Early Colonial Sexual Politics in the Massim." In *Sites of Desire/Economies of Pleasure: Sexualities in Asia and the Pacific*, edited by Lenore Manderson and Margaret Jolly, 48–71. Chicago: University of Chicago Press, 1997.

Senft, Gunter. "'Noble Savages' and the 'Islands of Love': Trobriand Islanders in 'Popular Publications.'" In *Pacific Answers to Western Hegemony: Cultural Practices of Identity Construction*, edited by Jürg Wassmann, 119–40. Oxford, UK: Berg Publishers, 1998.

Tree, Isabella. "Culture Shock." *Travel Intelligence.* http://www.travelintelligence.com/travel-writing/culture-shock (Accessed on September 20, 2012).

Weiner, Annette. "Trobriand Islands." *Encyclopedia of World Cultures.* 1996. http://www.encyclopedia.com/doc/1G2–3458000408.html (Accessed on September 20, 2012).

Weiner, Annette B. *The Trobrianders of Papua New Guinea.* New York: Holt, Rinehart and Winston, 1988.

Selected Bibliography

PRINTED SOURCES

Adhikari, Mohamed. *Not White Enough, Not Black Enough: Racial Identity in the South African Coloured Community.* Cleveland: Ohio University Press, 2005.

Alexander, Marc. *The Sutton Companion to British Folklore, Myths and Legends.* Stroud, UK: Sutton Publishing, 2005.

Ames, Michael, and Roberts F. Stone. *The World Beard and Moustache Championships: The First Official Book.* New York: Bloomsbury USA, 2005.

Azoy, G. Whitney. *Buzkash: Game and Power in Afghanistan.* 2nd ed. Long Grove, IL: Waveland Press, 2003.

Barrett, Leonard E. *The Rastafarians.* Boston: Beacon Press, 1997.

Beauchamp, Monte. *Krampus!: The Devil of Christmas.* San Francisco: Last Gasp, 2010.

Bennett, Margaret. *Scottish Customs: From the Cradle to the Grave.* Edinburgh, Scotland: Birlinn Ltd, 2005.

Benson, John. *Eyewitness Travel Guide: Japan.* New York: DK Publishing, 2000.

Bigalke, Terance William. *Tana Toraja: A Social History of an Indonesian People.* Singapore: Singapore University Press, 2005.

Brooking, Tom. *The History of New Zealand.* Westport, CT: Greenwood Press, 2004.

Broom, Richard. *Aboriginal Australians.* 3rd ed. Sydney, Australia: Allen and Unwin, 2001.

Brown, Callum G. *Up-Helly-Aa: Customs, Culture and Community in Shetland.* New York: St. Martin's Press Inc., 1998.

Buckley, Thomas, and Alma Gottlieb, eds. *Blood Magic: The Anthropology of Menstruation.* Berkeley: University of California Press, 1988.

Budak, Ali. *Fasting in Islam and the Month of Ramadan: A Comprehensive Guide.* Translated by Suleyman Basaran. Somerset, NJ: The Light, 2006.

Burt, Susan M. "Naming, Re-naming and Self-Naming among Hmong-Americans." *Names.* Santa Barbara, CA: ABC-CLIO, Inc., 2004.

Capone, Stefania. *Searching for Africa in Brazil: Power and Tradition in Candomblé.* Durham, NC: Duke University Press, 2010.

Carroll, B. Anthony. *The History of Junkanoo, Part 2: The Individual Junkanoo Participants and Performers (1940–2005).* London: Author House, 2007.

Chagnon, Napoleon A. *Yanomamo—The Fierce People.* New York: Holt, Rinehart and Winston, 1968.

Chasteen, John Charles. "The Prehistory of Samba: Carnival Dancing in Rio de Janeiro, 1840–1917." *Journal of Latin American Studies* 28 (1996): 29–47.

Clark, Mary Ann. *Santería: Correcting the Myths and Uncovering the Realities of a Growing Religion.* Westport, CT: Praeger, 2007.

Cobo, Father Bernabe. *Inca Religion and Customs.* Austin: University of Texas Press, 1990.

Collins, Sandra. "'Samurai Politics: Japanese Cultural Identity in Global Sport—the Olympic Games as a Representational Strategy." *The International Journal of the History of Sport* 24, no. 3 (2007): 357–74.

Connolly, Paul. "Tuna Tossing." *The World's Weirdest Sports*. London: Murdoch, 2007.

Cost, Bruce. *Asian Ingredients: A Guide to the Foodstuffs of China, Japan, Korea, Thailand, and Vietnam*. New York: William Morrow Cookbooks, 2000.

Covarrubias, Miguel, and Adrián Vickers. *Island of Bali*. Jakarta, Indonesia: Periplus Editions, 2008.

Daeschner, J. R. *True Brits: A Tour of Great Britain in All Its Bog-Snorkelling, Shin-Kicking, and Cheese-Rolling Glory*. New York: Overlook Press, 2004.

Davidson, D. S. "Disposal of the Dead in Western Australia." *Proceedings of the Philosophical Society* 93, no. 1 (1949): 71–97.

Davis, Rod. *American Voudou: Journey into a Hidden World*. Denton: University of North Texas Press, 1999.

De la Torre, Miguel A. *Santería: The Beliefs and Rituals of a Growing Religion in America*. Grand Rapids, MI: William B. Eerdmans Publishing Company, 2004.

Deutsch, Jonathan, and Natalya Murakhver, eds. *They Eat That? A Cultural Encyclopedia of Weird and Exotic Food from around the World*. Santa Barbara, CA: ABC-CLIO, 2012.

De Witte, Marleen. *Long Live the Dead! Changing Funeral Celebrations in Asante, Ghana*. Amsterdam: Aksant Academic Publishers, 2001.

Douglass, Carrie B. *Bulls, Bullfighting and Spanish Identities*. Tucson: The University of Arizona Press, 1997.

Edmonds, Ennis Barrington. *Rastafari: From Outcasts to Culture Bearers*. New York: Oxford University Press, 2003.

Ember, Melvin, and Carol R. Ember, eds. *Countries and Their Cultures*. 3 Vols. New York: Macmillan, 2001.

Enning, Cornelia. *Placenta: The Gift of Life—The Role of the Placenta in Different Cultures, and How to Prepare and Use It as Medicine*. Oregon: Mother baby Press. 2007.

Epstein, Irving, ed. *The Greenwood Encyclopedia of Children's Issues Worldwide*. Westport, CT: Greenwood Press, 2007.

Fishbane, Simcha. "The Ritual of Kapparot." *Jewish Journal of Sociology* 50, no. 1/2 (2008): 67–75.

Frater, Jamie. *Listverse. Com's Ultimate Book of Bizarre Lists: Fascinating Facts and Shocking Trivia on Movies, Music, Crime, Celebrities, History, and More*. Berkeley, CA: Ulysses Press, 2010.

Galván, Javier A. *Culture and Customs of Bolivia*. Santa Barbara, CA: ABC-CLIO, 2011.

Galván, Javier A. *Culture and Customs of Puerto Rico*. Westport, CT: Greenwood Press, 2009.

García Rodero, Cristina, and J. M. Caballero Bonald. *Festivals and Ritual of Spain*. New York: Harry N Abrams Publishers, 1994.

Gibbon, Pierce. *Tribe: Endangered Peoples of the World*. London: Castle Illustrated, 2010.

Gouin, Margaret. *Tibetan Rituals of Death: Buddhist Funerary Practices*. New York: Routledge, 2010.

Grandin, Greg, Deborah T. Levinson, and Elizabeth Oglesby, eds. *The Guatemala Reader: History, Culture, Politics*. Durham, NC: Duke University Press. 2011.

Grenhouse, Linda. "Court, Citing Religious Freedom, Voids a Ban on Animal Sacrifice." *The New York Times*, June 12, 1993, 9.

Gupta, Aman. *Human Rights of Indigenous Peoples*. New Delhi: Isha Books, 2005.

Hamon, Raeann, and Bron Ingoldsby, eds. *Mate Selection across Cultures*. Thousand Oaks, CA: Sage Publications, 2003.

Hast, Dorothea E., James R. Cowdery, and Stan Scott. *Exploring the World of Music: An Introduction to Music from a World Music Perspective*. Dubuque, IA: Kendall and Hunt, 1999.

Heine, Peter. *Food Culture in the Near East, Middle East, and North Africa*. Westport, CT: Greenwood Press, 2004.

Henderson, Helene. *Holidays, Festivals, and Celebrations of the World Dictionary*. Detroit: Omnigraphics, 2005.

Hobart, Angela. *People of Bali*. Oxford, UK: Blackwell Publishers, 2001.

Hogue, Charles Leonard. *Latin American Insects and Entomology*. Berkeley: University of California Press, 1993.

Hopkins, Jerry. *Extreme Cuisine: The Weird and Wonderful Foods That People Eat*. Berkeley, CA: Periplus, 2004.

Huber, Patrick. "A Short History of 'Redneck': The Fashioning of a Southern White Masculine Identity." *Southern Cultures* 1 (1995): 145–66.

Hughes, Susan, and April Fast. *Cuba: The Culture*. New York: Crabtree, 2004.

International Rogaining Federation. *Rogaining, 2010 & Beyond: Strategic Plan for the Sport of Rogaining*. Central Park, Victoria, Australia: International Rogaining Federation, 2007.

Jagannathan, Maithly. *South Indian Hindu Festivals and Traditions*. New Delhi: Abhinav Publications, 2005.

Jahnke, Robert, and Huia Tomlins Jahnke. "The Politics of Maori Image and Design." *Pukenga Kokero Journal* 7, no. 1 (Summer, 2003): 5–31.

Jensen, Robert, and Rebecca Thornton. "Early Female Marriage in the Developing World." In *Gender, Development, and Marriage*, edited by Caroline Sweetman, Vol. 11, No. 2, 9–19. Oxford, UK: Oxfam Publications, 2003.

Johnson, Andreas. *Baba Yaga: The Ambiguous Mother and Witch of Russian Folklore*. New York: Peter Lang, 2010.

Joseph, Suad, ed. *Encyclopedia of Women and Islamic Cultures: Family, Body, and Sexuality, Vol. 3*. Leiden, The Netherlands: Brill Academic Publishing, 2006.

Kaler, I. Gusti Ketut. *Ngaben: Mengapa May at Dibakar? (Ngaben: Why Corpse Is Burn)*. Denpasar, Indonesia: Yayasan Dharma Naradha, 1993.

Kalman, Bobbie. *India: The Land (Lands, Peoples, and Cultures)*. New York: Crabtree Publishing Company, 2009.

Kamachi, Noriko. *Culture and Customs of Japan*. Westport, CT: Greenwood Press, 1999.

Katz, Solomon H., and William Woys Weaver, eds. *Encyclopedia of Food Culture*. New York: Thompson Learning, 2003.

Khalaf, Sulayman. "Camel Racing in the Gulf: Notes on the Evolution of a Traditional Cultural Sport." *Anthropos* 94 (1999): 85–106.

King, Michael. *Moko: Maori Tattooing in the 20th Century*. Auckland, New Zealand: David Bateman, 1992.

Kislenko, Arne. *Culture and Customs of Thailand*. Westport, CT: Greenwood Press, 2004.

Knight, Dave. *Medellin, Colombia: Including Its History, the Festival of Flowers, Candelaria Church, Plaza Cisneros, and More*. New York: Earth Eyes Travel Guides, 2012.

Krieger, Michael. *Conversations with the Cannibals: The End of the Old South Pacific*. Hopewell, NJ: Ecco Press, 1994.

Kuper, Hilda. *The Swazi, a South African Kingdom: Case Studies in Cultural Anthropology.* Orlando, FL: Holt Rinehart and Winston, 1985.

Kuss, Melina. *Music in Latin America and the Caribbean: An Encyclopedic History.* Austin: University of Texas Press, 2008.

Lall, R. Manohar. *Among the Hindus: A Study of Hindu Festivals.* New Delhi, Asian Educational Service, 2004.

Lefeber, Yvonne, and Henk W. A. Voorhoeve. *Indigenous Customs in Childbirth and Child Care.* Amsterdam: Van Gorcum Publishers, 1998.

Leriton, Richard. *Weddings by Design: A Guide to Non-Traditional Ceremonies.* New York: Harper Collins, 1993.

Le Vay, Benedict. *Eccentric Britain: The Bradt Guide to Britain's Follies and Foibles.* Bucks, UK: Bradt Travel Guides, 2005.

Levine, Nancy E., and Joan Silk. "Why Polyandry Fails: Sources of Instability in Polyandrous Marriages." *Current Anthropology* 38, no. 3 (June 1997): 375–98.

Levy, Patricia. *Cultures of the World: Ghana.* New York: Marshall Cavendish, 1999.

Liedewij, Loorbach. *Sullivan's List: The 100 Most Amazing Events in the World.* Middlesex, UK: Lightning Publishing Ltd, 2011.

Lior, Noa, and Tara Steele. *Spain the Culture: Lands, People, and Cultures.* New York: Crabtree Publishing Company, 2001.

Lipsner, J. *Hindus: Their Religious Beliefs and Practice.* London and New York: Routledge, 1994.

Lonely Planet. *Extreme Cuisine: Exotic Tastes from around the World.* Oakland, CA: Lonely Planet, 2009.

Macintyre, Stuart. *A Concise History of Australia: Cambridge Concise Histories.* Cambridge: Cambridge University Press, 2009.

Magat, Margaret. "Balut: "Fertilized Duck Eggs and Their Role in Filipino Culture." *Western Folklore* 61, no. 1 (Spring 2002): 63–96.

Mason, Michael Atwood. *Living Santería: Rituals and Experiences in an Afro-Cuban Religion.* Washington, DC: Smithsonian Institution Press, 2002.

McAllister, Patrick. "Connecting Places, Constructing Tét: Home, City and the Making of the Lunar New Year in Urban Vietnam." *Journal of Southeast Asian Studies* 43, no. 1 (February 2012): 111–32.

McGowan, Chris, and Ricardo Passanha. *The Brazilian Sound. Samba, Bossa Nova, and the Popular Music of Brazil.* Philadelphia: Temple University Press, 1998.

McKay, Susan. *Spain: Festivals of the World.* New York: Gareth Stevens Publishing, 1999.

Melton, J. Gordon. *The Encyclopedia of Religious Phenomena.* Canton, MI: Visible Ink Press, 2008.

Melton, J. Gordon. *Religious Celebrations: An Encyclopedia of Holidays, Festivals, Solemn Observances, and Spiritual Commemorations.* Santa Barbara, CA: ABC-CLIO, 2011.

Metcalf, Richard, and Richard Huntington. *Celebrations of Death: Anthropology of Mortuary Ritual.* 2nd ed. New York: Cambridge University Press, 1999.

Momo, Comfort. *Female Genital Mutilation.* Oxon, UK: Radcliffe Publishing Ltd, 2005.

Monger, George. *Marriage Customs of the World: An Encyclopedia of Dating Customs and Wedding Traditions.* Santa Barbara, CA: ABC-CLIO, 2004.

Morgan, Jinx, and Jefferson Morgan. *The Sugar Mill Caribbean Cookbook: Casual and Elegant Recipes Inspired by the Islands.* Boston, MA: Harvard Common Press, 1996.

Moss, Jean. *The Day of the Dead: A Pictorial Archive of Día de los Muertos.* (Dover Pictorial Archive). New York: Dover Publications, 2010.

Mufana, Bill. *The Lobola System and a Few Other Topics*. Lusaka, Zambia: Zambia Educational Publishing House, 2006.

Mukundchandras, Sadhu. *Hindu Festivals (Origins, Sentiments & Rituals)* Ahmedabad, India: Swaminarayan Aksharpith, 2005.

Musgrave, Elizabeth. "Memento Mori: The Function and Meaning of Breton Ossuaries 1450–1750." In *The Changing Face of Death: Historical Accounts of Death and Disposal*, edited by Peter C. Jupp and Glennys Howarth, 62–75. Hampshire, UK: Palgrave Macmillan Publishers, 1997.

Mvududu, Sara C. *Lobola: Its Implications for Women's Reproductive Rights in Botswana, Lesotho, Malawi, Mozambique, Swaziland, Zambia, and Zimbabwe*. Harare, Zimbabwe: Women and Law in Southern Africa Research Trust, 2002.

Norbury, Paul. *The Essential Guide to Customs and Culture of Japan*. London: Kuperard, 2011.

Olsen, Dale A., and Daniel E. Sheehy, eds. *The Garland Handbook of Latin American Music*. New York: Routledge, 2000.

Omari-Tunkara, Mikelle S. *Manipulating the Sacred: Yoruba Art, Ritual, and Resistance in Brazilian Candomblé*. Detroit: Wayne State University Press, 2005.

O'Sullivan, Joanne. "Blackening the Bride and Groom." In *Book of Superstitious Stuff*, 168–170. Watertown, MA: Imagine, 2010.

Pearson, Mark Parker. *The Archeology of Death and Burial*. College Station: Texas A & M University Press, 2000.

Peleg, Yifat. "Gender and Ossuaries: Ideology and Meaning." *Bulletin of the American Schools of Oriental Research* (2002): 65–73.

Peoples, James, and Garrick Bailey. *Humanity: An Introduction to Cultural Anthropology*. Beverly, MA: Wadsworth Publishing/Cengage, 2011.

Peppas, Lynn. *Cultural Traditions in Japan*. New York: Crabtree Publishing Co., 2011.

Pérez y Mena, Andrés I. "Cuban Santería, Haitian Vodun, Ruerto Rican Spiritualism: A Multicultural Inquiry into Syncretism." *Journal of Scientific Study of Religion* 37, no. 1 (1997): 15–27.

Pounder, D. J. "Ritual Mutilation: Subincision of the Penis among Australian Aborigines." *American Journal of Forensic Medical Pathology* 4, no. 3 (September 1983): 227–29.

Pringle, Robert. *A Short History of Bali: Indonesia's Hindu Realm*. Crow's Nest, Australia: Allen and Unwin, 2004.

Roy, Christian, ed. *Traditional Festivals: A Multicultural Encyclopedia* (2 Vols). Santa Barbara, CA: ABC-CLIO, 2005.

Rubin, Arnold, ed. *Marks of Civilization: Artistic Transformations of the Human Body*. Los Angeles: UCLA Museum of Cultural History, 1988.

Salewicz, Chris, and Adrian Boot. *Reggae Explosion: The Story of Jamaican Music*. New York: Harry N. Abrams, 2001.

Salisbury, Joyce E., and Gregory S. Aldrete, eds. *The Greenwood Encyclopedia of Daily Life: A Tour through History from Ancient Times to the Present* (6 Vols). Westport, CT: Greenwood Press, 2004.

Santos-Granero, Fernando. *The Occult Life of Things. Native Amazonian Theories of Materiality and Personhood*. Tucson: University of Arizona Press, 2009.

Scott, Delilah, and Emma Troy. *The Upside-Down Christmas Tree and Other Bizarre Yuletide Tales*. Guildford, CT: Lyons Press, 2010.

Secretan, Thierry. *Going into Darkness: Fantastic Coffins from Africa*. London: Thames and Hudson Ltd, 1995.

Shekar, H. V. *Festivals of India: Significance of Celebrations.* Louisville, KY: Insight Books, 2000.

Shellgrove, David L., and Hugh Richardson. *The Cultural History of Tibet.* Bangkok, Thailand: Orchid Press, 2006.

Shilling, Mark. *The Encyclopedia of Japanese Popular Culture.* New York: Weatherhill Publishers, 1997.

Smith, Bardwell. "Buddhism and Abortion in Contemporary Japan: Misuko Kuyō and the Confrontation with Death." *Japanese Journal of Religious Studies* 15, no. 1 (December 1988): 3–24.

Smith, Susan L. *Japanese American Midwives: Culture, Community, and Health Politics, 1880–1950.* Urbana: University of Illinois Press, 2005.

Somaweera, Ruchira, and Nilusha Somaweera. "Serpent Jars: The Snake Wine Industry in Vietnam." *Journal of Threatened Taxa* 2, no. 11 (October 2003): 1251–260.

Sosnoski, Daniel. *Introduction to Japanese Culture.* North Clarendon, VT: Tuttle Publishing, 2006.

Stevenson, Robert. "Music in Quito: Four Centuries." *The Hispanic American Historical Review* 43, no. 2 (1963): 247–66.

Taylor, Richard P., ed. *Death and the Afterlife.* Santa Barbara, CA: ABC-CLIO, 2000.

Toivo, Raisa Maria. *Witchcraft and Gender in Early Modern Society: Finland and the Wider European Experience.* Burlington, VT: Ashgate Publishing Company, 2008.

Verma, Manish. *Fast and Festivals of India.* New Delhi: DPB (p) Ltd, 2007.

Vilhar, Gorazd, and Charlotte Anderson. *Matsuri: World of Japanese Festivals.* Boston, MA: Weatherhill Publishers, 2004.

Vincent, Jon S. *Culture and Customs of Brazil.* Westport, CT: Greenwood Press, 2003.

Walter, Tony. "The Empire of Death: A Cultural History of Ossuaries and Charnel Houses." *Mortality* 17, no. 3 (2012): 303–04.

Webber, Sara, and Toby Schonfeld. "Cutting History, Cutting Culture: Female Circumcision in the United States." *The American Journal of Bioethics* 3, no. 2 (Spring 2003): 65–66.

Weiner, Annette B. *The Trobrianders of Papua New Guinea.* New York: Holt, Rinehart and Winston, 1988.

Welchman, Lynn. *Women's Rights and Islamic Family Law: Perspectives on Reform.* London: Zed Books Led, 2004.

Werner, Robert J. *Bolivia in Focus: A Guide to the People, Politics, and Culture.* Northampton, MA: Interlink Books, 2009.

Wilson, Jeff. *Mourning the Unborn Dead: A Buddhist Ritual Comes to America.* New York: Oxford University Press, 2009.

Zimmern, Andrew. *Andrew Zimmern's Bizarre World of Food: Brains, Bugs, & Blood Sausage.* New York: Random House, 2011.

ELECTRONIC SOURCES

African Names. http://www.afrikannames.com (Accessed on August 20, 2012).

Akan Naming Ceremony. *The Earth Center.* http://www.theearthcenter.com/templates/fire fly/archives/ffarchivesdento.html (Accessed on August 20, 2012).

All Africa. "Cameroon: Campaign Launched to Counter Breast Ironing." *All Africa: Humanitarian News and Analysis.* June 28, 2006. http://allafrica.com/stories/200606290001 .html (Accessed on June 13, 2012).

Andrews, Brian. "Colombia's Hormigas Culonas." *NTN24 News.com*. April 24, 2012. http://brianandrews.ntn24.com/2012/04/colombias-hormigas-culonas/ (Accessed on September 20, 2012).

Armstrong, Luke Maguire. "The Burning of the Devil in Guatemala." *Perceptive Travel*. http://www.perceptivetravel.com/issues/0210/guatemala.html (Accessed on October 2, 2012).

Astor, Michael. "Brazil's Once-Banned Religions Gain Followers." *Los Angeles Times*. January 25, 2005. http://articles.latimes.com/2005/jan/02/news/adfg-brazil2 (Accessed on July 25, 2012).

Bakerjian, Martha. "Infiorata—Flower Art Festivals in Italy: Flower Petal Tapestries and Mosaics for Corpus Domini." http://goitaly.about.com/od/festivalsandevents/qt/infiorata.htm *About.com Italy Travel* (Accessed on January 24, 2013).

Bali Ceremonies. http://www.baliholidayisland.com/balinese_ceremony.htm (Accessed on July 25, 2012).

Barakat, Noorhan. "The History, Significance of Ramadan around the World." *Gulf News.com*. July 19, 2012. http://gulfnews.com/news/gulf/uae/heritage-culture/the-history-significance-of-ramadan-around-the-world-1.1051436 (Accessed on April 8, 2013).

BBC Nottingham. *History of Goose Fair*. September 4, 2008. http://www.bbc.co.uk/nottingham/content/articles/2005/09/15/goose_fair_history_feature.shtml (Accessed on November 26, 2012).

Betty, Stafford. "After the Abortion, Misuko Kuyo." *National Catholic Reporter*. July 25, 2008. http://ncronline.org/node/1462 (Accessed on June 25, 2012).

Bizarre Festivals of Asia. http://www.dyscario.com/travel-and-places/10-of-the-most-bizarre-festivals-of-asia.html (Accessed on July 2, 2012).

Bleacher Report. "The Nine Most Unusual Popular Sports in the World." http://bleacherreport.com/articles/82123-the-nine-most-unusual-popular-sports-in-the-world (Accessed on September 4, 2012).

Bonuccelli, Domenic. "Baby-Jumping: The Work of the Devil?" *Lonely Planet*. November 20, 2009. http://www.lonelyplanet.com/spain/travel-tips-and-articles/18856 (Accessed on July 12, 2012).

Candomblé in Salvador de Bahia, Brazil. http://www.bahia-online.net/Candomble.htm (Accessed on July 24, 2012).

Cheese Rolling. Official Web site of the Cheese Rolling Competition. http://www.cheese-rolling.co.uk/index1.htm (Accessed on September 5, 2012).

Child Rights International Network (CRIN). "Millions of Cameroon Girls Suffer Breast Ironing." *CRIN Network: Children and Violence*. June 13, 2006. Alert Net. http://www.crin.org/violence/search/closeup.asp?infoID=9218 (Accessed on June 15, 2012)

Fang, Liu. "Travel Peaks Ahead of Tomb Sweeping Day." *CCTV.com*. March 26, 2012. http://english.cntv.cn/program/china24/20120326/109627.shtml (Accessed on September 19, 2012).

Feria de las Flores Festival and the City of Medellin Official Web site. http://feriadelasflores.medellin.travel/ (Accessed on February 15, 2013).

Fiestas de Quito—Founder's Day in Quito. http://www.ecuadorexplorer.com/html/fiestas_de_quito.html (Accessed on March 1, 2013).

Fragala Smith, Karen. "Haiti: A Historical Perspective." *Newsweek*. January 16, 2010. http://www.newsweek.com/2010/01/15/haiti-a-historical-perspective.print.html (Accessed on April 14, 2013).

Hamre, Bonnie. "Inti Raymi, Festival of the Sun." *About.com*. http://Gosouthamerica.about.com/od/perartandculture/a/IntiRaymi.htm (Accessed on January 2, 2013).

Hinduism in Indonesia. http://www.hindu-indonesia.com (Last accessed on July 1, 2012).

History of Fire walking. http://www.firewalking.com/firewalk_history.jsp (Accessed on November 13, 2012).

Horn Dance of Abbots Bromley Official Web site. http://www.thehorndanceofabbotsbromley.co.uk/index.htm (Accessed on October 9, 2012).

Horowitz, Carol, and J. Carey Jackson. "Female 'Circumcision': African Women Confront American Medicine." *Journal of General Internal Medicine* 12, no. 8 (August 1997): 491–99. http://www.ncbi.nlm.nih.gov/pmc/articles/PMC1497147/ (Accessed on August 26, 2012).

Hunt, Katrina Brown. "World's Most Dangerous Foods." *Travel + Leisure.* October, 2009. http://www.travelandleisure.com/articles/worlds-most-dangerous-foods (Accessed on August 1, 2012).

Infiorata: Patrimonio d'Italia. Official Web site for the Annual Infiorata Cultural Celebration. http://www.infiorata.it/ (Accessed on February 25, 2013).

Japan Festivals. http://japan-fest.info/ (Accessed on July 2, 2012).

Krutak, Lars. "Scarification and Tattooing in Benin: The Bétamarribé Tribe of the Atakora Mountains." *Lars Krutak: Tattoo Anthropologist.* 2008. http://www.larskrutak.com/articles/Benin/index.html (Accessed on November 30, 2012).

Kumbh Mela Official Web site. http://kumbhmelaallahabad.gov.in (Accessed on September 6, 2013).

Lee, Mike. "Land Divers of Vanuatu." *ABC News.* http://abcnews.go.com/WNT/story?id=130132&page=1 (Accessed on August 20, 2012).

Leo Neto, Nivaldo A. *et al.* "From Eshu to Obatala: Animals Used in Sacrificial Rituals at Condomblé 'terreiros' in Brazil." *Journal of Ethnobiology and Ethnomedicine* 5, no. 23 (August 2009). http://www.nbci.nlm.nih.gov/pmc/articles/PMC2739163 (Accessed on April 14, 2013).

Lobola. "South African Traditional Marriage Customs: Lobola and Polygamy." http://www.southafricaweb.co.za/article/south-african-traditional-marriage-customs-lobola-and-polygamy (Accessed on October 12, 2012).

Lotus Births, Indonesia. http://www.cmindonesia.com/1/post/2012/7/kala-dokter-bicara-soal-lotus-birth.html (Accessed on November 11, 2012).

Maasai Association. "Maasai Ceremonies and Rituals." 2012. http://www.maasai-association.org/ceremonies.html (Accessed on April 5, 2013).

McCoy, Randy. "Redneck Olympics under Fire." *B98.5—Central Maine's Country.* 2012. http://b985.fm/redneck-olympics-under-fire/ (Accessed on April 4, 2013).

Mishima, Shizuko. "Setsubun—Bean Throwing Festival." *Japan Travel.* http://gojapan.about.com/cs/japanesefestivals/a/setsubun.htm (Accessed on January 10, 2013).

Mitchell, Ryan. "Maori Chief on Facial Tattoos and Tribal Pride." *National Geographic News.* October 14, 2003. http://news.nationalgeographic.com/news/pf/84577710.html (Accessed on June 25, 2012).

Monroe, M. H. "Aboriginal Mortuary Rites: Disposal of the Body." *Australia: The Land Where Time Began.* http://austhrutime.com/aboriginal_australia.htm (Accessed on December 13, 2012).

Ottery St. Mary Tar Barrels Official Web site. http://www.otterytarbarrels.co.uk/history.html (Accessed on October 14, 2012).

Pantone, Dan James. *Matis Indians: The Jaguar People.* http://www.amazon-indians.org/page01.html (Accessed on March 24, 2013).

Pegg, David. "Puffin Heart." *25 of the Strangest Foods from around the World.* http://list25.com/25-of-the-strangest-foods-from-around-the world/5/ (Accessed on January 14, 2013).

Popovic, Mislav. "Bone Houses." *Traditions and Customs from All over the World.* http://traditionscustoms.com/strange-traditions/bone-house (Accessed on March 23, 2013).

Porten, Mariya "Holy Cannibalism. The Aghori of India." *Tuscer Geographica* 7, no. 6 (2011). http://www.enewsbuilder.net/tusker/e_article002109245.cfm?x=b11,0,w (Accessed on April 13, 2013).

Portugal's Chapel of Bones. http://www.atlasobscura.com/places/portugals-chapel-bones (Accessed on March 3, 2013).

Public Broadcasting Station. "Maori Moko." *Skin Stories: The Art and Culture of Polynesian Tattoo.* PBS. http://www.pbs.org/skinstories/culture/role2.html#moko (Accessed on June 21, 2012).

Rastafari and Jamaican Culture. http://www.jamaicans.com/culture/rasta/culture.shtml (Accessed on July 28, 2012).

Rojas, R. Uriel, "Fiesta o Baile de los Diablitos." *Southern Costa Rica.* http://www.southerncostarica.biz/Buenos-Aires/cat-events-parties/Fiesta-o-Baile-de-los-Diablitos/341/ (Accessed on October 14, 2012).

"Scarification." *Body Arts.* Oxford: Pitt Rivers Museum, 2011. http://web.prm.ox.ac.uk/bodyarts/index.php/permanent-body-arts/scarification.html (Accessed on November 30, 2012).

Serwaa-Fobi, Maame Afia. "Child Naming Ceremonies in Ghana." *All Ghana Data.* http://www.allghanadata.com/?id=36-671-1&t=Child-Naming-Ceremonies-in-Ghana (Accessed on August 20, 2012).

"Tibetan Sky Burial." http://www.youtube.com/watch?v=b6hSK8CluxQ (Accessed on November 15, 2012).

Tiemoko, Richmond. "Preliminary Findings on Youth, Sexuality, and Marriage in Selected African Countries." *Sexuality in Africa Journal* 3, no. 1 (2006): 11–13. http://www.arsrc.org/downloads/sia/mar06/jan06.pdf (Accessed on September 7, 2012).

Tomatina Festival Official Web site. http://www.latomatina.org (Accessed on April 4, 2013).

Travel Channel. "Eating Tarantula (Deep Fried) in Cambodia." *Bizarre Foods with Andrew Zimmerman.* http://www.youtube.com/watch?v=vkTJWoUMbGk (Accessed on August 16, 2012).

Travis-Henikoff, Carole A. *Dinner with a Cannibal: The Complete History of Mankind's Oldest Taboo.* Santa Monica, CA: Santa Monica Press. 2008. http://users.rcn.com/salski/No18–19Folder/Endocannibalism.htm (Accessed on March 24, 2013).

UNICEF. *Female Genital Mutilation/Cutting: A Statistical Exploration.* 2005. http://www.unicef.org/publications/files/FGM-C_final_10_October.pdf (Accessed on August 26, 2012).

Upacara Adat Ngaben Umat Hindu Bali (Ngaben Adat Ceremony in Balinese Hindu). http://dewaarka.wordpress.com/2009/06/15/upacara-adat-ngaben-umat-hindu-bali/ (Accessed on November 5, 2012).

Weller, Ben. "South Korean Mud Festival Attracts Messy Behavior." *Reuters.* July 16, 2008. http://www.reuters.com/article/2008/07/16/us-korea-mud-idUSSEO31940820080716 (Accessed on August 1, 2012).

Wheewall, Adam. "Haxey Hood: 700 Years of Tradition." 2012. http://www.wheewall.com/hood/index.php (Accessed on November 7, 2012).

Wolchover, Natalie. "Five Strange Courting Rituals from around the World." *Life's Little Mysteries.* February 11, 2011. http://www.lifeslittlemysteries.com/1089-strange-courting-rituals-from-around-world.html (Accessed on April 14, 2013).

World Health Organization. *Female Genital Mutilation.* http://www.who.int/topics/female_genital_mutilation/en/ (Accessed on August 26, 2012).

Index

Page numbers in **boldface** reflect main entries in the book.

Contributors

Aguilar, Cindi
Santa Ana College, California

Ali, Nadia
Independent writer, Trinidad

Babb, Stefanie A.
Florida Gulf Coast University at Fort
Myers

Baeder, Steven A.
West Cypress Church, California

Blank, Sharla A.
Washburn University, Topeka,
Kansas

Blaylock, Matthew R.
University of Tennessee at Knoxville

Cioffoletti, Dawn
Florida Gulf Coast University at Fort ·
Myers

Courter, William F.
Santa Ana College, California

Duerr, Glen M. E.
Cedarville University, Ohio

Fabrykant, Marharyta
Belarusian State University, Belarus

Fandino, Daniel
University of Central Florida

Galván, Javier A.
Santa Ana College, California

Garlitz, Dustin
University of South Florida

Hamilton, Stephanie L.
Frank Slide Interpretative Center,
Toronto, Canada

Hara, Abubakar
Northern University of Malaysia,
College of Law

Harper, Misti Nicole
University of Arkansas at Fayetteville

Hassanali, Muhammed
Independent Writer, Ohio

Hicks, Raymond
Santa Ana College, California

Houle, Michelle E.
Lindsay Community School, San
Diego, California

Hussein, Nashaat H.
Misr International University,
Cairo, Egypt

Jacob, Frank
Heinrich-Heine University,
Dusseldorf, Germany

Jorgensen, Sara C.
University of Tennessee at Chattanooga

Kaganiec-Kamieňska, Anna
Jagiellonian University, Krakow,
Poland

Kikawa, Eve
Santa Ana College, California

Kladky, William P.
Notre Dame University, Maryland

Layne, Mark
University of Texas at Tyler

Logan, Gabi
Travel writer, United States

Luévano, Peter
Los Angeles Unified School District,
California

Mishra, Patit Paban
Northern University of Malaysia,
College of Law

Money, Kellie
Murray State University, Kentucky

Okwei, Veronny Odili
Musician and writer, Lagos, Nigeria

Pappas, Erin
University of Chicago

Qadeer, Haris
Gautam Buddha University, India

Reinherz, Adam
University of Pittsburgh, Pennsylvania

Robertson, Mario
Santa Ana College, California

Sanko, Marc
Edinboro University of Pennsylvania

Smith, Rachelanne
Independent writer, Sacramento,
California

Steckman, Laura
Independent writer, Oregon,
Wisconsin

Sukumaran, Biju
Independent writer, China

Tapia, Alejandra
Santa Ana College, California

Taylor, Ken
New Orleans Baptist Theological
Seminary

Team, Victoria
School of Psychology and Psychiatry,
Monash University, Australia

Tiegs, Bob
Louisiana State University

Veyna, Angelina F.
Santa Ana College, California

Watts, Linda S.
University of Washington at Bothell

Wexelbaum, Rachel
Saint Cloud State University of
Minnesota

Whalen, Kenneth
Universiti Brunei Darussalam,
Brunei

Williams, Victoria
Independent writer, London,
England

Wilson, Charles H., Jr.
University of Tennessee at Knoxville

Wozniak, Kevin
Independent scholar, New Jersey

About the Editor

Dr. Javier A. Galván is a professor of both History and Spanish at Santa Ana College in Santa Ana, California. Within the field of history, he follows a social history approach and specializes in the region of Latin America. In foreign languages, his academic training was focused on second language acquisition, and he regularly teaches the introductory levels of Spanish courses in both traditional formats and online delivery. At Santa Ana College, he has received various professional awards, including the Publication of the Year and multiple Research Travel Grants.

His latest publications include *Latin American Dictators of the 20th Century*. Jefferson, NC: McFarland, December, 2012; *Culture and Customs of Bolivia*. Santa Barbara, CA: ABC-CLIO, 2011; *Culture and Customs of Puerto Rico*. Westport, CT: Greenwood Press, April 2009. He has authored multiple entries on encyclopedias, including *Encyclopedia of World Empires, The International Encyclopedia of Revolution and Protest*, and *The Encyclopedia of Emancipation and Abolition in the Transatlantic World*.

Galván's interest in combining the theoretical approaches of two fields from humanities (foreign languages) and social sciences (history) is to blur the traditional academic boundaries and present information to students that is more interconnected by following the study of multiple cultures in a global setting. He proposes that a multidisciplinary approach to learning is more beneficial to university students because they can make meaningful connections of information while simultaneously developing crucial academic skills that include college-level writing, doing research, public speaking, and applying critical thinking strategies.